VICTORIA'S ISLAND VILLAGE

WHIPPINGHAM

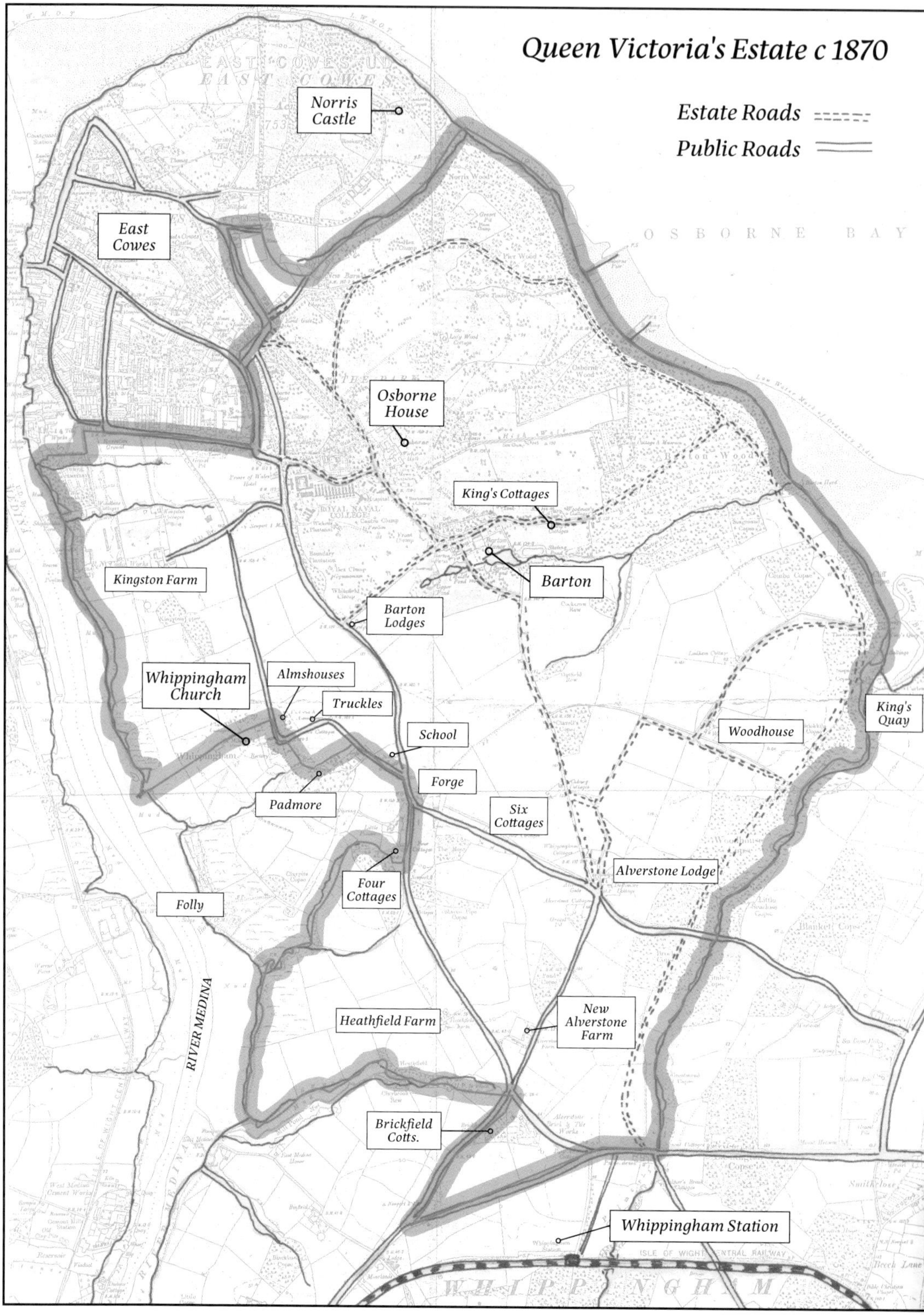
Queen Victoria's Estate c 1870
Estate Roads
Public Roads
Norris Castle
East Cowes
Osborne House
King's Cottages
Barton
Kingston Farm
Barton Lodges
Whippingham Church
Almshouses
Truckles
School
Forge
Padmore
Six Cottages
Woodhouse
King's Quay
Alverstone Lodge
Four Cottages
Folly
RIVER MEDINA
Heathfield Farm
New Alverstone Farm
Brickfield Cotts.
Whippingham Station
OSBORNE BAY
ISLE OF WIGHT CENTRAL RAILWAY

VICTORIA'S ISLAND VILLAGE

WHIPPINGHAM

By

SARAH BURDETT

KSW BOOKS

Published 2018
By KSW Books

A copy of this book is held in the British Library

ISBN 978-0-9574540-1-9

Cover photos: *Front: V&A cypher on St. Mildred's Church*
Back: Queen Victoria attends church at Whippingham

Printed by Crossprint
Isle of Wight
www.crossprint.co.uk

Contents

Prologue

Victoria's Island Village is an updated version of *The Book of Whippingham* which I wrote in 2006. The book had only a short run and it is now somewhat of a rarity. I was often asked by Whippingham residents and visitors where they could get hold of a copy. This new publication holds much of the text of the original but has been extensively updated with new information and photographs.

As a history of the village it spans time between medieval Whippingham and the 21st Century, but as the title suggests it leans toward the connection to Queen Victoria, Prince Albert and the Royal family. Victoria influenced the daily lives of the people of Whippingham and its surroundings and the evidence is recorded here.

Throughout the book measurements are given in Imperial format. Many of the quoted texts contain items in feet and inches, gallons, bushels, pounds, ounces and quarts. Converting them all into metric within the text would make it awkward to read and most people now have easy access to conversion tables if they require them.

For the enlightenment of those younger than the author, here is an explanation of pre-decimalisation money. I was taught in £..s..d (pounds, shillings and pence). We had to write it with two dots between the three characters - for instance: £3..4s..2d was 3 pounds, 4 shillings and twopence, pronounced tuppence, 3d was thruppence. The convention now is one dot.

There were 12 pennies in a shilling and 20 shillings in a pound. The halfpenny (hape-ney) and farthing were a half and a quarter of a penny respectively. My bus fare to school in the 1950s was a penny hape-ney (1½d). We all had to learn our 12 times table to cope with the 240 pennies in the pound!

Sarah Burdett 2018

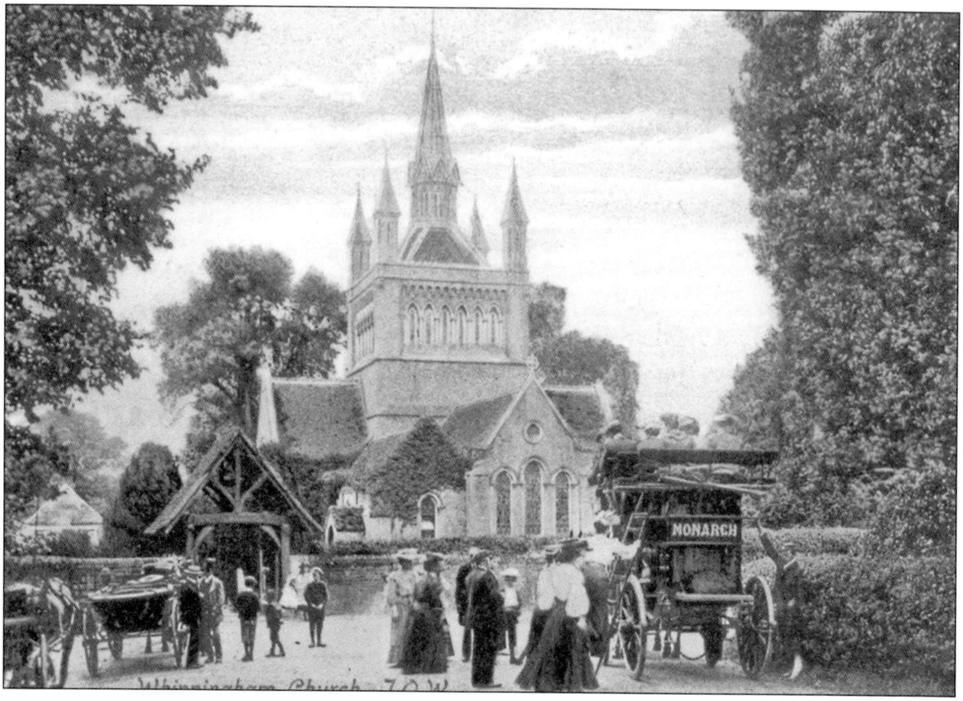

Visitors to Whippingham Church c.1910. Note the woman climbing a ladder to reach her seat on the coach. (WJ Nigh & Sons Ltd)

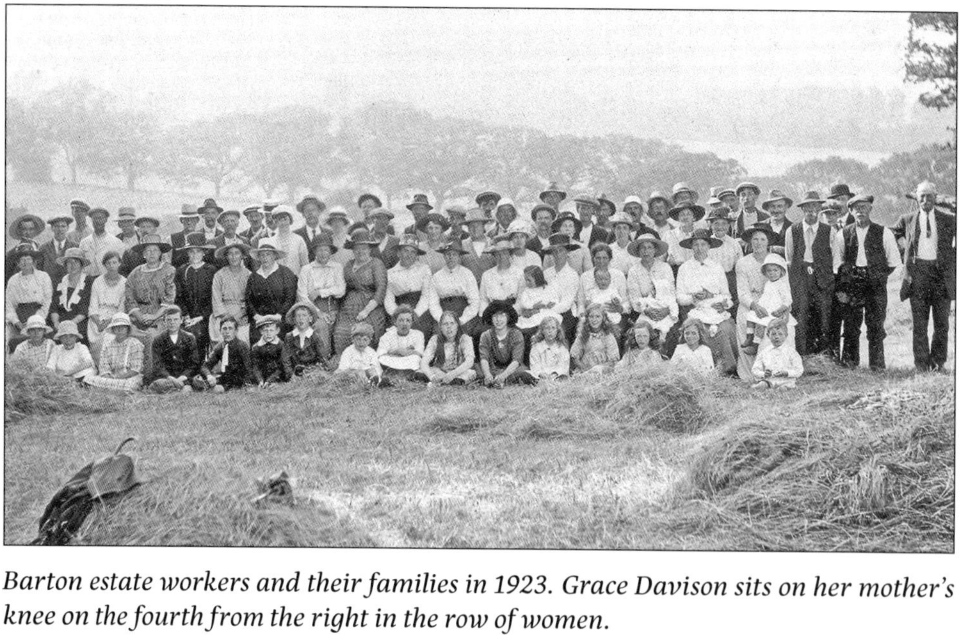

Barton estate workers and their families in 1923. Grace Davison sits on her mother's knee on the fourth from the right in the row of women.

Introduction

'There is a lot more to Whippingham than just the church!'

Whippingham is mentioned in the Domesday Book of 1086. Nine hundred years later Whippingham is now part of the Island's 'Tourist Trail'. In the summer months coaches decant their occupants for the obligatory ramble around the church and churchyard, before moving off half an hour later to visit Osborne House. By tea time all is quiet again. The almshouses bask in the evening sun, the river sparkles, the jackdaws squawk in the church chimney and peace returns.

So many people, now forgotten, have passed through the church gates. This book tells a few of their stories and describes their homes and work in the village.

Some of Whippingham's history can be gleaned from local names. Take Clavell, for example. Clavell's Copse still stands along Mount Road on the Barton Estate. Lord Robert de Claville probably worshipped at the old church of St. Mildred's in 1220. He had two sons, Henry and Hugh. Henry Claville's wife gave land to Stephen, Rector of Whippingham in 1266.

The family name, Snow, is another. Les Snow plays the organ at the church in 2017. His family lived and worked on the Osborne and Barton Estates. Grace Davison née Snow can be seen on her mother's knee in an estate workers photograph of 1923. A vast number of people are shown on that one picture, all working on, or supported by, the Barton Estate. Today, mechanisation has changed the face of farming, the dairy herds have gone, and the workforce has dwindled to just a handful.

Much of old Whippingham that we see in 2017 is a product of its Royal connection. When Queen Victoria bought Osborne and Barton in 1845, she and Albert embarked upon a massive rebuilding programme, not only of their own house, but also the church and all the cottages and farms on the estate.

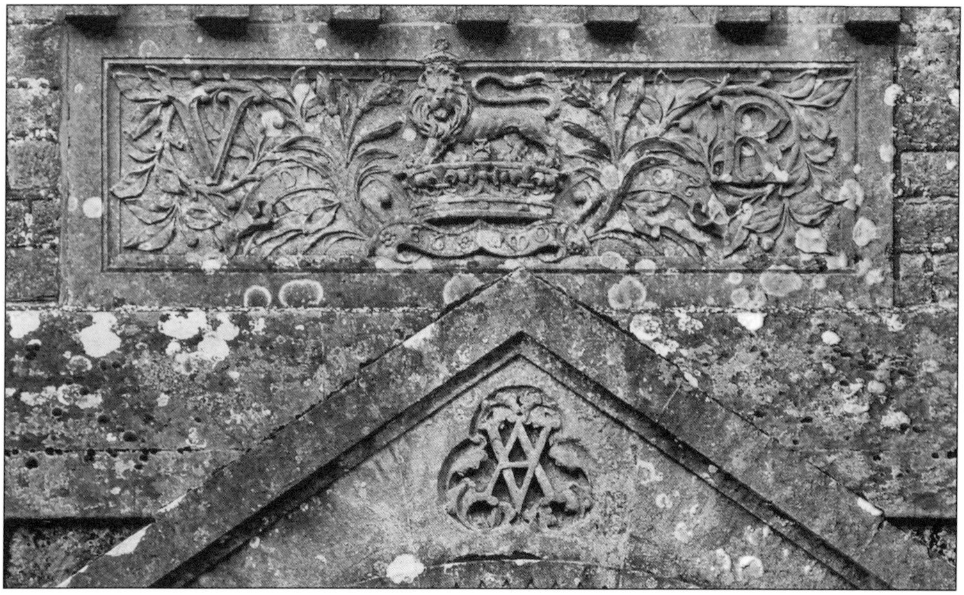

The Royal emblem of Queen Victoria and the later Victoria and Albert cypher over her own doorway to St Mildred's Church.

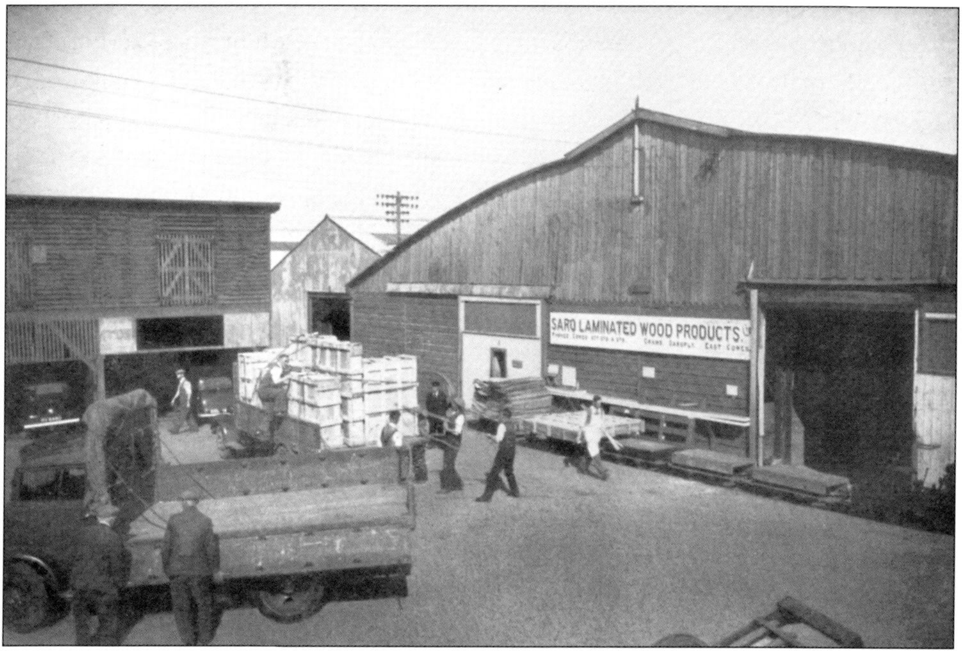

The Folly Works in the 1940s. Boxes of plywood products being loaded ready for export from the Island.

She wanted to visit 'her people', but if they lived in rough conditions it wasn't seemly. Prince Albert drew up plans for new cottages and most of the old ones were knocked down. These improvements continued after Prince Albert died in 1861.

Queen Victoria had the new school built in 1863, visited it frequently to look at the children's work, and gave prizes. What an incentive to always produce your best work! The almshouses were constructed in 1875 for aged retainers of the Queen's Estate. Six new farmhouses were built and the latest innovations appeared. Millions of drainage tiles and bricks were produced in the Queen's own brickyard, the bricks all with VR in the frog. Progress was the word.

After Victoria died in 1901, life carried on more quietly, although it was not without change. In 1910 the hospital for the Royal Naval College Osborne was built opposite Barton Gates. In 1913 Sam Saunders was producing aeroplanes just south of the Folly Inn. These took off from an airfield there, and the seaplanes taxied away along the river. The Folly Inn by the river served beer to the men from the sailing barges that might have to wait there before sailing on up to Newport with the tide for their cargoes to be unloaded.

During the Second World War 40% of the nation's plywood was being produced at the Saunders Roe (Saro) Folly Works. One night, in 1942, bombing sent much of it up in smoke. An anti-aircraft battery appeared at the Heights and the noise of the guns could be heard, and felt, as far away as Parkhurst. Saunders Roe took over the Naval College hospital site and the Osborne Works of GKN Aerospace continue there to this day. Thousands of people have worked there over the years.

In post war years the village became a quiet backwater off the main road. New houses were built on the Heights accommodating an increasing population and the Medina Park static caravan site grew to its 150 homes. The school grew in size until it closed in 2012. A private school, The Priory, arrived to take over the buildings. The Forge, in existence long before Queen Victoria arrived, continues to thrive in 2017.

Traffic now pours through the village on its way to and from the ferry terminal at East Cowes, but a visit to Whippingham is worth a detour as there is still so much to see of Queen Victoria's Island Village.

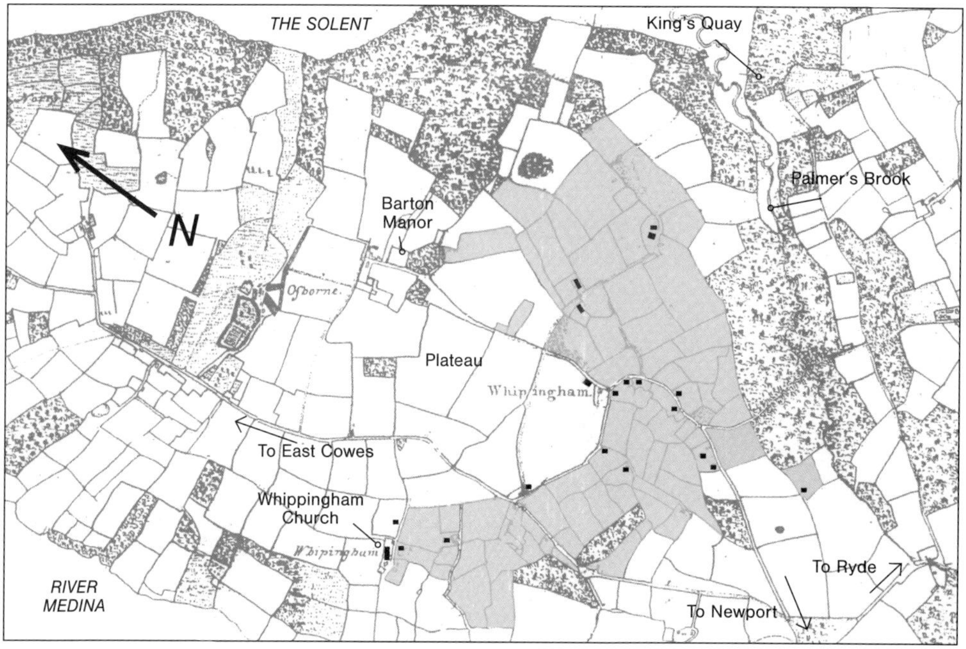

Map based on 1793 survey showing the crescent of settlement along, or just above, the spring line. Smaller fields around homes, larger ones on the plateau.

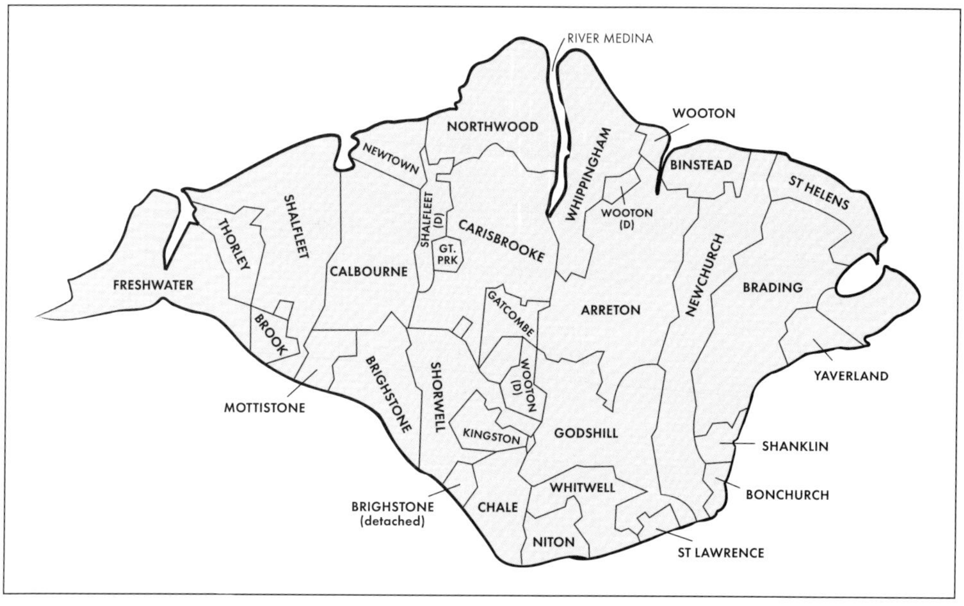

Map of the Island showing medieval parish boundaries based on Worsley's map of 1781. Several smaller parishes were carved out of the original eight.

One

Old Whippingham

The Medina Estuary gave easy sheltered access by boat to the centre of the Island. Evidence has been found of Middle Stone Age hunter-gatherers making shelters beside the Medina, and scatters of burnt flint have been found between Alverstone and Whippingham Roads. The Bronze Age people who followed made a ring ditch around a burial mound just south of Barton Manor, but no remains of Iron Age people have been discovered so far. Just a few Roman finds have turned up, near the river bank, which was probably a routeway as the clay lands were poor and difficult to farm.

The Anglo Saxon Chronicle reveals that in AD 530 and 631 groups of Saxons invaded the Island, and tried to introduce Christianity, with little success. In 686 the Saxon Caedwalla of Wessex laid waste to the Island, with the official reason that the people were not Christians. *'By cruel slaughter he endeavoured to destroy all the inhabitants thereof and to place in their stead people from his own province'.*

Whippingham may have acquired its name at this time. 'Whippa' was probably the Saxon leader put in charge of this area by Caedwalla. 'Ham' means settlement, and 'ing' means people, so the name means 'Whippa's people's settlement,' or manor in later terms.

Eight Island parishes were formed following conversion to Christianity, each with its own church and Whippingham was one of these. The parish ran north to south from the Solent along the river to Shide, south of Newport, by medieval times. Mildred was the name of a Saxon Saint from Kent, and was adopted by Whippingham for the parish church. In times of Viking raids, the Church of St. Mildred, high on the hill above the Medina, may have provided a safe refuge for the parishioners.

At the time of the Domesday record of 1086, the land belonged to the King, and Wulfward rented it from him. There was enough work for half a plough, and there were three villagers and two smallholders with one plough between them. Only about 60 acres were in cultivation, and the value of the land was only 10 shillings. This is quite low, and reflects the poor quality of the soil.

William Fitz Osbern was made Lord of the Island by King William in 1066, and in 1070 Fitz Osbern decreed that the rents from lands belonging to Whippingham Church should be sent to the Abbey of St. Mary at Lyre in Normandy, along with those of five other churches on the Island.

The Early Village

Whippingham does not fit the popular stereotype of an old village. There is no village green, no cluster of cottages around the village church or duck pond. In Medieval times the most necessary commodities were water and workable land. Whippingham grew up in an arc around the southern edge of a gravel plateau. Clay underlays the gravel. Springs emerge at the edge of the gravel with streams descending over the clay to the river. Wells could easily be dug through the shallow gravel and houses were built here. Even the Victorian settlements were built on the spring line. Looking at the 1863 OS map we see 'w' for well next to nearly every building.

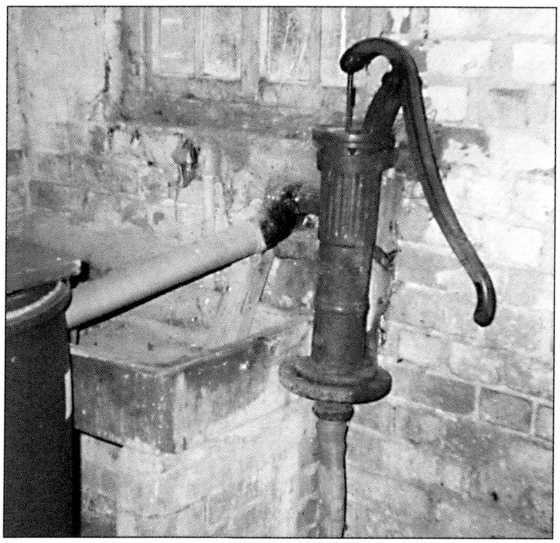

An original pump survives in one of the cottage outhouses built along the spring line.

From deeds in the County Record Office we can see various names appearing that give us a little insight into the people living here. Henry de Clavill was Lord of the Manor of Alverstone in 1222. We know then that his brother Hugh had *'land in the cultures called the Heth in the field of Whippingham in various strips.'* Heathfield was cultivated in the strip fashion, whereby different people farmed strips of land in the same field. The Clavills gave the revenue of some of their land to the Abbey of Quarr. In 1247 one acre east of Padmore owned by Mary Claville, widow of Henry, was being rented by Simon Othyn for 6d a year. In 1266 this land was given by the Clavilles to Stephen, rector of Whippingham and his successors.

A hundred years later, there were arguments over landownership between Thomas le Clavyle and Maud, late wife of John Othyn, in Whippingham. In 1342 the abbot of Quarr leased, for two lives, nine acres and a croft at Petheye, Whippingham to Thomas the elder and Thomas the younger.

The medieval farmer would have had a hard life and often would work for his Lord for a set number of days in lieu of paying rent. Mention is made of a 'croft', which would have been a smallholding. Houses were made of cheap materials readily available. Here in Whippingham this would have been wood and wattle and daub, none of which survive well so we have no examples of old wooden cottages. There was no usable stone with which to build. The manor of Woodhouse was bought by Sir Harry Worsley in 1620, Alverstone Farm being part of this. It was not until 1715 that Alverstone Old Farmhouse was built of stone and brick.

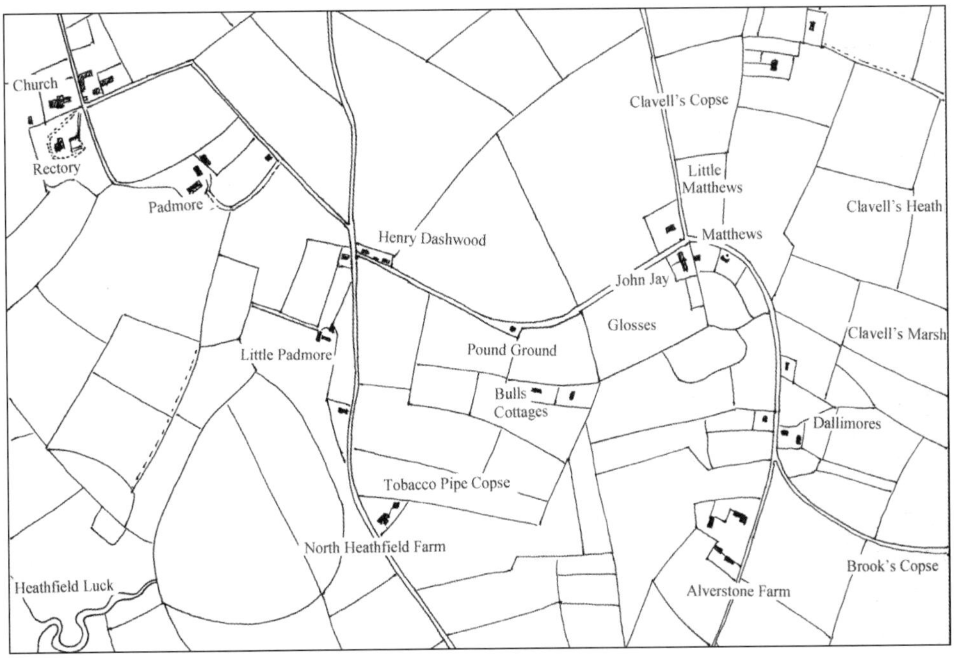

Based on the 1841 tithe map showing Whippingham Street area at Matthews, which may have been the village hub, near the present Coburg Cottage.

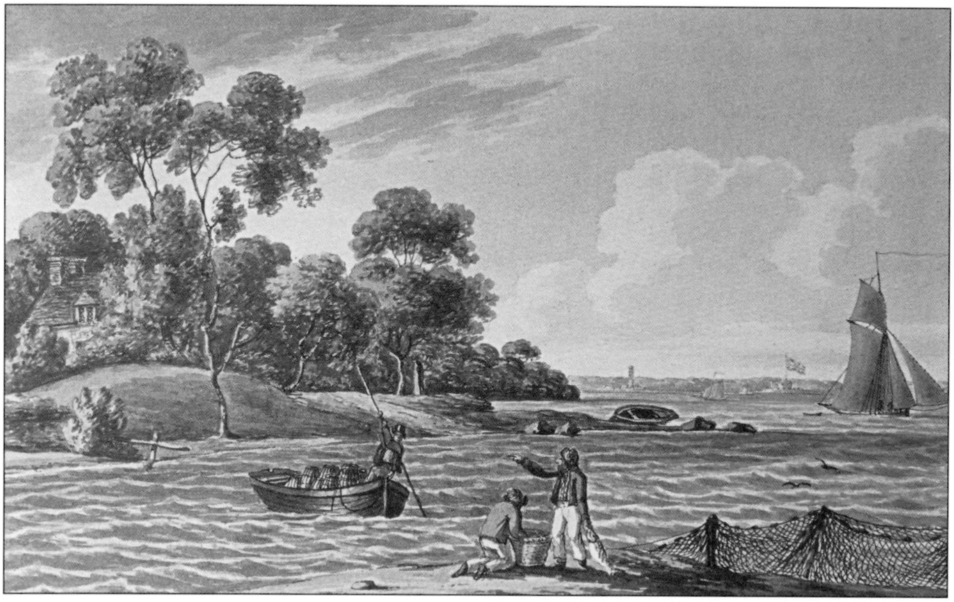

Described as King's Key [sic] this 1809 painting by Charles Tomkins shows scenes of fishing and a cottage built among the trees. A flag flies over Calshot Fort.

The Claville family appear to have moved south to Pann, where they owned the manor in 1657, leaving the name Clavell's Copse behind them in Whippingham. The Othen family continued to rent farmland. In the 1930s, Mr Othen rented the field south of the present GKN Osborne Works and ran a successful piggery and horticultural business with his son. Was he related to Simon Othyn who rented an acre east of Padmore in 1247? The Thomas family still farm in Whippingham – perhaps they are descendants of the Thomas family of Fayrelie?

At the eastern end of the village is an area called Whippingham Street on some old maps, and Alverstone or Elverton Street on others. This is beside the private road to Barton Farm, almost opposite Coburg Cottage. On the 1841 map several dwellings are shown, but these were later demolished.

This area had easy access to King's Quay, also called Shoflet many years ago. It was mentioned in the Domesday Book, with a manor, meaning an area of land, equating to Woodhouse today. The creek would have been important as a landing place before it started silting up in Victorian times. The name King's Quay is said to have originated in the arrival of King John here shortly after signing the Magna Carta, but this is unlikely as the name first appears in print in 1769.

There was also an important anchorage a mile north west of King's Quay, called Meade Hole, Osborne Bay today. Meade Hole was where pirates exchanged or sold their wares, especially during the 1500s. In 1570 the Spanish ambassador sent an agent to see what was going on and he reported back to King Phillip of Spain that there was a 'Great Fayre' of spices, wines, wool, saffron, oil, soap and a great number of other goods stolen from the Spanish King's subjects. In 1581 another witness spoke of people visiting over 30 ships, all buying, selling or bartering goods. He saw woollen cloth and linen, clothing, jewellery, shoes, beef, mutton, beer and bread, with the boatmen doing a good trade rowing customers from ship to ship. The people of Whippingham must have taken part in this, if they could, as it was right on their doorstep!

One can imagine smugglers using King's Quay, nicely tucked away from the excise men, who were stationed in East Cowes in the 18th century.

In 2017 the Shoflet, or King's Quay, has silted up and alders grow in the mud. The stream still flows under Palmer's Brook bridge and Brock's Copse bridge. Eels used to swim up it as little as 30 years ago as far as the old railway bridge by Whippingham Station, creating a seething, squirming knot in the pool there.

During Victorian times there was a footbridge across the stream at King's Quay. Workers on the Queen's Estate and children on their way to school at Whippingham would use the bridge, which provided a link to the Queen's property on the eastern side of the creek. Now the area is a haven for wildlife, inaccessible to the general public.

The Militia

Edward III embarked upon the 'Hundred Years War' with France in 1338. At Barton Oratory the arch-priest as landholder had to provide two bowmen or archers for the King's forces. Similarly, the other landholders in the area were called upon to equip men who would go to fight for the King or defend the Island.

Situated next to the sea, Whippingham was always vulnerable in times of war. The coastal land owner was the first in the line of defence on these occasions. There were French raids on the Island in the 14th and 15th centuries, and again in 1545. The Spanish Armada was seen from the south of the Isle of Wight as it passed up the channel. Militia units were formed, and these met twice a year for training during the reign of Queen Elizabeth I.

In 1625 there was a military muster of 2,020 volunteers on the Island. Whippingham men were combined with Wootton, Arreton and East Standen, and commanded by John Urry, Lord of the Manor of East Standen. He had 11 officers, 80 musketeers, 22 'corselets', (armoured men) or pikemen, and nine 'bare vickes'.

In 1681, the Worsley estate included Alverstone and the land towards Woodhouse, still known as Clavells. In the Worsley accounts we can see, *'Paid by the order of Mr Dowdeing for: A musket and bandoliers - 9s Two swords - 15s, Two belts - 5s, and a pike - 5s - To send to Clavells there being none there'* It fell to the landowner to protect his own property!

By 1782 a full time militia of 60 men was based on the Isle of Wight. They were marched from area to area and billeted where space could be found. In October 1782 they were in East Cowes. In 1795 worry about invasion by the French caused 13 Volunteer Militia Units to be formed on the Island. There were units in North Whippingham and South Whippingham. In the Worsley accounts we find an entry for, *'15 gallons of beer for the Vollunteers of South Whippingham.'* [sic] Training to be a volunteer soldier was obviously thirsty work. A 1799 review of troops in Parkhurst Forest in June noted that 3000 Island Militia volunteers were present.

A North Whippingham Volunteer belt badge was found in a field in the village. The GR stood for George III. The original owner was probably severely reprimanded for losing it!

When Queen Victoria bought Osborne, troops were stationed in East Cowes for her protection. It is believed that 20 soldiers were sometimes billeted at New Alverstone Farm. At one time there was rumour of a possible Fenian attack on Osborne, and these troops were called in to search the grounds. These, however, were regular soldiers, not volunteers.

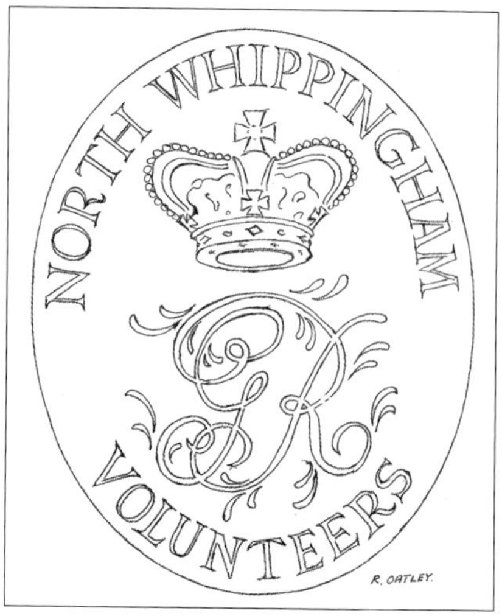

Two

The Church & Rectory

This chapter is not intended to be a guide to the present day St. Mildred's Church as there is an excellent illustrated guidebook available at the church. Here we describe some aspects that have not been included in that publication.

Little is known about the earliest Whippingham Church. Saint Mildred was a Kentish Anglo-Saxon princess who became an abbess, dying in about 700 AD. Her remains were buried at Canterbury in 1033. Only seven other English churches are dedicated to her.

The only authenticated carved stonework from the early Saxon church has been built into the west wall of the entrance porch, and there are two interesting small stones in the eastern wall. Just one engraving of the church as it was before 1800 survives, drawn by Tomkins in the 1790s showing a possibly 12th century nave and a 13th century chancel and a 14th century tower with a saddleback roof.

St. Mildred's was the only church of the large medieval parish of Whippingham, but there were just 17 households on the lay subsidy of 1334. Employees were not included in this, only those landowners liable to tax. An assessment of personal property was made and the same tax scale was used for the next 300 years. Whippingham had a lay subsidy of £1.2s., placing it at the bottom of the roll for the eastern half of the Island. In 1377 the lay subsidy considered the war damage to the Island after the French invasion. It revealed that there were only agricultural workers in Whippingham, no trades or craftsmen.

The Hundred Years War with France meant that it was difficult to pay the rents owed by Whippingham to the Abbey of Lyre in France. The payment in 1189 had been fixed at 10 shillings a year, but often this was not paid.

In 1415, all proceeds of Isle of Wight property previously paid to Lyre were taken by King Henry V and bestowed upon the Abbey of Sheen in Surrey which he

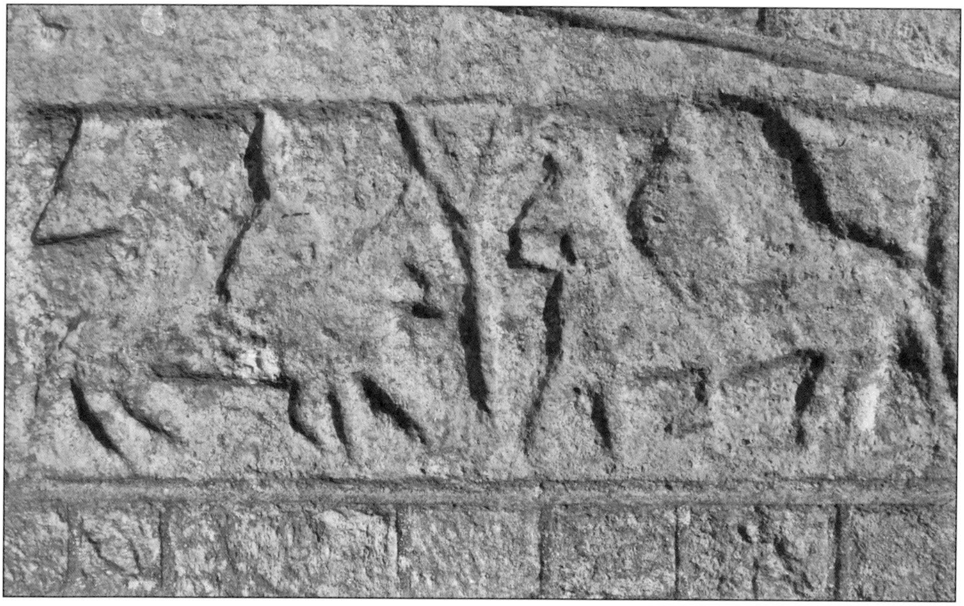

A carved stone recycled from the original church and set into the entrance porch. It depicts two soldiers meeting on horseback.

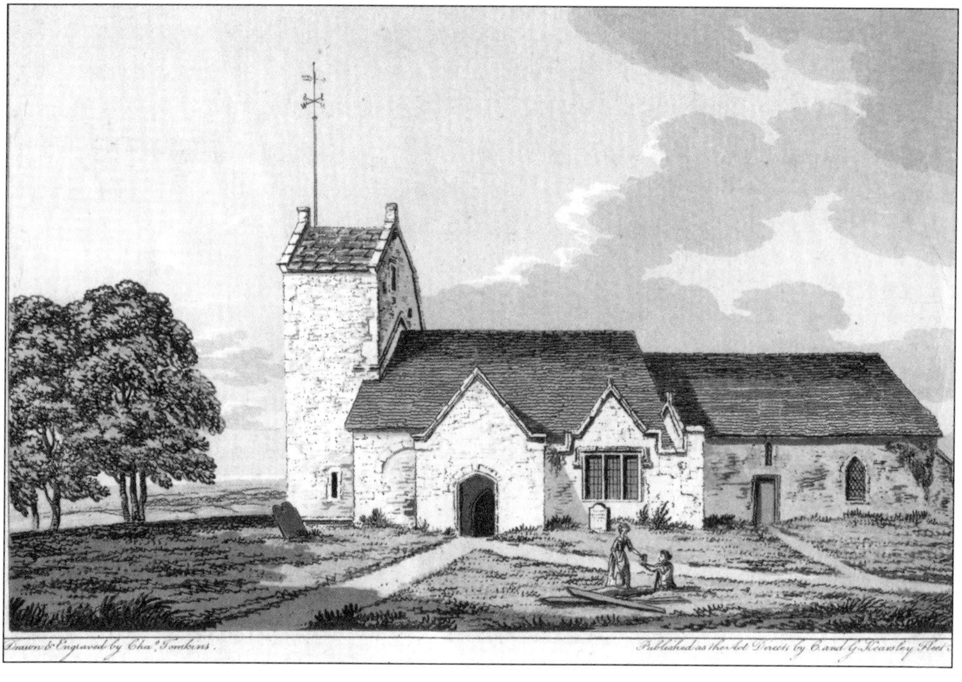

St. Mildred's Church depicted in an engraving dating from 1794.

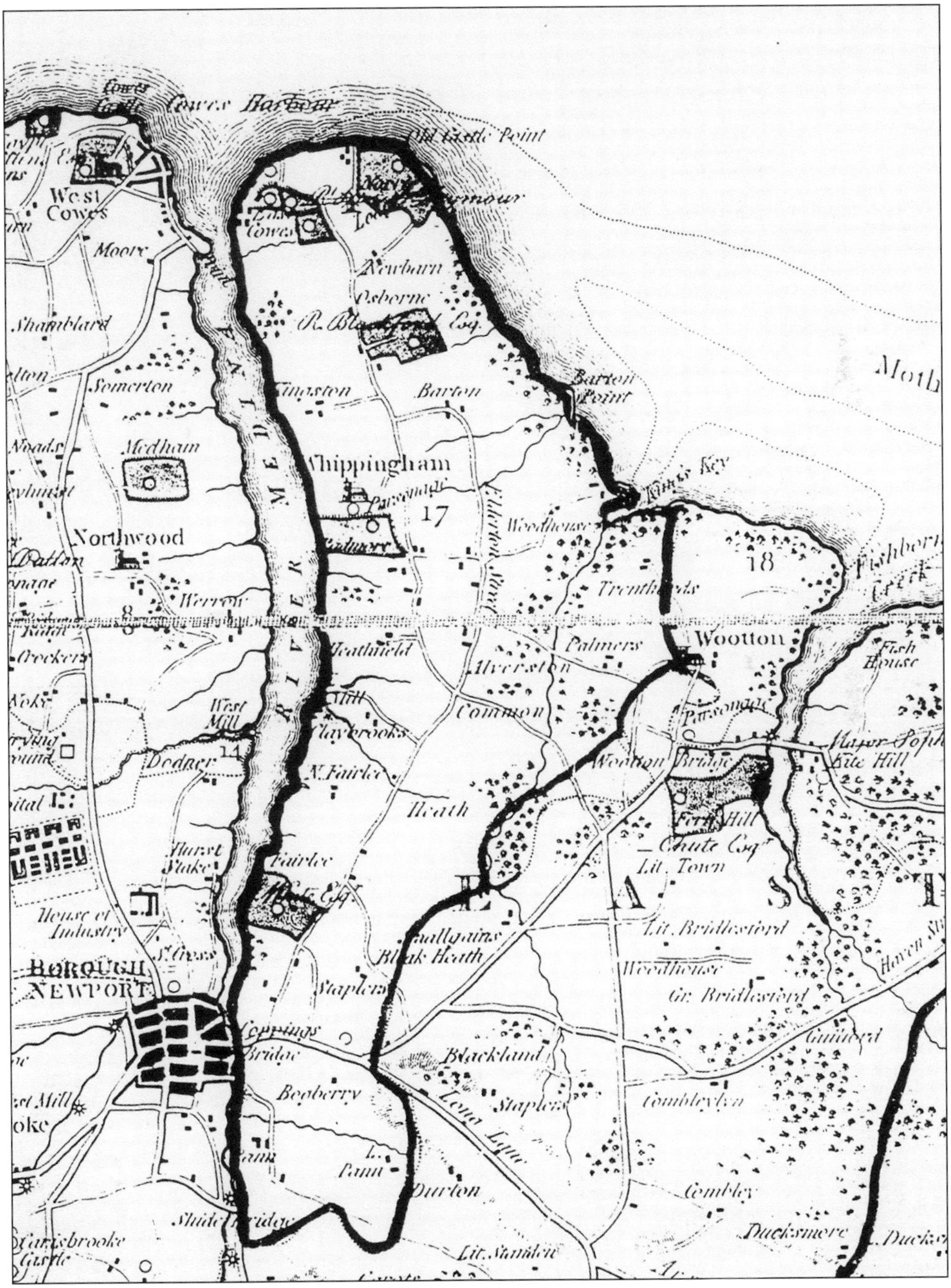

Map dating from 1810 showing the parish boundary of Whippingham. The parish was reduced in size when 'daughter' churches were built at East Cowes and Staplers, Newport in the 1830s and 60s.

had founded the previous year. Sheen now received the dues and also appointed the rectors of Whippingham.

Over a hundred years later Rector John Glazier was appointed by Sheen but in 1533 Whippingham was temporarily being served by, *'a layman only in reading the pistells and gospelles with the procession.'* [sic] Eventually Glazier became Bishop of Hereford, retiring in 1555 with a pension of £6.13s.4d. He died in 1563, having lived through the many changes to the English religion, probably guiding the parishioners of Whippingham in the new faith.

Life must have been very hard in the 16th century period. Whippingham Church was first Catholic until Henry VIII introduced Protestantism, but when Mary became Queen, Catholicism was reintroduced. Then followed Queen Elizabeth I, and the Protestant religion was again celebrated in Whippingham. Not everyone followed the changing faiths. Recusancy appeared in Whippingham! This meant that the person refused to go to church, preferring to maintain his own Catholic beliefs. Richard Hobson, a gentleman of the Isle of Wight, was in prison in 1592 for recusancy, and in 1607, Edward Hobson of Whippingham was cited as not having received communion. Perhaps life was becoming more lenient, as no mention is made of prison for him, nor for Samuel Pratt of Whippingham who was also, *'not receiveing communion, nor cometh he orderly to church!'* [sic]

Writing in the 1600s, John Oglander, the famous Isle of Wight diarist, dismisses Whippingham Church as being insignificant because nobody of note was buried there. Oglander probably touched on the reason for the church, and Whippingham itself, remaining something of a sleepy backwater. From medieval times the surrounding area mainly belonged to landowners who lived elsewhere, leasing to tenant farmers, some of whom may have been little more than crofters. The lack of any residential wealth, leadership and church patronage doubtless discouraged the development of a strong local community.

John Nash

By 1803 the parish church of Whippingham was, *'in a state of great ruin and dilapidation and in want of much repair.'* It was now, *'too small to receive and contain its number of inhabitants.'* The village of East Cowes was growing as trade and shipbuilding increased and several influential people from there were on the parochial church council. One of these was John Nash Esq.

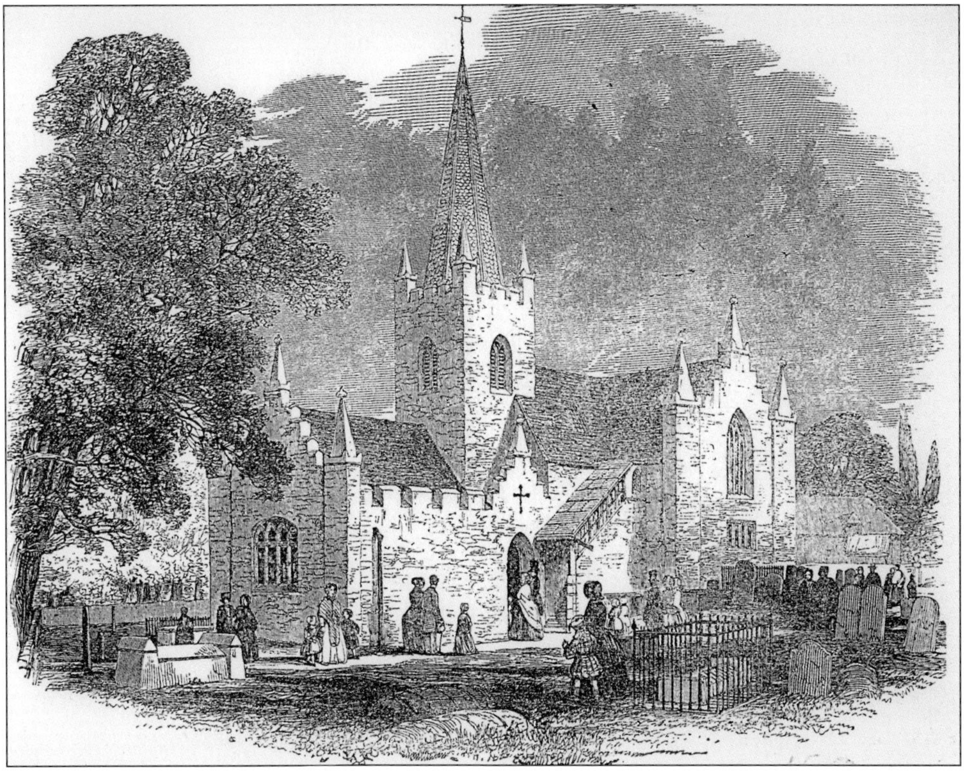

The engraving shows the church with new spire and external staircases to the galleries rebuilt between 1804 and 1811.

John Nash had built himself a home on the slopes above East Cowes, calling it East Cowes Castle. He was a renowned architect, building expensive terraces in London, the Brighton Pavilion for the Prince Regent, and then remodelling Buckingham Palace when the Regent became King. The Prince Regent visited Nash in East Cowes during regatta week. Nash had also bought the lease of North Heathfield Farm in Whippingham. This was on the left going down Whippingham Shute, opposite Heathfield Cottages.

The architect now turned his attentions to Whippingham Church, helping to draw up plans for extensions and improvements for the parochial church council. A builder by the name of James Guy was contracted to, *'perform the said repairs, additions, alterations and improvements...for the sum of six hundred and fifty pounds.'*

A new school room was to be built at the west end of the church, the church was to be enlarged on the north side, gable ends built and a new roof made,

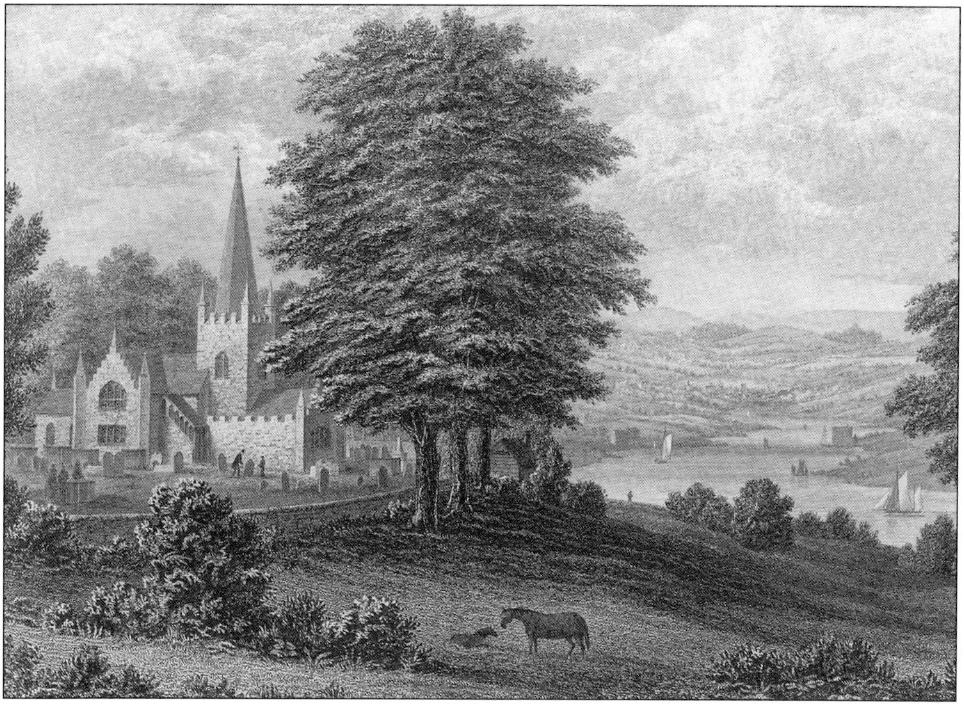

Brannon engraving of 1851 showing the 'Nash' church and the view up the River Medina towards Newport.

two galleries constructed with external staircases, the existing gallery was to be taken back, and the font to be moved. The ceilings were to be repaired and painted, old decayed wood replaced, and new pews to be fitted up. All this work was to be carried out in just three months, but we do not know if he kept to the deadline!

Several rich parishioners, many of them from East Cowes, contributed to the cost of rebuilding the church and agreed to pay for their own pews. Richard Whitmaich from South Heathfield Farm and John Nash also purchased their own pews. Mention is not made in the original contract of a spire, so this must have been an afterthought. The Nash alterations completed in 1804 do not initially show a spire, but later illustrations of the church do. Work continued on various parts of the church until 1813.

Other builders were used for work in the churchyard. One of these, Thomas Denyer, a bricklayer of Newport, was still trying to obtain his payment four years after the work was completed. His detailed invoice may throw some light on some

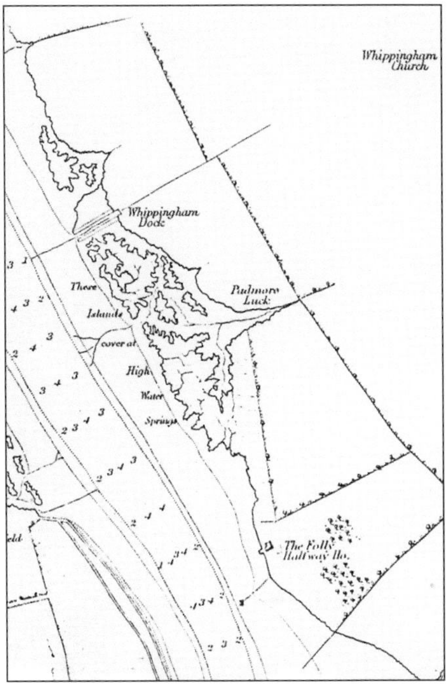

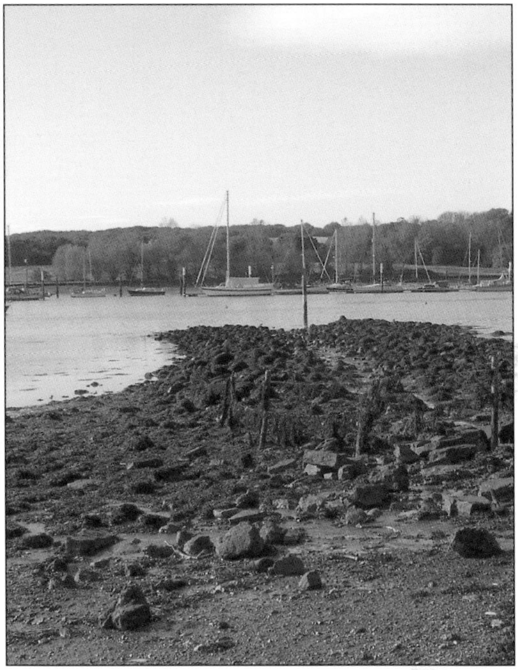

1856 Admiralty chart shows Whippingham Dock near to the church. The photograph depicts its remains at low tide. Stone is possibly from the original church.

interesting bricks which reappeared in the southern wall of the churchyard in the year 2000. These small yellow/grey handmade clay bricks are Flemish, and predate 1804. They possibly arrived on the Island as ships' ballast. Denyer states that he reused old bricks in building the wall near the rectory, and it may have been these that were found during repairs.

By 1813, little remained of the Norman church. Some of the stone was reused, but new stone would also have been needed. Transport at this time would have been by water wherever possible. On the Medina River, just below Whippingham Church, a 'dock' was constructed for the delivery of new stone to build the church. In 2017 the two arms of the dock project out into the river at right angles, each just a jumbled heap of stones covered thickly by seaweed, and marked at the western end by a warning pole. It is interesting to think that some of this jumble of stones may be waste Norman or even Saxon material from the old church. The builders of the pier would not have used costly new stone for its construction. This dock was used again in 1854 when Whippingham church was once more under reconstruction.

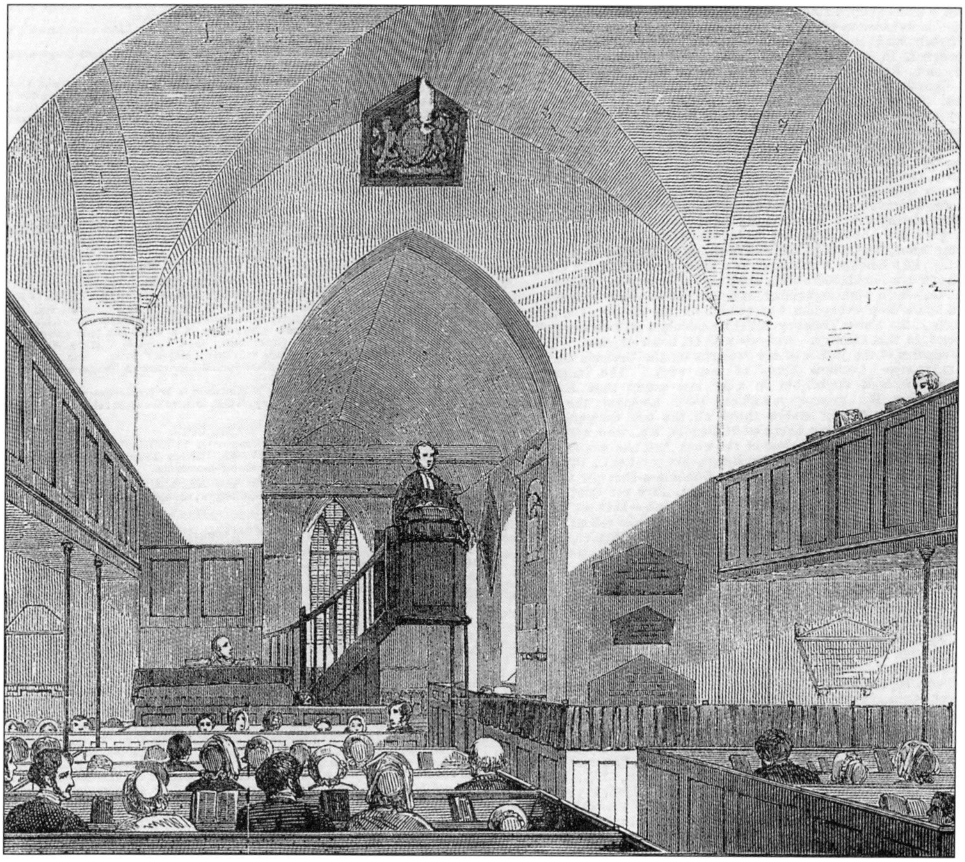

Inside the 'Nash' church. The galleries could be reached by the external staircases. The Queen's pews, at the front-right below the pulpit, were screened by low curtains.

Queen Victoria's Church

Queen Victoria and Prince Albert bought Osborne House in 1845. Although it was their own private residence, accommodation was built for numerous household staff, visiting officials and an increasingly large family. Naturally, attendance at church was expected, and the Royal family, if the weather was fine, would sometimes walk to Whippingham Church when in residence at Osborne, rather than driving there.

The Bishop of Winchester, writing in 1854 comments that, *'the parish church of Whippingham does not afford sufficient accommodation for Her Majesty, the Prince and their Royal family and suite at Divine Service, and ...it is desirable that for such purposes adequate and appropriate accommodation should be provided.'*

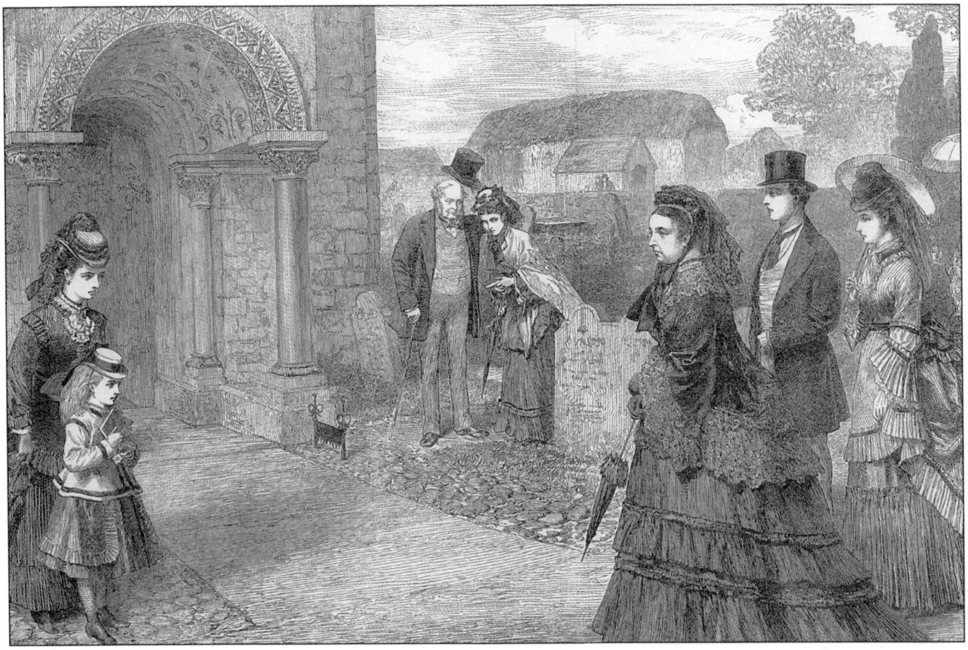

The Queen arrives for morning service. Dated before 1875 as Truckles Farm can be seen in the background. (IWCRO)

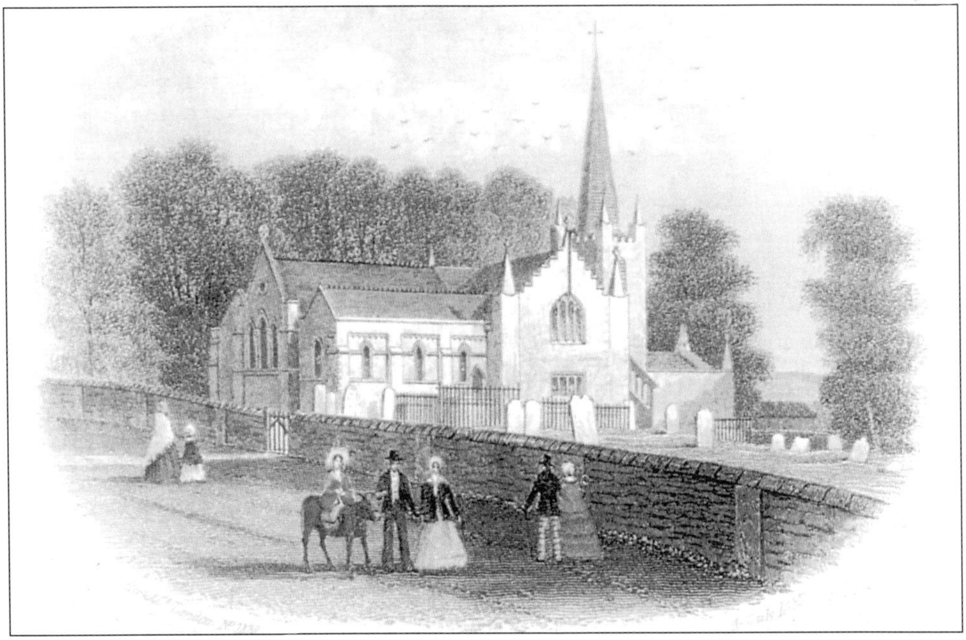

An 1855 engraving showing the new chancel, which was added to the 1804 church.

Designs for the enlargement of St. Mildred's were prepared. The Prince Consort had considerable input into these, working with the architect Albert Jenkins Humbert.

The chancel was enlarged first. The Bishop wrote, *'It is proposed to take down the present chancel and to rebuild in an inspired manner, and build in the churchyard two aisles – looking into such new chancel but separated therefrom by a series of six arches.'* The fact that part of the churchyard was to be incorporated into the building necessitated the removal of some of the graves and copious instructions were provided as to how this should be done.

The Queen was given her own private entrance door to the church, leading directly into the southern of the two Royal chapels either side of the chancel. Chairs, not pews were provided for the Royal family and the household. After the Queen's death Edward VII ordered pews for the southern chapel, and most of the chairs were removed.

In 1860 the plans were made for the rebuilding of the remainder of the church. This was to be one of Albert's last projects, as he died in 1861. The lantern tower, 98ft high, has at its centre a replica of the Order of the Garter. The two transepts have rose windows which are based on the designs of those at Notre Dame Cathedral in Paris. Externally, the spire and turrets have a rather Germanic feel to them, reminiscent of the Prince's homeland.

Many small touches were added later to the church by the Royal family. The new font was designed by Princess Louise and given by the Queen, who also donated the simple handmade wrought iron candelabra with glass shades. These still give the church a special touch, especially when lit at Christmas. Princess Beatrice and Princess Louise made a font carpet, and the lych-gate was given by the Queen.

The newly completed church became very important to Victoria after the death of Albert. Despite his dislike of memorials, Queen Victoria immediately had an elaborate marble one to Albert carved for the Royal Chapel. Other memorials followed, one to Prince Leopold who died quite young, and to various grandchildren who died in their youth. The windows were added by the Queen in memory of her second son, Prince Alfred. Two windows were sent to an exhibition, and Victoria was asked if more could be removed for display. Her emphatic answer came back, *'No, certainly not.'*

Queen Victoria took an interest in the services, to the extent of giving £10 in 1898 to pay for the organist, Ronald Jackman, to take further instruction. The

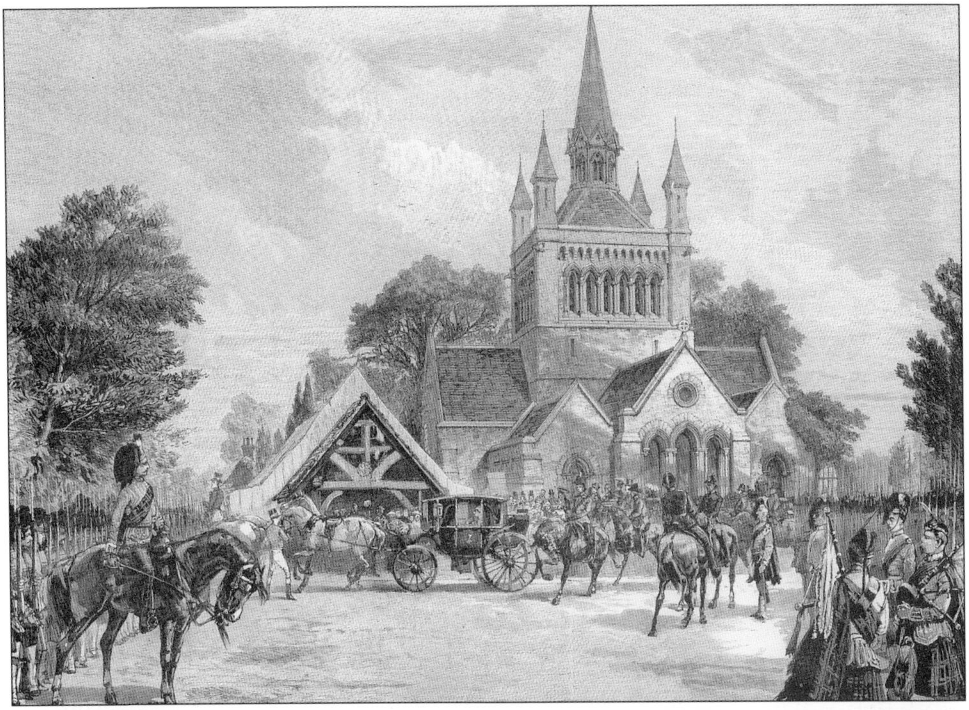

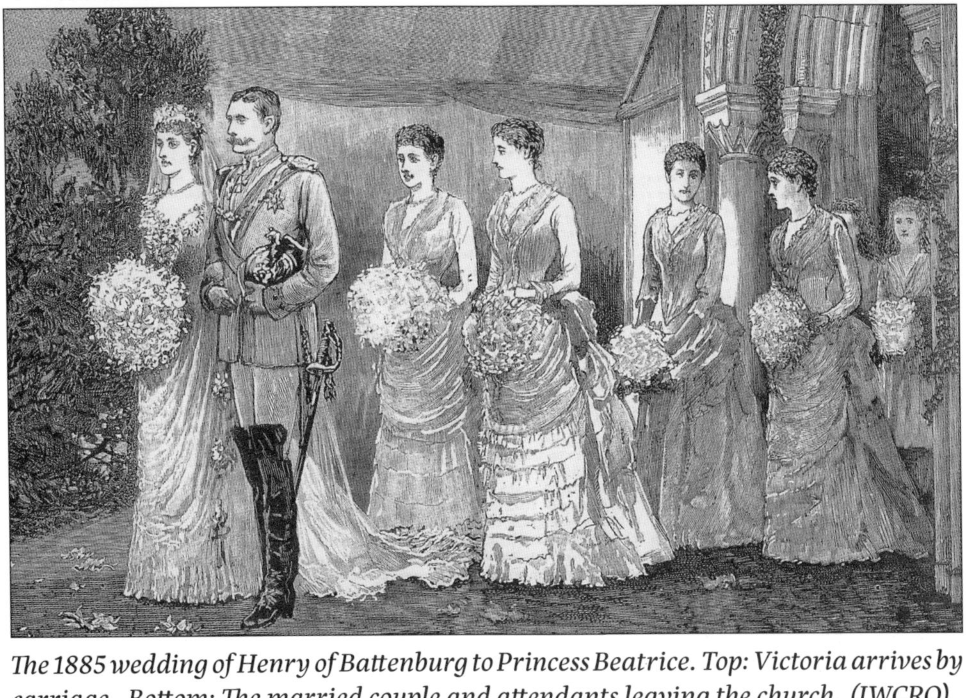

The 1885 wedding of Henry of Battenburg to Princess Beatrice. Top: Victoria arrives by carriage. Bottom: The married couple and attendants leaving the church. (IWCRO)

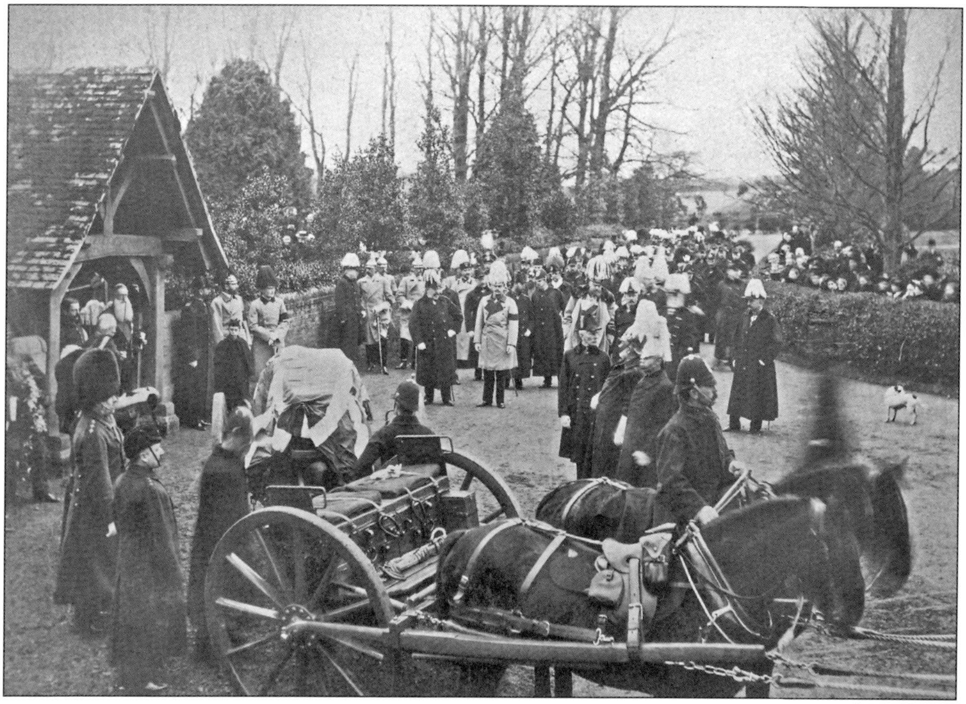

The funeral of Henry of Battenburg in January 1896. His coffin lies on a gun carriage. Edward, Prince of Wales, stands in a dark coat and white gloves at the centre.

Queen thought that, *'he seemed to distinctly benefit from the hints given to him by Sir Walter Parratt.'* The East Cowes Rector at the time, Reverend Barnaby, wrote to Mr Jackman, *'It is indeed something for you to be jolly proud of and thankful for that the Queen wishes you to have lessons and offers to pay for them for free!'*

The Queen's youngest daughter, Princess Beatrice, was married at Whippingham Church in 1885 to Henry of Battenburg. The wedding was a grand affair for Whippingham, with numerous Royalty from various countries. The church was filled with beautiful flowers for the occasion. It had been intended to open the church afterwards to visitors so that they could see these flowers, and raise money for a worthy cause, but unfortunately these plans failed as the congregation at the wedding helped themselves to bouquets before they left!

Sadly, Henry of Battenburg died eleven years later. By this time, Queen Victoria had had her own chapel built at Osborne House as she was unable to attend Whippingham as frequently as before. It was decided to create a Battenburg memorial chapel out of the northern 'household' chapel at Whippingham and he was laid to rest there. Henry had been made Governor of the Isle of Wight, a role that was now taken on by his widow. In 1914 Princess Beatrice moved into Carisbrooke Castle, and at the outbreak of the Second World War the government decided she should move to the safer mainland. She died in 1944, but after the war, her remains were returned to Whippingham to lie beside her husband

The Battenburg link is still strong in Whippingham. The name was changed to Mountbatten in 1917 because of anti-German feelings. For the same reason, Lord Louis Battenberg resigned as Admiral of the Fleet in 1915 when he and his wife Victoria, granddaughter of Queen Victoria, were living in East Cowes and subsequently both were buried in Whippingham churchyard. Their eldest daughter, Alice, was the mother of Phillip, Duke of Edinburgh and their youngest son became Lord Louis Mountbatten of Burma. Members of the Royal family and the Mountbatten family visit St. Mildred's from time to time.

The Churchyard

The Churchyard was enlarged in 1897, taking in a parcel of land belonging to the Queen called Pond Piece to the north. New stone walls were built to the north and by the road.

Various local characters are buried here, including Sam Saunders the aircraft builder, John Samuel White the shipbuilder, and Uffa Fox the boat builder. Uffa's tombstone depicts the airborne lifeboat he designed. Sam Saunders coffin was shaped like a boat, and regrettably nobody had thought to measure the family vault. When the time came to lower the coffin it was found that it was too large, so bricks had to be knocked out of the entrance to the vault to allow sufficient space!

The grave of John Lord, a managing director at Saunders-Roe, takes the unusual form of a broken propeller mounted on a stone. He died in 1936 at the age of 57, but not, as some presume, in an air-accident.

Some of the earliest graves are to the east of the church. One of the smallest tombstones depicts a skull and crossbones, *memento mori*, symbol, a reminder of death, which is most easily visible just before noon if the sun is shining. Close by the north wall of the church are several large chest tombs, some belonging to members of the Goodrich and Shedden families, rich merchants of East Cowes. These once had iron railings around them which were removed for recycling during the Second World War.

Many of those working for Queen Victoria are buried here, sometimes with a headstone given by Her Majesty, as in the case of Mr and Mrs Warne who were

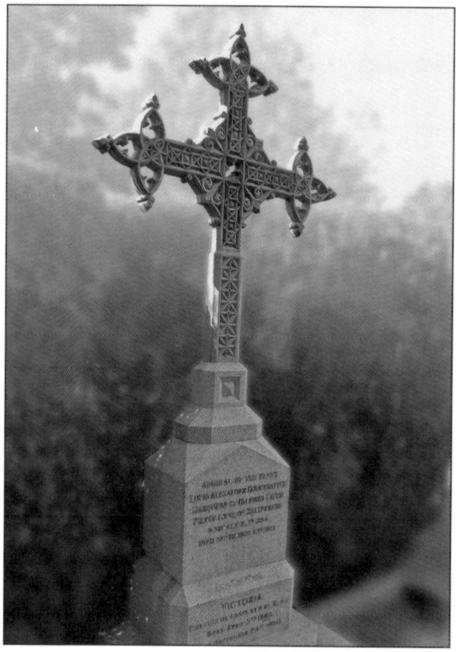

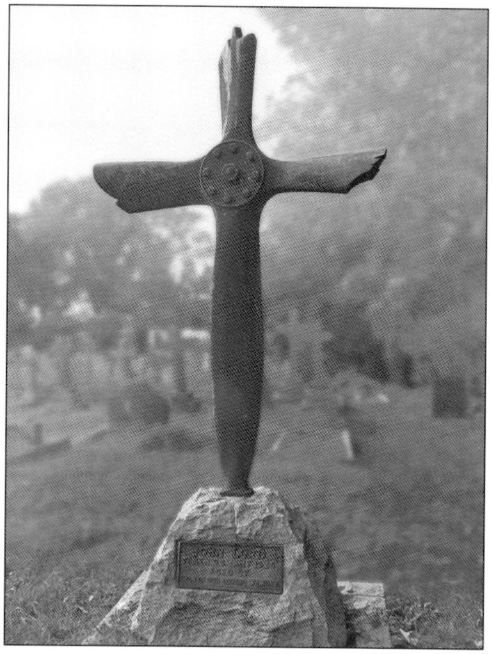

Left: The bronze and granite memorial of Prince Louis of Battenburg and Victoria of Hesse, the Queen's grand-daughter. Right: John Lord's bronze propeller grave.

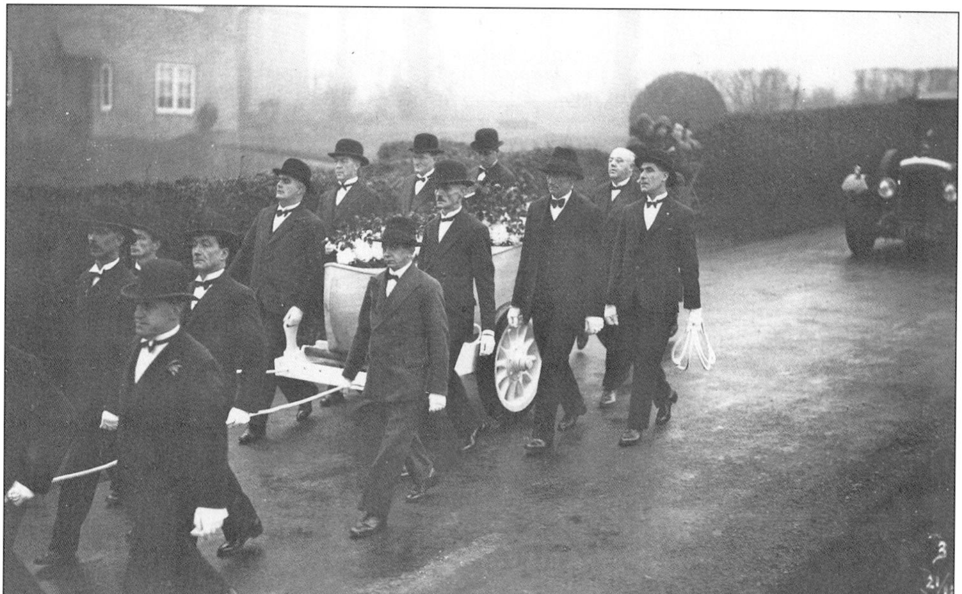

Sam Saunders' funeral procession passes Truckles Cottages on the way to St. Mildred's churchyard in 1933.

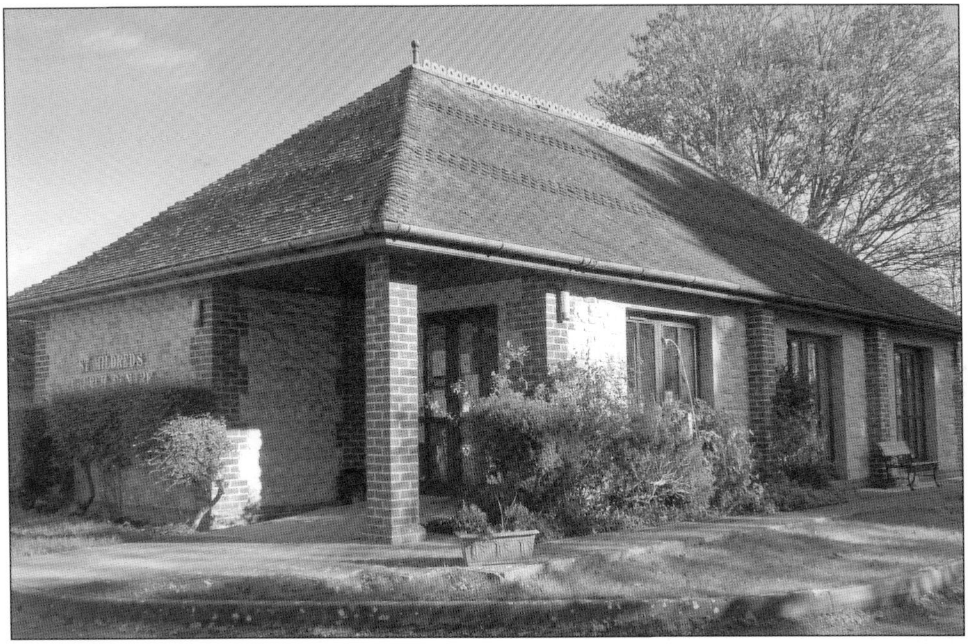

St Mildred's Church Hall, built in 1991 in the grounds of the Rectory.

the caretakers at Swiss Cottage on the Osborne Estate for 27 years. Andrew Toward, the *'faithful Land Steward to the Queen and Prince Consort'* lies by the vestry door. A red polished granite cross to Sir Henry Ponsonby, the Queen's private secretary, is next to the Battenberg grave, and nearby is George Warren, the Queen's telegraphist for 37 years.

The estate carried on in Royal ownership after Queen Victoria's death and several headstones proudly record the fact that some men worked for three monarchs, Queen Victoria, her son Edward VII and also George V.

The village war memorial, given by Princess Beatrice, stands beside the south door to the church. On the wall of the church is a plaque inscribed with the names of those Whippingham men who gave their lives in two World Wars. The first name on the list is Maurice Battenburg, son of Princess Beatrice, who died at the first battle of Ypres in 1914.

The Church Hall

A school room was added to the church in the 1804 rebuild. After the church was rebuilt again in 1854, Sunday school classes were held in the village school by Mrs Prothero, the rector's wife.

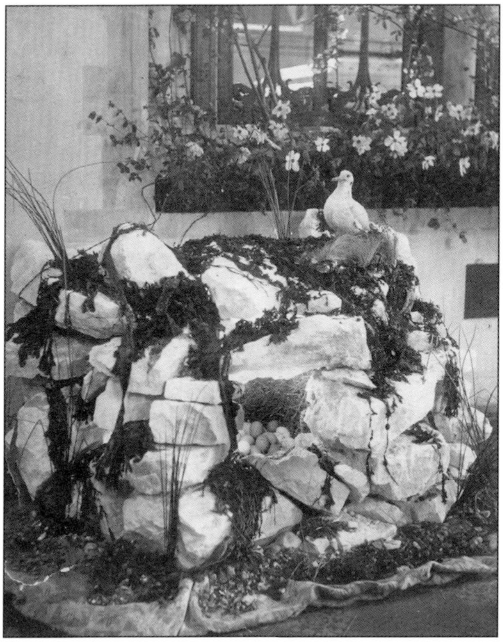

Rev Pritchard's Egg Sunday seagull nest in the church over Easter in the 1930s.

The present church hall was built in 1991 and at the same time the car park and a garden were laid out in the old rectory walled garden. This makes a delightful place to rest and also is ideal for church events and social functions such as the village show and the church fête.

When Queen Victoria was alive the choirs of St. James' in East Cowes and St. Mildred's would perform Christmas carols at Osborne House. The tradition returned in the 1980s when the Durbar Room was used for this by the Friends of Osborne. In the 1920s there was only a ladies choir, but by 1937 there was a choir of boys.

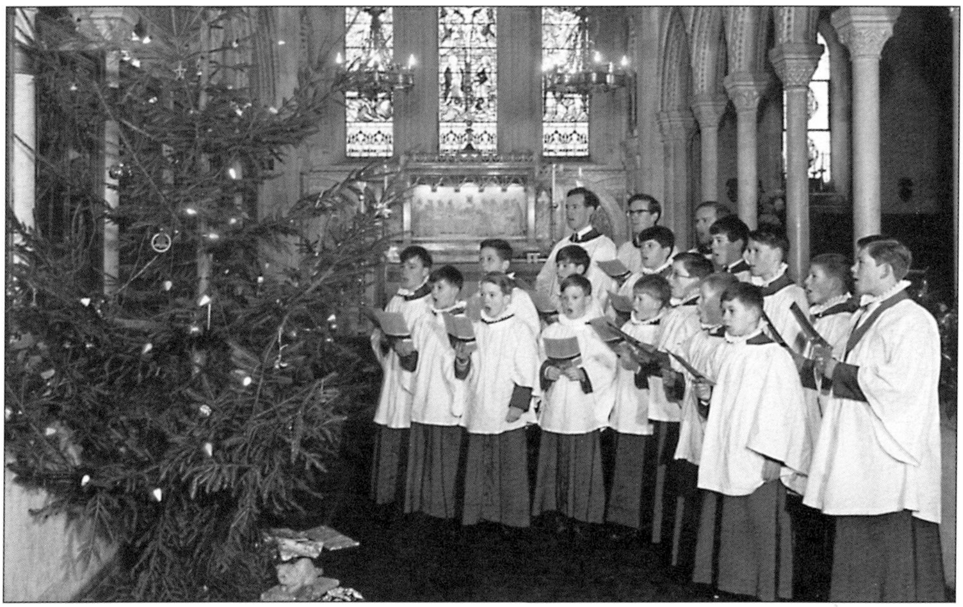

The church choir singing Christmas carols in the 1960s.

Revd Mostyn Pritchard was the Rector in the 1930s and he introduced a number of innovations, many of them with children in mind. Children's services were held twice a month, with special services with 'children's surprises' held on Feast Days. Egg Sunday at Easter saw the children who had chickens bringing eggs, which they took up to an egg nest. The eggs were later given to the sick or needy in the village. Mostyn also introduced the annual candle-lit service, and his Sunday services were so popular that Newport Omnibus Company agreed to rearrange their timetable and route to bring people to church! Between 1931 and 1937 he took 64 baptisms, 65 weddings and 46 funerals.

An old carriage-house next to the church car park functioned as a tea shop for many years. Margaret Caws served the teas then Pam Tuckwell took over until it finally closed its doors in 2004. An exhibition on the history of the church, local buildings of Whippingham and the Victorian Royal children has been on display in the church and hall for several years. Before there was a shop, Mrs Flux would sell postcards, sweets and tobacco from a stall just outside the church gate. Later she started selling teas to visitors at her garden at Truckles. Exhibitions on the history of the church, local buildings of Whippingham and the Victorian Royal children have been on display in the church and hall for several years. In 2017 there are sales tables in the church as well as in the hall, where delicious teas, coffees and cakes are served.

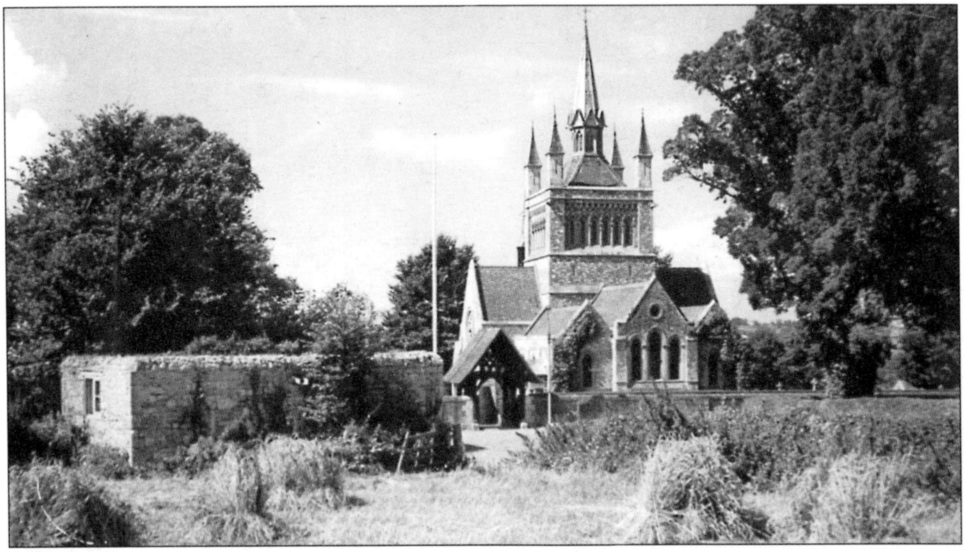

Corn stooks in Padmore Field in the 1950s. The church shop is in the foreground, originally the carriage house for the Queen. (WJ Nigh & Sons Ltd)

Tourists have visited Whippingham Church ever since Prince Albert rebuilt it and after the Queen's death, parts of Osborne House were opened to the public from 1904. Tourism blossomed as excursions were organised to East Cowes, and these frequently called in at Whippingham Church. This continues today, with visitors arriving throughout the season. The church welcomes visitors from Monday to Thursday from Easter to the end of October and stewards act as guides in the church to answer any questions that arise. People arrive from all over the world and the guides have a most interesting time showing them this beautiful church.

Whippingham Rectory

Records show that there has been a secular building associated with Whippingham Church for hundreds of years hidden away behind the trees to the south of the church.

The eastern side of the building is the older, stone-built with flagstone floors and thick walls and comparatively small windows. This became the domestic area when the western rooms were added, possibly in the early 1800s. It is thought that the building was extended to plans by John Nash. A sketchbook begun in 1805 by George Repton, who worked with Nash, depicts the extension. Reverend Ridley occupied the rectory from 1802 to 1817, and the plans show a study for the rector by the front door and two large reception rooms. The western of these was built with curved corners, an attractive feature, and the dining room was made octagonal. A spiral staircase led up to Miss Ridley's rooms. The large bay windows to the west are typical of Nash. Initially the new extension remained separate from the other rooms upstairs. Later, possibly in 1859, a staircase was built in the hall and a galleried landing added to make all the rooms accessible from it. The spiral staircase was removed.

In 1828, John Albin in his *'Companion to the Isle of Wight'* describes Whippingham Parsonage as a very beautiful and distinguished feature. From the house, lawns stretched out to west and south, where there was an uninterrupted view looking across the fields and up the Medina Valley. Queen Victoria sketched the view on 15 August 1864, during one of her visits to Canon and Mrs Prothero. Behind the house, to the south east, was a walled garden, with fruit trees and sufficient space for vegetables to be grown to keep the rector's family self-sufficient. Lord Ernle, Canon Prothero's son, speaks of growing up at the rectory in the 1850s and the family eating all their own produce.

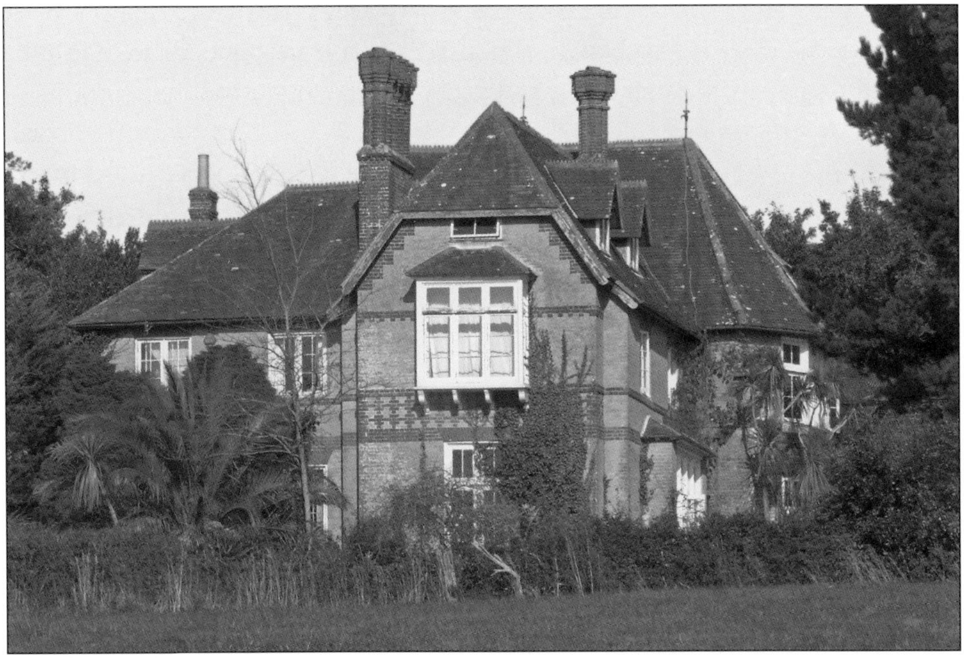

Whippingham Rectory.

Rev. Prothero had several hunters. His coach house and stables were next to the church, at what is now Glebe Cottage.

In 1859 some plumbing was carried out. A new seat of one-inch thick Honduras mahogany was to be fixed to the water closet, and a five inch brass bolt fixed to the door! The plumber was to, *'refix the present water closet seat to one of the servants' closets,'* and to, *'lay on water to the housemaid's sink with proper drain from same.'*

In the 1930s the Reverend Mostyn Pritchard was almost the last rector to be in residence at the rectory. He had come to the Island from a rich Kensington living and was given furnishings for his new home by his grateful parishioners as a wedding present. Carpets on the floor in the hall included tiger skins! His wife took in lodgers to help with expenses, and to help heat the house as it was very cold in winter.

After the Second World War, the rector of East Cowes became the rector of Whippingham as well. Whippingham Rectory was re-allocated for church use. The two main reception rooms of the rectory, linked by folding doors, became the 'Church Rooms' where meetings and Sunday School were held. The bedrooms of the west wing were converted into a flat, and the rear part of the house was let separately. By 1980, the Reverend Snape and his wife Evelyn were living in the flat upstairs above Church Rooms. Mrs Snape ran dancing classes for children in the two reception rooms downstairs.

Once the new church hall was complete in 1991, the old rectory was sold and split into two homes. The incumbent, serving both St. James' Church and St. Mildred's, had been living at East Cowes Rectory in Old Road for some years. That rambling building was sold in 2001, and now the Rector of Whippingham and East Cowes lives in Victoria Grove, East Cowes, half way between the two churches.

Life at the Rectory in the 1850s and 1860s

Rowland Prothero was born at Whippingham in 1851. His father was the rector of St. Mildred's at that time, and chaplain to the Queen. Rowland later became Minister for Agriculture during the First World War and then as Lord Ernle wrote about his life in a book entitled *Whippingham to Westminster.* He remembered the rectory as a roomy, comfortable home, with sunken fences separating the garden from the fields and view of the river.

Whenever the Queen visited the rectory the children would be sent for. Her presence inspired awe in the young Rowland, and she exuded a simple kindness. The church was being rebuilt and the boy had been reprimanded by the builder for playing in the mortar. When Rowland saw the builder on the tower with another man he took a shot at the builder with his catapult. Unfortunately the builder's friend received the missile in the back and turned to reveal he was Prince Albert! Rowland felt very guilty the next time he was brought before the Queen, but nothing was said.

The household was fairly self sufficient. Bread was baked weekly and was a major event. When it was fresh it was delicious and the crust was unforgettably crisp and sweet but by the fifth day the bread was tough and dry. Milk, butter, eggs, poultry, fruit and vegetables came from their home resources. They brewed their own beer and Rowland remembered always having his own silver mug of beer with dinner as a child. The butcher came once a week for orders, and fish was fetched from West Cowes. Pigs were kept and the village postmaster, an elderly villager, was the pig-killer.

Rowland's mother did have some groceries sent specially from London, and sometimes Rowland would accompany a villager on a trip to the market in Newport. This excursion would be on Hollis's passage boat – which called twice a week at the Folly Hard. Embarkation at high tide was easy, but more of a problem at low tide. Hollis was a red-faced, hoarse-voiced mariner, with rings in his ears and wore a blue jersey.

Their own soap and pomatum were made at the rectory, perfumed after old-fashioned recipes with a variety of scents. Wax candles were used downstairs, but the nursery only had tallow candles. If the boy's nose or lips were chapped by the wind then his nurse applied tallow which smelt musty.

Rowland remembered some of the regular callers at the rectory. The postman came every day and sometimes the pedlar would arrive to sell his wares, his pack a miracle for the variety of its contents. He was a cherry-cheeked merry fellow. The organ-grinder visited with his marionettes dancing in a glass case on top of the organ. One figure stood with its hand out with a tray for money. If Rowland added a penny to the tray the puppet bowed and added it to the pile, but if Rowland gave it a stone this would be thrown out! Between 1857 and 1860 a little shrivelled man from southern India made an annual visit to sell Madras curry powder.

Rowland and his brothers enjoyed only formal relations with their parents. As a young child he would be deposited in the drawing room at six in the evening to spend an hour with his mother. He had been washed and put into clean clothes for this occasion. As the boys grew older, their mother took on their education, she herself was a linguist and Latin scholar. While living at Whippingham Rectory she clung on to two luxuries – parcels of books from Rolandi's Foreign Library, and a London dressmaker!

From the age of six, arithmetic and writing were taught to the rectory boys by the village schoolmaster, who came three evenings a week. Rowland remembered using quill pens. He also had the pleasure of his father's servant reading to him between the intervals of answering the bell. When he was ten years old Rowland was sent to boarding school, but the next year he was so ill that he was sent home. Another year was passed at the rectory before he was sent to school at Marlborough in 1864.

Rector Prothero ran the parish single-handedly. Sundays were, of course, a special day. First there would be family prayers, then at a quarter to ten Rowland would walk with his mother to the village school where she held a Sunday school class for the older village boys. Each boy would say by heart the collect for the day, and then he would be questioned by Mrs Prothero on the meaning of what he had learnt. At eleven there was a morning service at the church.

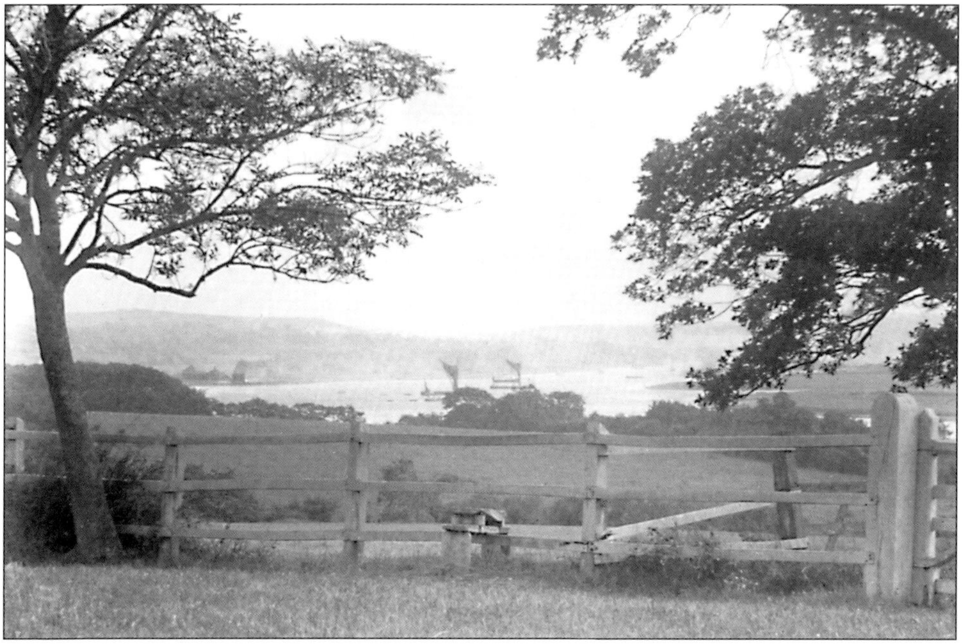

Rowland would have been familiar with this view looking down the fields to the river. This c1910 photo shows sailing barges and East Medina Mill in the distance.

After morning service, Rowland's father would go into the servants' hall and carve a sirloin of beef into dinners for the half dozen or more old people who had been unable to come to church. A daughter or grandchild would come to collect the food with a basin tied up in a handkerchief, and Rowland would add a baked potato to the dish.

In the winter, evening service was at 3pm and in the summer at 6pm. Afterwards, Rowland's mother held a Women's Club. Some 20 women paid three pence a week, and Mrs Prothero doubled the fund. These savings were paid out at Christmas.

On Sundays the boys had dinner and tea with their parents, when there would often be visitors from Osborne, perhaps members of the household and guests, sometimes a famous politician or a clever preacher. Officers from the barracks at Parkhurst, or, if the tide and season was right, regatta-goers from Cowes, might also visit the rectory for tea. The visits would have been arranged before hand by correspondence. All the guests would go to the church service. The children were not to play any outdoor games on Sundays, and only given a small range of suitable reading books. Spelling games were permitted, but only biblical names could be used! Newspapers were not allowed and *The London Illustrated News* remained in its wrapper until Monday morning.

At Christmas the rectory had a decorated tree, but cards were not sent. Christmas plays were dying out, but a party of young fishermen from East Cowes acted out one of the old mummers plays at the rectory. On New Year's Eve a wooden silver-banded punch bowl was decorated with holly, the children walked round the table three times and received gifts from all the diners. On 6th January there was a Twelfth Night cake, and a children's party. Pictures of different characters were drawn and put into a hat. Each child drew out a card and those receiving the King and Queen would sit on a made-up throne and preside over the party. On Valentine's Day, 14th February, the postbag would be full of messages and when Shrove Tuesday arrived, all the village children trooped down to the rectory, singing a song asking for food.

In 1855, aged four, Rowland remembered going to Southampton with his parents on the *Gem*, at that time a vessel of the Isle of Wight Steam Packet Company. His parents travelled on the steamer but the carriage and horses, held by a groom, went in a low-sided 'horse boat' towed behind the steamer. Inside the carriage sat the children and their nurses. At the Brambles Bank the seas were choppy and lopped over into the 'horse boat', splashing the carriage. The horses began to plunge about. Once round the corner the seas calmed down, but it must have been a very frightening experience for all concerned.

Looking down from the Rectory towards the river young Rowland saw the boats passing. There were sturdy brigs arriving laden with coal from Cardiff and other vessels carrying goods of all descriptions. He saw the many brown- sailed barges carrying cement on their way to the mainland, or returning empty. The cement mills on the west bank of the Medina, already operating in the 1850s, were generally wreathed in a cloud of smoke.

Rowland's childhood memories give us a rare insight into what life must have been like in Whippingham at the rectory, and glimpses into a different world 160 years ago.

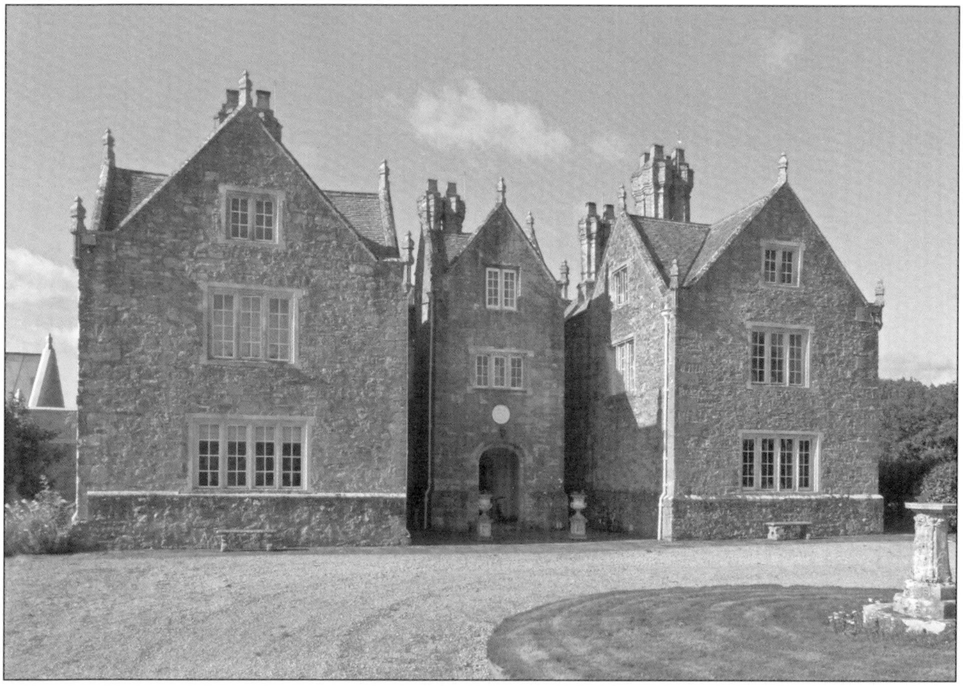

The east-facing front door to Barton Manor.

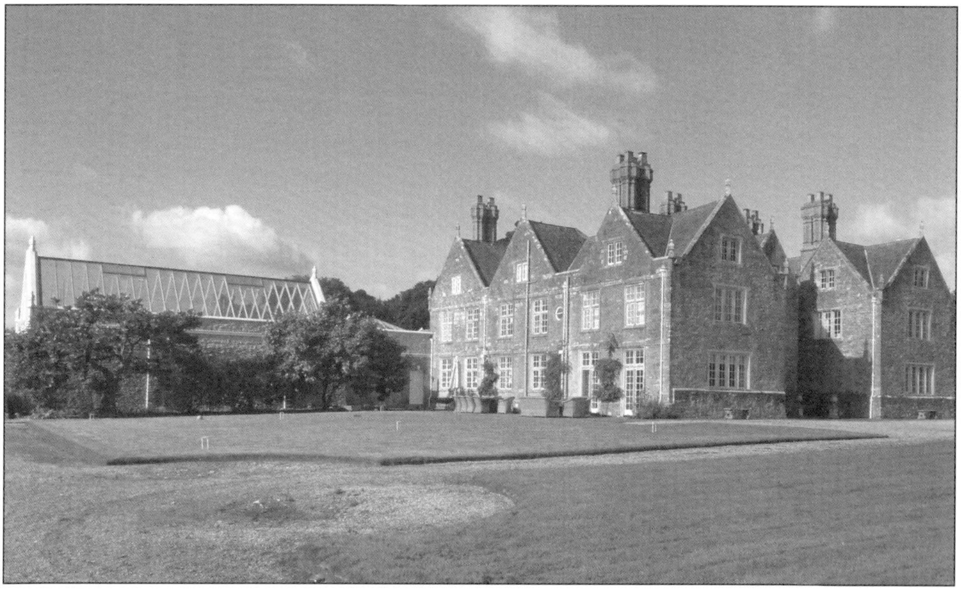

View of the south elevation showing the wall of the kitchen garden and newly refurbished swimming pool. This was constructed on the site of the greenhouse.

THREE

Barton Manor & Farm

The recorded history of Barton dates back to 1275 when an oratory was founded here. This was planned for the retreat of six priests and a clerk, following the rule of Saint Augustine. They were to choose an arch-priest from among their number, and this man would be ratified by the Bishop of Winchester. Otherwise, they were an independent body. Copies of the charter of the foundation still exist at Winchester, with their ornate seals attached.

Strict rules were laid down as to what they should wear; rusty black habits and hats and a new cloak lined with lamb's wool each winter, and what they should eat; one main meal with a second course and on feast days a third course if the resources of the house allowed. The clerk was to read something edifying to them while they dined. Their old clothes were to be given to the poor, and they were required to supply 13 poor people with bread, beer and soup every day.

Cridmoor Farm at Carisbrooke was purchased specifically to provide funds for their almsgiving. The priests were all to sleep in one dormitory, unless illness prohibited this, and to follow all the many religious services of the day, including prayers for their founders and benefactors.

Barton Oratory was endowed with numerous parcels of land from all over the Island, farms, grazing land, two mills in Newport, - one of them Cross Mill, and a warehouse in Southampton. Over £625, a massive sum for those days, was spent in setting up the oratory. Lay brothers ran the day-to-day work, leaving the priests to spend their time in study or meditation.

From 1321 Barton was given the responsibility for maintaining the oratory at St. Catherine's Hill, where a light was to be kept burning at night for the safety of seafarers.

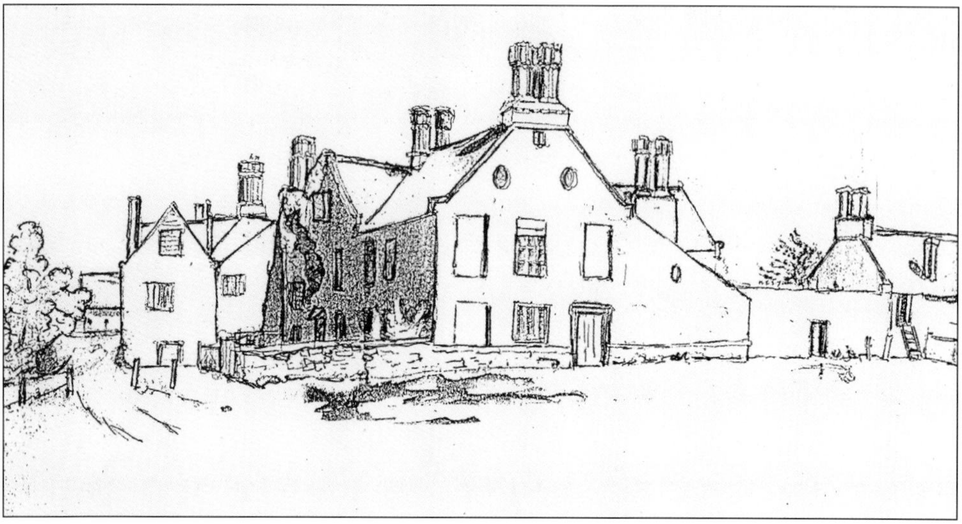

How Barton Manor looked before Queen Victoria bought it in 1845 and it was remodelled by Prince Albert.

Perhaps because of their independence, discipline became lax, and there were complaints to Winchester in 1365. William Love, the arch-priest in 1389, appears to have been guilty of several misdemeanours, and let Barton Oratory get on without care. In 1390 arch-priest Love was captured and carried off to *'parts beyond the seas,'* and the buildings became dilapidated.

He must have been returned to Barton, with better intentions, as in 1403 a formal contract was entered into between William Love and a mason, Richard Lathbury, to undertake the necessary repairs. The Oratory continued to function until 1439, when all Barton lands were given to Winchester College.

Barton was owned by the college for the next 400 years, leasing out the lands to a variety of tenants. The duty of maintaining a priest at the chapel at Barton continued with Winchester. There was a chapel there until 1547. In that year an act was passed to abolish all chantries, Barton among them, as protestant feeling was against them.

Later a substantial Jacobean house was constructed. It included several small lancet windows which may have survived from the oratory building. In 1790 Hassell wrote *'A Tour of the Isle of Wight'* and commented that Barton had recently been the residence of Lord Clanricarde. Hassell tells us that;

'All the sides of the rooms are of wainscot, formed into small panels, in which are fixed a number of representations of the cross. Here was likewise a chapel, but the

building is now appropriated to less sacred purposes, being converted into a warehouse for wool. The mode of construction of the house, with so many gable ends towards the front, gives a great formality to its appearance, so do the tall chimnies.' [sic]

The Queen buys Barton Manor

Queen Victoria rented Osborne in 1844 for one year, to enable the Royal couple to assess its suitability as their family home. They decided it was too small, so a new building was started as soon as they bought Osborne in 1845. The same year they bought Barton Manor from Winchester College for £18,600. The house would provide additional accommodation for the equerries, diplomats and visiting family.

The house was remodelled according to Albert's designs. The walls and chimneys of the house were carefully repaired with matching masonry and bricks made at the Queen's own brickyard. The panelling was removed and the house gutted. A suite of kitchens was added that could be used to prepare additional food for Osborne when the need arose. Insulated carts were built specially for the purpose of transporting food there from Barton.

Prince Albert had the old farm buildings to the east removed and in their place he designed gardens that would enhance the view from the house. He planted many new trees, including a *Cupressus lambertiana* on his 27th birthday on 26th August 1846. This new introduction from America grew to a great height, but blew down in the hurricane of 1987, along with many other trees on the estate.

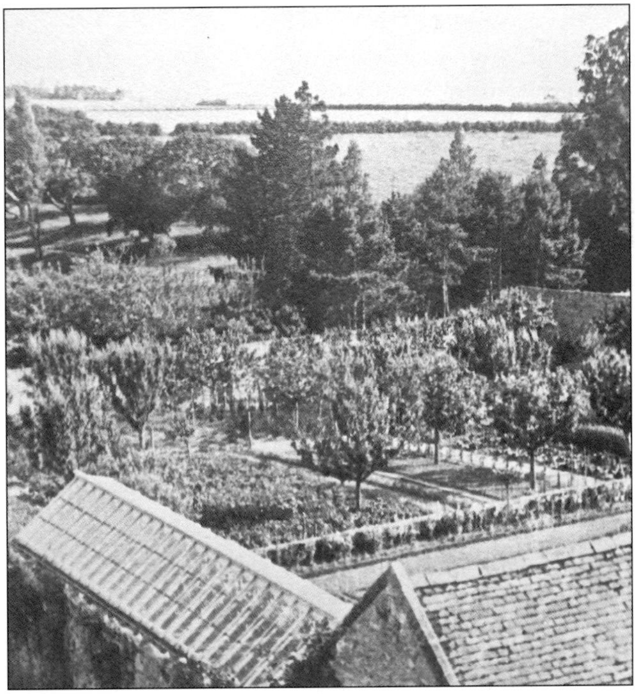

Overlooking the walled garden in the 1950s. It had numerous fruit trees.

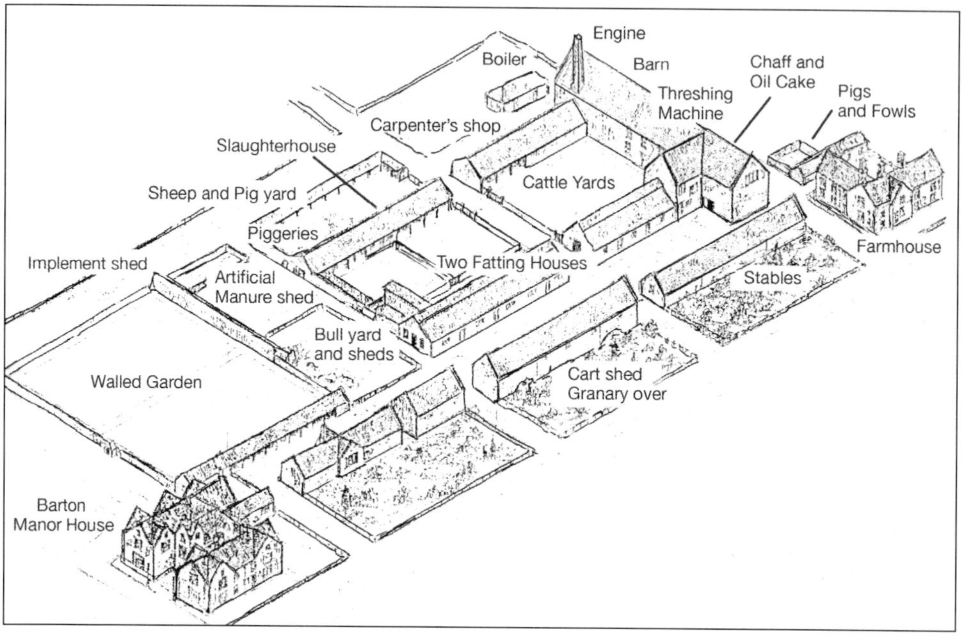

The large complex of buildings which made up Albert's Barton Farm. It includes barns for the animals,grain storage and machinery to help with the harvest.

Prince Albert's Barton Farm

Barton Farm was run as the 'home farm,' without a tenant. It was to supply the Royal needs as well as to run as a commercial farming enterprise. Prince Albert created a 'model' farm, to give the tenants of the other farms ideas that they could copy if the new techniques proved useful.

To the west of the house Albert had an extensive range of modern stone and brick farm buildings constructed in 1852. Stone was used on elevations of the buildings that showed as you approached the complex and the cheaper bricks were used inside the farm yard. These buildings incorporated the latest innovations. There were two steam engines. One was used to pump water to the house and fountains at Osborne and the other was used to drive a shaft that ran the length of the building to belt-drive a chaff cutter, a mill, a threshing machine, corn elevators and other machinery. A hand-operated tramway enabled trucks of prepared fodder and bedding to be pushed easily along to the stables, cowsheds, piggeries, calf fattening sheds and bull pens.

The cart sheds incorporated cast iron beams to support a cement floored grain store above to prevent vermin. The carts were another innovation. Sets

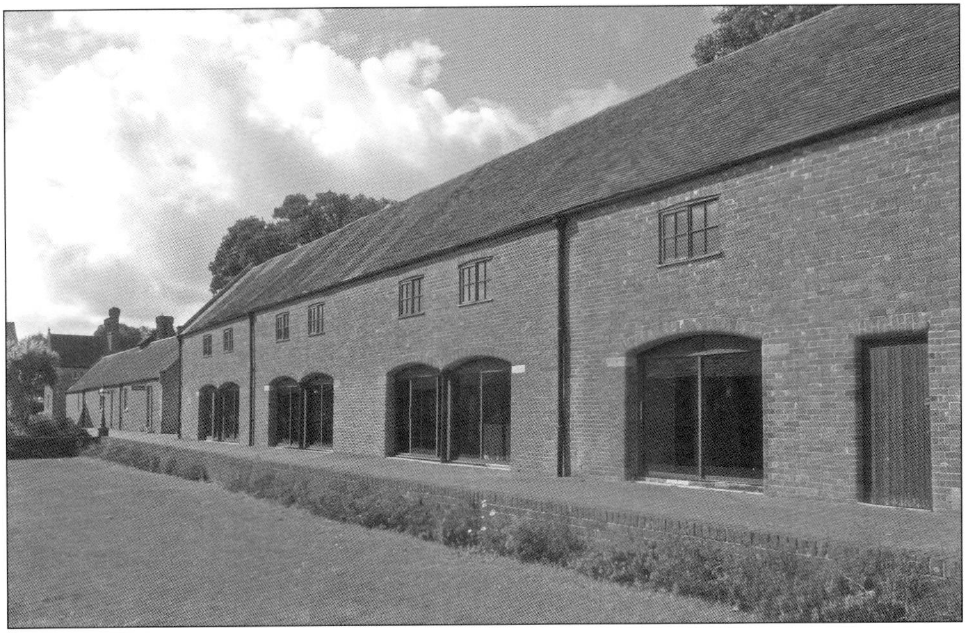

The long cartsheds and stables have been sympathetically restored and are now used for events and exhibitions.

of axles and wheels were constructed that could have interchangeable beds laid on them. There were cart beds, harvest beds and dung beds. When not required these were stored vertically like plates in a plate rack.

Metal supports were constructed for the hay and grain ricks. This kept them off the ground, and the rats away. A vast underground reservoir was constructed, with brick barrel vaulting, to collect water from a nearby spring.

The Prince had thousands of drainage tiles made at the Queen's brickyard which were used to drain the heavy clay fields of the lower pastures. The soil was also greatly improved by adding 30 tons of chalk per acre. This was brought across the Solent from Portsdown Hill, delivered at Barton Hard. This was cheaper than using chalk from the Island. Dung for the fields also came from Portsmouth.

By 1860, Albert had considerable stock at Barton. There were 31 horses, 64 cattle, 783 sheep, and 51 swine. Most of the working horses were Clydesdales, the milking cattle Alderneys, the fattening beasts Galloways, and the sheep mainly Southdowns.

The farm accounts were submitted annually to Prince Albert and generally showed a loss, although the woodland was making a profit. In the ten years from

1848 to 1858 the profit on Barton Estate amounted to £857.13s.0d. Land steward Andrew Toward pointed out to Prince Albert in 1858 that he had expenses not normally incurred on a farm:- *'There is the daily expense, not needed by tenant farmers, of sweeping and cleaning about the buildings for the sake of appearance. The coppice wood on the estate will annually become of less value in consequence of the introduction of so many ornamental trees, which causes the undergrowth to be destroyed at an increase in labour with a decrease in profit.'*

Barton Farm was visited by the Queen and Royal children on their walks, and guests would be shown the farm, hence the sweeping and cleaning. From the lodge gates at Barton and Alverstone avenues of elm trees were planted leading to the house. The elms died in the 1970s of Dutch Elm Disease but Albert's large cork-oak plantation survives.

Four hundred acres were under cultivation, and a further 400 were under pasture by 1860. At that date the farm had a Smith's Steam Cultivator for some fields, which drew a plough back and forth across a field on wires. Queen Victoria was careful to pay the going Island rate for workers on their estate as she did not want to encourage a rise in pay all over the Island by excessive pay. Her staff did however receive free medical care, and useful gifts at Christmas.

The work at the farm continued after Albert's death in 1861. When the Isle of Wight Agricultural Shows started the Queen was a frequent prizewinner. Sometimes she would have a cup made with her cash prizes to celebrate her wins, and at other times she would put the monies into the school prize fund.

Surplus stock was sold locally. In 1901, Slades, the local East Cowes butcher, had a photograph taken of his Christmas meat display, with labels proclaiming, *'Stock fattened on Her Late Majesty's farm at Barton.'*

A shallow pond was built that could be used for skating if the winter weather permitted. Constructed in 1861, it was enlarged and made more watertight in 1872. This facility was much appreciated by the Royal children, and grandchildren. Victoria, however, would not allow mixed skating by the adults, as it was much too unseemly should a slip occur!

The farm after the Queen's death

When Queen Victoria died in 1901, her son Edward gave Osborne House to the nation. The household wing became a convalescent home for officers. He retained Barton Manor as a holiday home on the Island and continued the work that his father had started on the gardens, building the terraces leading down to the lake,

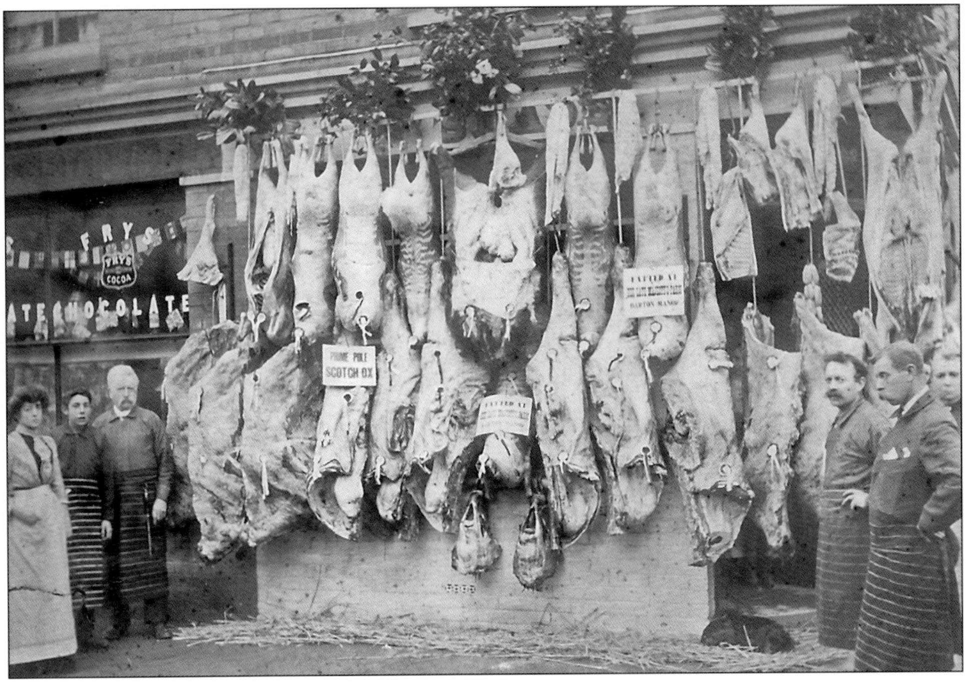

The staff of Slades Butchers, East Cowes and their produce, Christmas 1901. One label reads; Fattened at Her Late Majesty's Farm Barton Manor.

the walled garden and planting more trees. King Edward used the house for entertaining, one of his visitors being his cousin the Kaiser of Germany.

In 1909 the Tsar of Russia, Nicholas II, and all his family paid a visit to Barton. The King and the Tsar reviewed the fleet on 2nd August at Spithead, and the next day watched the racing at Cowes. They visited the Naval College at Osborne on 4th August and took tea on the lawn at Barton.

Mount Cottages were built between 1901 and 1907. They are a pair of semi-detached cottages made of stone in the style of Barton Manor itself. After King Edward's death in 1910, Royalty appeared to lose interest in Barton Manor, and in 1922 the Barton Estate with Barton and Woodhouse Farms was sold. Crown Estates continued to own the outlying farms until 1956.

The Tillett family were the next owners of Barton Manor Estate. The farms provided an occupation for many people, as the photograph taken in 1922 shows *(page viii)*. Families had worked for generations on the estate, and some still live there in 2017. Today, with modern mechanization, the farms no longer need the large numbers of workers.

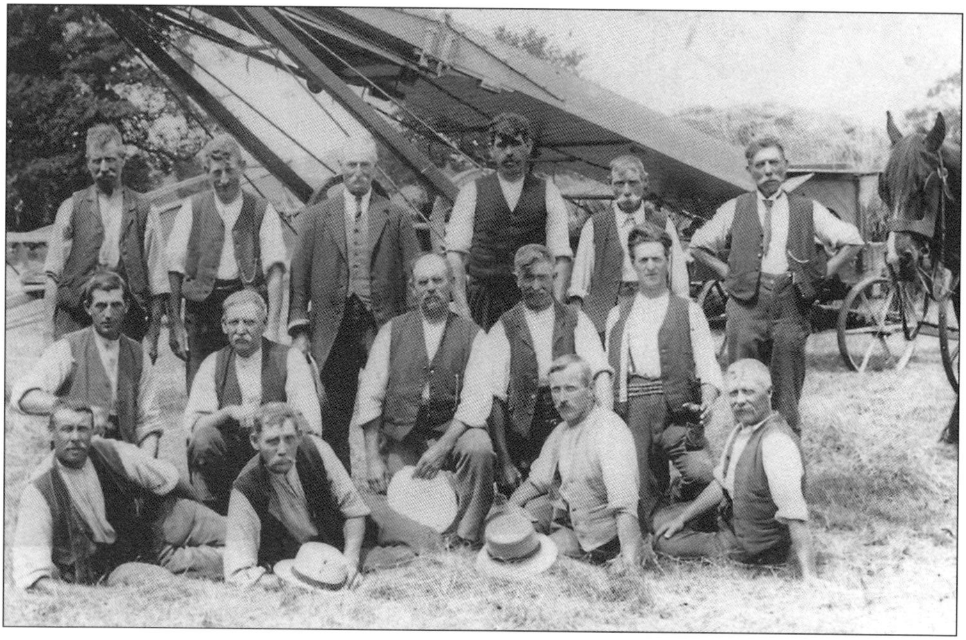

Workers on Barton Manor Farm take a break from using an elevator to build a haystack in 1923.

In 1922 the estate was profitable and the house a pleasant place to live. Princess Beatrice, the Queen's youngest daughter, visited Mrs Tillett several times. The Princess related the story that the Queen would sometimes put up families with young unruly children at Barton, rather than having them running riot at Osborne House.

Most of the farm buildings were still in their original use, including Albert's dairy. This had tiled floors and walls to keep the milk cool on the stone shelves and an elaborate central fountain cooling the air in the summer.

Grace Davison writes about growing up as a child at Barton, where her father became farm manager for the Tillett family. *'As a child I thought that every farm looked like Barton, with its stone and brick outbuildings. It was only later that I learnt that it was Prince Albert's model farm, and rather special as farms go.*

I remember the dairy well, with its tiled floor and tiled walls. In my mind I can still see the cooler and the vast vats of cream. I stuck my finger in one of these while Miss Thorpe, the Dairymaid, was not looking but discovered it was sour cream for butter. So I just had to swallow it before she turned round!

The main stone barn used to house a threshing drum and in that area there was a

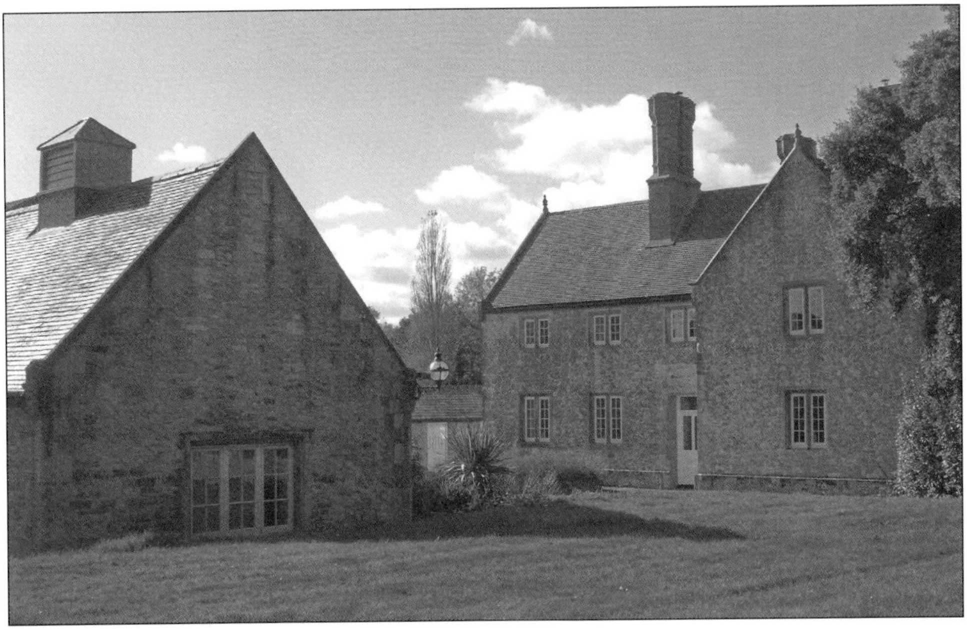

Barton Manor Farmhouse with the dairy in the foreground.

grinding drum and mangolds were chopped for feed. There was a chaff house with a granary over the engine house.

The cow sheds could house sixty five animals and there were two bull boxes with feeding passages and open yards. Eleven horses could be stabled and there were six pigsties. The range of buildings on the north side included a hayloft.

Mr Tillett's herd were lovely Guernseys and we were allowed so many pints of milk a day. As children we drank pints of rich creamy milk and mum made us big rice puddings. The skimmed milk was fed to the animals. When Tuberculin testing came into being, the cowmen had to wear milking hats and smocks and wash the cows' udders thoroughly before milking. My father had to impress the importance of this to the older cowmen as their previous less stringent methods were hard to break. The milk was taken to Sandown to the Isle of Wight Creameries.

As children we were always interested in picking up bits of cork from the cork-oak trees. There were always swans on the pond below the farm. We also used to play on the beach and in the creek at King's Quay with other estate children. We would be sent off for the day with a bag of jam sandwiches. Once the boys lit a fire and cooked a very elderly dead rabbit which they found. It made them ill! We would collect cuttlefish bones for our chickens, and eat wild strawberries. We swam in King's Quay above the sluice and had mud-ball fights across the stream. King John's treasure was said to be buried in the creek, but we never found it.

Old Mrs Tillett at the big house was a small, dainty lady who always dressed perfectly, with her white hair back in a neat bun. She was very kind and looked after my mother for several days during a severe illness. She took calve's foot jelly and so on to Lily Snow at Matthew's Cottage when she was ill. Mrs Tillett visited all her cottagers and helped them all.'

Mr Ablitt came from Newtown to manage Barton Farm from 1936-41, with children George and Sue. In 1942 they moved to Heathfield Farm.

During the Second World War life at Barton changed. Officialdom visited and said that all the iron railings around the Osborne fields rented by the Tilletts, and the ornate gates, were to be taken for scrap. This would have caused considerable inconvenience to the farm, and the loss of the V and A embossed gates would have been sad. Ivor Tillett offered the authorities the boiler and engine from the engine house at Barton instead. This had not been used for several years as the coal consumption had been enormous and the only man who could work the engine had died! The men agreed and carted it off, thus saving the railings and gates, which can still be seen in 2017.

The Manor House was host to several visitors during the war. The RAMC officers from the hospital unit based at Osborne Stable Block were quartered at Barton, and German officer prisoners of war were lodged at Barton while undergoing treatment. Orderlies had to carry the stretchers the half-mile between buildings. On one occasion, a German aircraft came over firing its machine-guns as a German officer was being taken to Osborne. The orderlies unceremoniously dumped the stretcher on the road and dived for cover. Fortunately nobody was injured!

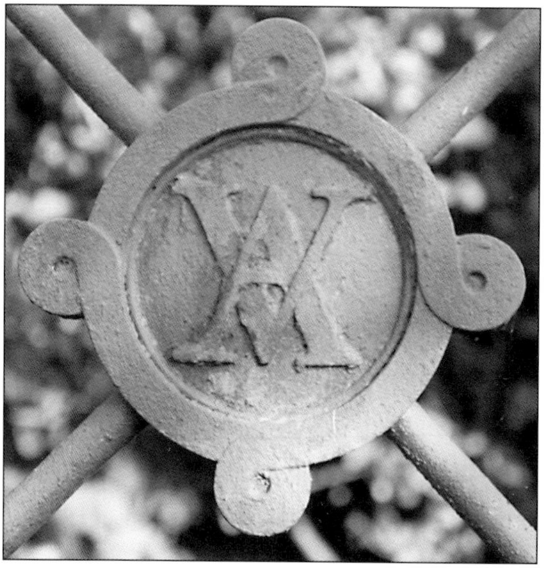

The V and A cypher which features on many of the gates on the estate.

After the Second World War

In 1952 the Tillett family moved to Devon. Barton Manor was sold and the Estate was split up into its constituent farms. Barton Manor house then had a variety of owners. The first was Peter McDonald, MP for the Island. Next for a short time, Barton Manor was called 'Brookfield', a school for boys intending to make a career in the Royal Navy. A model boat found under the floorboards of the classroom may date from this time. Subsequently Barton was owned by Miss Holt and later by Lady Price.

In 1976 Anthony and Alix Goddard bought Barton Manor and set about planting a vineyard on the warm sunny slopes. They opened the grounds to the public. Spring daffodils and huge herbaceous borders provided colour and the old skating lake was turned into a delightful garden with a stream. The middle lake was home to a black swan and numerous, enormous, hungry carp. The 'secret garden' was full of the scent of roses. The wine, bottled on the premises, was popular and won competition medals.

In 1987 the Barton home farm buildings came up for sale. These adjoined Barton House and were no longer needed for farming. The Goddards bought them, not only because the size of their vineyard and tourist business had expanded to bursting point, but also because they were itching to restore the old buildings to something like their former glory. This they achieved. Four out of five of the buildings required re-roofing. By luck, 12,000 second- hand clay

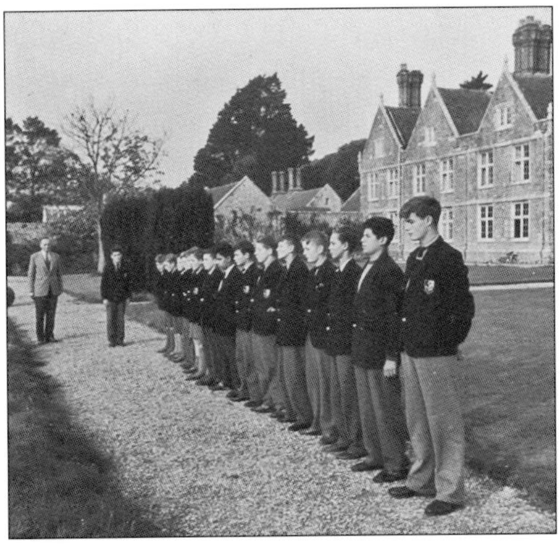

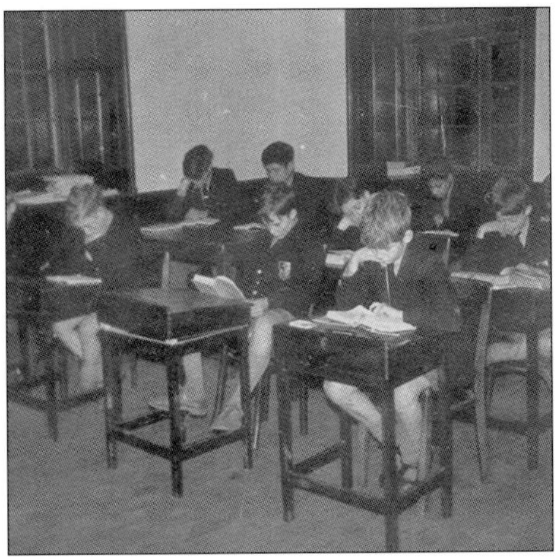

Barton Manor as Brookfield school for boys in the 1950s, preparing them for a career in the Royal or Merchant Navy.

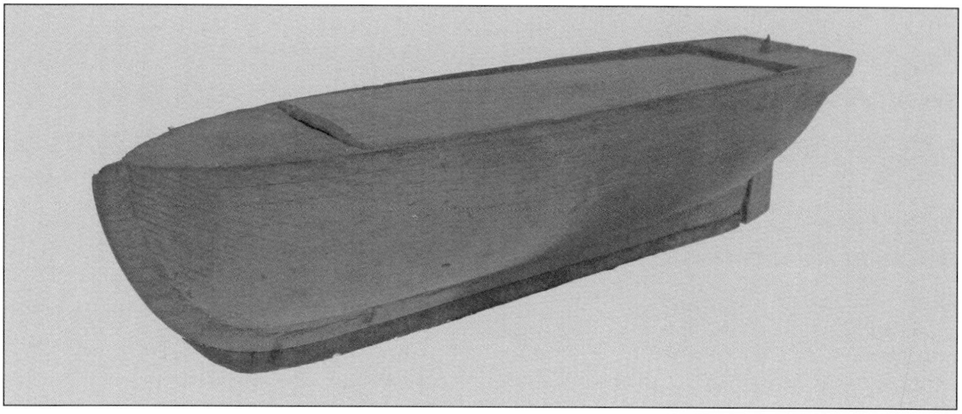

The handmade toy boat found under the floorboards of one of the classrooms. It may have been hidden by a Brookfield boy and forgotten before he could finish it.

tiles were purchased just a day before the 1987 hurricane, which tripled their value overnight! The cart shed and granary became the kitchen, restaurant and function room. The stabling became the toilets and shop, and the dairy became the ticket office. The old farmyard became a very pleasant place to sit, enjoy the sun and eat.

Mr Goddard was a Lloyds name and when funds had to be found after the Lloyds crash, regretfully he sold Barton Manor in 1993.

Robert Stigwood bought Barton that year for £1.15million. He had arrived in Britain from Australia with £3 in his pocket in 1959 and soon became an agent for various pop stars. The Bee Gees and Cream were among his clients and he also worked with the Beatles and Brian Epstein. His first pop musical was *Hair*, followed by *Jesus Christ Superstar*, *Evita* and *Grease*. Stigwood made his millions, bought a yacht (with a crew of 28), a Bermuda home, and Barton Manor. He entertained his friends and spent much of his time quietly at Barton, flying in and out by private helicopter. He removed the vineyards.

For several years the grounds were given over to the Island's Earl Mountbatten Hospice to use for fundraising events four times a year. The owners in 2017, Alex and Dawn Haig-Thomas, carried out yet more restoration work of the house and grounds, and hosted a very successful Classic Isle Music Festival in 2017.

Barton Farm

After Barton Estate was split up in 1953, Barton Farm had a series of managers and owners. Mr R J Billings bought Barton Farm in 1964 and John Broughton came from Dorset to become farm manager. They soon included Woodhouse and several fields were rented from Osborne, covering a very large mixed acreage.

In 1971 Richard and Ann Orlik bought Barton Farm to add to their Kingston Farm holding and managed it themselves. They built a new rotary milking parlour to replace the two obsolete existing dairy units in 1973 and were milking 300 cows by 1985, three times a day. Three full-time herdsmen and two students were employed. In 1985 milk production became uneconomic and the herd was sold. Since then, Barton Farm has been turned to arable production, growing cereals, oilseed rape and hay for horses.

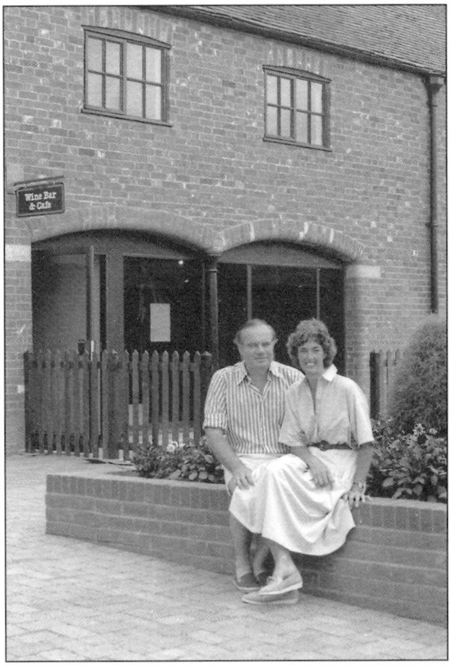

The Goddards in 1988.

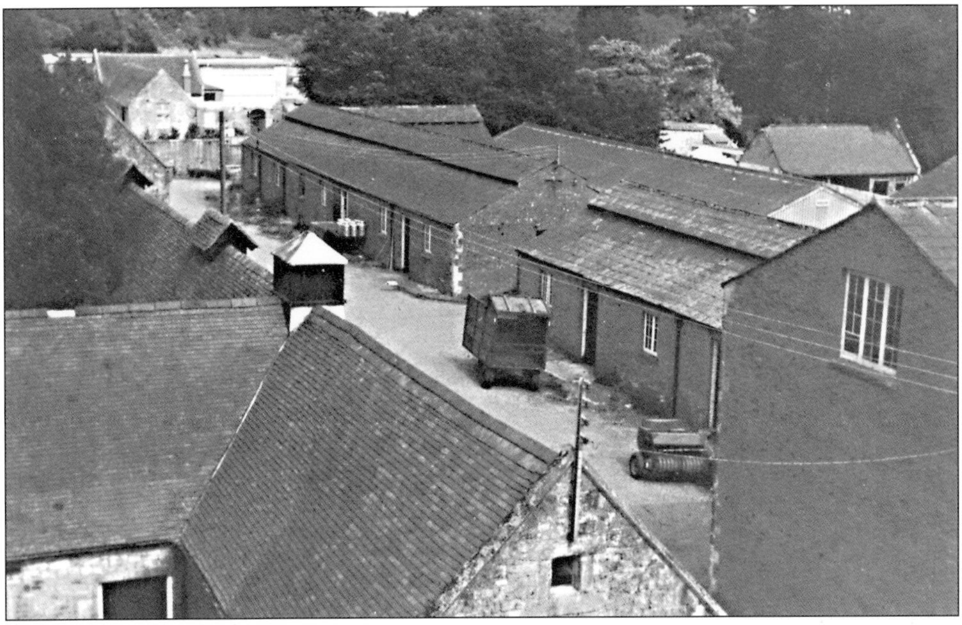

A view over the farm buildings, still very much in use in the 1970s.

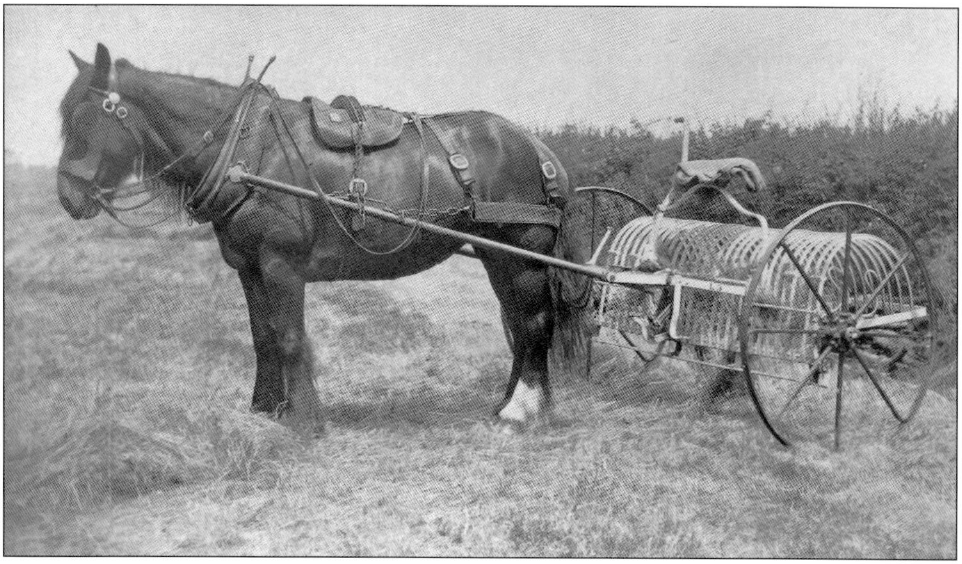

A 1930s horse-drawn swath turner, for drying cut grass before storage, on Barton Farm. The machine survives in a barn on the estate.

Four

Padmore House

Padmore House is a large residence near to the church with excellent views looking up the Medina Valley. In references from 1637 it is called Great Padmore, to distinguish it from Little Padmore, the farm at the top of Folly Lane. Little Padmore Farm paid 14 shillings tax, while Great Padmore paid only eight shillings. By comparison, Osborne House paid £2 and 9 shillings at that time.

In 1640 a London merchant owned Great Padmore, whose descendent sold it to Reverend Benedict Ball, Rector of Whippingham three years later. The hearth tax records of 1673 showed that Padmore House paid tax on four hearths. This was a money raising venture by the government to pay for the Monarchy and expensive overseas wars.

The earlier stone-built house was enlarged and a Queen Anne-style frontage was added. By 1742 Mr Blachford of Osborne was also the tenant at Padmore. Twenty years later Doctor Benjamin Cook, a surgeon at Newport, was living at the house. Soon after 1791, the Jolliffe family owned both Padmores and by 1820 young James Jolliffe was the rector of Barton Stacey in Hampshire.

When he retired in 1851 James took up residence at the family home of Padmore with his three daughters, Frances Elizabeth, Mary and Emily Ellen. Their father died in 1864 and the three spinster daughters remained at Padmore until at least 1914, when they were aged 87, 85 and 81. The youngest had arrived there in her teens. Frances Elizabeth was buried at Whippingham in 1915 and her sister Mary in 1919. Emily Ellen, the last of the sisters, is sadly not mentioned on the family grave, which is on the left as you look at the Queen's door to the church.

We know a little of the way of life of the three Victorian ladies in their old age from the book, *Arreton All My Days* by Hilda Alice Moore. In 1913 at the age of

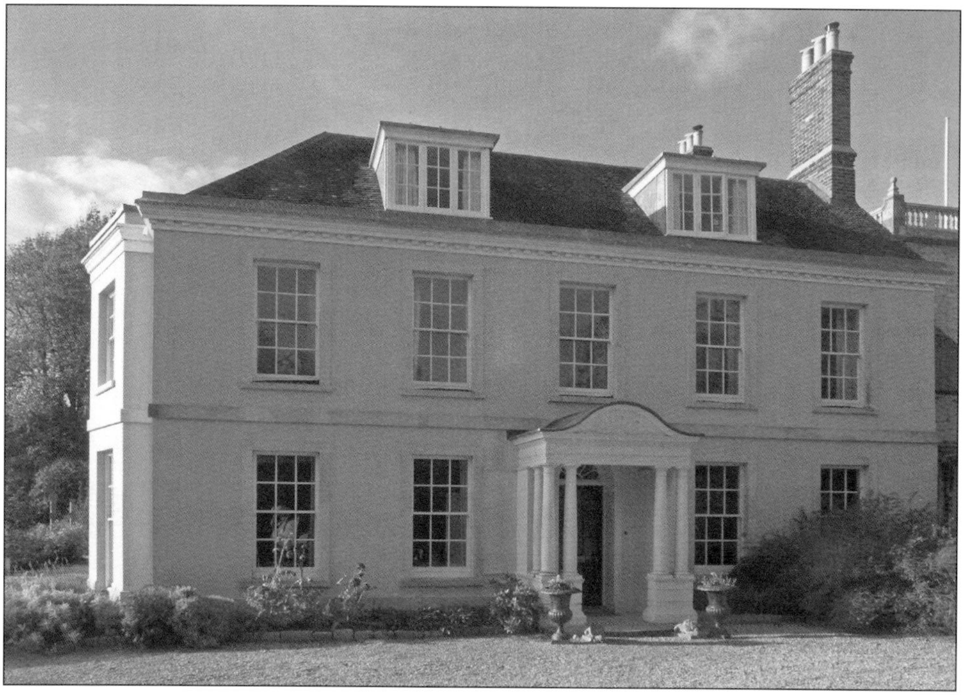

The present-day front of Padmore House created around 1800 with its multiple-columned portico and curved pediment.

16 Hilda had answered an advertisement for a 'between-maid' at Padmore. She was interviewed, with her grandmother, in the ladies waiting room at Newport Railway Station, by Mary Jolliffe. Mary must have been about 85 at the time. Hilda was told she had to have a cotton print dress for the mornings, and a black dress with a white apron for the afternoons. Hilda's salary was to be £10 a year, and after six months she would be allowed every other Sunday afternoon off.

Hilda found that the 'between maid' had a wide variety of tasks. The Misses Jolliffe liked their own butter, so Hilda had to skim the milk daily and then two or three times a week had the task of churning butter. Once made, the butter was put into round pots and stamped with a wooden pattern.

Daily tasks included cleaning out and making up the fires in the bedrooms so that these could be kept going all day, cleaning and filling the oil lamps and trimming the wicks. There was no gas or electricity. She collected the large stoneware hot water bottles from each bedroom, emptied them and filled them with fresh water. These were placed, un-stoppered, in the kitchen oven where they remained for the whole day, so that in the evening Hilda could stopper them

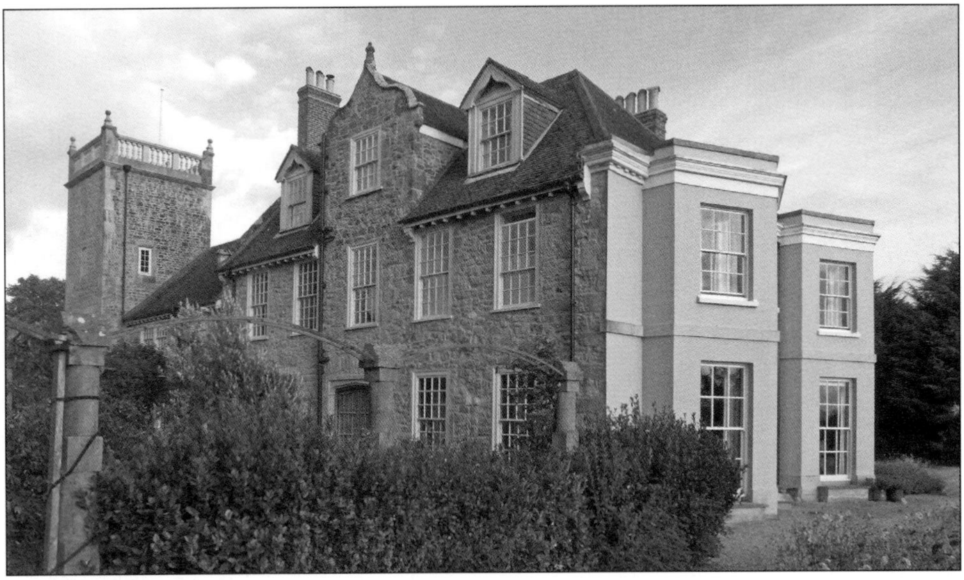

The original front of the house overlooking the river. The tower contains a water tank to work a fountain in the rose garden. The bay windows date from around 1800 when the entrance was changed to the south side of the house.

and take them upstairs. She could only carry one at a time as they were so heavy!

The drawing room and study were cleaned each day, and the stairs, decorated with red felt, were brushed. The walls and doors were white, and Elizabeth had painted attractive pictures of flowers in the panels on the doors. Hilda's favourite job was to check over the Misses Jolliffe's court clothes. These were the dresses, tiaras, ostrich plumes, shawls, stockings, gloves and shoes that the three young ladies had worn for their 'coming out' when they were presented at court. Each was arranged in a separate compartment, and had to be checked for moths, then the dresses taken down to the pantry and pressed with the flat irons. It would take her a day, between her other jobs, and had to be done once a week.

Her least favourite job was cooking up the offal that was brought three times a week by the butcher to feed the cats. There were 16 indoor cats, and several more outside. The smell of the food was so disgusting that the cooking had to be done in the brew-house outside, and the cats were very demanding. So too were the donkeys which had to have numerous carrots and two brown loaves cut in strips. If Hilda was late with their food they would start braying very loudly.

The donkeys were kept to pull the low four-in-hand coach in which the ladies travelled on the few occasions when they went out. Mr Downer was the coachman, and he also helped around the house, carrying coal and so on. The gardener, who also looked after the cow, was Mr Shaw, who lived in the small lodge on Beatrice Avenue.

A washerwoman who came in on a Monday to do the laundry, and on Thursdays the ironing, was paid a couple of shillings a week. The servants ate in the kitchen and enjoyed the same food as was served to the Misses Jolliffe. It was very plain, such as cold brisket of beef with baked potatoes. The sisters disliked puddings, eating fresh fruit instead, much of which came from the Padmore garden, including green figs.

Hilda was expected to attend St. Mildred's church every other week and sit in the family pew in line with the rest of the servants. After two years at Padmore she felt that she was rather missing out on life as the Misses Jolliffe did not entertain much. They were very kind to Hilda and in many ways she was quite happy with her job, but it was time for her to move on to the bright lights of West Cowes.

In 1915 Sam Saunders, boat and aircraft manufacturer, bought Padmore House and moved into it in 1920. His daughter Ethel had already died, from meningitis, and his family consisted then of his wife Kate and son Hubert. Hubert was a director of the Saunders Company. Sam Saunders had moved from his home in East Cowes, where his business had been expanding. He sold the land by the river belonging to Padmore to his company for seaplane workshops. At Padmore the stables were demolished and garage for the family motor cars was built, incorporating two bedrooms for staff.

Sam Saunders retired in 1929 and devoted the last four years of his life to planting an orchard of 800 apple trees at Padmore, and an extensive rose garden. He was active in doing things for the village, such as having the Community Hall built. He regularly left a basket of apples outside his gates for the school children to help themselves! Sam Saunders had 'The Chalet,' now known as 'Malacca', built for his grand-daughter Ursula and her husband Guy Hummel in the grounds.

In December 1933 Sam Saunders died. His funeral took place at Whippingham Church, in dense fog, the boat-shaped coffin leaving from Padmore being drawn by some of his devoted staff. His wife died six years later. Padmore House was sold by Hubert in 1935.

In 1974 the house was converted into a delightful hotel but this closed in the late 1980s and it became a family home again. Recently the owners uncovered delicate painted ceiling decoration in the dining room, possibly dating from Georgian times.

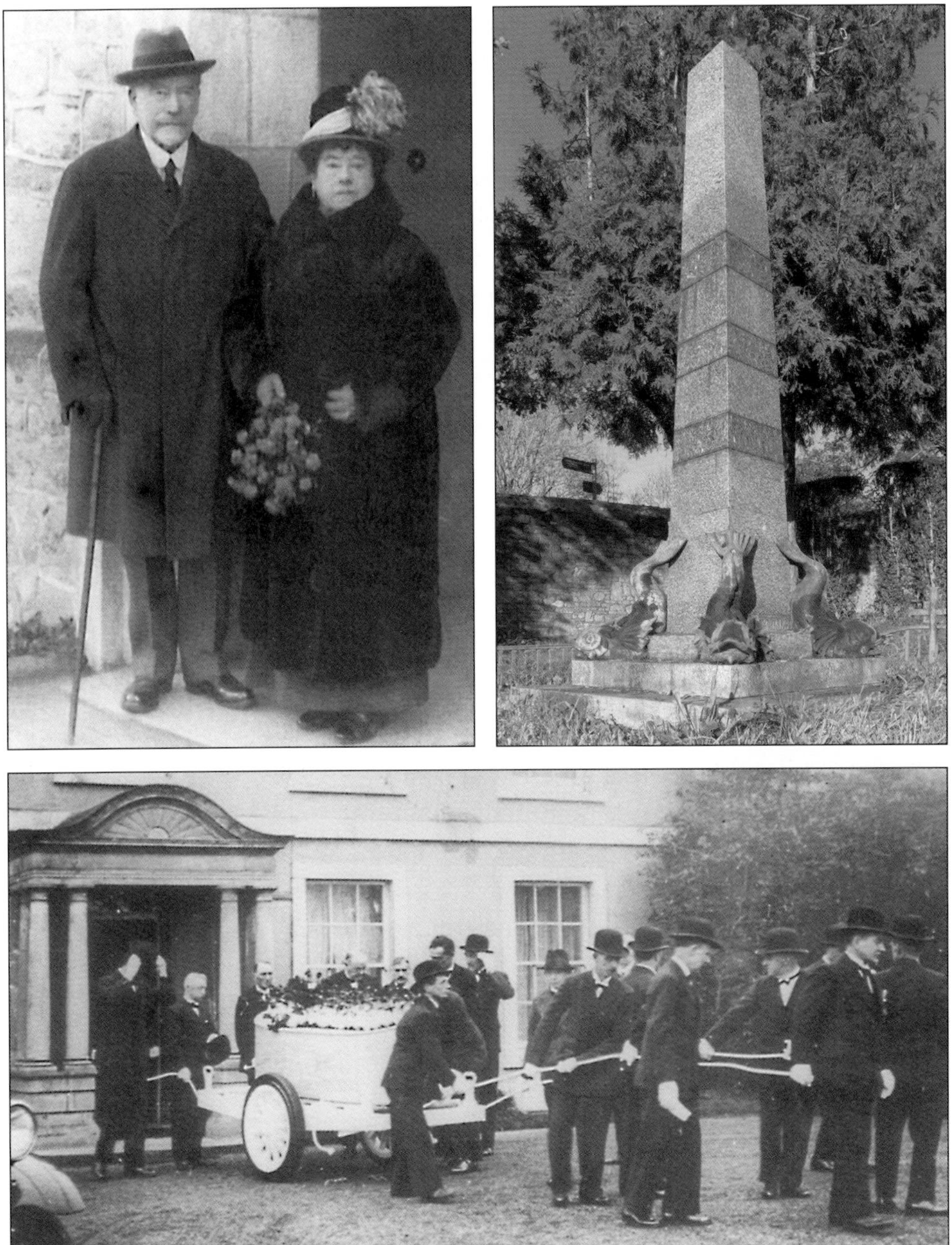

Left: Sam and Kate Saunders at the door of Padmore in 1927, on their golden wedding anniversary. Right: Their grave at St. Mildred's. A granite obelisk with copper dolphins at the base. Bottom: Sam's boat-shaped coffin leaves Padmore in December 1933.

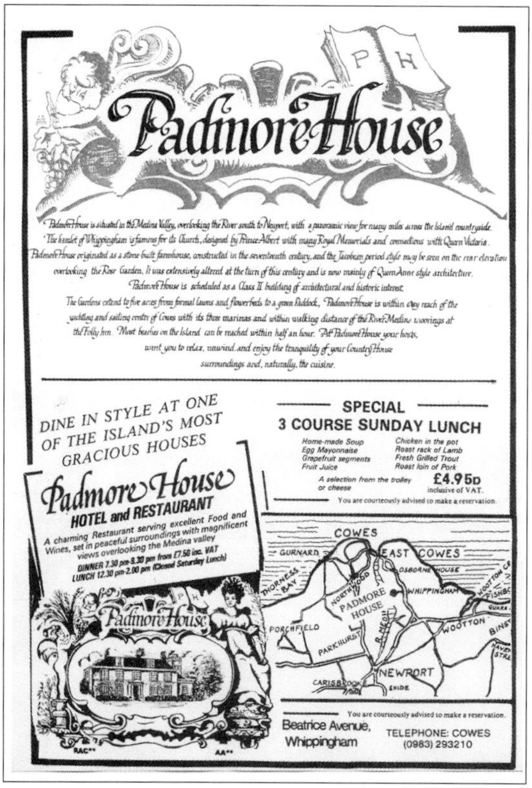

Left:
Newspaper advert for Padmore House Hotel. Three course Sunday lunch was £4.95.

Below:
The delicately-painted trompe-l'oeil ceiling rose discovered during renovation work at Padmore. It dates to the time when the 1800 frontage was built.

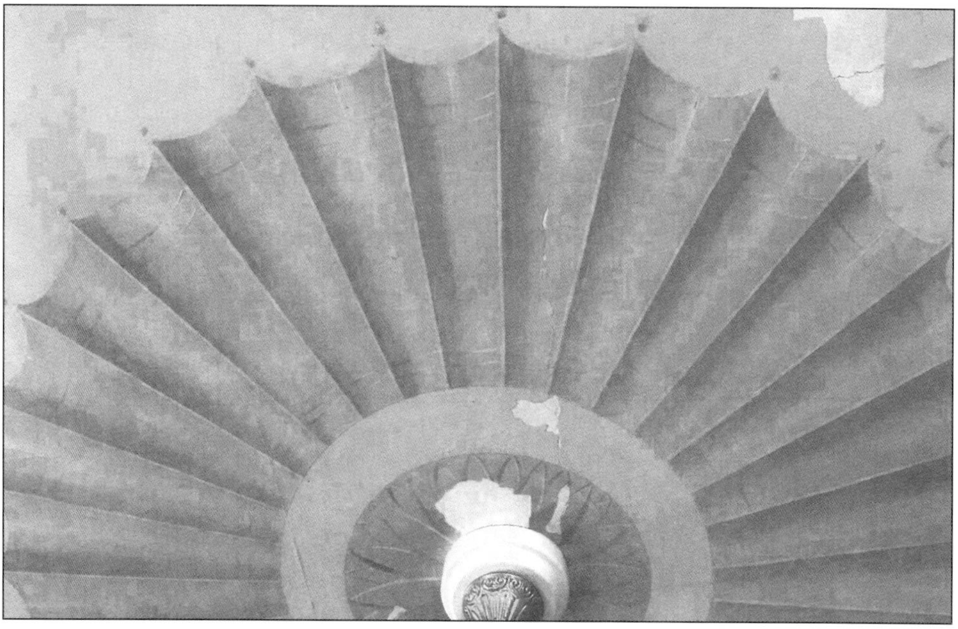

Little Padmore

Little Padmore always had close associations with Padmore House. Once Padmore was upgraded into a gentleman's residence, there needed to be a farmhouse for the tenant farmer to occupy.

Hubert Saunders, son of Sam Saunders, lived in Little Padmore at the time of his father's death in 1933. Although this had been built as two cottages, it had been turned into one large house in 1930. There was *'a pretty rock garden with lily pond and streamlet, miniature waterfalls and splashes'* that featured in the sale document of 1935. The house was offered for sale with a small paddock beside the road.

The farm buildings were sold separately with the 75 acres of farmland. The land was bought by a building firm for development, but nothing came of the venture and in 1936 Frank Thomas took on the tenancy of Little Padmore Farm and the farmhouse as well. The Thomas family continued the farm as a mixed dairy farm during the war, buying Little Padmore in 1948. Eleanor Thomas and her sons, Trevor, Viv, and Don, took over after Frank's death. In those post war days the farm provided a living for them all. Gradually the brothers extended their holdings, and ran three farms in partnership, Alverstone Farm, Binfield Farm and Little Padmore.

In 1997, some of the land east of Whippingham Shute was sold into Alverstone Farm. Little Padmore now caters for the equestrian market.

George's Field - also known as The Pony Club Field

This field between Padmore House and Whippingham Church was known as Wall Mead in around 1900. It was part of the Padmore Estate, and the only completely walled field in Whippingham.

Some children walked from East Cowes to attend school at Whippingham and enjoyed running along the top of the wall on their way home. The slower children would be pushed off by those catching them up. Uffa Fox was one of the boys who took part in the early 1900s. They never played the game on the walk to school as it was an uphill run that way!

In March 1975 Wall Mead came up for sale. The Isle of Wight Pony Club, part of the National Association of Pony Clubs, thought it would be an excellent idea to have their own facilities and the eight and a half acres of Wall Mead suited their requirements perfectly.

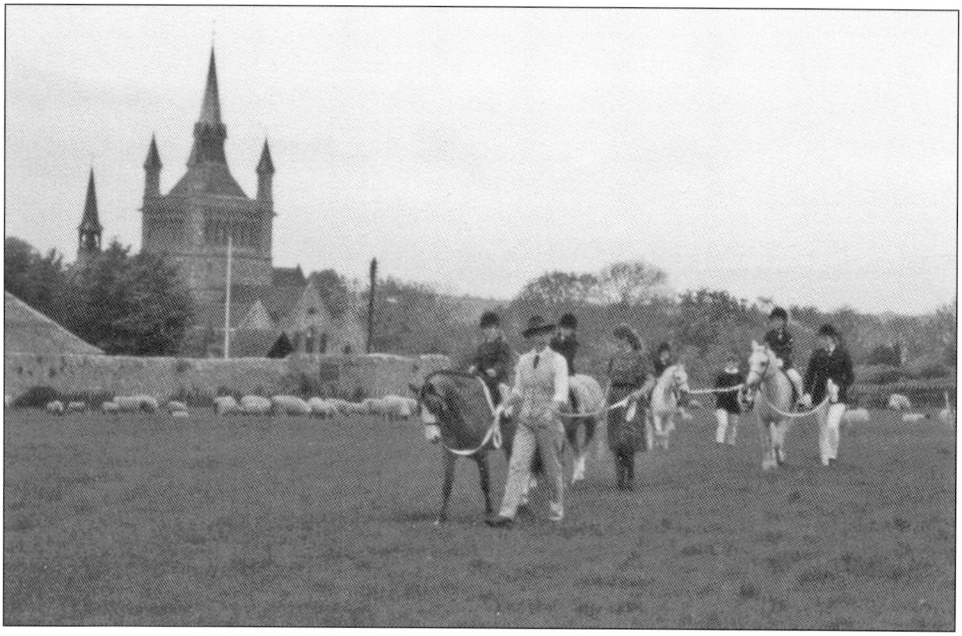

The Pony Club meets in George's Field between Padmore and the church.

It was just off the main road, but in quiet, attractive rural surroundings with good pony-proof boundaries in the form of stone walls on all four sides. Mrs Lacon of Norris Castle was in favour of the idea, and offered to put up some of the purchase price of £4,300 in memory of her son George, a keen rider, who tragically died at the age of 21 in a car accident.

At this time, there were 280 members of the club on the Island, ranging in age from six to 20 years old. George's Field, now also known as the Pony Club Field, was to become the venue for their working rallies, instructional camps, horse shows and various annual camps. There was also a camp for disabled riders and their helpers. At the camps, instruction was given in care of horses, grooming, cleaning tack, first aid and of course, riding. Following the purchase of the field, membership of the pony club on the Island gradually rose to a peak of about 500.

In recent years at George's Field a fenced ménage has been constructed of a washed grit surface over a compacted chalk base. Now dressage can be taught, and competitions in this discipline held. A highlight in the history of George's Field was the visit of Princess Anne in the 1990s to observe a camp run by 'Riding for the Disabled'.

Five

Agriculture before Prince Albert

In 1681 there was still a common somewhere in the village. Animals found straying there were rounded up and taken to the village pound, where their owners would have to pay a fine to retrieve them. The following entry comes from the Worsley Accounts:

'To two bailiffs and a boy for driving the beasts in Whippingham common (and ought not to go there) to pound'. Today no trace of the pound remains. The clue to the site of the pound lies in a couple of field names half way along Alverstone Road on the south side behind Six Cottages. These were called Pound Field and Pound Close on the 1841 inventory that goes with the Tithe map of the area.

Several interesting documents are held at the Isle of Wight County Records Office. An early estate map exists of Osborne Farm – approximately the present Osborne House Estate. It is dated 1734, and shows all the field boundaries, with little drawings of various animals – sheep and cattle. A granary on staddle stones is also drawn in as part of a range of farm buildings, and the house is shown in an Elizabethan style of architecture.

The Board of Agriculture for England carried out a survey on the Island in 1802 recording the amount of land that had been enclosed. Agriculturalists had realized the advantages of breeding stock more carefully to improve the quality and improving crops by methods which were only possible on enclosed fields. Mr Bell, the surveyor of the Island found most of the Island was now enclosed, apart from Niton.

He found, elsewhere on the Island, that before a crop of wheat, the land would be left fallow for a year. Wheat was cut and then left to dry on the ground. *'It is not bound into sheaves until the day before it is carried to the barn or rick.'* Barley and oats were mown and put into small stacks to dry.

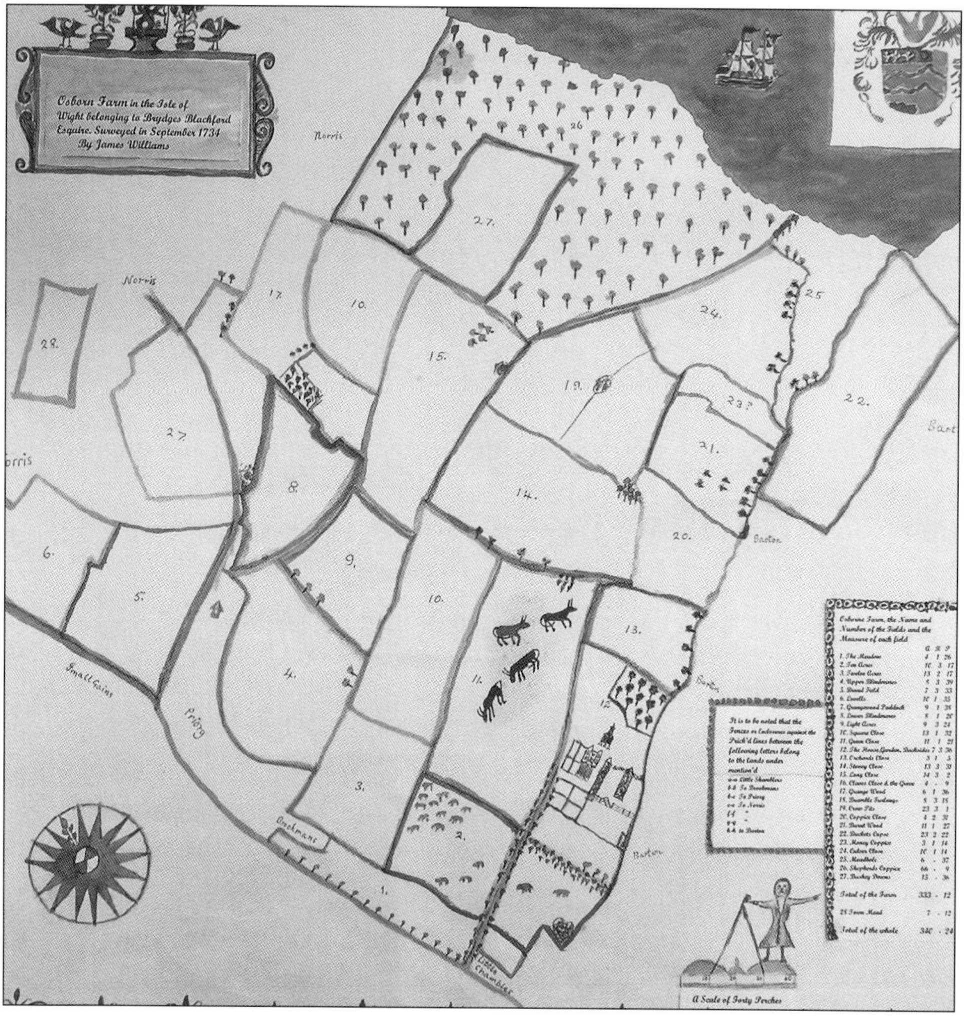

An approximate copy of the 1734 estate map of Osborne Farm. The Tudor-style farmhouse and barns are shown bottom right beneath the livestock.

Men took no part in the weeding of crops. *'Weeding with small hooks - (or rather cutting up the thistles, for no other weeds are thought of) is performed by women and children.'* and also *'Hoeing is a system never practiced, on the Isle of Wight.'*

Mr Bell regretted that so much emphasis was being put on growing grain crops. However, with the French wars underway, grain crop prices were high and the Island was close to Portsmouth and the great victualling demands of the

Navy. *'It is much to be lamented that the cold clay lands to the north are not more generally adapted to grass.'*

The farmers in Whippingham were cashing in while they could and trying to improve their clay soils for grain crops. Farmer Rolf of Barton *'carries 3 tons of chalk to a load and puts 20 loads to an acre costing £10.6s.'* Mr Walker of Kingston Farm said that less chalk an acre was sufficient. *'He thinks 10 loads an acre would answer sufficiently to allow it to be more easily tilled.'*

Lord Seymour at nearby Norris was experimenting with a variety of manures including seaweed. At Barton Farm a field had 30 loads of sea sand carried upon an acre, giving an amazing improvement. In 1802 the usual cattle were Normandy or Alderney breeds. The carthorses were very large, pulling waggons in line. Only Lord Seymour at Norris had a fine team of the smaller Suffolk horses.

The general food for servants was pork or mutton. Mr Bell found that there was a food called Dunch – a pudding made of flour and water - that the labourers seemed to prefer to bread. They would down two quarts of very strong beer at a meal and as much 'small' beer as could be drunk. No brown bread was seen, only white. Most farm houses had a half acre of orchard.

The woods at Barton and Osborne were extensive. A survey in 1782 for Worsley had put the value of the timber on Woodhouse and Alverstone Farms at £1,327. The coppice wood at Woodhouse was valued at £215.

Some of the landowners paid Mr Bell to do a more specific survey of their property as at Alverstone Farm at Whippingham. Of 20 fields, 16 were arable, and only four pasture. Bell's first observation is somewhat damning. *'This farm consists of various soils, all of which have been impoverished by bad management, but are capable of Improvement by Chalking.'* He suggests a rotation of crops should be implemented; perhaps fallow then turnips, barley, clover and wheat. Proper drainage was also suggested and more profit could be made from dairy cattle and a flock of sheep.

Another suggestion that he makes is that some Alverstone Farm land should be considered on the Newport side of the farm, *'for the purpose of erection of small villas upon.'* Bell was possibly ahead of his time in suggesting housing development on the poor land!

Where 'Chalking' is suggested the chalk had to be burnt in a kiln, and then the resultant lime powder was applied to the soil. An old lime kiln was discovered on the lower slopes of Heathfield Farm near the marina creek when

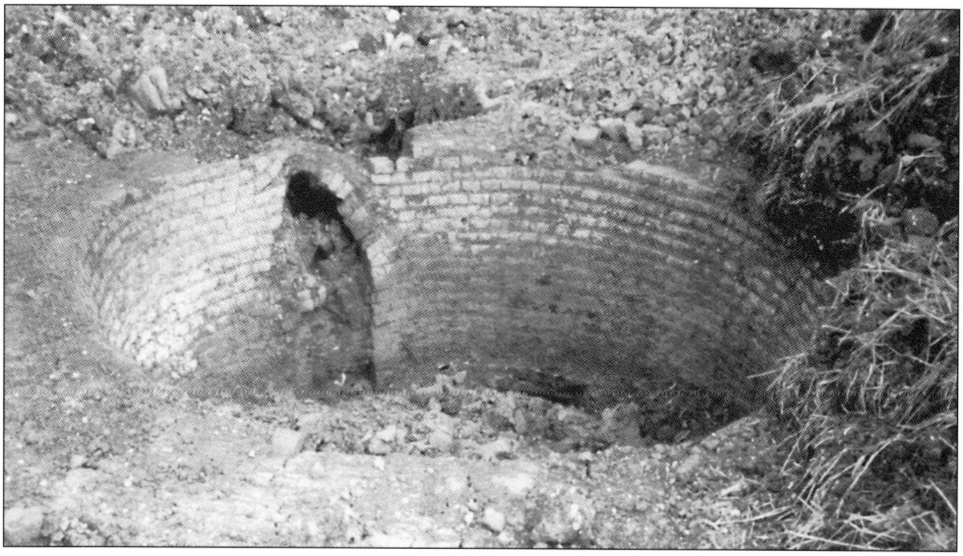

The remains of the lime kiln at Heathfield Farm near the marina creek, uncovered by Southern water in 2000.

Southern Water were putting in their sewage pipeline in 2000. Mr Bell had said that the tenant should, *'chalk within his lease every acre of Arable Land with fifteen loads an acre.'* Probably the kiln was built around 1800. It was of the 'flare' type and the bricks were laid using the surrounding clay, rather than mortar. The chalk could have been brought from Shide chalk quarry at Newport using boats on the Medina River. Another field next to Palmers Brook by the Ryde Road had the field name 'lime kiln ground' on the 1841 tithe map.

At the Island County Records Office there is a little gem of a book relating to 'Padmore.' Started in 1804, the notebook is described by the writer as a, *'Daily account of Expenses and Receipts for farming business at Padmore.'* The book is like a child's exercise book of today in size, and difficult to read. However perseverance pays off, revealing that the leases of Padmore cost £66 and the Property Tax was £8.5s.5d. The quarterly Poor Rate was £1.14s.0d., and later we read the second Highway Rate was paid at £1.7s.6d. The occupier also had to pay Window Tax in 1804 and it cost him 15 shillings.

Two ricks of hay were valued together at £18.8s. The mowing of the next crop of hay and clover grass was done by Vine, who was paid 2/6 an acre in June. Farmer Gladdis was paid 15s a day for ploughing, with his own team. One field, Short Close, took him seven days. The molecatcher, Mr Bull, was paid 12/6. The

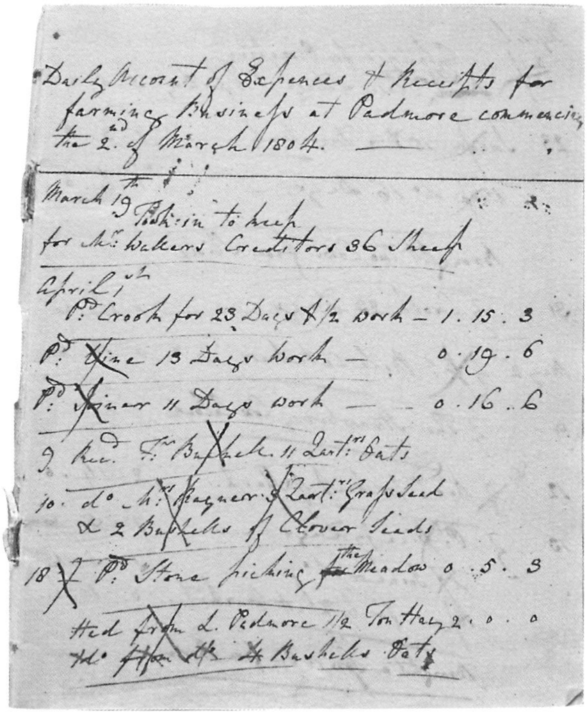
Daily Account of Expences & Receipts for farming Business at Padmore commencing the 2d of March 1804.
March 19th Took in to keep for Mr Walkers Creditors 36 Sheep
April 1st Pd Crook for 23 Days & 1/2 work — 1. 15. 3
Pd Vine 13 Days work — 0. 19. 6
Pd Joiner 11 Days work — 0. 16. 6
9 Recd 5 Bushels 11 Qrts Oats
10 do Mrs Rayner 5 Quarts Grass Seed & 2 Bushels of Clover Seeds
18 Pd Stone picking the Meadow 0. 5. 3
Had from L. Padmore 1/2 Ton Hay 2. 0. 0
Do 4 Bushels Oats

Daily expenses and receipts for farming business at Padmore commencing 2nd March 1804.

March 19th. Took in to keep for Mr Walkers creditors 36 sheep.

April 1st. Paid Crook for 23½ days work 1.15.3

Vine 13 days work 0.19.6
Joiner 11 days work 0.16.6

9th. 5 bushels and 11 quarts oats

10th. ditto, Mrs Rayner 5 quarts grass seed and 2 bushels clover seeds.

18th. Paid stone-picking the meadow 0.5.3

Had from Little Padmore Half ton of hay. 2.0.0
Ditto 4 bushels of oats.

weeders, Messrs Joiner and Bridles, were paid 9d per man per day over eight days. Joiner's daughter received only 6d a day for weeding.

By 1808 Joiner was being paid seven shillings a week. Another farmworker, Bridle, was paid £2.7s for threshing the wheat, and for 10 days work and six rats he received 16/9. Some of the threshing was carried out in March, and some in May. For haymaking Mary Hollis was paid a shilling a day for her casual work, while Ned Ralph had 2/6 a day for reaping. Once the rick was made it cost 10/6 to get it thatched.

Livestock details are also included in the notebook. For instance, Padmore bought three pigs that cost £2.2s.0d in June 1804. An entry on July 4 reads, '*N.B. White faced cow took the Bull the beginning of June or latter end of May.*' A later entry notes that the Strawberry Cow had calved. In 1808 seven calves were sold for a total of £17.

In the winter Padmore land was grazing sheep for other farmers. Mr Jolliffe sent 21 more sheep on 12 December, removing them in April. The previous year £2.14s had been received from sheep pasturing.

Looking at the book, it is fascinating to see the farmer's handwriting, his corrections, and his checking of the accounts. *'Omitted last reckoning £0.8s.6d'* shows on one page! It is good to note that he paid for his worker's beer when they went to market for him; *'Beer for both (Vine and Joiner) 1s.6d'*

Tithes

One thinks of tithes to the parish as being an expenditure that the landowners had to pay only in medieval times. Tithes were a form of taxation paid to the church in some cases right up until the 20th Century. The tithe map of 1841 and its accompanying survey is one of the earliest detailed records of the last two hundred years. All the landowners are listed, and their tenants, together with details of all the land and whether it was arable or pasture. By an 1836 Act of Parliament, tithes were based on the price of grain.

Looking at an inventory of 1853, it shows the tithes paid to Whippingham Church amounted to £685.18s.1d. However, less than half this sum was received by the rector. He had to pay Property tax, Financial tax, and Land Tax, pay the curates their stipend, pay for repairs to the church and rectory, subscribe to the East Cowes school, pay for stamps, printing receipts, and pay to have the accounts audited.

It was surprising to hear that when Fred Blackman took over North Fairlee Farm in 1957 he was still paying tithes of £12.3s.7d to the church every two years. In 1964 the option was granted to end the requirement to pay tithes, so £200 was paid as a final payment. Looking at the sale document for the Osborne Estate of 1956, we see in the initial remarks that, *'Tithe ...[payment is] believed to have been redeemed.'*

Acts of Parliament reflected changed circumstances. In 1936 it was decided that all tithes should cease by 1996. Land holders were able to redeem their tithes with a lump payment. In the 1980s those still paying tithes were told to stop.

Old Alverstone Farmhouse

In 1716 a new farmhouse was built at Alverstone. Some maps call the area 'Elverton', and this is the name used in 1718 when an account was paid to, *'James Dennett and partners...building a new house in Elverton Street in 1716. £35.8s.6d.'* Alverstone Farm was part of the Worsley Estate from 1620 to the early 1800s, the main seat of the Worsley family being Appledurcombe at Wroxall. Alverstone

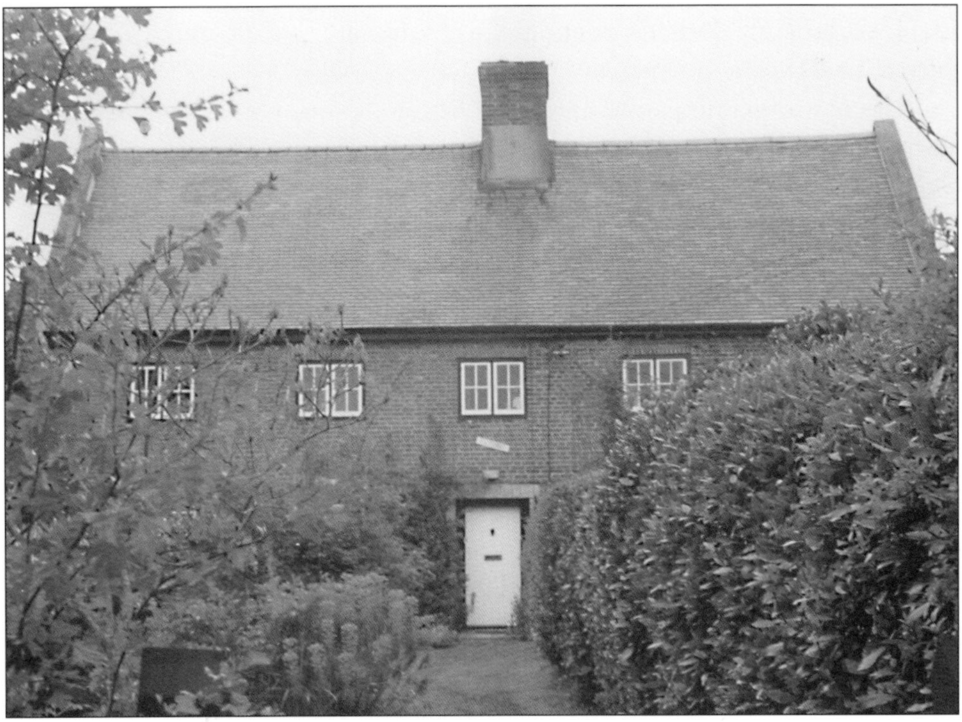

Old Alverstone Farmhouse in the 1990s. One of the oldest buildings in Whippingham. Originally one house but converted to two cottages during Victoria's ownership.

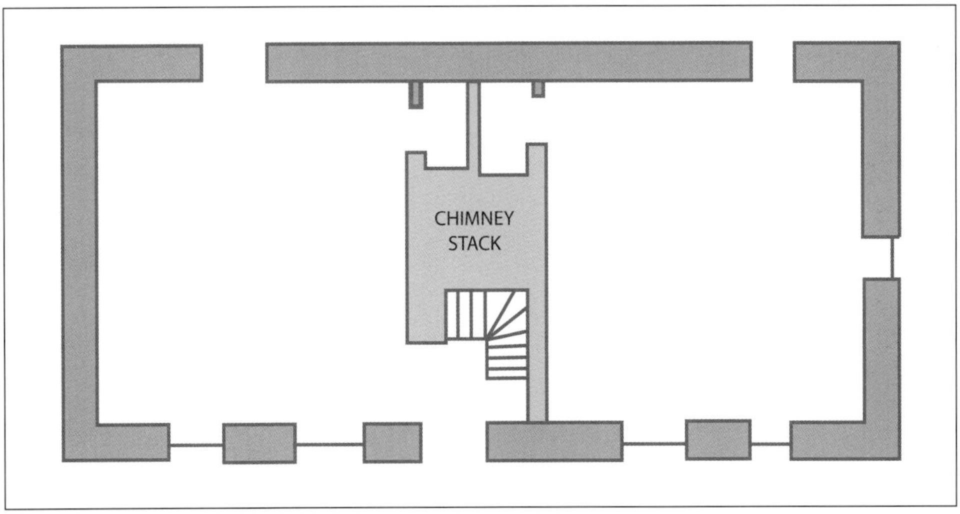

The layout of Alverstone Farmhouse, with a large, central fireplace, when it was first built in 1716.

Farm was large at 360 acres, but gradually parts were sold off and by 1840 it had been reduced to about 75 acres.

The house is one of the oldest in Whippingham with the date 1716 on the lintel over the front door. It was built with an eastern central doorway, and a room each side of this. These rooms both had fireplaces in the centre of the building and the staircase went up to the two rooms on the first floor beside the fireplace. The house has a stone lower course below the ground-floor window level, stone quoins (corners) and then Flemish bond brickwork above. The front elevation of the house is decorated with a horizontal row of chequerboard bricks.

When Queen Victoria and Prince Albert bought Alverstone Farm in 1845 Alverstone Farmhouse was one of only three on the estate that was not demolished and rebuilt. In later years the building was made into two cottages for the farm labourers and two new cottages with gable fronts were built in the old rick-yard.

A new Alverstone Farm house was built at the bottom of Alverstone Road in 1854 and is an impressive building with a range of 'model' cowsheds and barns. (see page 73)

In 2017 Old Alverstone Farmhouse is still two cottages. The building is one of the most charming in Whippingham and holds nearly 300 years of history within its walls.

Six

Queen Victoria's Estate

In the same year as buying Osborne House and Barton, Victoria and Albert spent another £13,000 on adjacent land. They bought Woodhouse and Alverstone farms, four cottages from John Tiley and three cottages from Joseph Cross and Joseph Hearn. The following year, 1846, North and South Heathfield Farms, Six Cottages and gardens at Brook's, Brook's Copse and also Matthews' Cottage were purchased. The name Brook's very soon became written as Brock's in all the records.

More small portions of land were acquired in 1847, including six acres of Glebe land from the Rector of Whippingham. This marked the boundary of the Queen's Estate for some years, and it was not until 1862, the year after Prince Albert's death, that Truckles Farm was purchased, with Kingston Farm bought shortly afterwards. The popular impression is given that Queen Victoria shut herself away at Osborne after Prince Albert's death and did nothing except grieve, but her journals show that she still carried out many activities, enlarging and improving her estate being one of them.

In 1873 J W Hill wrote in his *'Historical and Commercial Directory of the Isle of Wight'*, The Osborne Estate *'now extends from the high road between East Cowes and Newport to the wooded shores of King's Quay, bounded on the south by the highway between Newport and Ryde, and on the north by the Solent. Thus from north to south it extends about two miles and a half, and from east to west nearly two miles, embracing every variety and charm of scenery, the woodland, valley, hill, brook and lea; the sheltered cove, the village church, the leafy copse, and the broad sweep of undulating plains.'* The western boundary of Queen Victoria's land extended to the banks of the River Medina.

Albert and Victoria had acquired a mixture of farms south of Osborne, some of which had been improved a little. The first necessity was to drain the fields and for this Albert needed thousands of drainage pipes.

The Queen's Brickyard

In 1845 a tile-kiln and drying hacks were put up at the junction of Ryde and Newport Roads. Mr Cubitt, the master-builder employed by Prince Albert to construct the new Osborne House, had a brick kiln at the same site to make the bricks for Osborne House and for all of the estate lodges, cottages and farm buildings.

The following year, 621,500 drain tiles were made, and between 50 and 60 acres of land were drained in different parts of the estate. In 1847 the length of the covered drains laid was more than 35 miles. This work went on for several years, 33 miles in 1848, 29 miles in 1849, 46 miles in 1850, and so on until all of the estate was drained to Prince Albert's satisfaction.

The 1863 Ordnance Survey map shows the brickyard in detail. There were pug mills for mixing the clay which was dug on site and as each brick was made it was set out to dry in the hacks before firing in the kiln. The hacks were open-sided sheds, clearly shown on the map. The clay was red after firing, and these bricks can be seen used

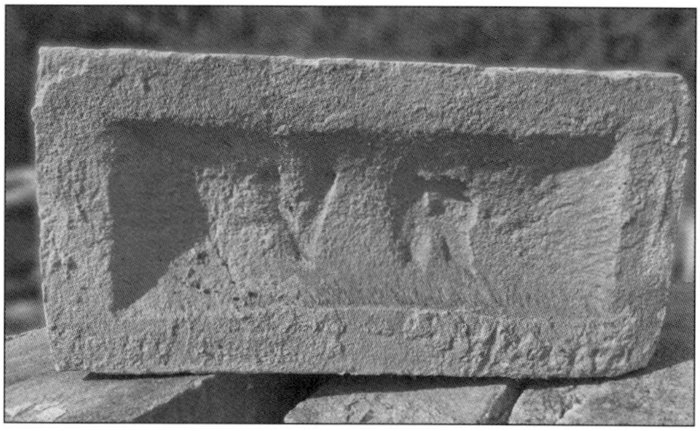

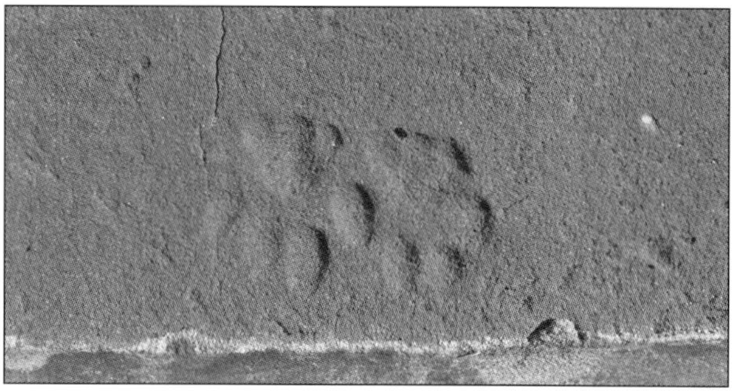

Bricks from the Queen's Brickyards had VR stamped into the frog. Red bricks came from Alverstone and buff-coloured from the King's Quay site.

Paw-prints from a cat survive on a brick at Primrose Cottage on the estate.

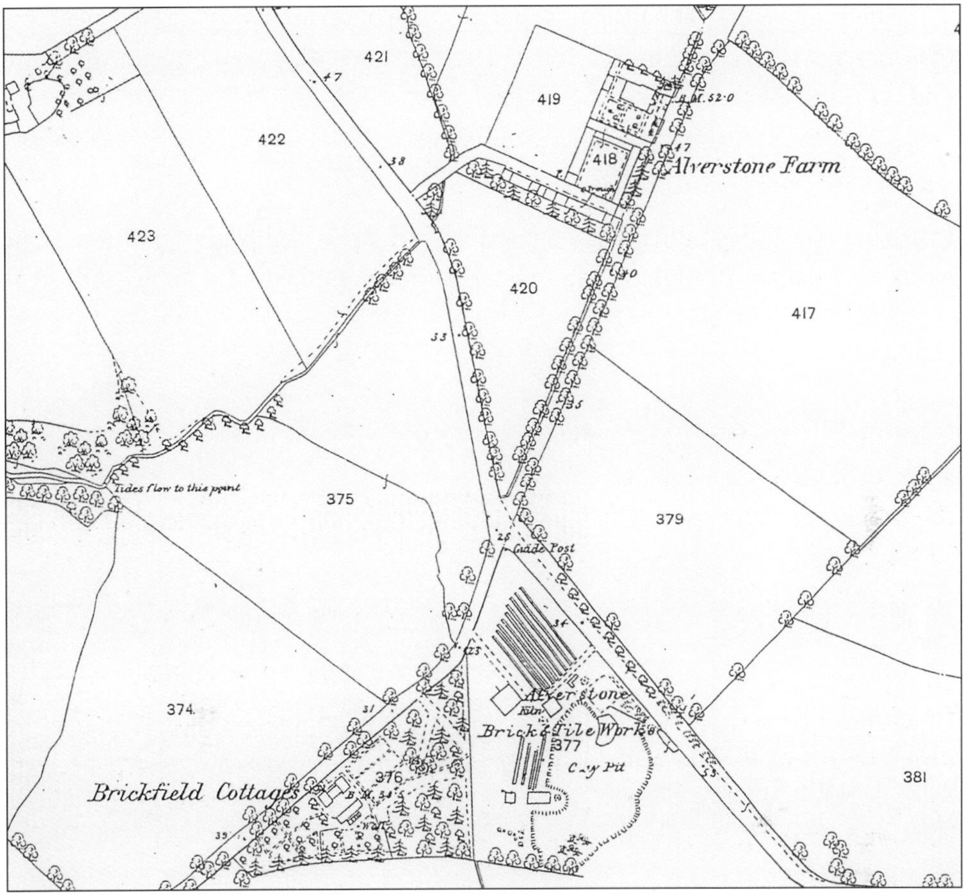

The drying hacks and clay pit of Alverstone Brick and Tile Works can be seen clearly on this map from 1863.

in buildings all over the estate. At Osborne House the bricks were rendered to resemble stonework.

The bricks made at the Queen's brickyard all had the initials VR in the frog, or dip. Ridge tiles were also made, again imprinted with VR. Occasionally the bricks or tiles became imprinted with the paw marks of cats or dogs, as they hunted mice around the hacks while the clay was still soft. A second brick kiln near King's Quay was started where buff yellow bricks were made.

In 1846 William Pierce is recorded as being a brick-maker at the Queen's brickyard. He served Queen Victoria for 49 years, retiring in 1894 at the age of 78 as foreman of the brickyard. He was granted a pension of £11.14s quarterly,

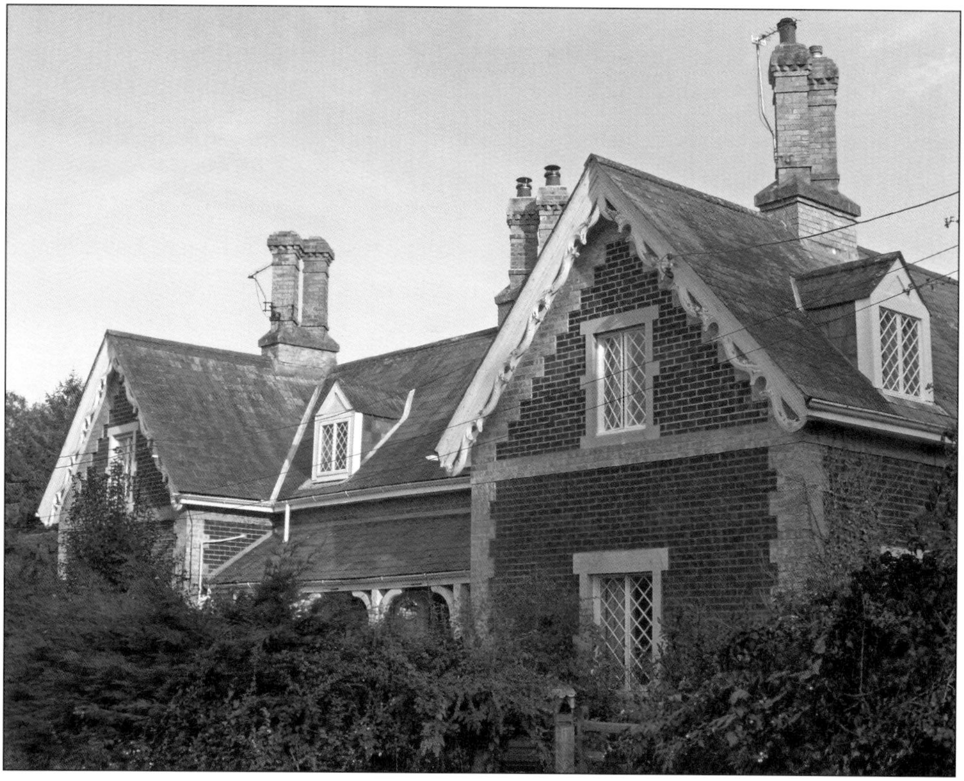

Brickfield Cottages built to a design by Prince Albert.

which was the same as the foreman of the Queen's pleasure-grounds, and higher than any other pensioner living on the estate at that time. William lived at Brickfield Cottages.

The Avlerstone Brick and Tile Works continued to function until 1914. Decorative pots were made for the tourist market, finished with a pictorial Osborne House clay motif.

Brickfield Cottages

Three tenements were constructed adjacent to the brickyard in 1853 and are still known as Brickfield Cottages. They were built in the 'Old-English' style to the design of Prince Albert, and constructed of red brick with buff dressings. It is thought that Prince Albert may have been present at the 'topping out' ceremony for the cottages, as something very like his signature was discovered in the lead flashing by the ridge.

On the Ryde Road two more tenements for brickyard workers were built the same year, known then as Ryde Road Cottages and later as Point Cottages. These were on the site of the present crematorium roundabout but were completely destroyed in the major air raid of 1942.

The Estate Roads

The Queen and Albert had bought a peaceful retreat where they could stroll unhindered by the local people. They would walk to church along the public roads, or drive in their carriage in inclement weather. People usually respected their desire to be private, although there were occasions, such as the Queen's arrival in her Royal Yacht at Trinity Pier, when the local population would turn out to greet her and welcome her back to the Island. In fact the school in East Cowes had such a problem with truancy on these occasions that they decided to call a half-holiday whenever the Queen was expected, otherwise the attendance figures took an unhealthy dip!

The Royal couple set about improving the roads within their estate. Being on top of 'plateau gravels' it was easy to have new gravel pits opened up for use in road construction. The writer in *The London Illustrated News* of 1858 extols the virtues of the Osborne Estate roads; '*...roads, which, for solidity, width, and uniformity in appearance, cannot be surpassed. ....they extend over many miles, intersecting the estate in those parts most convenient for farming purposes, and yet forming ever-varied drives and scenery through which Her Most Gracious Majesty can pass unmolested and unnoticed in the pure enjoyment of rural life.*' By 1900 there were over 20 miles of private drive within the estate.

Some roads that had previously led straight through farmyards were re-routed, decorously by-passing the yards, and skirting cottage gardens. Albert was particular about hedges being kept cut, which was relatively unusual in the mid-nineteenth century. It was good for thickening up the hedges and making them stock-proof and would also have enabled Victoria and the children to see into the fields from their carriage while out driving.

New roads were created, such as the Ring Road around Osborne House itself, the drive to King's Quay and the Boundary Drive. The latter required much construction work to stabilize the cliff. The route was not a farming necessity, but instead provided attractive views of the Solent in glimpses through the trees. The roads also provided good access to the woods for rough shooting. Mount Road on the Estate was re-routed in 1858, inserting a road between the site of

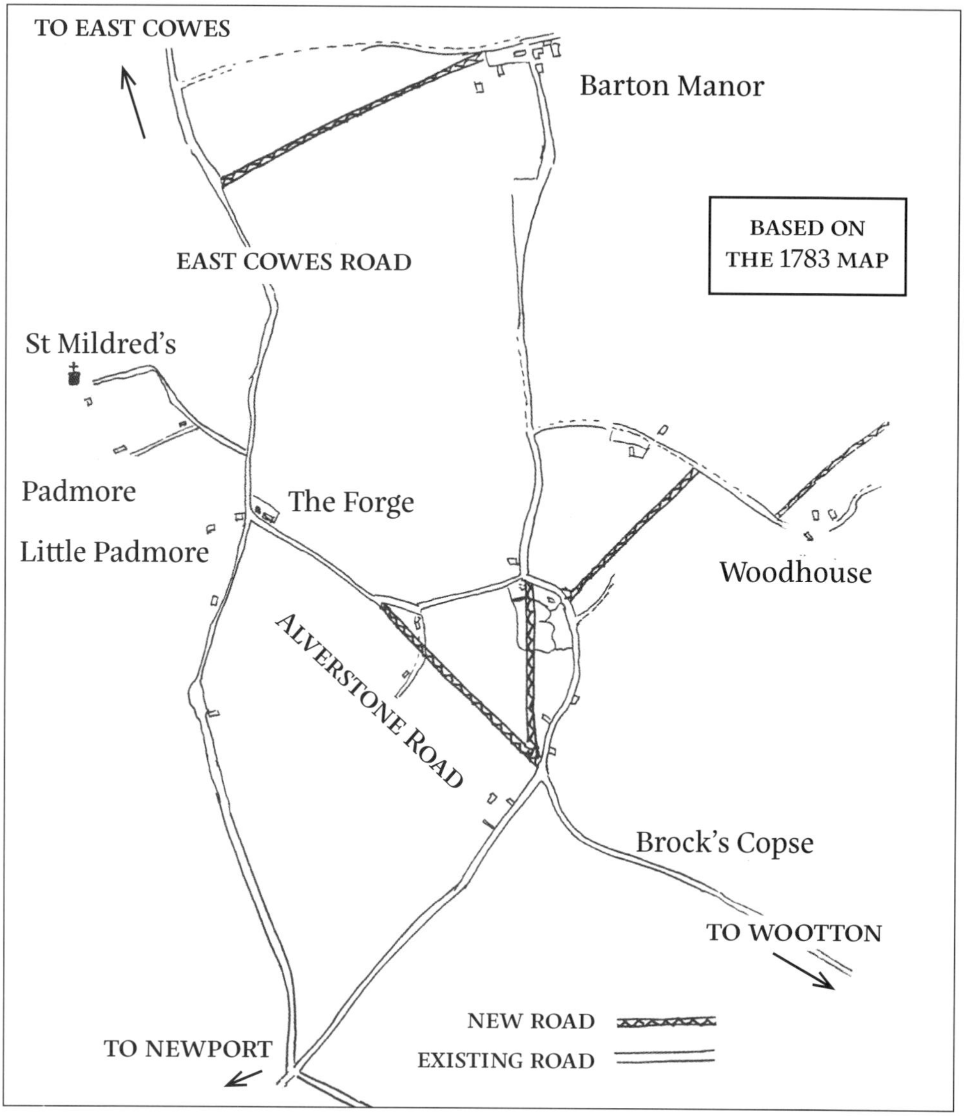

Prince Albert had the roads re-routed to make the estate more private around Whippingham Street and Alverstone. He also made the public road straighter.

Coburg Cottage and the Alverstone Gate, passing behind Primrose Cottage. The ditches beside all the roads were always kept clear to allow for good drainage, and the surfaces kept smooth and pot-hole free.

When the Queen was driving around the estate outriders would precede her. Cottagers would be alerted and would hurry to remove their washing from the

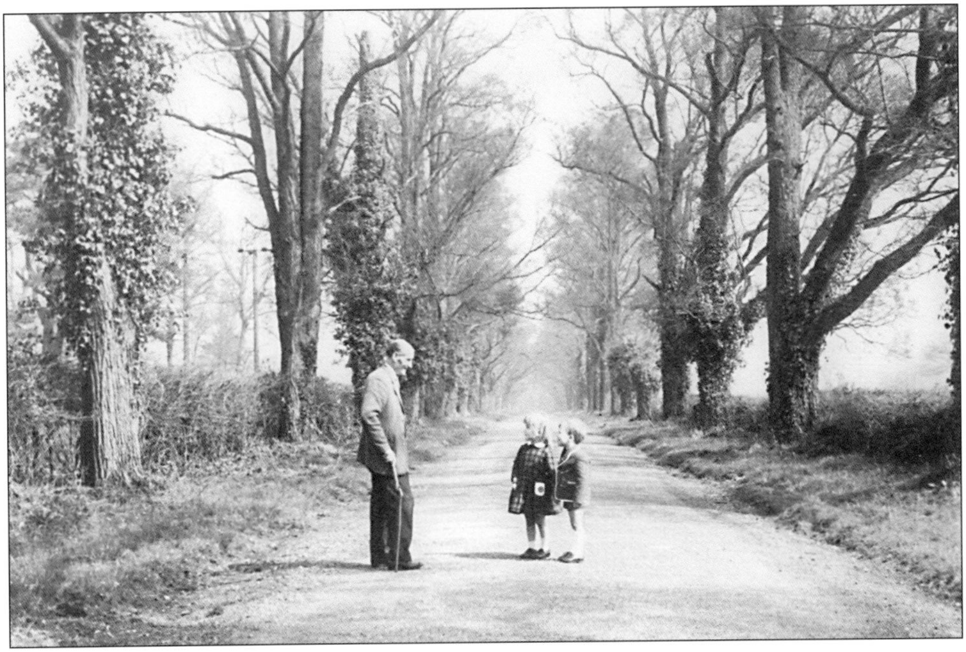

The avenue of Guernsey Elms at Barton. George Jones talks to two young children in the 1960s

line. Children would be whisked inside and put into clean smocks, ready to be at the gate to curtsey or bow to the Queen as she passed. Workers too would bow to her Majesty.

Prince Albert set about re-routing the public highway, Alverstone Road. Travelling from The Forge, one travelled about 100 yards before veering left to reach Mount Road near Coburg Cottage. This road was closed off, and replaced with a footpath on the line of the old road. In 1858, the old pack-horse track across Alverstone farmland was widened and straightened to meet up with the previous road system at Alverstone Lodge. The new road gave the estate more privacy and impressive gate pillars were constructed at the two entrances to the Queen's Barton and Woodhouse estate, either side of Alverstone Lodge.

The Race Course

Thousands of people drive along the road known as 'The Race Course' every week on their way from Ryde or Whippingham to Newport. Some are oblivious to the name, but others may wonder what lies behind it. It passes through land that once belonged to the Queen.

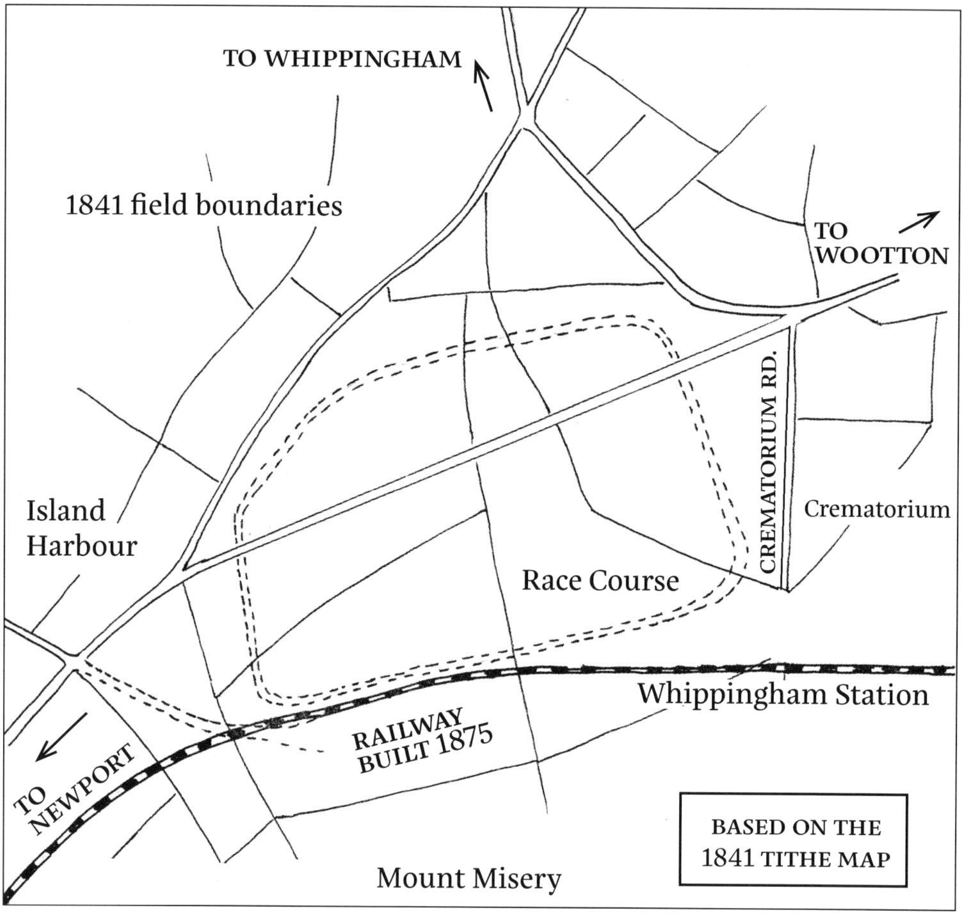

The location of the race course, the railway line and Whippingham Station. The present road between Newport and Ryde runs through the centre of the course.

According to Brettell, writing in the 1848 edition of the *Handbook to the Isle of Wight*, there was horse-racing here. After passing Whippingham going towards Newport, *'To the left is the new Race Course: the races are held generally in the month of July, and are well supported.'* A race card of 1842 shows that races were held here on 2nd and 3rd August, with four races each day. In 1843 there were only three races held each day, on 19th and 20th July. A newspaper listed the gentry who attended, and it was noted that the colt 'Little Wonder' did not win, only gaining third place. Presumably he had been the favourite!

The land was owned partly by Lord George Seymour and partly by Mr Holmes prior to 1845, and these gentlemen may have created the race track. The Queen

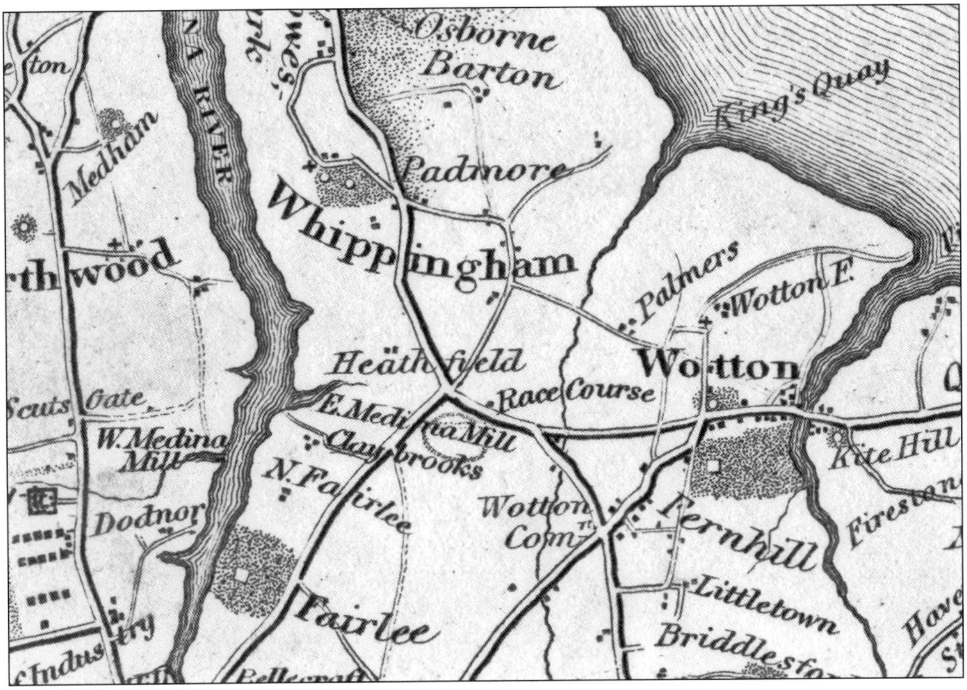

A pocket edition of Brettell's 1848 map with 'Race Course' prominently marked. The track itself is picked out with the finest of dots on the engraving plate.

bought this as farmland in 1845 as part of Alverstone Farm. Perhaps racing ceased soon after. One other guide book mentions the race course, a Brannon map in an 1847 *Guide to the Isle of Wight.*

In 1865 140 acres of the outlying southern portion of the estate, including Mount Misery, were sold by the Queen to Mr Henry Pinnock for £2,500. This would have included the race course land.

Queen Victoria's Farms

Alverstone Farm

In 1854 Prince Albert set about having a new farmhouse and buildings constructed at the lower end of Alverstone Road. This became a very large and impressive building, somewhat in the Italianate style, built of brick with rendered dressings. Both gable walls have a large plaque bearing the garter ribbon, and the date 1854.

An additional wing was added to the rear of the farmhouse and it is believed that 20 troops of the Queen's Lifeguard were billeted here. This would account

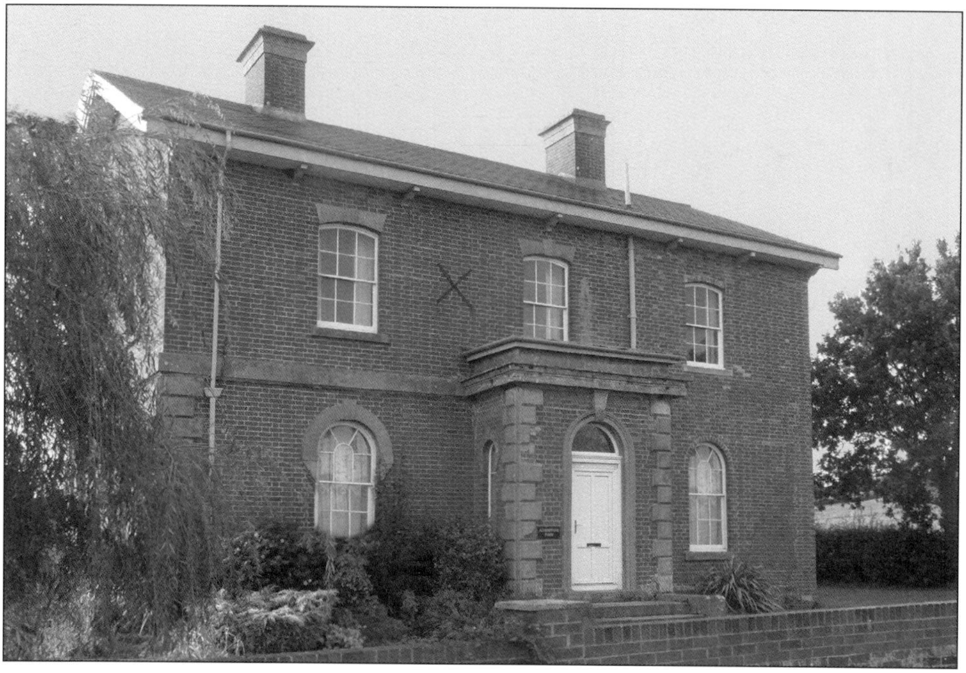

The new Alverstone Farmhouse built in 1854. The house and yards became another 'model farm' built to the designs of Prince Albert.

for the size of the accommodation, more than twice the size of any other farm house on the estate, with two very large ground-floor rooms.

The whole complex at Alverstone has a unity which epitomises the early Victorian ideal model farm. The farm buildings stand in a rectangular arrangement with a cow shed, a separate long range of stabling and cart sheds, barns and a large walled rick-yard. They were originally single storey and built of the red bricks from the Queen's brickyard just across the road. In 1877 the straw barn was altered and the west range given a second storey, enabling loaded carts to enter. A granary was created on the first floor in the north-west corner.

The Victorian farm buildings have changed very little. The original troughs remain, as do many of the roof vents, and the wooden hooks for hanging the harness. The wooden partitions where the loose grain was stored, the hatch and chain for the pulley for lifting sacks, and a grain chute to the mill below still survive, together with a small winnowing machine on the ground floor.

In 1873 a lease was drawn up between Her Majesty and Thomas and Henry Knighton. They were described as butchers of Northwood and their yearly rental

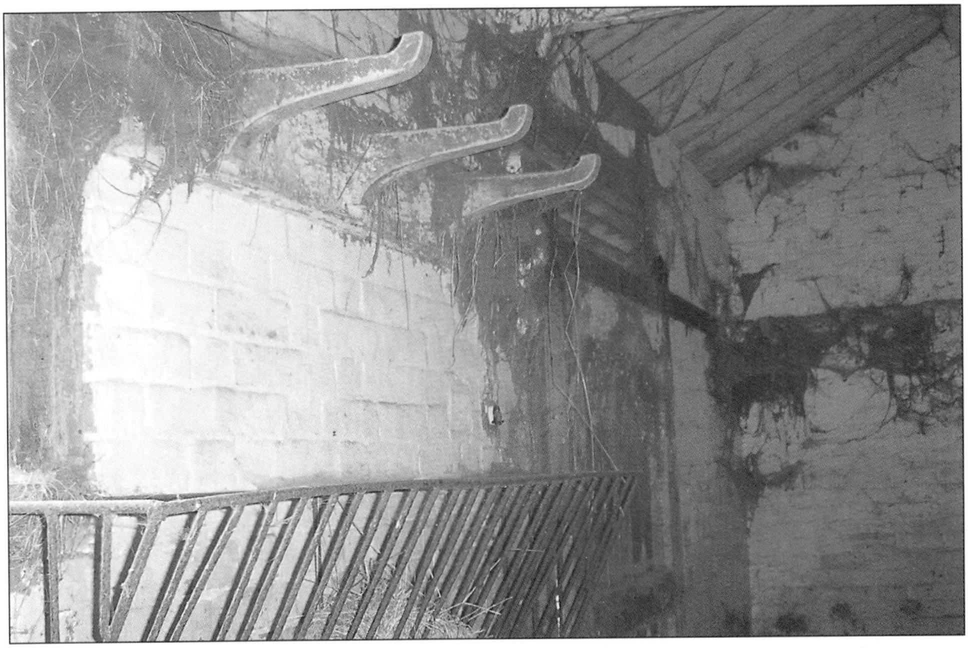

Wooden hooks for the hanging of harnesses survive in one of the stables.

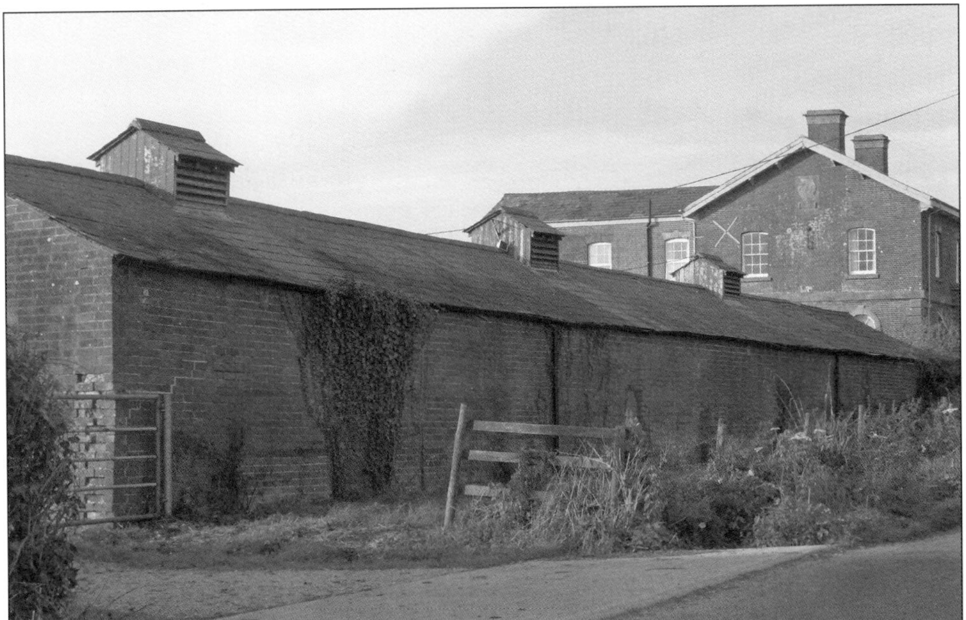

The old cowsheds, with their vented roof sections for better air circulation, are now used as stables.

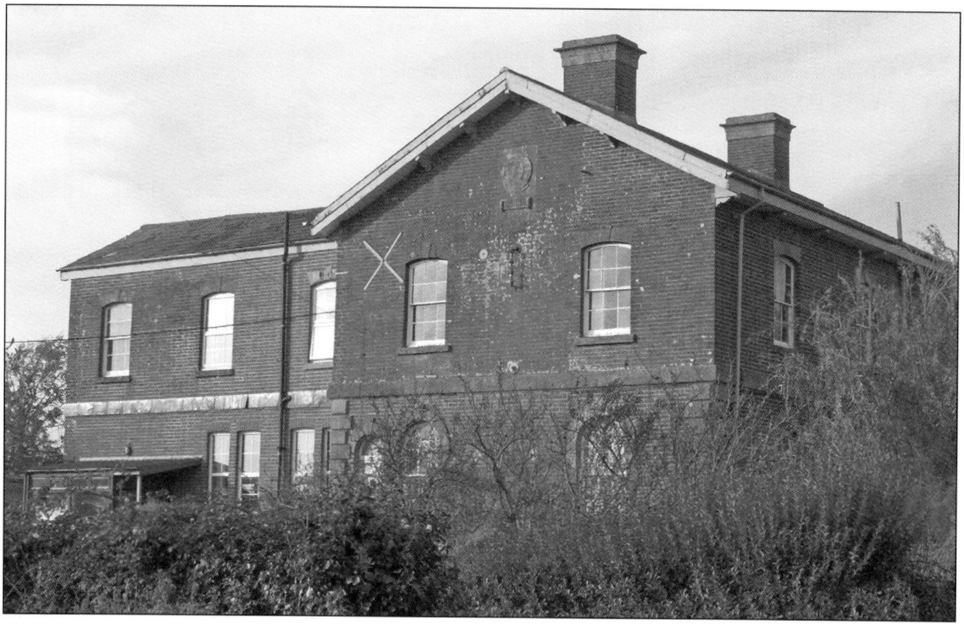

A view of the rear of the farmhouse showing the extension built to house the 20 soldiers of the Queen's Lifeguard.

was to be £130. The Knighton brothers were to be responsible for adding bone meal and manure to the fields annually. In the valuation of the farm that year the land was said to be in a fair state of cultivation. It was suggested that the lessor should pay for more chalking of the fields, with the tenant paying for the carting and spreading of it. Only four cottages would go with the farm.

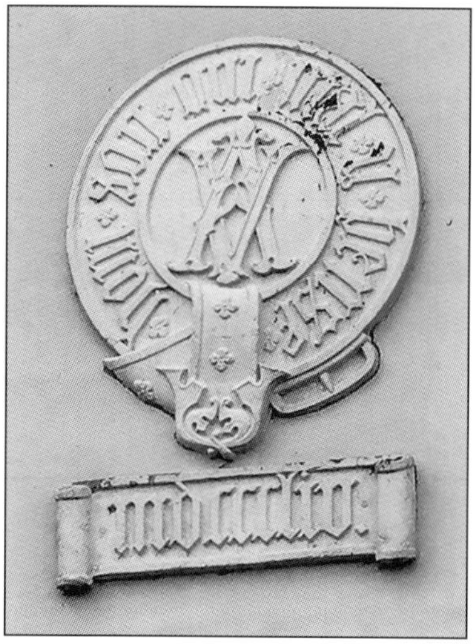

Alverstone Farm's V and A garter ribbon plaque dated 1854

Mr and Mrs Knighton were to move into the farmhouse, but there was some discussion with the Queen's land steward as to the condition of the decoration in the house. A letter was sent to the Keeper of the Privy Purse giving instructions that before the Knightons moved in, *'The walls usually papered in such a house might be thus furnished instead of being coloured with distemper as usual – of course with cheap papers'.*

After the death of Queen Victoria in 1901 Alverstone Farm remained part of the Crown Lands until 1956, by that time being rented to Don Cheshire for £649 per annum. It was auctioned with other remaining parts of Queen Victoria's lands in Whippingham. By that time the tied cottages for the farm were Ivy Cottage and numbers 1 and 2 Brickfield Cottages. The land being sold was 237 acres, with 25 acres of woodland, the timber being valued at £687.10s.

The farmhouse had hot and cold running water laid on, and had eight bedrooms. The outbuildings had been extended by a four-bay Dutch barn and the yard had been concreted. A red-brick shed for milking 40 cows with electrically-driven machinery was installed in the 1950s. Viv Thomas bought Alverstone in 1964 from Don Cheshire.

As well as helping with the farm, Mrs Cheshire had been running bed and breakfast accommodation in the enormous farmhouse, and Mrs Thomas continued this for a few years, letting out the front of the farmhouse.

Mr Thomas started at Alverstone Farm with an 80-strong Guernsey herd, with one cowman to help. An average of eighteen 10-gallon churns were filled each day, collected from the wooden stand next to the dairy by a lorry every morning and taken to Isle of Wight Creameries in Newport. When Isle of Wight Creameries went over to the tanker system the pipes went straight from the dairy to the tank, and thence to the tanker lorry. Lorries collected milk from 300 farms on the Island in 1964.

In March 1996 Viv Thomas went over from milk production to beef. The price received for the milk was going down and the process became uneconomical. By 2017, the farm was still the same size, but the majority of the land was under pasture. There is also stabling for horses and a sand school for riding.

Heathfield Farms

North Heathfield Farm no longer exists. In the early 1800s it was leased to John Nash, the architect, who lived at East Cowes Castle. When he died in 1835 it passed to his wife. She sold the copyhold to Her Majesty in 1846 for £1000 and in 1853 the Queen purchased the freehold from Winchester College.

The farmhouse and yard were on the left as you go down Whippingham Shute, just below the copse and opposite the present Heathfield Farm Cottage. In 1853 the entire site was levelled, but in dry summers the outlines of some of the buildings are visible in the paler grass growth. The North Heathfield land to the east of the main road was combined into Alverstone Farm, and that to the west into South Heathfield Farm.

South Heathfield Farm was run by the Whitmaich family for many years until it was bought by the Queen in 1853. John Whitmaich continued to rent the farm until his death in 1874. The land was taken into the estate management to improve it, and then was let to Thomas Knighton, one of the brothers from Alverstone Farm. It would seem that there were several bad harvests, and the Queen kindly remitted a half-years rent in 1893 and again in 1896.

It was on Heathfield Farm land that Sam Saunders built his first sheds where he constructed amphibious aeroplanes in 1913, and a small airstrip was created.

Fred Warne took over the tenancy of Heathfield Farm. His grandson John remembered that the terms of the Crown tenancy were very strict. 'Not even a nail could be put into a tree, let alone cut one down.' The Warnes had a dairy herd, and bottled their own milk on the farm. In one drought summer in the late 1930s they were permitted to cut branches for cattle feed.

In 1956 Heathfield farm was sold by Crown Estates. George Ablitt and his son were renting the farm at £315 per annum, having come to the farm in 1942

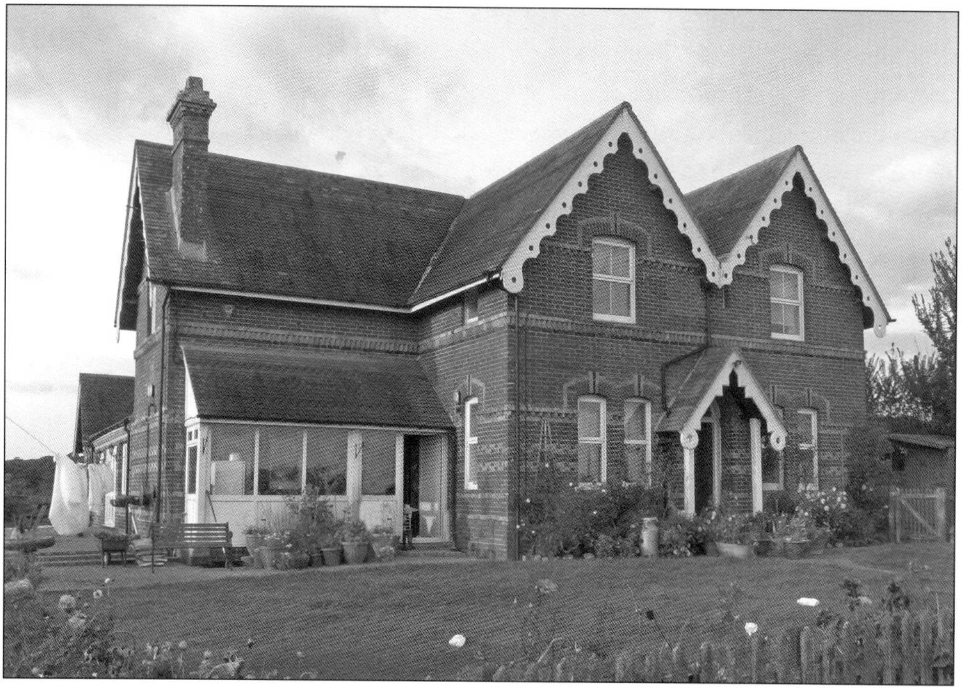

South Heathfield Farmhouse.

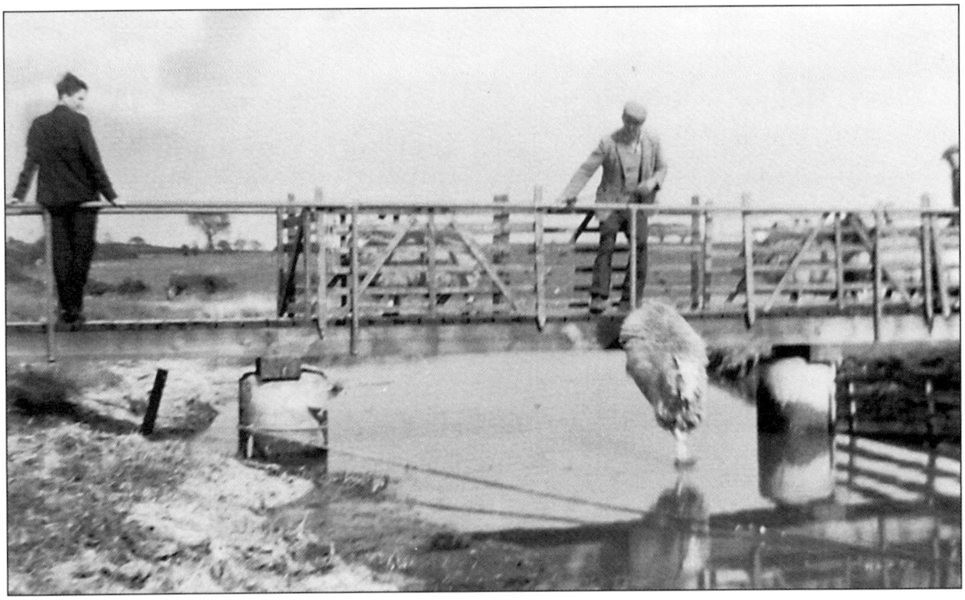

George Ablitt's unusual method of dipping his flock of sheep from the bridge over Heathfield Luck in the 1960s.

from Barton. Also sold were the two Heathfield farm cottages that had been constructed in 1872 at the bottom of Whippingham Shute.

In the 1960s George Ablitt was running a flock of sheep on the land and had a novel way of dipping them. Between Heathfield Farm and Twenty Acres (Medina Park) is a small stream, Heathfield Luck, where the riverside footpath crosses by a bridge. With the help of a few hurdles and helpers, George would persuade his flock to jump, or dive elegantly, off the bridge one by one into the water below, and swim to the shore!

In the late 1970s there was a suggestion to turn the farm into a golf course. However this did not take place and instead Mr Orlik bought the 150 acres of Heathfield Farm in 1996. The house was sold and the farm buildings became dwellings. The land is now farmed with Barton and Kingston. For all these three farms, just two men were employed, a very different scenario from 100 years ago.

Kingston Farm

The farmland belonging to Kingston once reached from Victoria Grove in East Cowes to south of Whippingham Church. In 1864 Kingston Farm came up for auction. The owner was Sir Hamilton Seymour, who had inherited the Norris

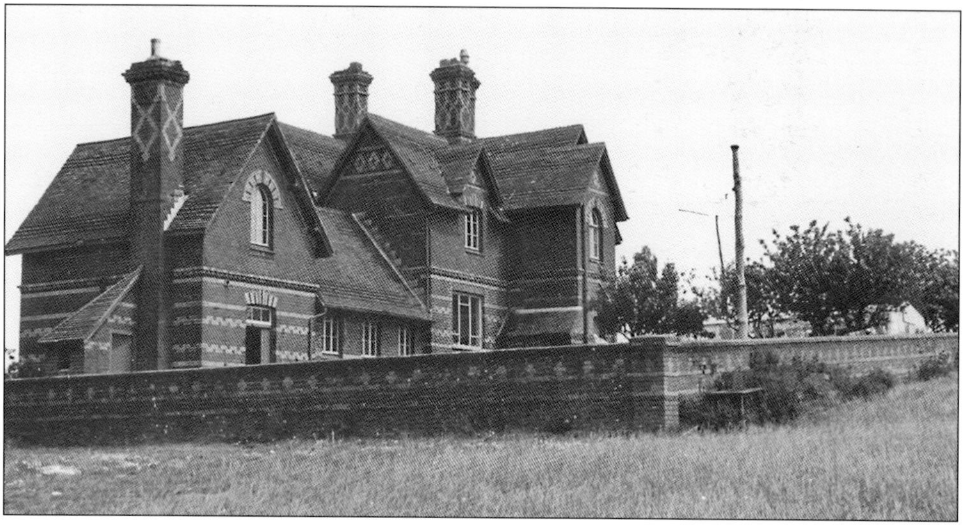

Kingston Farmhouse in the 1960s.

Castle estate in East Cowes. Letters at the Royal Archives show that the Queen's land agent Andrew Toward went to some lengths not to let it be known that the Queen was interested in buying the land, for fear of the price rising. Toward did not want the farm, *'falling into the hands of a stranger.'* An unknown agent stood for the Queen at the bidding, and after two other bidders had raised the price to £5,400, he bid £5450 and was successful. The other bidders had intended, *'..to try to let it off in small plots for building, which would not have improved the respectability of the neighbourhood,'* wrote Andrew Toward.

The building of a new Kingston Farmhouse began in 1866. Soon two labourers' cottages were built on the road down to Hallidays Boatyard, now Cadets Walk, in East Cowes. The farmhouse was constructed of red brick with much decoration. The outbuildings were numerous, and carefully arranged. Prince Albert would have been proud of them.

In Queen Victoria's time the southern boundary of East Cowes was Victoria Grove, abutting Kingston farmland. She gave land from the farm for a cemetery by the river in 1875. The road leading to it was named Kingston Road. From this time the size of Kingston farm continued to decrease. She gave land for allotments and the Victoria Recreation Ground was created on Kingston farmland given by the Queen in 1898. The same year the Queen had Beatrice Avenue extended from Crossways to Victoria Grove. During the First World War Victoria Rec. was ploughed up again to grow cereals.

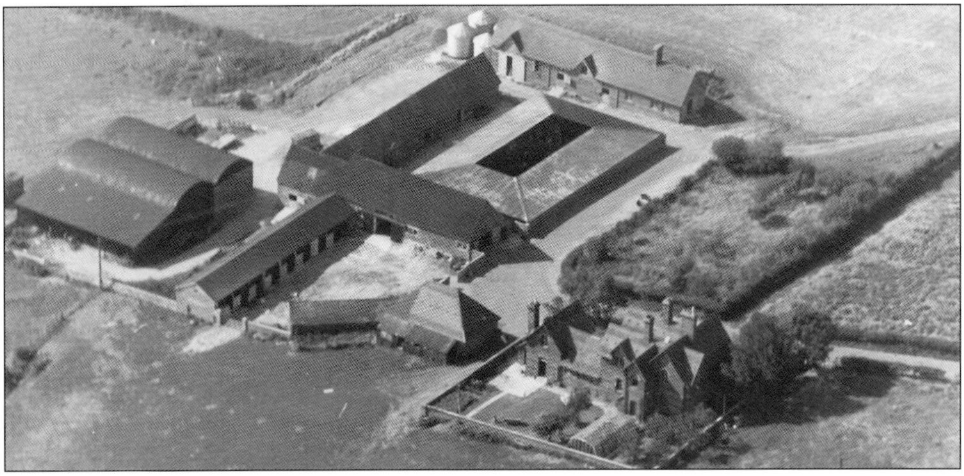

An aerial view of Kingston Farm and its surrounding buildings in the late 1960s.

When the Royal Naval College Osborne was developed in the early 1900s, fields of Kingston Farm were given to the Admiralty to allow engineering training workshops to be built by the river. After the Naval College closed in 1921, the Gas Works and Electricity Power Station were built on this land, and on additional Kingston fields.

An early Crown tenant of Kingston Farm was William Drudge, followed by Edwin Harvey, whose son carried on after him until 1944. Older people in East Cowes remembered going on annual Sunday School picnics to Farmer Harvey's fields, each carrying their mug tied on to their clothing with a ribbon or string. The picnic was an exciting day for the children in the 1920s. The name Harvey is remembered in Harvey Close, built on land near Kingston Farmhouse. Even before the Second World War Kingston land was being sold for a council housing estate, and a larger area was given over to allotments during the war. In the 1950s the council estate was extended.

In 1956 the remaining 158 acres of Kingston Farm was put up for sale by Crown Estates. Mr Starke bought it in 1959, and in 1961 Richard and Anne Orlik bought a reduced Kingston Farm of 120 acres with 60 cows and all the machinery and outbuildings. By 1970 there were 100 cows and cereal production had been reduced. In 1973 the milking system at Kingston became obsolete and it was decided to build a new dairy unit at Barton.

The Kingston farmhouse was sold, together with the outbuildings and nearby field. The latter was bought by an electricity company to use while re-building the power station and the buildings were later demolished. Consequently, those farm-buildings at Kingston were the first of Queen Victoria's to disappear from the Whippingham map.

The part of Kingston Farm south of Crossways Road as far as East Cowes Vics football field had been sold to the council and Osborne Middle School was built there in 1973. More of Kingston farm was sold for housing in the early 1970s, Greenlands Road being built at this time.

In the 1990s permission was given for housing on the fields south of Kingston farmhouse despite concerns about the contraction of the green belt of farmland between Whippingham and East Cowes. It was felt the two settlements should remain visibly separate and the Conservation Area that now surrounds the church should be protected. In 2006 planning permission for 550 houses on the fields between Osborne Middle School and the river was obtained, and the green belt between Whippingham and East Cowes was reduced. Building work still continues on this site, Hawthorn Meadows, in 2017, and a marine industrial site is being created by the river.

Truckles Farm

This farm was bought for the Royal Estate from Admiral Sir George Seymour in 1862 for the sum of £7,000 and incorporated into Kingston Farm in 1874. The farmyard was levelled so that The Almshouses could be built there, and shortly afterwards two new wash-houses were built for the use of the tenants living at Truckles old farmhouse.

The thatched farmhouse has large brick chimneys on the outside walls as thatch is always a vulnerable building material. Unfortunately on 26 July 1890 there was a fire at Truckles which destroyed the farmhouse. By 1892 Truckles was completely rebuilt as two cottages.

The first tenant in the rebuilt Truckles west cottage was Henry Cooper and his large family. He had been working as a carter on the Queen's Estate since 1846. His daughter Eva married Albert Thorne and they continued to live there. Subsequently their son Ray took on the tenancy, and together with his wife Audrey looked after the 'family' cottage until 2002 when they moved next door to The Almshouses.

Around 1910 the Russell family were living at Truckles east cottage. Mrs Flux lived there in the 1930s and 40s and served teas to people visiting the church.

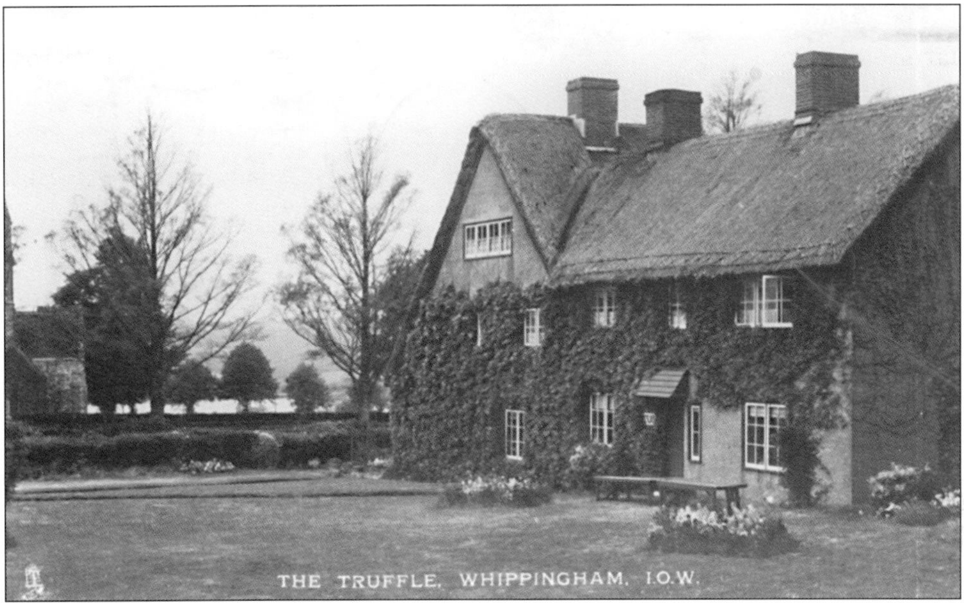

An early postcard, pre 1910, printed in France. Confusion over the spelling resulted in it being titled 'The Truffle'

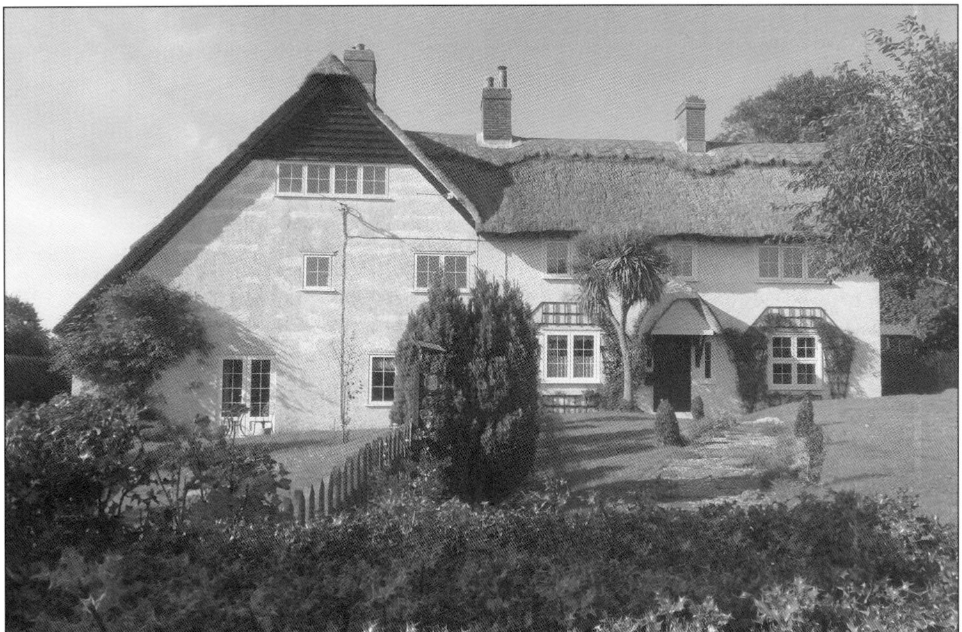

Truckles is one of the two remaining thatched properties in Whippingham.

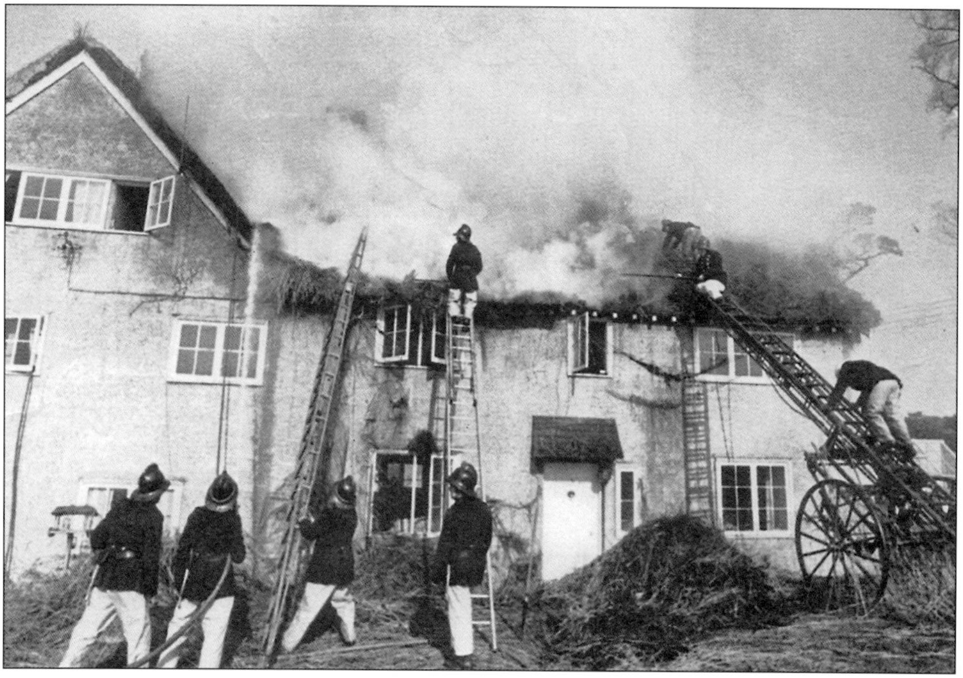

Firemen rake off the thatched roof of Truckles and damp down the straw during the 1973 blaze.

The roof fell victim to yet another fire in 1973, when sparks from the chimney set the thatch ablaze. By this time the IW Council owned Truckles, which was one of the very few thatched houses on the housing association stock on the Isle of Wight before being sold into private ownership. With the nearby almshouses they make a very picturesque corner of Whippingham, classified as a Conservation Area.

Woodhouse Farm

Woodhouse was the most easterly farm of the lands purchased by Victoria and Albert. It stretched down to the sea and King's Quay. In 1846 Prince Albert combined Woodhouse Farm with Barton as the 'home farm' for Osborne. The present farmhouse was built as labourer's cottages, and converted later to one house for a tenant farmer.

The Tillett family bought the Barton estate in 1922 including Woodhouse Farm. During the Second World War the Ministry of Agriculture said that some of the fields had to be used for growing potatoes. The farmer said it wouldn't work, but the 'Min. of Ag.' were adamant and seed potatoes were planted. However, when the time came to lift the crop, the ground was so wet that it was impossible.

In 1953 Barton and Woodhouse Farms were sold separately when the Tilletts left the Island. Roy Richards sold Woodhouse Farm to Eric Taylor and his wife Carol in 1967. Most of the fields were laid to grass for a flock of about 150 sheep and a prize-winning herd of Friesian milking cows. Eric, with his daughter Barbara, had considerable success with their cattle which were very good milk producers and in 1994 one of the Woodhouse cows was supreme champion at the Isle of Wight County Agricultural Show.

From 1984-1994 Carol Taylor ran 'Country Produce', a greengrocers in East Cowes. The farm provided all the potatoes for the shop. In 1994 the Taylor family sold Woodhouse to Nick Johnson who continued the dairy herd until 2002.

The number of dairy farms on the Island had decreased from about 60 in 1993 to 20 in 2003. In 2017 there are just 10 milking herds on the Island, none of them in Whippingham. Woodhouse Farm was sold in 2003 and the livestock and farm equipment were put up for auction. The milking equipment, which would have cost many thousands of pounds to install when new, fetched only £100.

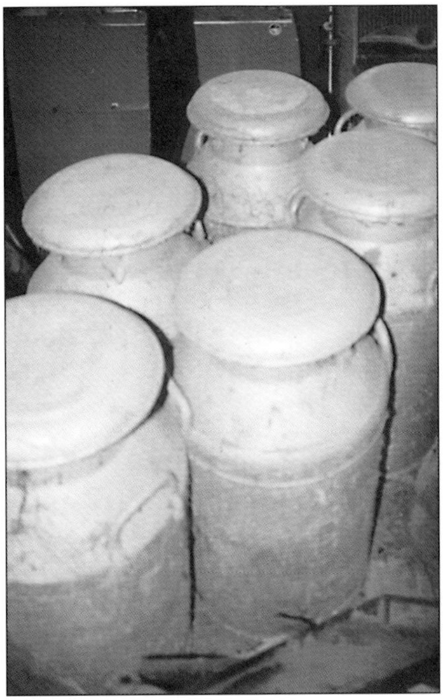

Milk churns gather dust in a barn at Alverstone Farm.

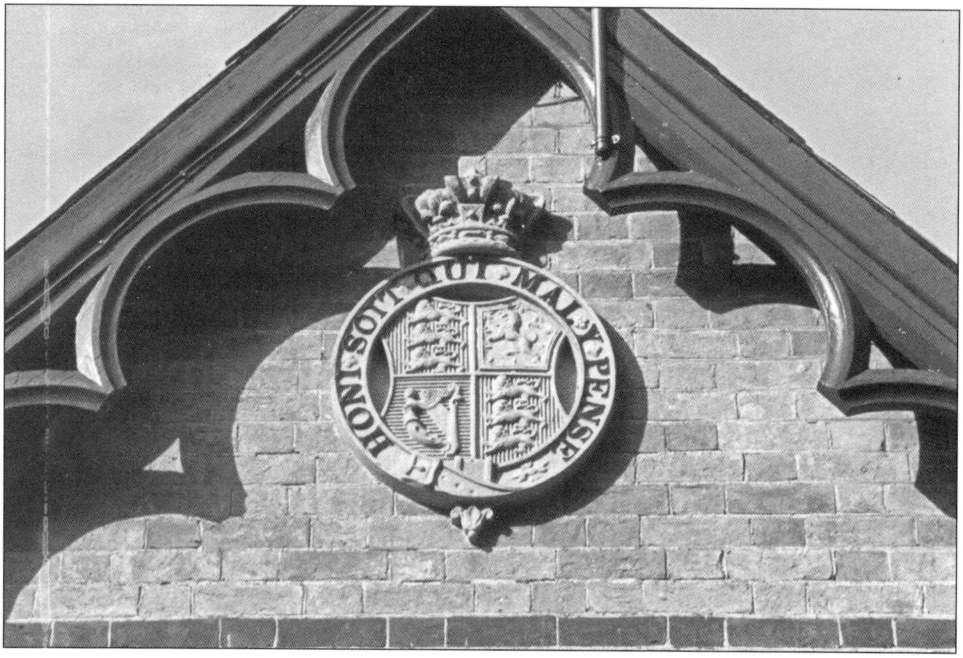

Royal plaque on the gable-end wall of Brock's Copse Lodge.

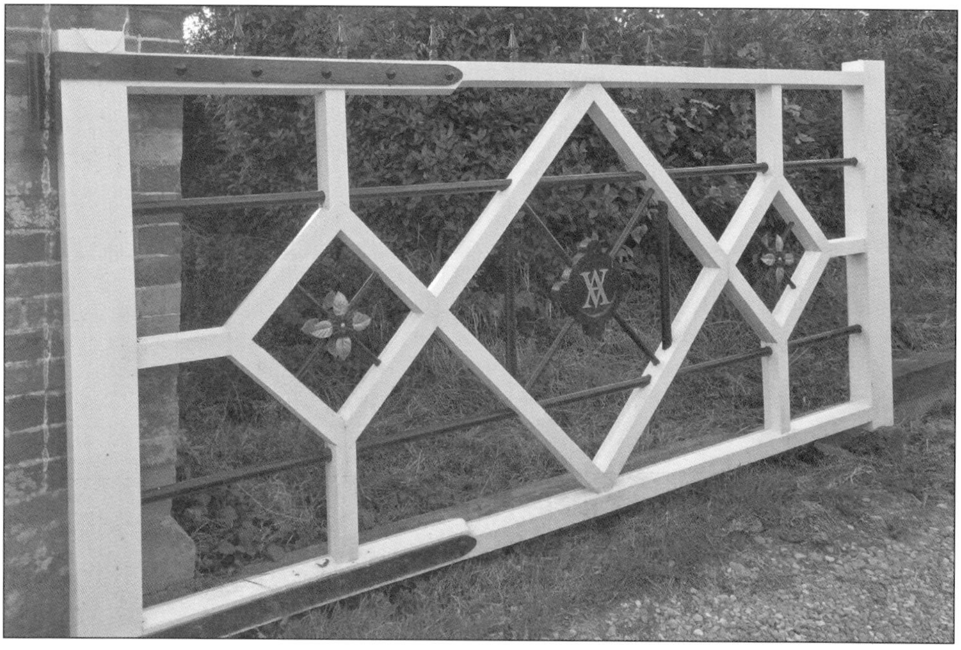

The restored gates of Alverstone Lodge showing the V and A cypher.

Seven

Cottages on the Queen's Estate

When Victoria and Albert bought Osborne and Barton they found that they were responsible for the quality of life of the people in the 31 cottages that were sold with the estates.

The Queen wrote in her journal at Christmas 1848; *'I take such an interest in all our labourers and people here, also their children, and hope that when their cottages are in better order, I may be able to go and see them, which, with two or three exceptions I cannot easily do now.'*

The cottages were occupied by farm labourers and in a bad state of repair. Families of six or seven people were crammed into two rooms in *'miserable'* cottages, very small and uncomfortable according to the Queen. Albert set about improving his farmworkers' homes as he aspired to become a model agriculturalist. He had Master Builder, Cubitt, instructing his men to mend pumps, kitchen ranges, windows and the leaking roofs. Walls were repaired, replastered and repainted.

Many of the cottages were torn down and rebuilt, with no record of what the original cottages looked like. Some of the new cottages were built on exactly the same site, but others in new positions. One field north of Primrose Cottage shows the outlines of previous buildings in a dry summer. This was the settlement called variously Alverstone, Elverton Street or Whippingham Street on old maps.

There are two areas of Whippingham where cottages have completely disappeared. One is located on the south side of Brocks Copse Road in the field before the copse as you travel east. Here there were four tenements and another cottage owned by Richard Whitmaich and James Taylor. It is a possible site for the original Poor House, given up in 1759, which had been rented from

Richard Whitmaich. These cottages were demolished in 1895. In dry conditions the outlines of the buildings can be seen, and Colin Thomas 'found' an old well when his tractor wheel got stuck in it in the 1990s. These may have been Pryor's Cottages as the adjacent field today is known as Prymore.

Another area is to the north of the churchyard where 'Church Cottages' existed by the old gravel pit. They were demolished after having been used by soldiers practicing house-to-house combat before embarking for D-Day, during the Second World War. They were told they could use these cottages for practice and they used them to destruction!

The Queen enjoyed visiting her people on the estate. She knew them by name, and all about their circumstances. The Queen wrote frequently in her journal about these drives, or walks. For example, *'6 February 1864. Walking with Lenchen and Katherine to Whippingham Church...Walked about the lovely church, my beloved's own design, the church yard and visited some of the cottages close by.'* and *'17 February 1864. After lunch drove with Louise and Katherine B, visiting some of the cottages, most of which I found very clean and tidy.'*

The work of improving the cottages continued until there were 36 cottages divided into 61 separate dwellings owned by the Queen in East Cowes and Whippingham. The new cottages were a considerable improvement on the old, but still primitive in their facilities compared to modern standards. The toilets were simply earth closets in the shed at the end of the garden, and in many cases these continued in use for a long time beyond 1901. Around the estate some of the cottages were provided with a private sitting room for the Queen. In addition a separate water closet was reserved specifically for her use.

Each tenant on the estate was allowed to keep a pig, and to work a garden or allotment. This would supplement the wages earned by providing fruit, vegetables and meat.

The Royal Estate Lodges

Barton Manor Lodges

South Lodge was built in 1848 and North Lodge in 1850. Their style copies that of the manor house itself, using similar stone and features. The design originated from Prince Albert, and his drawing for the proposed lodge is in the British Museum. After his first draft, a porch was added and the rear wing became 'T'-

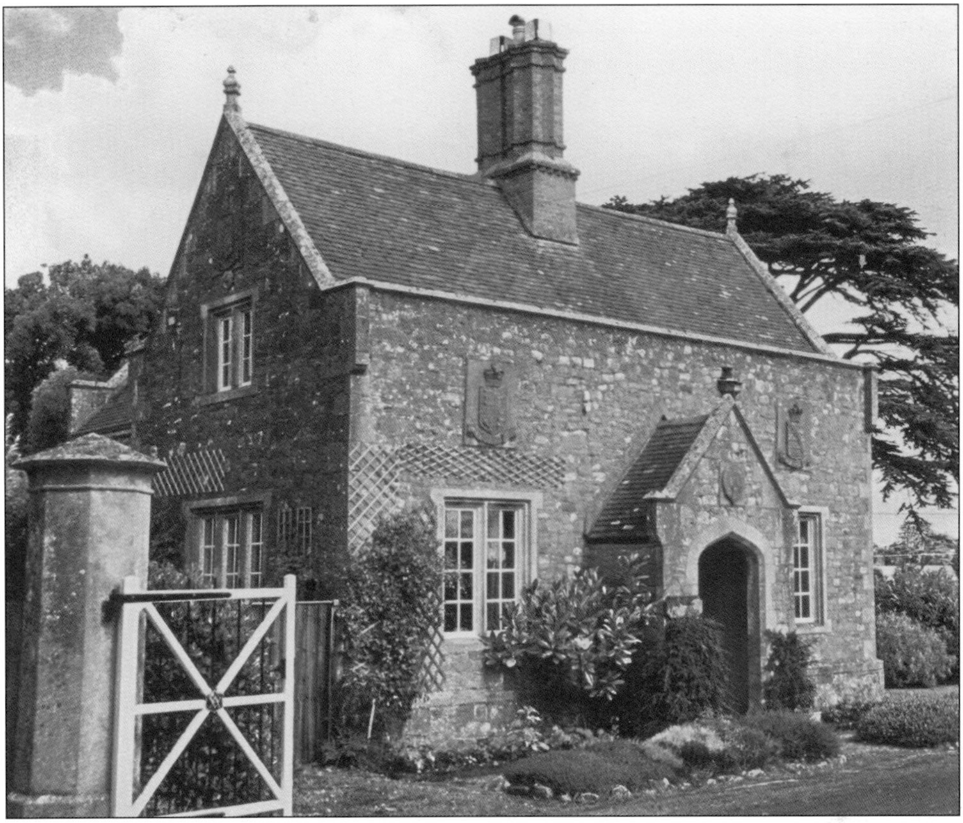

The North Lodge at the gates of Barton Manor. The central gate and pillars were removed leaving the smaller pedestrian gates.

shaped. Heraldic devices were applied externally recording the connection of the Barton Estate with Winchester College as well as the Queen and Prince.

Between the two lodges were three gates. The central gate and the two wooden gate posts for it were removed in the late 1970s. All the gates had the intertwined letters V and A.

Various estate workers lived in these two lodges through the years. Near the end of Victoria's life one occupant was Thomas Foakes, who had been working for the Queen since 1846, when he was just ten years old. He started by weeding the grounds, but by 1888 he was a carpenter on the estate as his father, George, had been before him. George Foakes was a foreman wheeler and carpenter in 1846 earning £1 a week. He was the second most highly paid man on the estate, and his final position was as estate carpenter for Barton Manor.

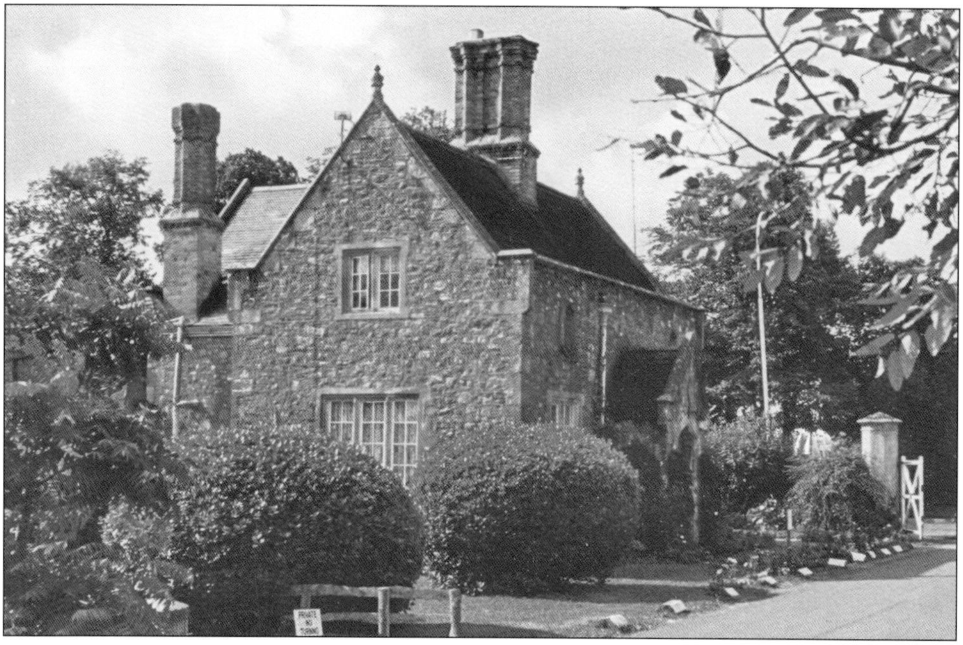

The South Lodge taken from inside the gates of Barton Manor.

Mr Streeter the chauffeur lived at one of the Barton Lodges while the Tilletts were living at the manor.

At the end of the twentieth century Mary Cox lived at North Lodge. In the 1970s she had propagated an apple tree in the garden that was both good for eating and cooking and with excellent keeping qualities. A nursery took it up and the trees were produced commercially in the year 2000 under the name Mary's Millenium.

The cottages still look much the same in 2017 as when they were built and still proudly guard the entrance to Barton Manor when seen from the main Whippingham Road.

Alverstone Road Lodge

The Lodge at Alverstone Gate was constructed in 1858 at the same time as Mount Road was extended from the site of Coburg cottage to the Lodge. Previously the only road here to the estate had been to the east of the new lodge, past Dallimores.

Consequently the occupants had two gates to attend to on the east and west. Each gate had brick-built piers using red brick coursed with bands of buff brick,

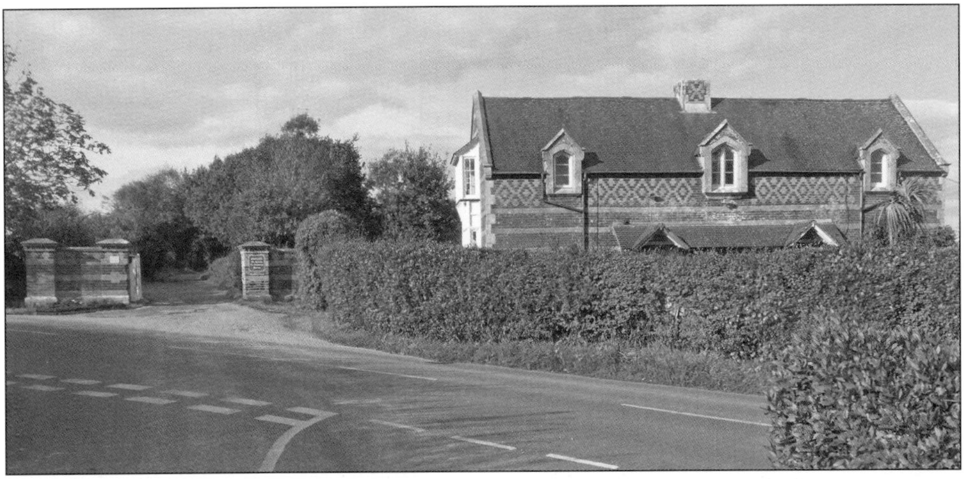

Alverstone Lodge after restoration in the 1990s minus the grand chimneys. Compare with the engraving over the page.

and screen walls to further piers on the west side, creating a strong visual feature. The gates themselves were of a slightly more countrified style than that at Barton main road entrance, but still sported the entwined initials V and A. One of the gates and its post has recently been restored.

Alverstone Lodge was once an entrance fit for a Queen. The building formed a pair of lodges with a central chimney stack. It is built of red bricks coursed with bands of buff brick. Two attractive first-floor bay windows feature in the end walls, overlooking the two driveways and gates. These were carefully restored in the 1990s. The tall chimney stacks were removed then.

In 1860 Henry Hurst and Eli Jenkins were occupiers of Alverstone Lodge. Henry had a young family and records in 1864 show his children, Victoria and Morris, received Christmas presents from the Queen. Victoria received both a dress and a doll, but Morris, who was older, was given a book. The same year Mrs Hurst and Mrs Jenkins both received a Christmas gift of a petticoat from the Queen. The task of gate opening fell upon them while their husbands were working on the estate.

In the 1880s Mrs Gallop was the sick-nurse on the Estate, and lived at Alverstone Lodge. By 1888 Henry Hunt and George Lock were living as tenants at Alverstone Lodge. George Lock had been working for the Queen for only four years, but Henry Hunt had retired as foreman of the pleasure grounds at Osborne three years earlier. He had been working as a gardener for the Queen since 1845.

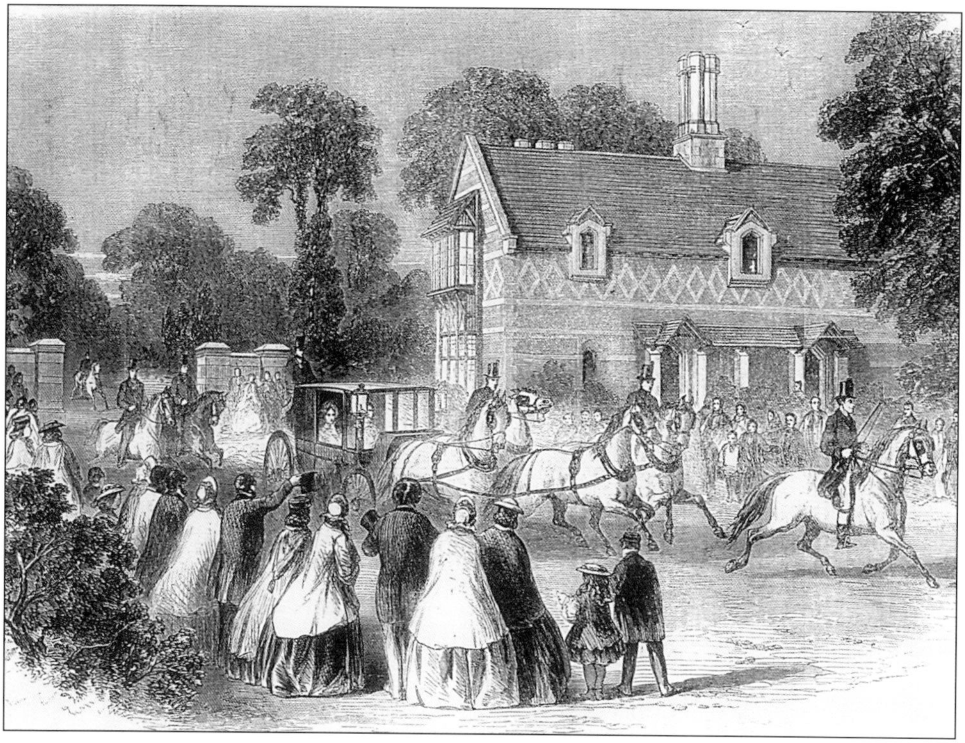

Princess Alice leaves Osborne with her new husband Prince Louis of Hesse Darmstalt via the gates of Alverstone Lodge in 1862. (IWCRO)

Also in 1888, the estate steward Andrew Blake noted in a letter to the Queen that there were 16 of her elderly, pensioned estate workers still occupying cottages on the estate. A further 11 men living on the estate were either nearing retirement, or were invalids. He feared that able-bodied workers would have to be sought from outside the estate if this continued to be the case. This was despite The Almshouses having been opened for a dozen years for pensioners.

Mr and Mrs Billy Snow started their married life at Alverstone Lodge in 1894. Billy was foreman of the pleasure grounds, roads and avenues of Osborne and Barton estates. He was made foreman in 1885 when he was 25 years old, and had a gang of 11 men working under him.

When Queen Victoria, or other members of the Royal household, came through the gate on their official drives, Mrs Snow had to open the gate for them. The outrider would ride ahead and call out, *"Gate, gate!"* giving the signal. She received a shilling a week for doing this.

Brock's Copse Lodge

Down the hill from Alverstone Lodge towards Wootton one passes through Brock's Copse. The original name for this area was Brook's Copse, bought by the Queen in 1846, but the name soon appeared as Brock's.

In 1864 Brock's Lodge was built just above the bridge at the same time as a driveway, Boundary Drive, was created through the copse towards the main Ryde to Newport Road. The south side of the Brock's Copse road has a V and A monogrammed gate, but traces of the drive have disappeared.

Brock's Lodge today is often in the shade of the surrounding trees. It is built of the estate red bricks and buff bricks, but in this lodge the buff bricks form the major part of the building with red banding. It also has ornate timber barge boards. Crossed brick decoration is used on the chimney stack and the side of the house, together with the same cross-work on the gate piers. The gate matches the others at Alverstone Lodge. The building is still largely intact and has been little altered, still retaining its original Elizabethan-style chimney pots and crests mounted on the gable ends. It presents an excellent example of the estate architecture.

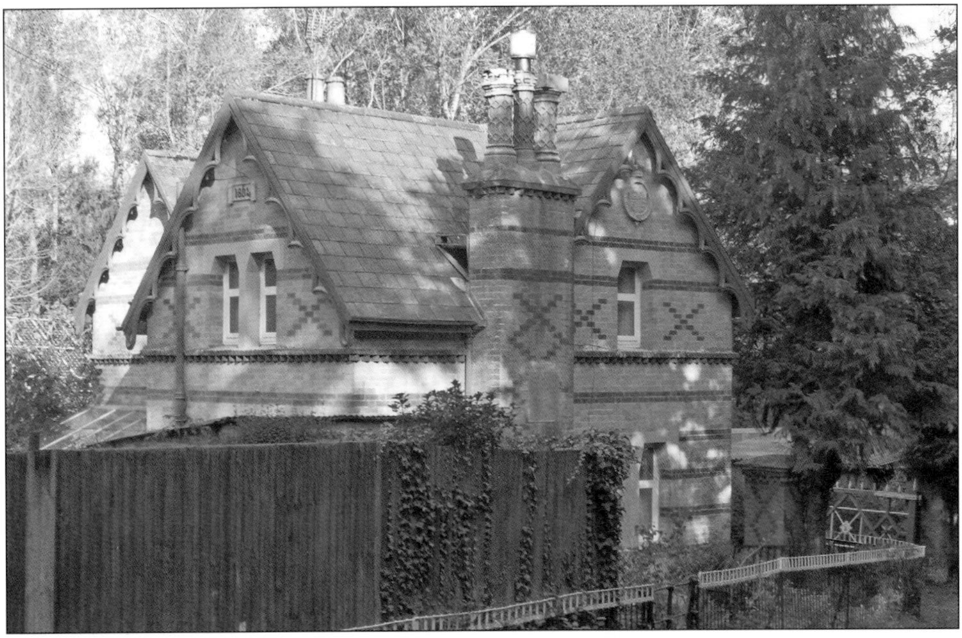

Brock's Copse Lodge displaying all the fine charecteristics of an estate lodge. Decorated with contrasting brickwork and fine gable-end woodwork.

Mr and Mrs James Hollyer were tenants of Brock's Lodge in 1864. They had moved into the new lodge from Primrose Cottage with their three children, James, Lucy and Harriet. James senior had been working on the Queen's Estate since 1846, when he was described as a farm labourer who was paid 12 shillings a week.

Like many of the cottages, Brock's Lodge was reliant upon a well for water. In 1888 a new well was dug, but it was found to be rather brackish and failed completely in the summer and autumn. When this happened the lodge had to be supplied by water cart. In 1900 a piped water supply was laid on to the lodges at Alverstone and Brock's Copse from a supply found 14ft down behind Six Cottages in Alverstone Road.

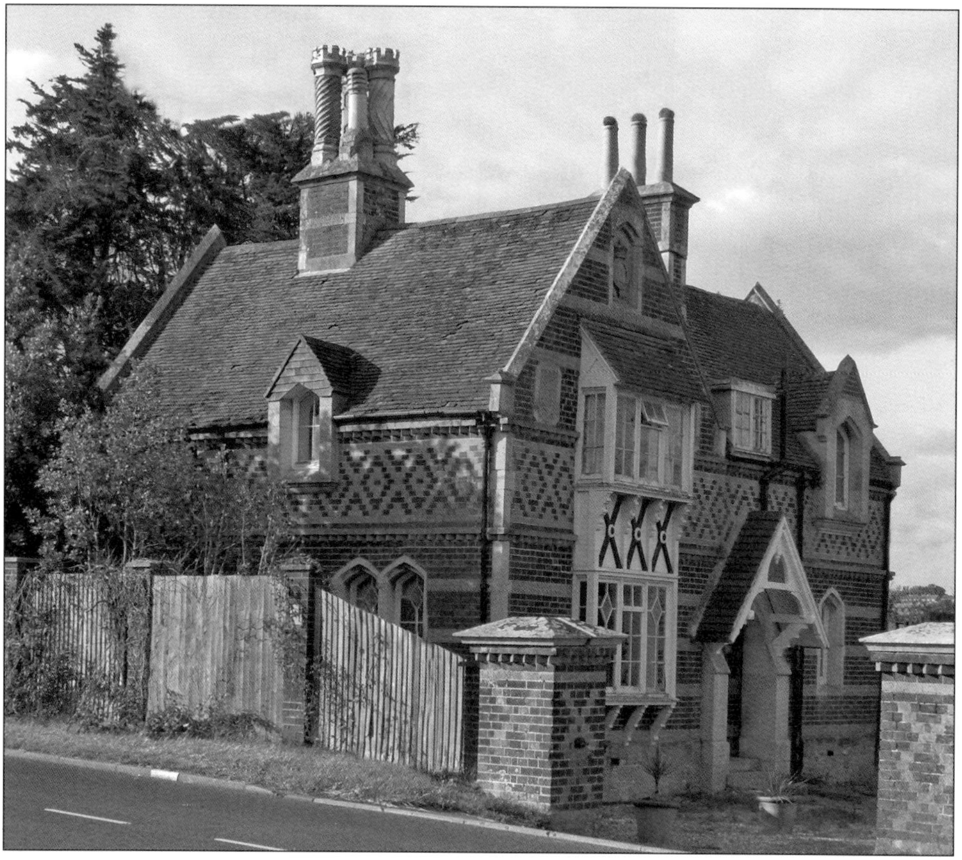

The prominent Ryde Road Lodge of 1864 stands near Palmer's Brook. It is highly decorated with ornate chimneys and diamond diapering brickwork on all sides, including the gate piers.

Ryde Road Lodge

This impressive lodge opposite Palmer's Brook Farm was the southern-most of Queen Victoria's lodges. It was built in 1864 and the drive led north to Brock's Copse Lodge. Built mainly of red estate bricks, it has buff bricks used as banding and decorative diamond patterning (diapering) around the upper walls. It is very ornate, and still has some of its decorative chimneys, the brick-built gate posts and gate. Heraldic arms and a plaque on the gable end confirm the date of its construction.

It has been said that the lodge was built for the Queen to use when she went to catch a train at Whippingham Station. Unfortunately this is untrue as the station and railway line were not constructed until 1875. It is believed that Victoria only used the train once at Whippingham. However, the lodge did give access to the estate for those arriving from Ryde by train, when a carriage would be sent to meet them.

William Cook was resident at Ryde Road Lodge in 1888. He had already served the Queen for 14 years. The lodge was sold by Crown estates in 1956 and called Palmer's Lodge in the sale document.

The Cottages inside the gates

Coburg Cottage

Perhaps one of the most ornate and unusual cottages on the estate is Coburg Cottage. Prince Albert had come from the principality of Saxe-Coburg which is in present-day Germany, near the old East German border. Queen Victoria visited Saxe-Coburg several times, including three times after Albert's death. When further cottages were necessary on the estate in 1870 she may have suggested that this Germanic regional style might be suitable. Hence we have in Whippingham a faithfully reproduction of a Saxe-Coburg building.

Coburg Cottage was built as a pair of cottages and completed in 1872. They are a unique architectural expression on the estate and possibly in the whole of England. The north cottage had a sitting-room for the Queen which was part-panelled and had a large marble fireplace. A flush toilet for her personal use was installed in a small room almost two storeys high and was illuminated by a high window which afforded extra privacy for the Queen.

Externally the ground floor has decorative dark wood beams with white render, giving a slightly Tudor impression. All of the first floor, the central

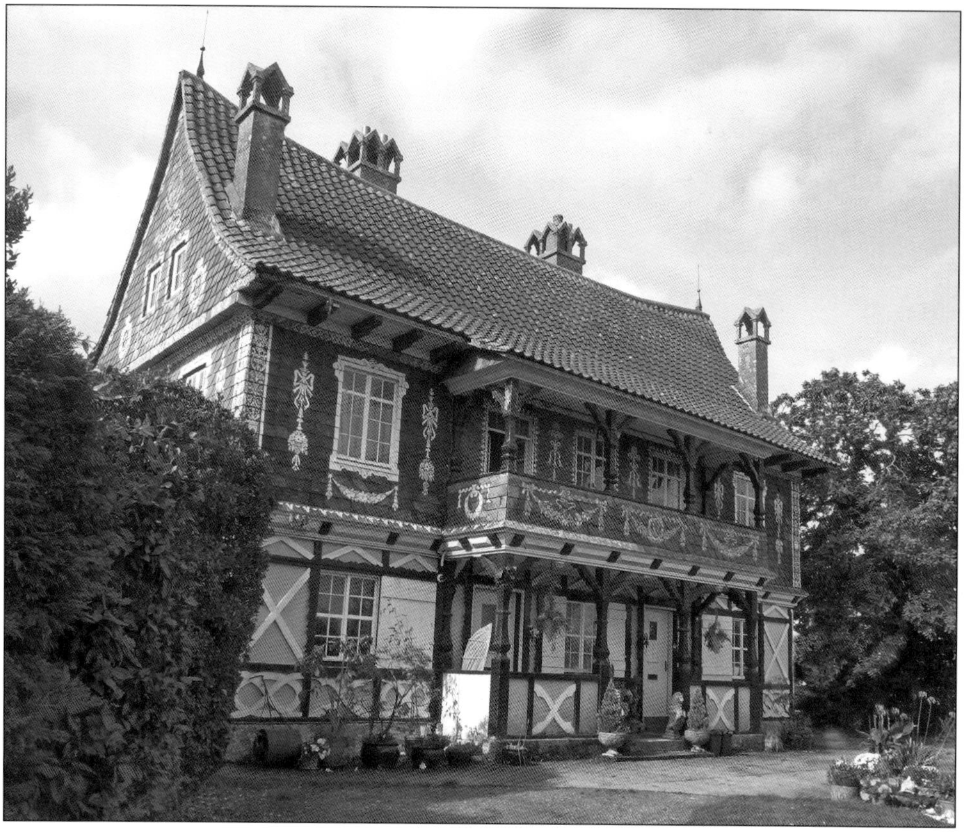

Coburg Cottage built in 1872. Designed to emulate the Saxe-Coburg style, birthplace of Prince Albert. Victoria chose the design after Prince Albert's death.

balcony over the wide porch, and the third-floor gable ends are hung with slate. This slate is decorated with white-painted garlands and ribbons, crowns and a 'V' motif for the Queen. It is a beautiful and stunning decoration, which has been restored in recent years. The decoration is signed 'Louise', the name of Victoria's artistic sixth child. It is quite possible that the design for the painted decoration could have been produced by Princess Louise.

On the rear elevation of the house the slate roof becomes a 'cat-slide' roof to cover the ground-floor rooms. A wash house and privies were built in the garden to the rear. The earth closet was still in use in 1953, although the northern cottage by then had the use of the Queen's water closet.

The ridge of the cottage has a distinct dip in it, and this odd-shaped roof can be seen across the fields from the main road.

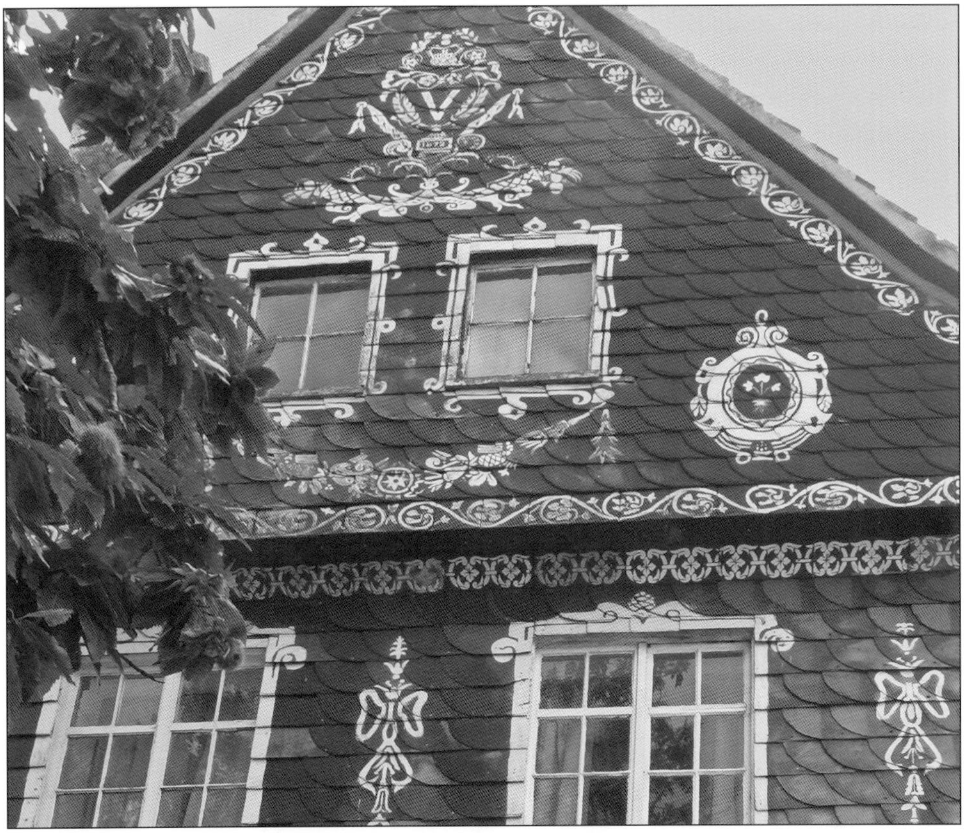

The gable-end wall of Coburg Cottage painted with garlands and ribbons over the slates. The fish-scale slates were carefully restored and re-painted in the 1990s.

Dallimores Cottage

In 1859 a new gamekeeper's cottage was constructed near Alverstone Gate on the site of Dallimores Cottage. The building looks continental, with a low pitched roof and shallow gables. It is built of brick with a rendered first floor and a slate roof with a porch under an attractive first floor balcony over the front door.

The same year a range of kennels, now converted into a bungalow, were constructed to the west of the keeper's cottage. The gamekeeper's dogs were kept here, ready to help him in his work and to provide retrievers for the shooting parties. In 1953 the sale catalogue describes them as, *'a very useful range of buildings providing three Boxes, two with large runs enclosed by iron railings and Fodder Room with copper and ovens...'*

In 1953 Dallimores Cottage was still in the Barton Estate. There were three rooms downstairs and three upstairs, proving that the keeper's position was a cut above the average estate worker. By 2017 the house had been carefully extended, but to the casual observer looks little different from Queen Victoria's time.

Mr Land was the head gamekeeper living at Dallimores until his sudden death in 1878. The *Isle of Wight County Press* reported that, *'Mr Land had won for*

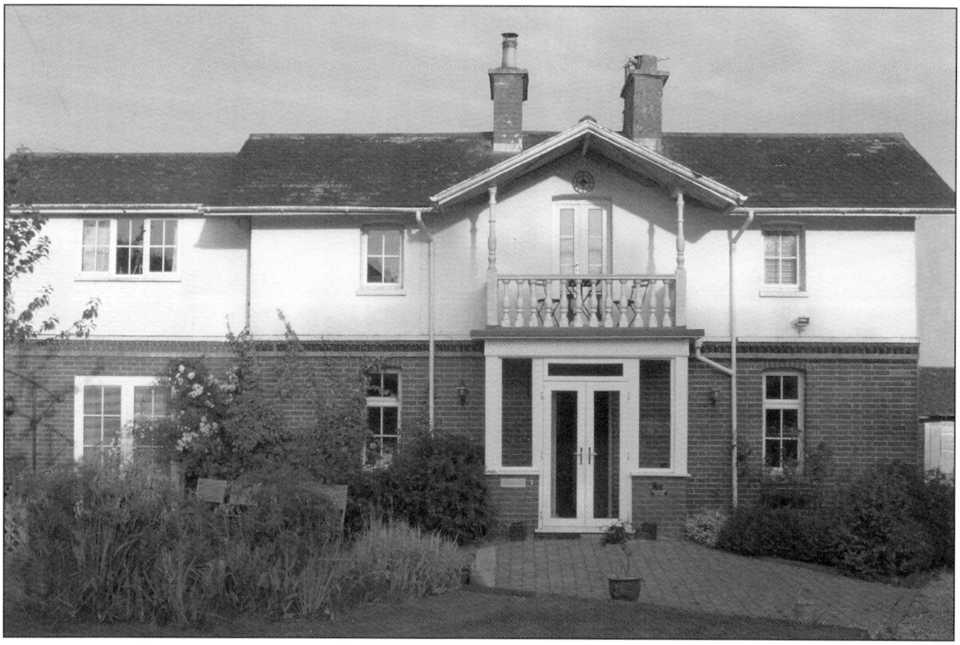

Dalimores Cottage has been extended and modernised but retains many of its original estate features.

himself a character of the highest kind, and was esteemed and respected not only by those on the estate but also by the farmers and others with whom he came in contact.' He died a day before the Queen's arrival at Osborne, and Victoria visited Mrs Land an hour after arriving on the Island. Mrs Land was given a pension of £45 as she had no children, and she moved into Coburg Cottage to make way for a replacement keeper in Dallimores.

In 1885 another new head keeper was appointed. His name was Wheeler and he was described by the land steward Andrew Blake as, *'a nice looking pleasing man who must keep the rabbits down.'* Four years later, in December 1889, Blake told the Queen in a letter, *'Wheeler says there are 30% fewer rabbits than when he first came here.'* Wheeler was also of the opinion that the present keepers could keep the numbers down and they were not in need of any outside assistance. He mentioned that the keepers also kill the rats, as many as 1,200 were killed in 1889 alone.

The Queen replied to Blake on 28 December 1889, *'I wish that the keepers should be told by you that I wish the rabbits to be kept down, but not entirely destroyed... And that the rats should be exterminated!'* Signed *'VRI.'* The underlining was done by the Queen herself, probably horrified at the thought of those 1,200 rats - but she had a soft spot for fluffy rabbits!

Some of the dogs kept at the kennels may have been terriers to catch rats. Others would have gone out with the keepers when summoned from the house to attend gentlemen intending to shoot. We know that another gamekeeper lived at King's Quay and he also had kennels. In 1874 that keeper had complained about the hounds of the local hunt disturbing the game in Osborne Woods when hunting at Palmer's Brook that November. The keeper asked the Queen if they should be stopped from hunting. Letters were sent to the Master of the Hunt, John Harvey of 'Marvel', near Newport, informing him that the Queen refused access to the hunt over her land at Palmer's Brook.

Numerous records exist of the shooting on the Osborne Estate. In the last quarter of 1890, Prince Henry of Battenburg, Princess Beatrice's husband, shot 69 pheasants, one partridge and two woodcocks on Christmas Eve, and even more on New Year's Eve with Lord Lorne. Prince Arthur, Duke of Connaught, the Queen's seventh child, went out shooting on the 27 December, bagging a total of 178 pheasants.

It is notable that the keepers had been keeping the rabbits down since September, shooting 404 of them, and had shot 210 partridges, leaving few of

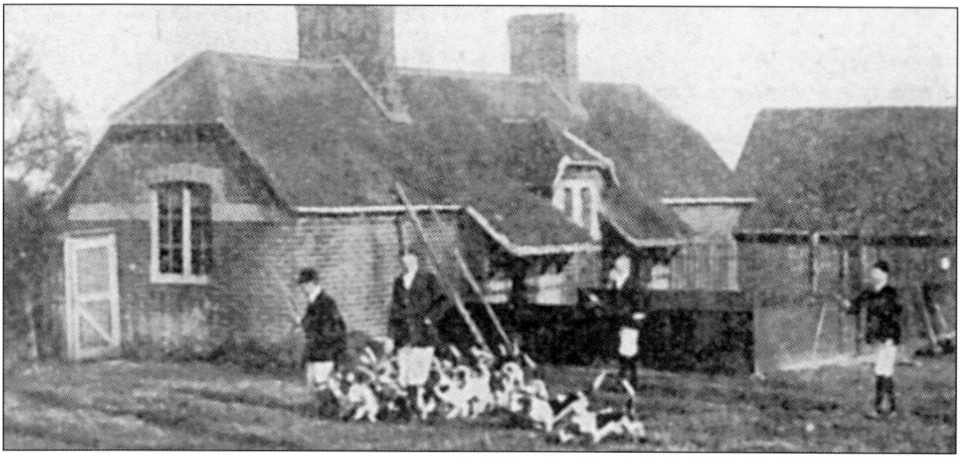

By 1908 a pack of hounds were kept at the kennels. The Naval Cadets from Osborne Royal Naval College went out on foot with these beagles on the Barton estate. (IWCRO)

these for the Royalty. However the pheasants had been left. These would have been bred on the estate especially for the sport. The 210 partridge shot were all sent up to Balmoral, but 408 pheasants shot in that quarter were all consumed at Osborne, as were six woodcocks, 26 hares and just 20 rabbits.

Of the rest of the rabbits, 162 of them were listed as being given away on the estate, and 240 of them were sold. The keeper had a separate book to record the amount of game sold, probably to the local butchers in East Cowes. Rabbits in 1890 fetched ten shillings a dozen, but hares three shillings each. This money was passed to the land steward for the estate accounts.

After the Queen's death, the land steward wrote to the King on 5 November 1901. *'What are his Majesty's commands as to the shooting of the pheasants in the Osborne Covers? About 150-200 might be shot.'* The reply was, *'The King has given Princess Henry of Battenburg's son permission to shoot a few pheasants and as many rabbits as he likes.'* Some of the birds were to be sent to Princess Henry (Beatrice) and the others sold. This side of the business of running the estate is often forgotten today.

King's Cottages (earlier known as Barton Cottages)

In 1848 three tenements were built just north-east of Barton Manor on the Barton Hard road. This leads down to Osborne Bay. They were the first of the new cottages on the estate and still stand today. All are similar in design to the

Brickfield Cottages on the East Cowes Road, red brick with buff banding. The central cottage has a projecting gable to the front and a small porch. The cottages either side have their doors at the ends of the building. The windows have small diamond-shaped panes.

By 1864 William Jackman, James More and Arthur Shepherd lived at Barton Cottages with their families. William Jackman had started as a carter on the Barton Estate in 1845, at a wage of 12 shillings a week. He retired in 1890 with a quarterly pension of £6.10 shillings. The couple were chosen as foster parents for the two Bulgarian children that the Queen was looking after. More details of this can be found in the chapter 'The Queen's Benevolence.'

The Barton Cottages gained the name King's Cottages at some stage after the Queen's death, as King Edward VII and King George V retained Barton for their own use until 1922. In 1953, while mains water was laid on and water closets provided, these were still in the original wash house outside. There was no electricity.

King's Quay Cottage

King's Quay Cottage was in existence before Victoria bought Osborne. A building and quay are shown on the 1783 map, and by 1809 a cottage ornée appears near the shore of the Solent with land running down to King's Quay.

The virtues of King's Quay are extolled in Englefield's writing about the Isle of Wight in 1799. *'The mouth of the little inlet called King's Quay has some pretty scenery about it. The inlet itself runs a winding course through...overhanging woods for above half a mile.'*

In 1809 the artist Charles Tomkins completed a series of 58 watercolour scenes of a tour around the Island. One of his paintings was of 'King's Key [sic] and Barton Point, Wootton.' (See illustration on page 8). This delightful view shows not only the cottage ornée on the rise just above the shore, but also the fishermen with their net and a lobster fisherman with his pots and boat. The cottage has solid brick chimneys, with ornate brick tops, a dormer window and the roof would appear to be tiled. It is reminiscent of similar cottages designed by John Nash, who was living at East Cowes Castle at that time, although there is no record of him having built King's Key cottage.

A stone-fronted dam and sluice were constructed across the inlet in Albert's time, presumably to help with drainage, and a footbridge. The inlet is now a Site of Special Scientific Interest for wildlife, and the silting creek has changed

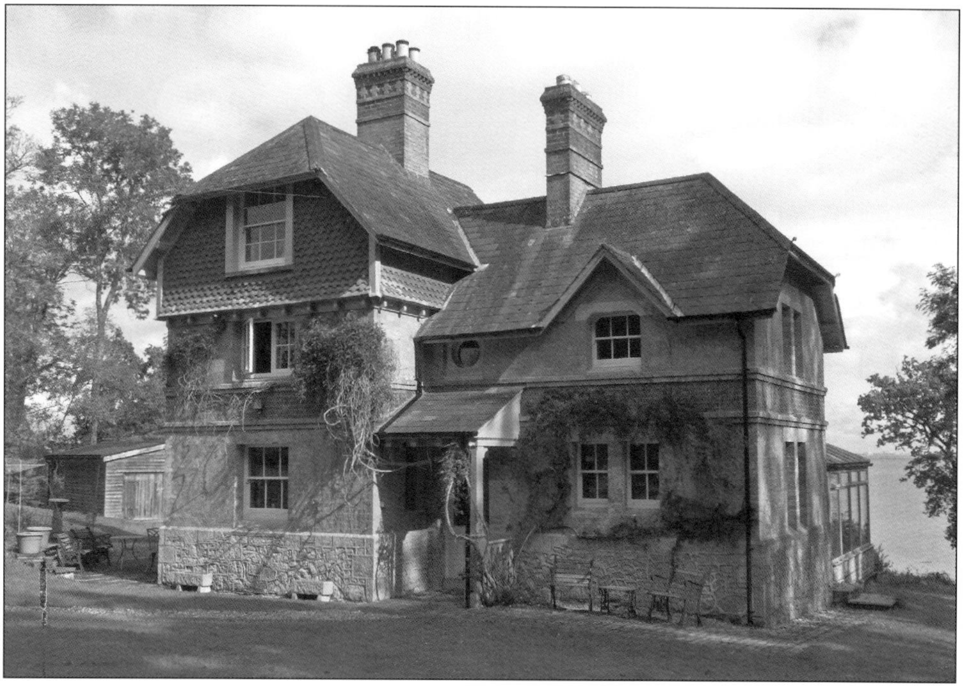

King's Quay Cottage of 1862, situated in its idyllic and secluded location overlooking the sea.

considerably since Tomkins painted his picture in 1809 and even since the Naval Cadets explored it in 1908.

The Queen purchased the property and in 1862 the old King's Quay Cottage and its outbuildings were pulled down. A new cottage was erected on the site and dog kennels built close by.

The new cottage is of three storeys in brick, with the top storey tile hung. In 1867 rooms were added to King's Quay cottage for Her Majesty's use. A separate porch-covered entrance was constructed leading to a sitting room, a retiring room and lavatory. The addition did not do a lot for the appearance of the cottage when seen from the sea, but the Queen did have a good view of the water from her simple sitting room! A carriage shed was erected in 1868, but removed and reconstructed at Swiss Cottage seven years later.

In the 21st century the cottage, now a private home, looks much the same as it did in the Queen's day, but the drive that had been created along the sea shore and through Brock's Copse is no longer the feature that it was. The sea is eroding the shore and what may have been the original pre-Victorian quay, and Albert's

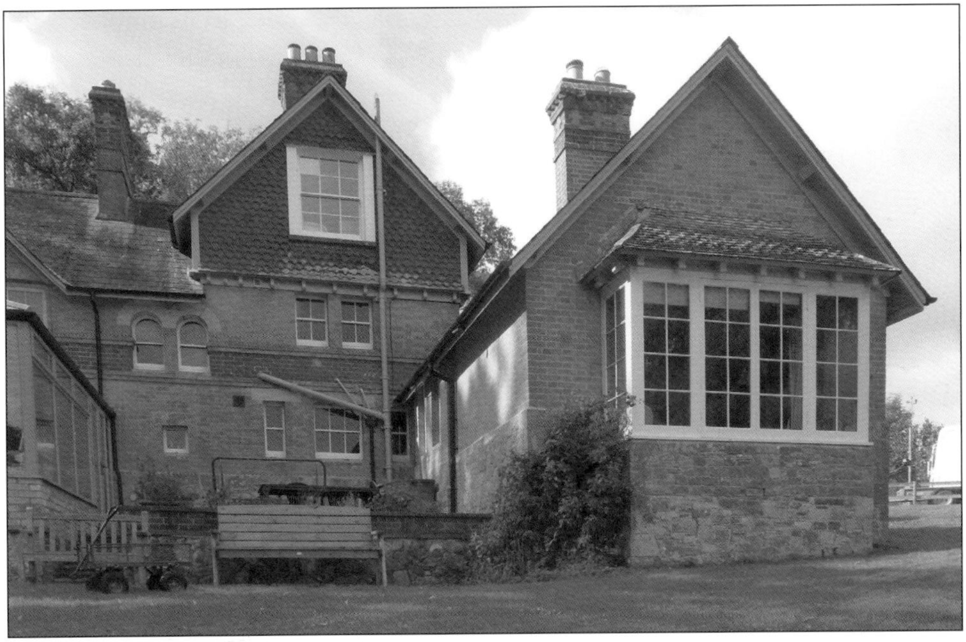

King's Quay from the rear. The extension has rooms added for Queen Victoria to use when visiting the cottage.

dam and sluice are no longer serviceable. Because of its SSSI classification there are difficulties in restoring the shore to its original Victorian configuration, and so the land will continue to erode.

Ludham's Cottage

There is a private gravel lane that runs from Mount Road to King's Quay. Along this road lies Woodhouse Farm and beyond that is Ludham's Cottage. It was farmworkers' accommodation.

This cottage is one of the few that Victoria did not have completely rebuilt. It is constructed of rendered brick and stone, white-painted, with a thatched roof, and was originally a pair of cottages. Additions were made to it in the 1900s. It remains an example of the Isle of Wight vernacular style and is quite different from anything else on the estate. The only other thatched building in Whippingham is Truckles Cottage near the church, although the Post Office Cottage opposite The Forge was thatched until 1961.

When Ludham Cottages appear in the Barton Manor sale document of 1953, they were part of the labourers' accommodation for Woodhouse Farm and to be sold in the same lot. They were described as *'excellent cottages set in large gardens.'* Each had two rooms up and two down, with an outside washhouse and earth closet. Water was procured from a well, and lighting would have been by candle or oil lamp.

Matthew's Cottages

The original Matthew's Cottage and land bought in 1846 by the Queen was in the field just north of Primrose Cottage off Mount Road. It does not appear on the 1863 map because the Queen had it demolished.

The new Matthew's Cottages were built after 1908, near to Woodhouse. In the Barton sale document of 1953 they are described as *'a pair of very superior modern brick and tiled cottages, substantially built and in good order.'* No.1 had a front sitting room with a fireplace, a kitchen with a tiled floor, a kitchener and sink with water laid on, and a pantry. There was an outside washhouse with a sink and a copper, also with water laid on, and an earth closet. Mains water and electricity were connected, and sink drainage was to a soakaway.

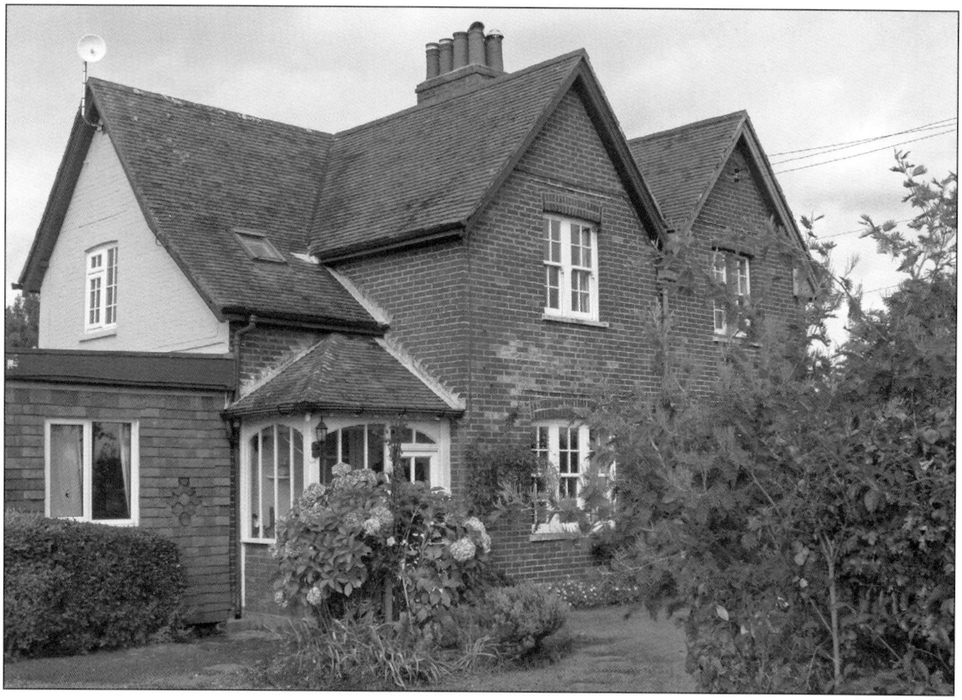

Matthew's Cottages, a pair of modern, well appointed houses with water and electricity, built for the estate soon after 1908.

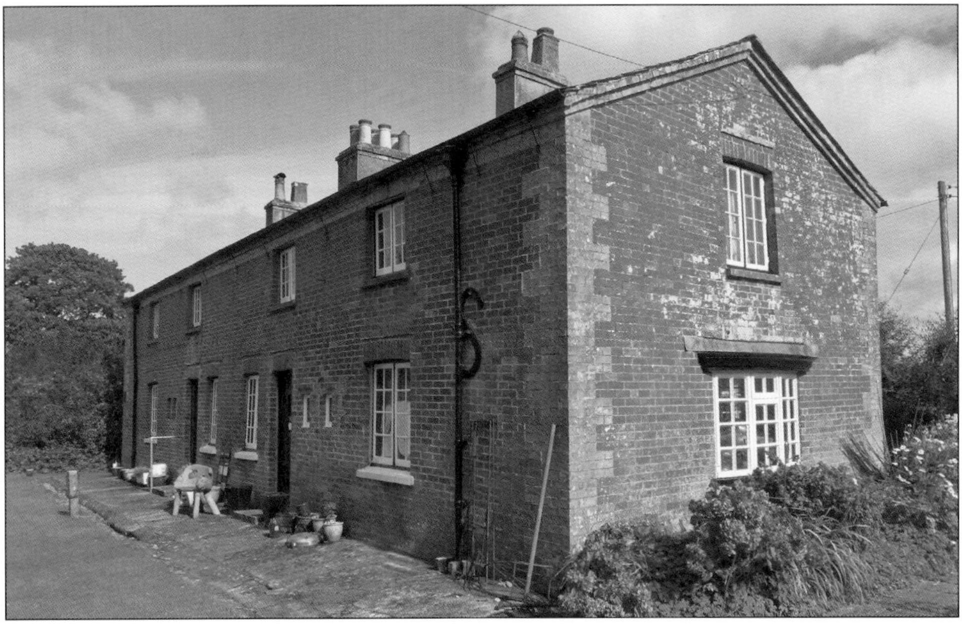

Primrose Cottage, built 1849, originally four homes and known as Whippingham Street Cottages, they later became two.

Primrose Cottage

One cottage in particular that still has a vegetable patch that would have been approved of in Victoria's time is Primrose Cottage, along Mount Road. The garden has changed little, apart from some of the new modern varieties of vegetable. The produce keeps Grace Davison and her daughter in fresh fruit and vegetables throughout the year. Fruit trees there still survive from Victorian times.

Built in 1849 as 'Whippingham Street Cottages, four tenements,' this was one of the earliest of the sets of cottages to be built on the estate. They were very functional, with little of the adornment that characterised the lodges that all the public could see. At that time their 'front' was to the original road to the east, and so the wash house and privies were built to the west. In 1864 the four cottages were converted to just two, giving the occupants more space.

When the Barton estate was sold to the Tillett family in 1922, 1 and 2 Primrose Cottages were sold to them as well. They were occupied by the same workers now working for a different landlord. Shortly after The Second World War a scullery was added to each cottage and an internal WC.

By 1953 when the Barton Estate was being sold, the Snow family was occupying No.2 at a rental of 11 shillings a week. Charles Snow, who had become foreman on the Barton Estate, bought this cottage. A sale document quotes the cottages as having a bathroom and a scullery. However, the bath was actually in the scullery, which also had the back door! Number 2 was later owned by Charles Snow's daughter Grace and her husband Tony Davison.

Many school children would remember a Whippingham school outing to visit Primrose Cottage and Mrs Davison for a glass of 'rhubarb wine' (rhubarb juice!) Goats were sometimes encountered in the field next door. Grace helped as a school dinner lady, (Meals Supervisory Assistant in modern parlance), for 22 years, and included a stint as school crossing warden.

Woodhouse Cottages

Initially Woodhouse Farm was part of the 'home farm' for the Queen's Estate and consequently farm labourers' cottages were constructed. The main pair of these became the farmhouse in later years.

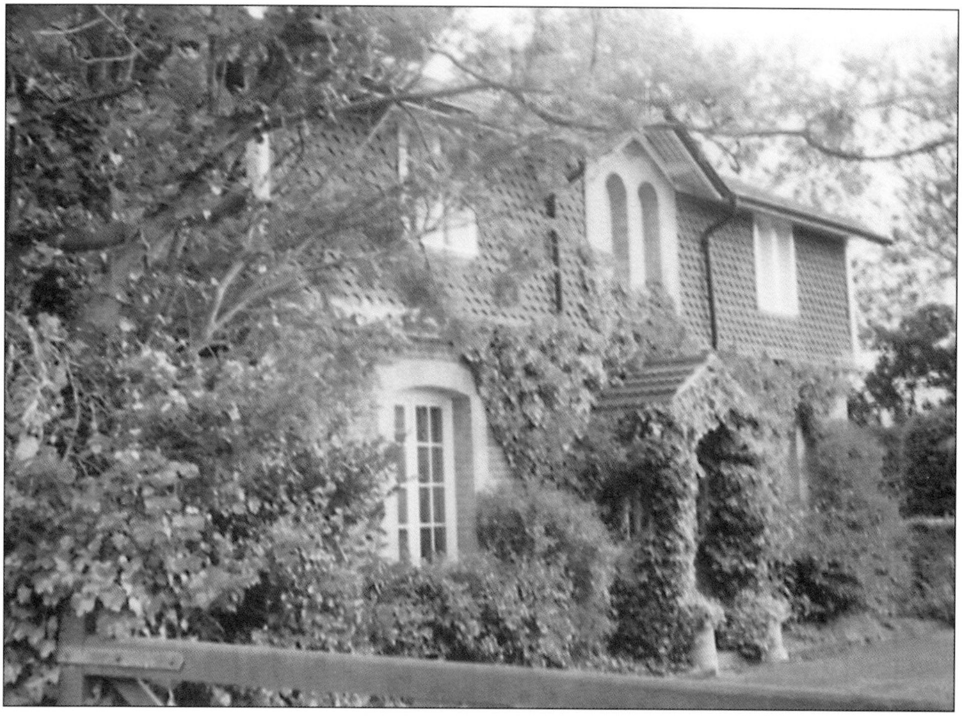

Woodhouse Cottages later became Woodhouse Farmhouse.

In 1856, the Queen wrote in her journal, *'Walked with Vicky and Arthur to Woodhouse, where cottages are to be built.'* The new farm buildings were completed in 1855, and the Woodhouse double cottage in 1859.

The design was similar to the Keepers Cottage at Alverstone, but with entrance porches at each end. Brick was used for the ground storey and the upper storey was tile hung. The roof has a low-pitched gable at the centre of the long elevation, and originally there was a pair of chimney stacks on the ridge of the roof.

Woodman's Cottage

This existing cottage was bought with the estate in 1845. Three years later we are told in the summary that it was altered and greatly improved. By 1953, in the Barton Estate sale document, the Woodman's Cottage is described as *'a picturesque bungalow cottage, situated in a charming and secluded spot between Barton Wood and the Osborne Estate'*. The house was brick-built, part-rendered, with a verandah on three sides. It was let to Mrs E Wiles, who later bought the cottage. She became the district nurse, known to many simply as Nurse Wiles, who drove a battered old blue Landrover, quite useful as the gravel road between the cottage and Barton Manor often deteriorated to a series of puddles.

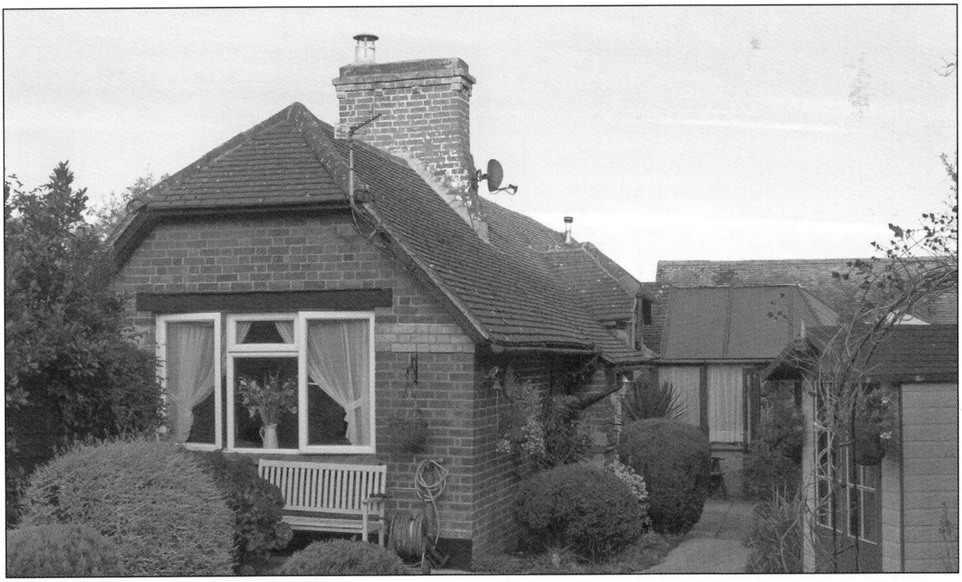

Dog Kennel Cottage, built to house the hunting hounds on the Barton Estate, now a family home. *(see pages 98-100)*

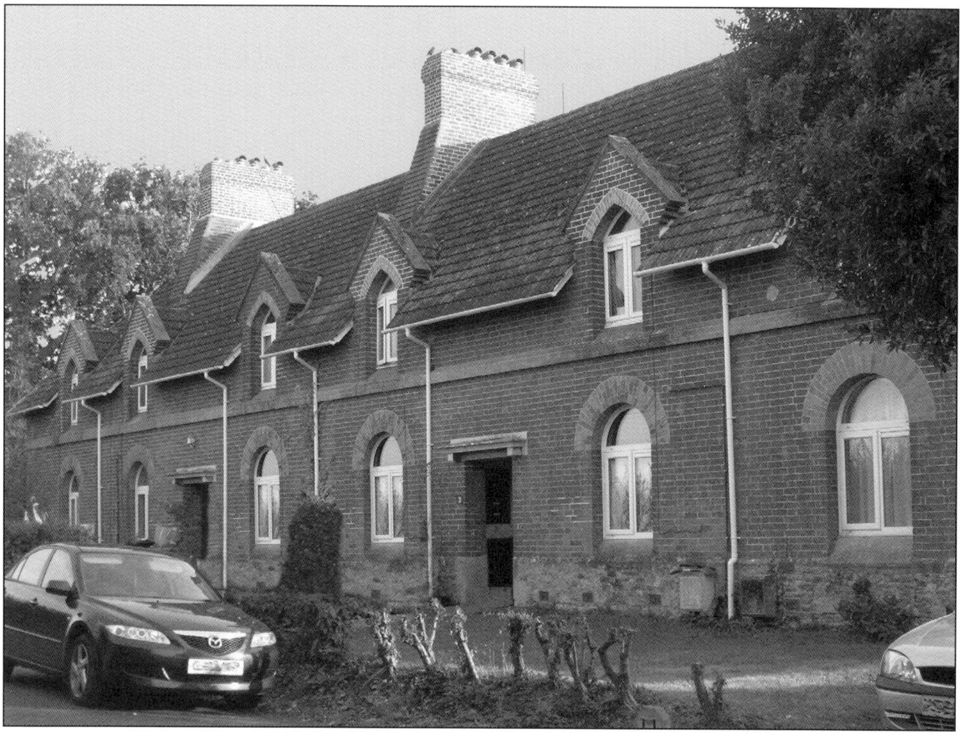

Six Cottages in Alverstone Road were built in 1859.

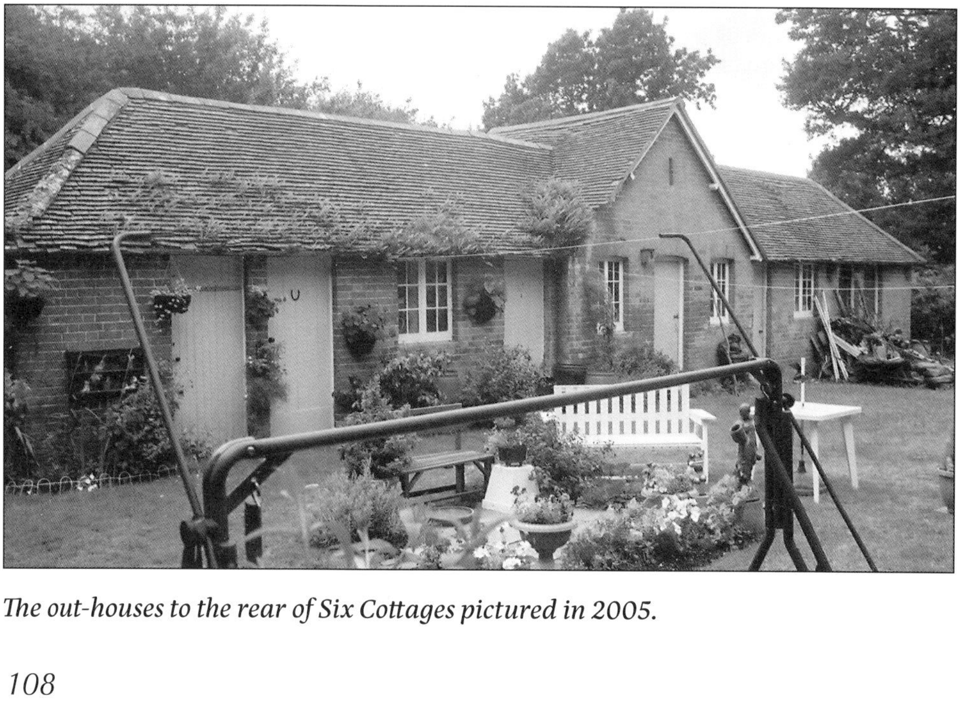

The out-houses to the rear of Six Cottages pictured in 2005.

Eight

Cottages outside the gates

There were several cottages built for the estate workers situated outside the Queen's gates, but owned by the Queen.

Six Cottages, Alverstone Road

Six freehold cottages were bought into the Queen's Estate in 1846 at a cost of £582.10s. Following the realignment of the public highway on Prince Albert's instructions, a terrace of six new cottages was constructed nearby in 1859 and the original cottages, several of which were occupied by members of the Bull family, were pulled down.

Six Cottages are of red brick with buff lintels and a string course which becomes the sill of the first floor windows. The building has been described by Pevsner as, *'one of the most sophisticated of all the estate buildings.'* It is a simple design, with its pairs of dormer windows and three substantial chimney stacks. Porches were added to the back doors of each of the cottages in 1898.

The new cottages were first known as Bull's Cottages. Frederick and William Bull were labourers at Barton Manor Farm, and Frederick retired in 1873 with a pension of £3.18s a quarter, which he was still receiving in 1895. In 1885 Widow Maria Bull started receiving her husband's pension, and she moved into the Almshouses. James Bull, another labourer on Barton Farm, retired in 1894.

The outhouses still survive as a tidy block at the rear of the cottages. The two boilers that were used for doing the washing still exist as does a pump from a well to supply water. In 1953 these cottages were no longer tied to Barton Manor, and had been bought by the county council.

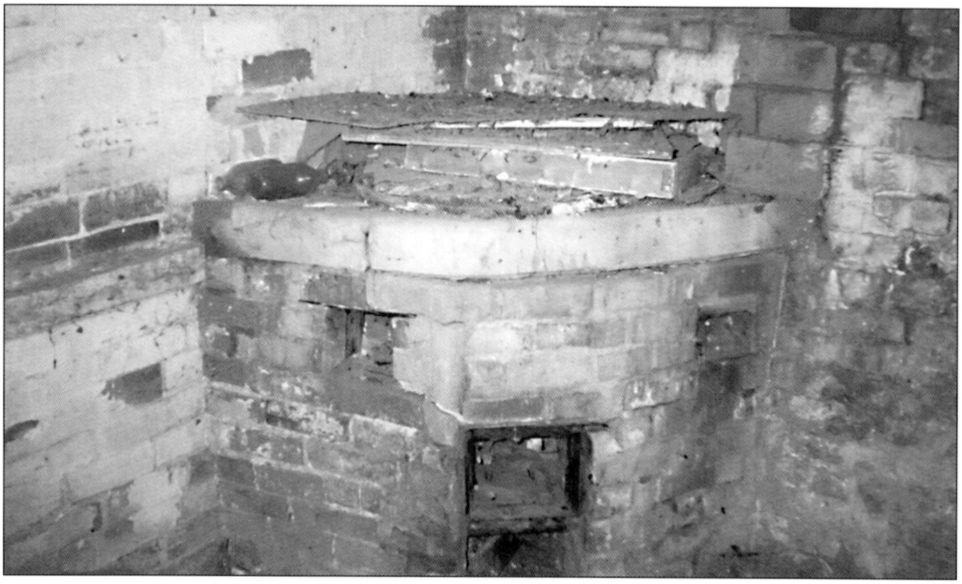

One of the copper boilers in an outhouse of Six Cottages. Water was heated for washing clothes and filling baths for the residents.

Four Cottages, Whippingham Shute

These were bought by the Queen in 1845, rebuilt in 1855 and called 'Post Office Cottages' perhaps because they were near to the cottage used as a post office. By 1863 the name 'Four Cottages' is on the OS map.

The houses are built of the red bricks from the Queen's brickyard. Some of the internal dividing walls use a 'VR' brick that is in the form of a hollow brick-shaped tube. The two outer dwellings have their doors at the ends of the block, and all shared the wash houses and privies built across the yard on the uphill side.

Four Cottages were occupied by the Royal Estate workers, Charles Tucker, James Salter, Henry Greenen, William Rose and their families. At Christmas 1864 their wives all received petticoats as presents from the Queen, and eight children from the families were attending school.

These cottages were comfortable homes for large families. The spacious gardens were given new piggeries in 1880. By the 1920s some of the people living there were still those retired from the Queen's service. One of these was Thomas Foakes, who had been carpenter at Barton Manor Farm. He was a respected sidesman at Whippingham Church in the 1920s, reading a lesson every week.

Another occupant was Mrs Ward, who had worked at Osborne House for Queen Victoria. She had the distinction of having helped to lay Her Majesty out when she died.

Four Cottages still stand at right angles to the road as you drive up Whippingham Shute. The productive gardens face south down the slope of the hill towards the copse, where the hazel catkins and primroses are always a welcome sign of spring.

Post Office Cottage

This is situated on the main Whippingham Road opposite the Forge, and now called Old Cottage. A post receiving house was appointed in Whippingham in 1843, and the first cancelling stamp to be used had the inscription 'Whippingham St.' on it. By 1855 the '*Post Office Directory*' states that Jane Groves was the receiver of letters, living opposite the Forge. The post arrived at Whippingham at 8.30

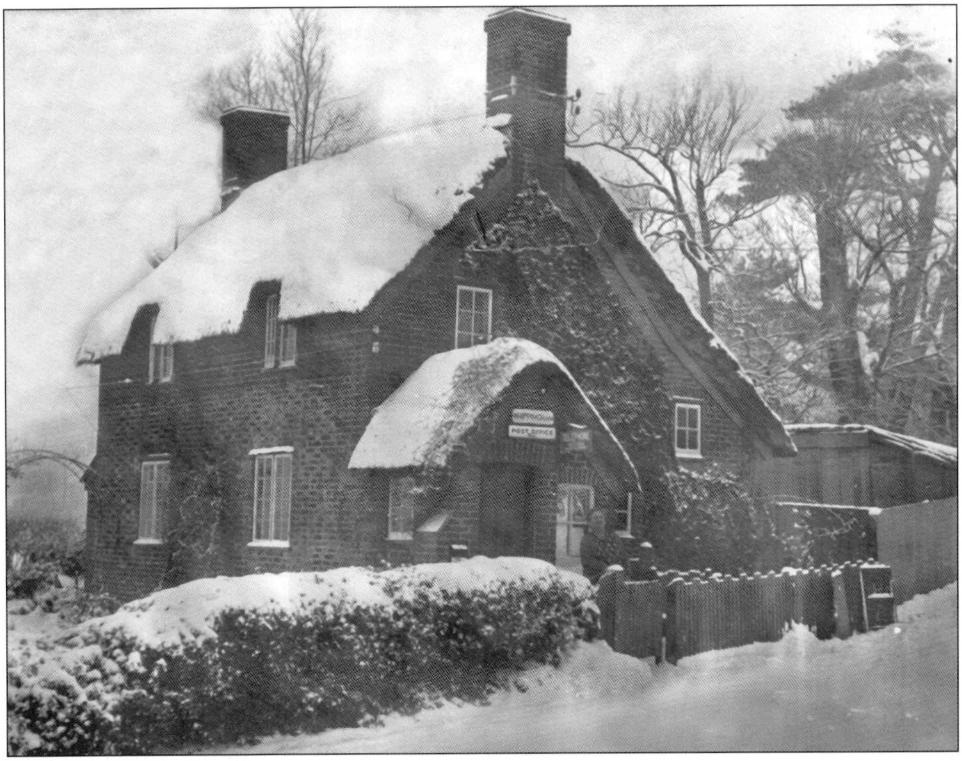

Post Office Cottage after a heavy fall of snow in 1938. A sign next to the doorway advertises a telephone inside.

in the morning and 6.30 in the evening and was dispatched at the same times. Letters went through West Cowes which was also the nearest money order office.

In 1878 it was William Groves who had the post office. John Hawkins the blacksmith was the receiver of mails and ran the post office at Whippingham in 1899. A new Whippingham Post Office Cottage was built on the Queen's orders in 1890. She received a letter from her land steward explaining that the cottage was in need of repair.

'Mr Blake and Mr Mann fear that the Whippingham Post Office Cottage will fall down if not repaired. But as your Majesty will allow a new cottage to be built here Mr Mann says that this can be done on the lines of the present cottage. But the piece of land for the back yard is very small and Blake suggests that [more] might be purchased from Miss Jolliffe.' A small section of Padmore land was duly bought. The cottage was thatched, and had a porch to the road entrance. It was this porch which constituted the post office.

In 1920 Frank Rann took on The Forge and moved into the Post Office Cottage. His wife, Fanny, became the sub-postmistress until she retired in 1946. She also had the job of caring for their family of 12 children.

By 1938 it was possible to telephone from the post office as can be seen in the photograph of the Post Office in the snow in 1938. In 1946 the Post Office moved to Dashwood's, opposite the Community Hall in Alverstone Road. One side of the house had a general store and the post office. The postbox was housed in a brick pillar by the entrance path. Mr and Mrs Anderson worked there first, and then latterly Stan Foreman. Dashwood's closed as a post office in February 1987.

In May 1987 Maddi Chessell opened a new sub-post office and general store at 8 Alverstone Road. Sadly she retired in 2014 leaving Whippingham with a part-time post office in the Community Centre.

Dashwood's Cottage

The Dashwood family was quite extensive. Many of them were involved in carpentry, building houses, and coach making, mainly in Newport, Ryde and East Cowes.

In 1748 William Dashwood was overseer for the Poor Rate in Whippingham, a responsible position, and in the 1790s Thomas Dashwood was doing *'carpenters work'* for the highways commission in Whippingham. Dashwood's Cottage and land was bought into the Queen's Estate in 1845 from Winchester College. At the time Henry Dashwood leased the house and the adjacent forge.

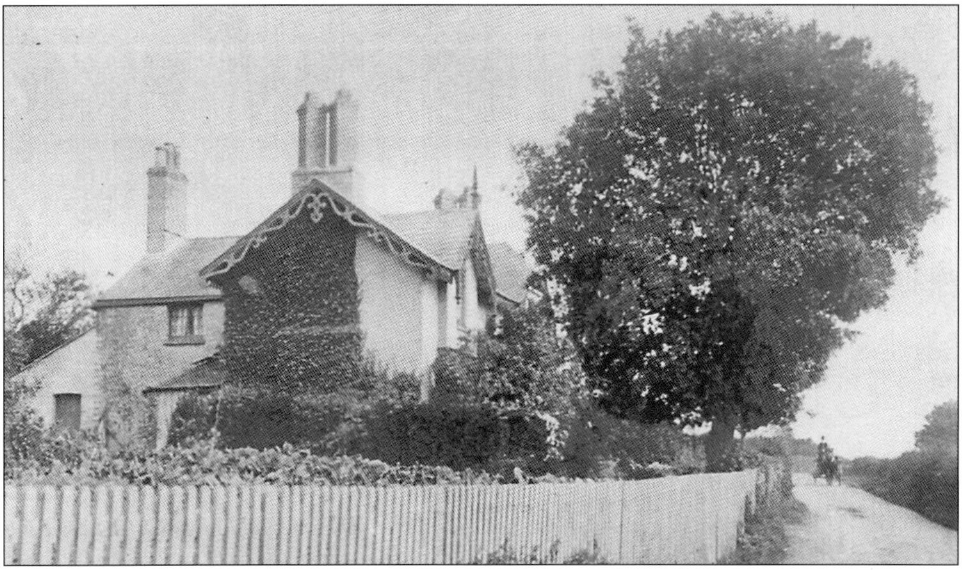

Alverstone Road pictured around 1910, with Dashwood's Cottage on the left.

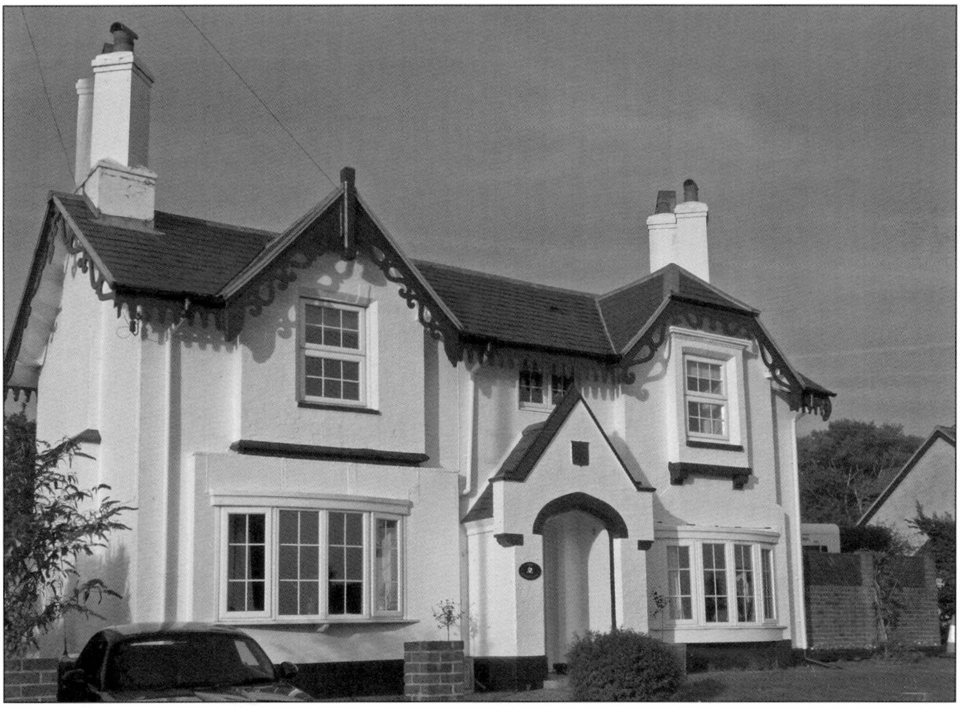

Dashwood's Cottage, now a private home, became Whippingham's Post Office and store between 1946 and 1987.

The Forge

By 1861 a William Dashwood, aged 63, was described as a wheelwright but 20 years later he was only doing carpentry work. Blacksmith John Hawkins took over the tenancy of the Forge in 1878 and walked to and from home in Newport every day until eventually moving into the Post Office Cottage. Hawkins was described as *'a hard working respectable man'* and was farrier to the Queen.

Bill Gray was the blacksmith by 1905. He too lived at Post Office Cottage with his step-son Percy Hardy. In 1919 Bill sold the lease on The Forge to Frank Rann who, for a year, walked daily back and forth to Newport until moving into the Post Office Cottage. His son, Bob, joined him working at The Forge, taking over in 1946 and buying it from the Barton Estate in 1953.

At that time The Forge was still shoeing horses, and also making and repairing farm machinery, as it had done in Victorian times. Bob Rann built up the trade in steel fabrication and on-site welding. His son, Trevor, with a workforce of six, expanded this, producing a wide range of steel-fabricated items. These include fire-escapes, balustrades, balconies and railings. Clients have included GKN Aerospace, and English Heritage, for whom Trevor constructed the walkway arches in the Osborne House walled garden. Boat trailers and cradles were also made for the RNLI. Trevor Rann retired in 2017 but the business continues to thrive under new management.

The end of the link with Crown Estates

It was not until 1956 that the agricultural portions of the Osborne Estate were put up for sale. This included Kingston, Heathfield and Alverstone Farms each with their attached 'tied' cottages, Palmer's Brook Lodge, and various adjacent individual fields that had been rented to different people. This sale effectively cut the ties that had bound Whippingham to the Queen.

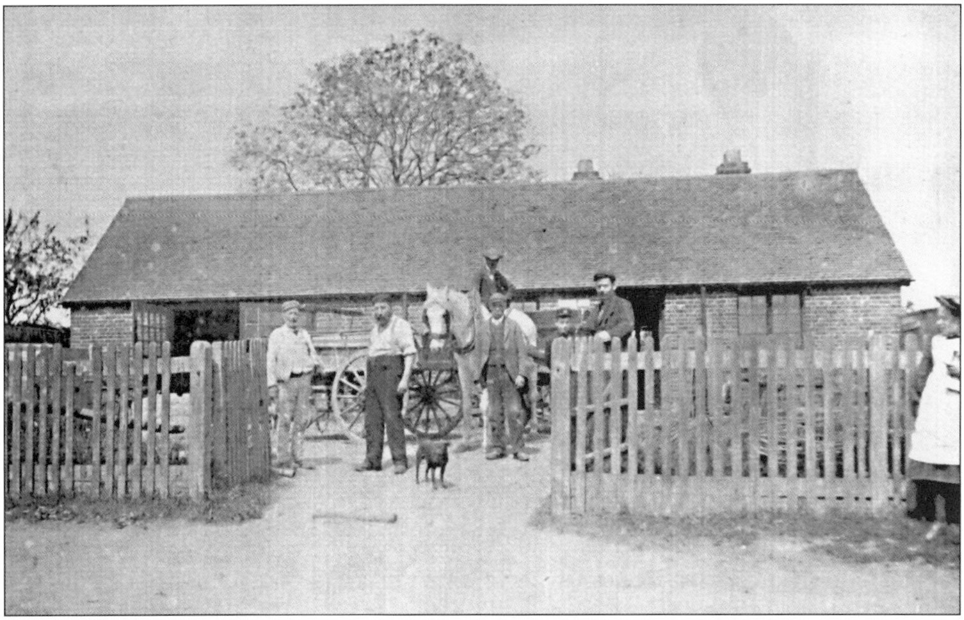

Blacksmith Bill Gray and his staff outside The Forge in 1910. The building remains largely unchanged today.

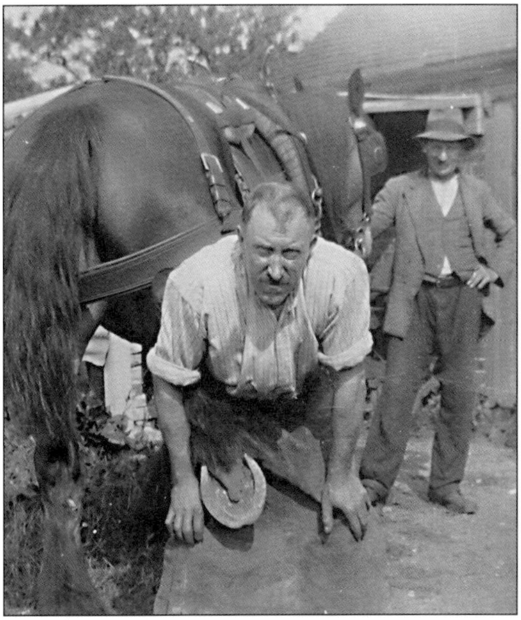

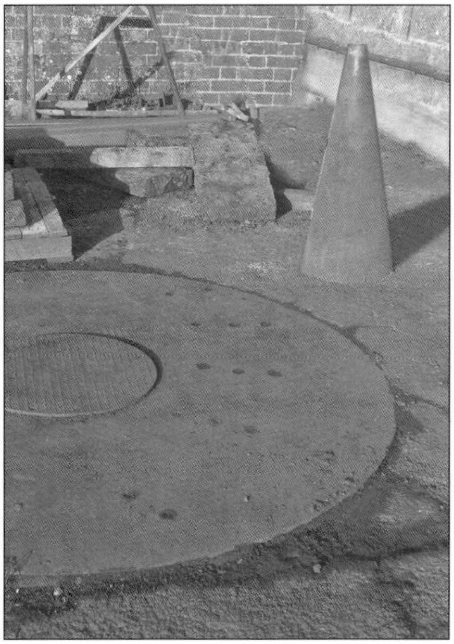

Left: Frank Rann shoeing a horse in the 1930s. Right: The wheelwright frame for cartwheels and cone mandrel for making rings at The Forge.

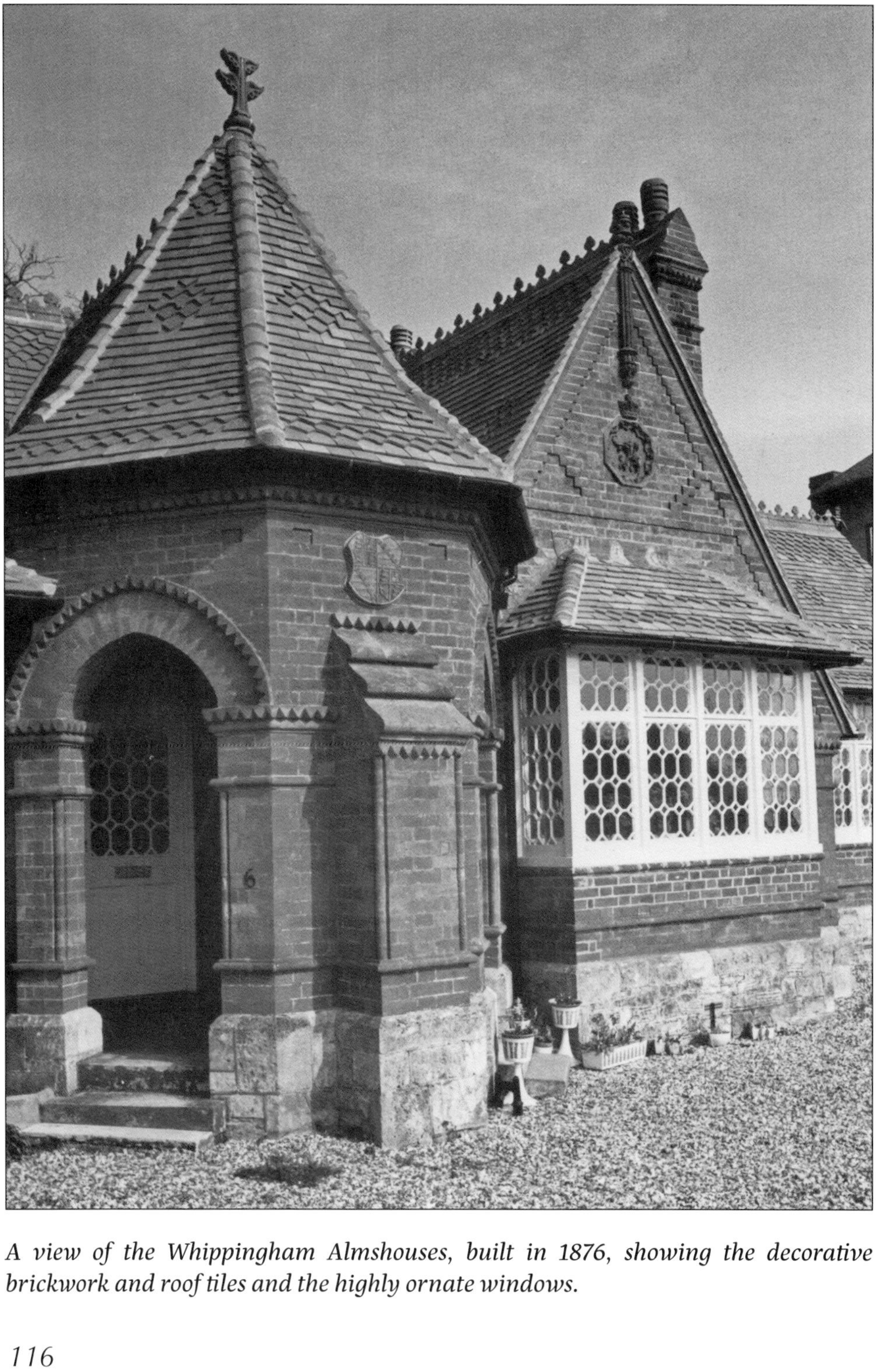

A view of the Whippingham Almshouses, built in 1876, showing the decorative brickwork and roof tiles and the highly ornate windows.

Nine

The Queen's Benevolence

Whippingham's Poor Rate book of 1748 shows how much landowners paid for the relief of the poor of the parish, *'at two shillings ye pound for the year.'* William Dashwood was the overseer for Whippingham. That year farmer Walker of Barton Manor paid £11.9s.6d, with Mr Blachford at Osborne paying only £7.10s. Clavells Farm, at £1.15s.6d, was half the value of Woodhouse, and both were held by W Sheath. The holdings Matthews and Dallimores were paying 10s each.

Whippingham Poor House was rented from Mr Whitmaich in 1759 at a rent of £22 a year. He lived at South Heathfield Farm but also had property near Brooks Copse.

Going into the Poor House was a last resort for those villagers incapable of looking after themselves, and with no home or means of making money. On May 17th Widow Odle was taken to the Poor House and died there in June. Her funeral was paid for by the parish Poor Rate, costing 16s.7d, which included 6s.1d for bread and beer. Her coffin cost 10s.6d. Widow Young was in charge of the Poor House, and she was paid 36s a year. Expenditure was made on furze faggots (kindling) and wood for cooking.

Some assistance was given to other poor people in the village. Andrew Hollis, an orphan, was being kept by Farmer Brading of Truckles, who received 6s for this. 3s.6d was spent on a new coat and waistcoat for Andrew. Arthur Weay's family had fallen on hard times so clothes and money were given to his wife. Five pairs of stockings for the children cost 3s.4d in March 1749.

The vestry decision was made in 1759 to give up the Poor House because a new workhouse had opened in Parkhurst, and all the poor of the Island were to be sent there.

Responsibility and welfare

The Queen had a great feeling of responsibility for the welfare of 'her people'. The Royal couple set about renovating and rebuilding the estate cottages. At work, the farm labourers were under similar conditions to those elsewhere in England. Rates of pay were no higher at Osborne, but in other ways the people were much better off.

The Queen paid an annual retainer to the local doctor who then looked after any sick people on the estate without them having to pay for themselves. There was also an estate nurse paid by the Queen. Mrs Gallop held that position in 1885, and Mrs Critchley was given £25 when she retired as estate nurse in 1898.

If the men fell ill they could expect sick-pay until they recovered. Elsewhere men would think themselves lucky to get a few weeks half-pay under similar circumstances. If the illness resulted in death, the Queen often contributed towards the funeral expenses.

When her head gamekeeper Mr Land died in 1878 the Queen visited Mrs Land immediately after arriving on the Island the following day and went personally to Whippingham Church to select the ground for a grave. On the day of the funeral she visited the house and joined the procession at Whippingham School on the way to the church. A wreath of white camellias from the Queen was laid on the coffin, together with one from Princess Beatrice. The *Isle of Wight County Press* commented, *'The above will, we are sure, be read by our readers with interest, as the kindly acts of Her Majesty, so well known here, show the deep sympathy felt by her for all classes of her subjects.'*

Pensions were paid to her employees in relation to the pay received, but if a man was fit and healthy he continued to work as there was no automatic retirement age. William Pierce, foreman at the brickyard, retired at the age of 78. His service and knowledge were obviously appreciated. Four men were recorded as being on invalidity payment in 1888, and five others in their 60s and 70s that year were expected soon to be receiving pensions and were being given lighter duties.

A school was built at Royal expense and contributions given for improvements. The Queen took over the entire expenses of the school paying all the outstanding annual expenses from 1894 until her death.

Parties were given to the estate children at Christmas, and they received gifts according to their age. Older children either received a book, or on alternate years, a dress or material for the girls or suiting for the boys. Children between the ages of four and seven received a toy every year. The Queen's Christmas list for 1864 comprised of; 17 dresses, eight dolls, 15 books and 10 toys for boys. That year all the wives of the estate workers received a petticoat as a present.

A Knecht Ruprecht Bisque doll was given to one of the children of the estate workers in 1885 by Queen Victoria at the Christmas party. The German legend is that Knecht Ruprecht (servant Rupert) was a little elf who accompanied Santa Claus, often dressed as a furry creature. This doll was given to 'The Lilliput Antique Doll and Toy Museum' at Brading by the recipient, aged 93 at the time, who had treasured it all of her life.

If every girl on the estate had similar quality dolls given them, there must have been quite a collection on the estate by the end of the Queen's reign. Probably the fact that there were so many meant that the children were allowed to play with them, and being fragile bisque ware, accidents happened.

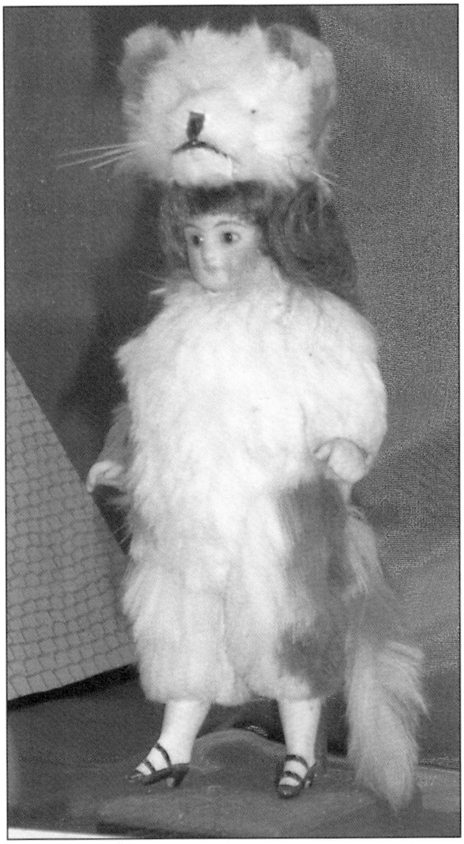

A Knecht Ruprecht doll given to an estate worker's daughter by Queen Victoria. Now at the Lilliput Antique Doll Museum, Brading.

In the Royal Archives is a letter from the land steward explaining the Christmas gift situation to the King in the autumn of 1901. It was suggested that action should be taken if the gifts were to continue. The answer was received, *'The King does not see any necessity of giving these presents this year.'* So although the estate was still in the Royal domain, the tradition of gifts from the sovereign ceased.

Comparing school photographs of the children at Whippingham School and those at East Cowes, it is noticeable just how well dressed the children of the Queen's Estate were. There is a story about a little boy splashing in a puddle at the side of the road as the Royal carriage passed him. *"Get out of that puddle young Jimmy! Your mother only*

Alvestone Farm
Whippingham
January 15th 1893

Sir,

I respectfully and gratefully acknowledge, on behalf of myself and my Brother, the kindness, and generosity of Her Majesty, in remitting us a half years Rent, by reason of the late unfortunate season.

My Brother and I have been tenants of Her Majesty over 20 years and we have at all times received the greatest kindness and consideration and encouragement.

I cannot express all that we would wish to say but we are indeed very, deeply grateful to Her Majesty.

I am, Sir
Your obedient Servant,
Henry Knighton

Gent.Rt.Hon.
Sir H F Ponsonby., KCB

Transcription of a letter from farmer Henry Knighton thanking Henry Ponsonby, the Queen's Private Secretary, for the reduction in his rent because of a poor harvest.

bought those shoes last week!" Queen Victoria is reported to have said. It gives you a feel for the care and interest she took in 'her people', even if the story cannot easily be verified.

Gifts had not only occurred at Christmas. Mr and Mrs Chambers celebrated their golden wedding in 1886 and received a present from the Queen. Mr Chambers had been an Osborne estate labourer since 1845.

The Queen's concern at those suffering loss in East Cowes is also well documented. When seven local Trinity House men died as they attempted to explode a wreck on the Brambles Bank in 1894, Queen Victoria invited all the widows to meet her at Osborne and offered her condolences. The youngest, Mrs Snow and Mrs Oatley, had only been married for one and three weeks respectively.

The Queen sent each family £10, and ensured that Trinity House would be giving them pensions.

In 1892 there was a disastrous harvest, and Victoria's farmers were finding themselves in difficulties. The Knighton brothers, who were farming both Alverstone and Heathfield Farms, had their rent reduced by half for that year, and the same reduction was given to Kingston Farm.

Elizabeth Groves, who lived at Whippingham Post Office was a deaf mute. As a girl she had been educated at the expense of Her Majesty, receiving her tuiton in the new 'Silent Language'. The Queen took pains to learn the finger alphabet so that she could communicate with Elizabeth.

The Bulgarian orphans

In 1855 the Crimean War was at its height. The Queen and Prince Albert had been closely following the proceedings, watching the troop ships leaving Portsmouth, and writing to Florence Nightingale. After a battle at Custëndje, sailors from *HMS Firebrand* found two small boys lying injured beside their dead parents. They took the boys on board ship, where Captain Hyde Parker adopted them. Gunshot wounds in the arms of both boys were treated, and a goat was procured to provide milk. The children were christened John and George Firebrand and were on board for two more battles at Sebastopol, where sadly Captain Hyde Parker was killed.

The Queen became aware of the incident, and announced her wish to take the infants under her wing. They were the same age as her youngest boys, Arthur and Leopold, aged five and two respectively. She consulted her land steward Andrew Toward, who suggested that Mrs Jackman, at Barton Cottages, would be the best person to care for them, her house being the most spotlessly clean on the estate.

As soon as the boys arrived, the Queen went straight over to see them. Despite having the scars of five bullets in his right arm, the Queen described Johnny as, '*very merry and intelligent and speaks English perfectly.*' She described little Georgy as '*delicate and gentle.*' Victoria visited frequently, and the children were allowed licence beyond the norm. When one of them stole her parasol and galloped off using it as a hobby horse, the Queen just laughed! The boys were renamed John and George Hyde, and remained with the Jackmans until they joined the Navy.

The Almshouses

In 1875/6 the Queen had the Almshouses built opposite the church for her retired employees or their widows. The old farmyard of Truckles Farm was cleared for the purpose, and an excellent terrace of cottages built of red brick with much decoration. There were six apartments and, adjoining the southern-most, a room and cloakroom were created for Victoria's personal use.

The Queen frequently visited to see the work in progress. In her journal for 21 January 1876 she wrote, *'Drove with Beatrice to the Almshouses at Whippingham, where I got out and I settled with McPherson where the peoples' gardens and the road is to be.'*

On 14 August 1876 the Queen wrote: *'Out to tea with Beatrice, and later went with her to look at the Almshouses at Whippingham which are now furnished and the ground in front laid out which looks very pretty. Old Mrs Isaacs is the only one yet living there. She was so delighted and as usual very funny. Another old woman, Mrs Kingswell is to live with her and I made her laugh by saying old women generally quarrelled, but I hoped they would not.'* Mrs Isaacs lived at the Almshouses until her death in 1896, aged 88.

In 1888 Widows Bull, Isaacs, Gallop, Gosh and Harding were living there, and also George Foakes who had been estate carpenter. It was the Queen who had the final say in who was to live in the Almshouses, after examining the recommendations put forward by her land steward. In 1896 the then steward, Andrew Blake wrote to the Queen's secretary suggesting William Houndsell.
'10 February 1896. Sir, I beg to recommend William Houndsell for a pension and the vacant Almshouse. He has been farm labourer for over fifty years and is now in his 78th year. During his service here he has been a very steady and trustworthy man and a thoroughly good labourer. Dr Hoffmeister does not think that he is fit to be about now, as he is subject to giddy attacks and falls down.' The Queen's secretary added a note saying, *'William Houndsell has a wife so perhaps Your Majesty will allow him to have the Almshouse.'* The reply comment from the Queen on the letter is the word, *'Approved.'*

Several women were employed over the years to work as attendants at the Almshouses, often these ladies were married to an estate worker. They would visit daily, checking up on the residents and do various tasks for them. Queen Victoria had set a form of sheltered accommodation in place in 1876 at Whippingham, but it was on a much grander and kinder scale than the old Poor House.

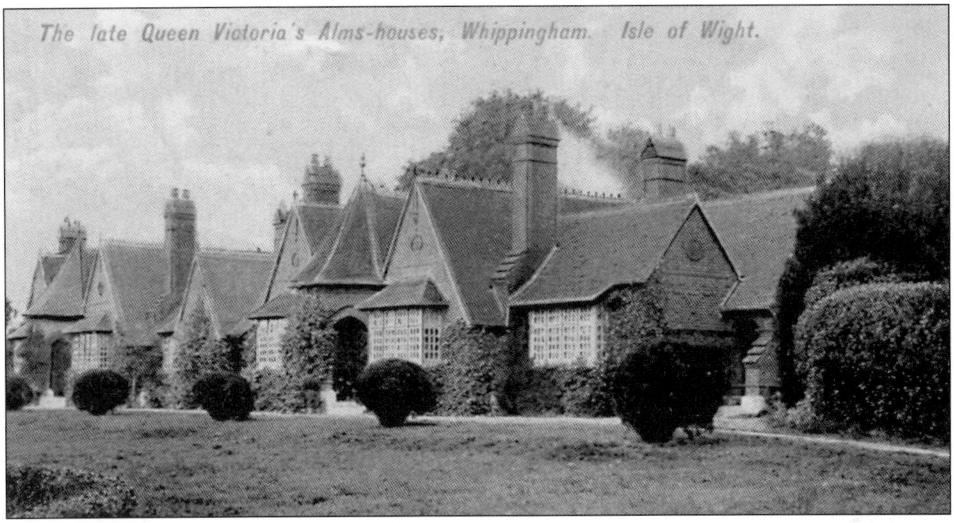

A postcard of 'The Late Queen's Alms houses' probably dating from 1905.

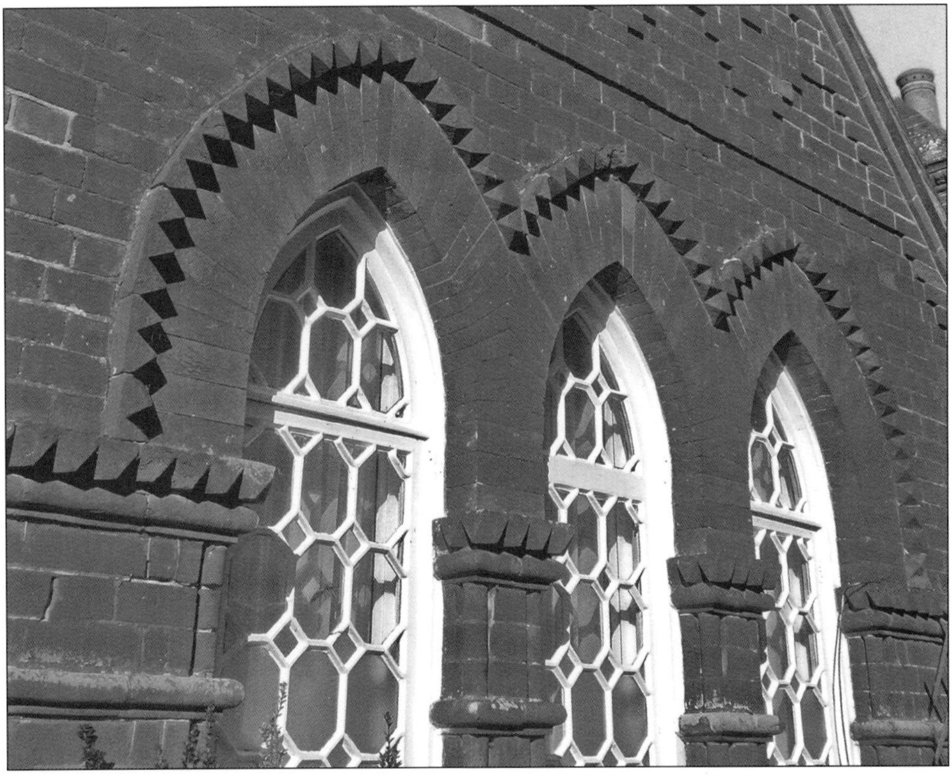

Queen Victoria's architects incorporated many pleasing design features to enhance the appearance of the building. The Almshouses were restored in 1980.

In 1935 the Crown Estate no longer required the Almshouses for retired employees of the estate and the criteria for eligibility were widened as the County Council took over the upkeep. The Queen's room had been incorporated to form another bungalow and in 1952 electricity was installed. In 1980 the Almshouses were completely renovated and bathrooms added at the rear. The building is now Grade I listed and is a fine example of Victorian architecture.

Queen Victoria looked after her people from their cradle to their grave, continuing the concern and attention that both she and the Prince Consort had shown from the beginning of their residence at Osborne in 1845.

Without the input from the Queen and Prince Albert, the village would look a very different place. Rows of cottages we take for granted would not have been built. The Almshouses would not grace the land opposite the church. The school would not have its royal links. The church would certainly not have been rebuilt in its present style. Similar buildings may have been constructed, but if one person of wealth had not tied the whole community together as Her Majesty did, there would not have been the extra design put into all the buildings and their brickwork.

Ten

Whippingham School

A school at Whippingham has been on the present site since 1848. The land, a quarter of an acre, was given by Lord George Seymour to the Reverend Bouverie and to the Rural Dean of East Medene *'for the education of poor persons of the village.'* The first National School was a simple building with accommodation for the schoolmaster to the east. There was a single, long, school room which had a gallery at one end with the seats raised in tiers. The National School organisation was a charitable body interested in extending education to *'the lower classes,'* encouraging local landowners and clergy to subscribe to erect a school and pay for a master. Guidance was given as to what should be in the curriculum.

Queen Victoria probably contributed to the National School fund for Whippingham, as by 1848 the Royal couple owned much of the surrounding land. Prince Albert was a paternalistic landowner and in 1850 conducted a survey of all the young people on the estate establishing whether they could read or write. 26 of the children in the 5 – 14 age range could read well or fairly well. Of the thirty four 15 – 20 year olds on the estate, only 14 could read. There were 62 children at the school in 1850, the majority of whom came from the Queen's Estate.

This survey also reveals that some children as young as 11 had already left school and were in employment. If a child had reached a certain standard he, or she could leave school at the age of 10. James Baker was the schoolmaster in 1851 and his wife Elizabeth was the schoolmistress.

Plans were drawn up in 1859 for a new school. Prince Albert decided on a complete rebuild, which the Queen paid for entirely out of her own funds. Albert died before the school was completed. The early name for the school on some

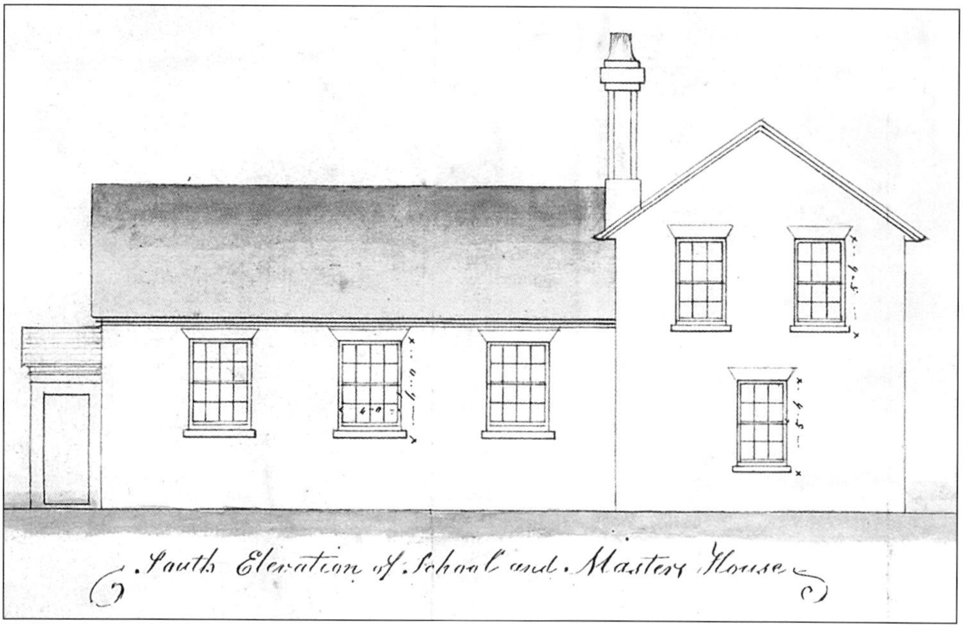

The south elevation of the original 1848 school taken from the architectural plans.

documents is written as, *'The Queen's School, Whippingham'*, although it remained a National School.

The new school, which forms the basis of the present building, was erected in 1863 to the north of the original school. The old building was then demolished and became the gardens for the two school houses.

Two acres of land adjoining the school to the north were levelled, enclosed and planted round with a row of elms, pines and laurels. The whole of this was sown with grass and became the playground for the children. 41 pine trees were planted on the perimeter, one for each year of Albert's life. Very few of the original pines remain as the top of the hill is very exposed to the wind. Several blew down in the 1987 hurricane, blocking the main road into East Cowes.

On 4th February 1864 Queen Victoria officially opened the school, accompanied by Princess Feodore of Leinigen, (her half sister) and four of the Royal children and Princess Feodore's daughter. The Queen's journal reads, '... *Went with Feodore and all the Children, to the new school at Whippingham, which was opened by a tea given to all the school children. They sang a hymn, then grace, after which they sat down to tea, consisting of bread and butter and plum cake, enormous quantities of which they ate, drinking equally as much tea. This over they*

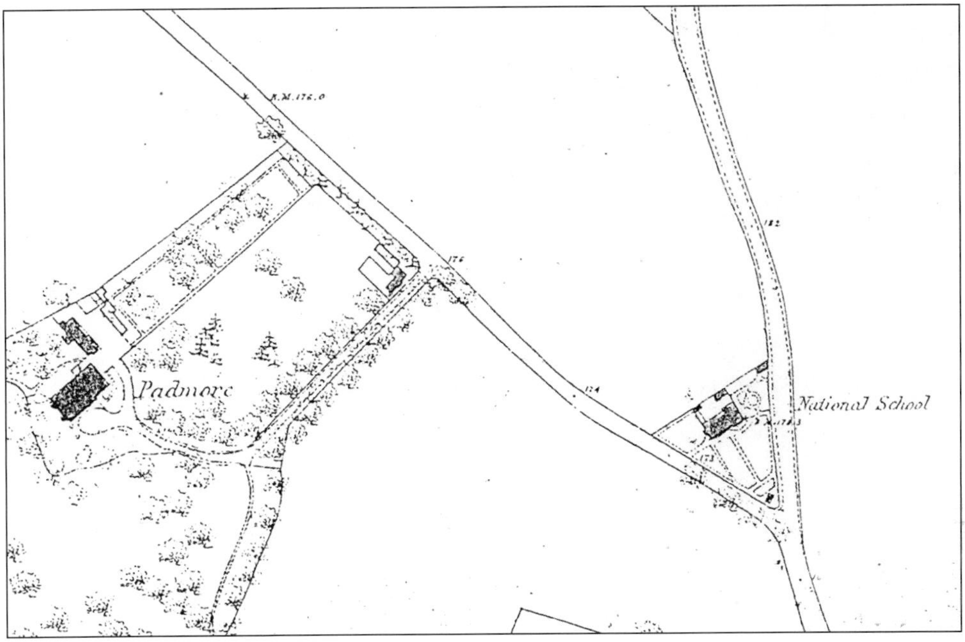

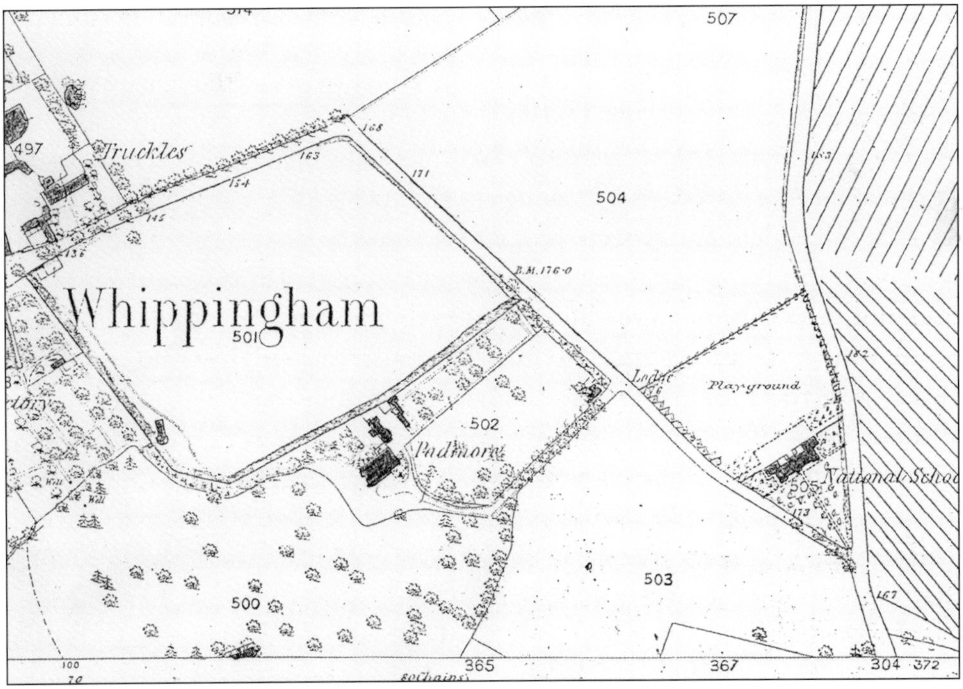

Top: Map of 1854 showing the first school. Bottom: 1863, the school has now been replaced by larger building and has an adjoining playground.

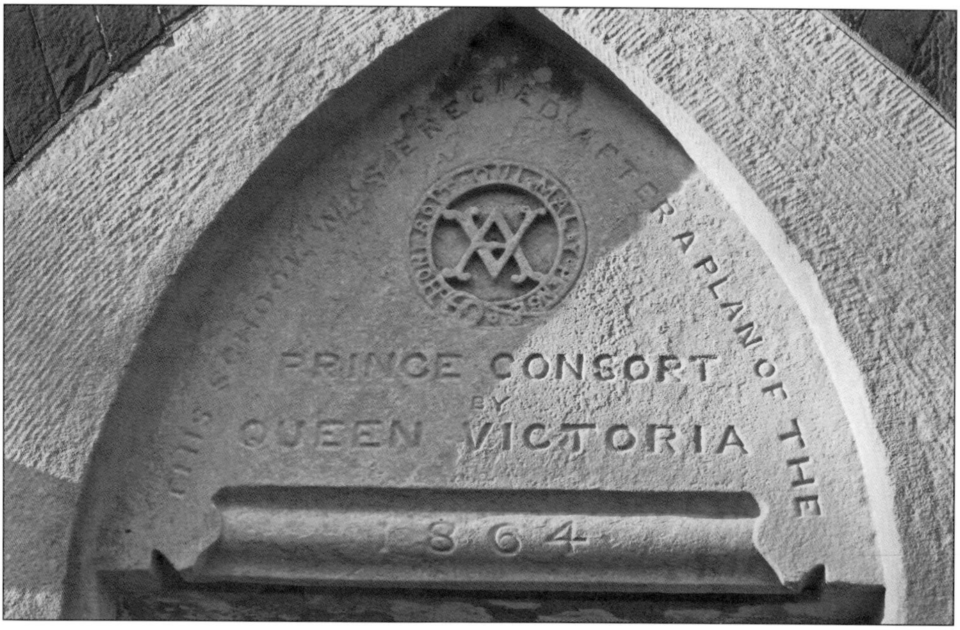

Datestone over the door. 'This school was erected after a plan of the Prince Consort by Queen Victoria. 1864'.

again sang Grace, followed by 'God save the Queen...' The inscription above the entrance informs us that, *'This school was erected after a plan of the Prince Consort by Queen Victoria – 1864.'* The drainpipes are dated 1863.

The school had one main room, which could be divided by means of two folding screens. This was deemed sufficient accommodation for 195 children, although in 1865 there were only 89 children. By 1871 there were 47 boys and 39 girls on the registers. In 1855 Charles Thomas became the headmaster and was still there in 1871, with Mrs Thomas recorded in the census as being the schoolmistress. The couple had five children of their own by then, one of whom, Charles William, is recorded as being a school monitor at the age of 12. Miss M E Hooper was an additional school mistress. In 1881 Mr and Mrs Thomas are still schoolmaster and mistress, but their son has moved on. Instead, their daughter Ida Thomas is a pupil teacher at the age of 19.

Mr Thomas died in 1886, having been at Whippingham for 34 years Ida took over as schoolmistress, with Miss Kate Stevens. These two ladies continued to run the school during the rest of Queen Victoria's reign, being 39 and 38 years old respectively in 1901.

Queen Victoria was a frequent visitor to the school. At Christmas she would attend, sometimes with Princess Beatrice, in order to give gifts or prizes to the children. By 1897 she was visiting with her daughter and grandchildren, as she recorded in her journal for 13th January: *'Went to Whippingham School with B, D and Ena, Mr Clement Smith meeting us there. I got out and went into the infants school where the children all had dolls in their arms and sang and recited little rhymes with actions on the 'Kindergarten' system after which they made way for the bigger boys and girls who went through their musical drill, first together and then separately. They did it wonderfully. The books and work were shown me, also drawings, all most creditable.'* Visits from the Queen must have been an excellent way for teachers to encourage the children to work hard!

While government grants were forthcoming for teachers training pupil teachers, the capitation grant was dependent on sufficient numbers of pupils being entered for examination, with extra payment if the children passed. If for some reason, such as illness, they could not sit exams, then the school received less money. This sometimes resulted in the school having a deficit. The financial statement for 1865 shows this, and also that each child paid the school 2d a week. The results of those children examined in reading, writing and arithmetic were excellent, a 97% pass rate, and the inspector said that this was better than any other school in the neighbourhood.

A fever epidemic in 1877 had resulted in the closure of the school for several months. The school pence income was lost, and the rector, Canon Prothero, reported that the deficit was £89.9s.11¾d. The Queen's secretary wrote in May, *'I have spoken to the Queen about the school finances....Cannot allow the burden of the deficiency to fall on you, as it has been caused by a misfortune that you could not avoid. If you can obtain no assistance from the Committee for the Council for Education, or from other sources...the Queen is willing to contribute...'* The Queen sent a cheque for £89. When in November 1877 the school received a £38 rebate from the council, £38 was returned to the Queen.

The main income for the school was from subscriptions from the few wealthy landowners living nearby. Subscribers gave £65.5s in 1865. Salaries for staff that year cost £93.10s.10½d.

In 1894 the Queen contributed £45. The message was sent that Her Majesty, *'wants to have complete control'* of the finances. When the school drainage had problems, it was the Queen who paid the bill. *'The cost of alteration to the drainage etc. at Whippingham School required by the Education Department will be £130 but*

Sir Fleetwood fears it is unavoidable and must be done.!' A room for the teaching of cookery was also deemed necessary by the school inspector.

There was a certain amount of confusion about just where the money was to come from. At one time requests were to be made to the Privy Purse, but this was corrected in April 1897, *'The Queen has now undertaken to pay all expenses at School,'* so the money was to come from Osborne estate funds.

1901 onwards

After Victoria's death, the county council took over the finances, but the King kept the land and a rent of £1 a year was paid to him.

A 1902 survey for the county council showed that there were three partitions in the main school room. Two classes of infants occupied the two west rooms. The surveyor was very scathing about the cookery room that had been added, which he considered entirely unsuited to its supposed use. The headmistress occupied the western school house.

The infants and girls 'sanitary offices' were poorly placed off the main corridor entrance and the staff toilet was in the teacher's house. The boys' toilets were in a detached building next to the poultry house. It had, *'a trough closet with four seats over same; there are no divisions, the boys having to sit in a row. At the end is a small urinal without water to flush; it is badly ventilated, the only opening being the door; when I made my survey it was very foul.'* He suggested that partitions and doors should be installed, and adequate flushing provided. The drains led to a cess pit in the teacher's garden, which then overflowed across Beatrice Avenue!

In 1907 Ida Thomas was still the head of the school which had 150 children on the roll. Soon after this, James W Rogerson became the headmaster and in 1914/15 had two assistant mistresses, Miss A Cooke and Miss A Board.

The early photographs of the pupils at Whippingham School show groups of perfectly dressed children. While Queen Victoria was alive each child received material as a gift every other year, so there was no excuse for poor dressing. The boys' sailor suits would have been passed from child to child and the white pinafores would have been repeatedly boiled and starched.

Uffa Fox (later a famous yacht designer) attended Whippingham School with his elder sister Mahala, starting in about 1903. He remembered each older child had their own desk which they could lock up if they wished and in which Uffa kept his conkers, toffees and pens. They had a break of one and a half hours for lunch, for which most children ate at home.

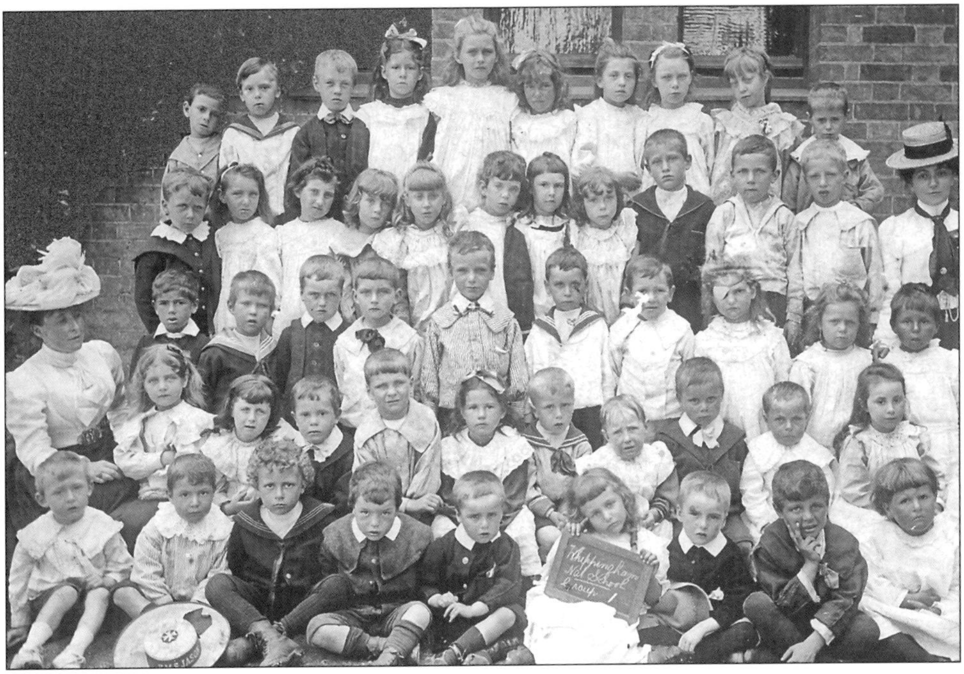

Sailor suits and starched pinafores were the order of the day in 1905. Though smartly dressed the children appear unhappy to have their photo taken.

Uffa enjoyed playing games on the school field but the boys were much better at cricket than football. Another school beat them at football 10-1, so when the Whippingham boys started their cricket training early in the spring Mr Rogerson coached his boys until they could bowl and bat accurately and effectively. The day arrived for the cricket match against the school that had defeated them at football. Whippingham batted first and made 120 runs. Billy Bullimore bowled first for Whippingham, and took four wickets in the first over, Uffa Fox took four wickets in the second, so the opposition were eight wickets down having scored nothing. The Whippingham boys had an attack of the giggles at this stage and it took three more overs to finish off the other school for 13 runs. Revenge had been taken.

The education committee decided that school children should be taught to swim when they were ten years old. Whippingham children were marched down to the Folly for their swimming lessons twice a week in the River Medina, instructed by Bob Savage, the Folly landlord. Uffa and a few of his friends were already known to Bob as good swimmers, so they were allowed to swim across

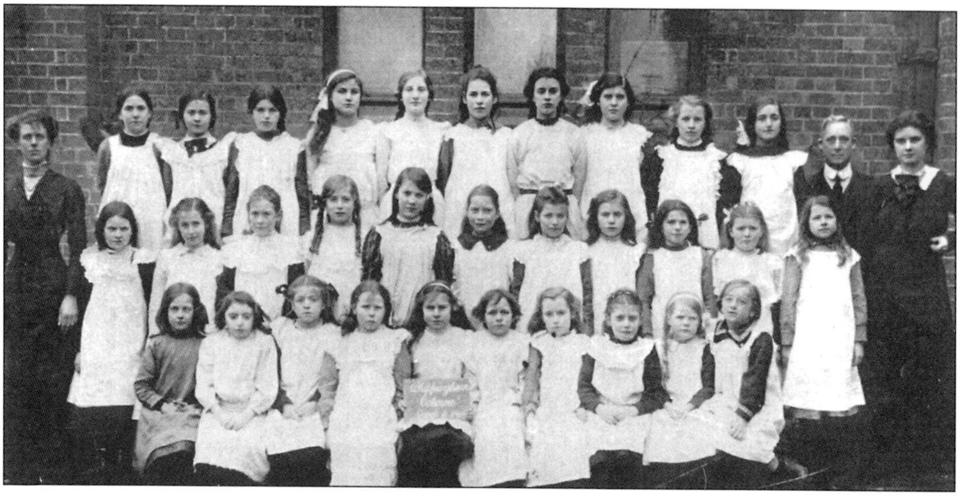

Older girls with their teachers and Mr Rogerson, the Headmaster. c.1910.

the river while Bob taught the other children. 24th September 1919 the log book reads, *'Girls attend for swimming instruction at 11 and boys attend at 1.30 as the tide is suitable about mid-day.'*

Gardening occurred frequently on the timetable for the boys at Whippingham, especially during the First World War. The school log book for 3rd September 1917 reads, *'Boys lifted one and a quarter cwt of late crop potatoes in the school gardens.'* Four days later, *'Instruction for boys for two hours, mostly planting out winter greens.'* 14th December, *'Boys attended to school gardens getting in a load of manure and spreading it over the beds!'* In the photograph it is interesting to note how well dressed the boys are for the job in hand. Many have proper gardening aprons on and there are an abundance of tools. Perhaps the lady is Ida Thomas.

Efforts were made to harvest blackberries and horse chestnuts for the war effort. *'23rd October 1918. Nearly 2cwt of chestnuts have been gathered by the scholars, and are being used by the army authorities.'* The starch from the horse chestnuts was used in the making of acetone for the explosive, cordite.
'9th September 1918. Elder girls went out during the afternoon to gather blackberries, by permission of the L.E.A. and the Government Authorities. About 10lbs of blackberries were gathered.'

After the First World War

Miss Cooke was the teacher that many remembered. She ruled by the cane and there were frequent punishments. One sulky boy with a hot temper was

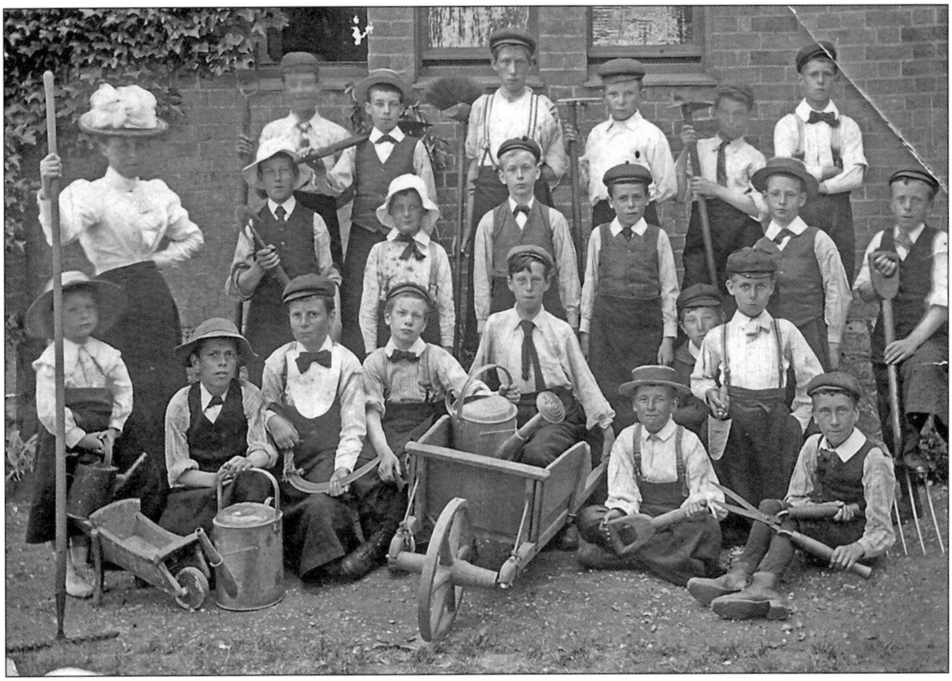

Gardening was part of the curriculum and was taken up by children of all ages. The photo dates from 1905. The subject became important in the First World War.

sometimes locked in a room at the back of the school by Miss Cooke. He kept shouting loudly which frightened the other children. On one occasion the miscreant fell silent. He had managed to escape through the window!

In 1930 Miss Marion Moody, known as Madge Moody, took over as headmistress of the school. She was only 23 years old, and, as Phyllis Jerome put it, *'full of bright new teaching ideas which we enjoyed.'* A different regime ensued. Miss Winter was appointed as assistant mistress for the infants.

Children attended Whippingham School until they left to go into employment. There may have been the occasional scholarship to Newport Grammar School. In 1934 the Island school system changed and Whippingham became only a junior and infants school. The main transfer of senior children was to be on 1st April each year, and, *'would include all children aged 11 or over, and any others who have spent a year or more in standard IV.'*

Whippingham shrank overnight to a school of 39 pupils. The school was remembered by everyone as being a very happy place under Miss Moody. In 1933 she and a local benefactor, Mr Upward, took ten of the children on holiday to

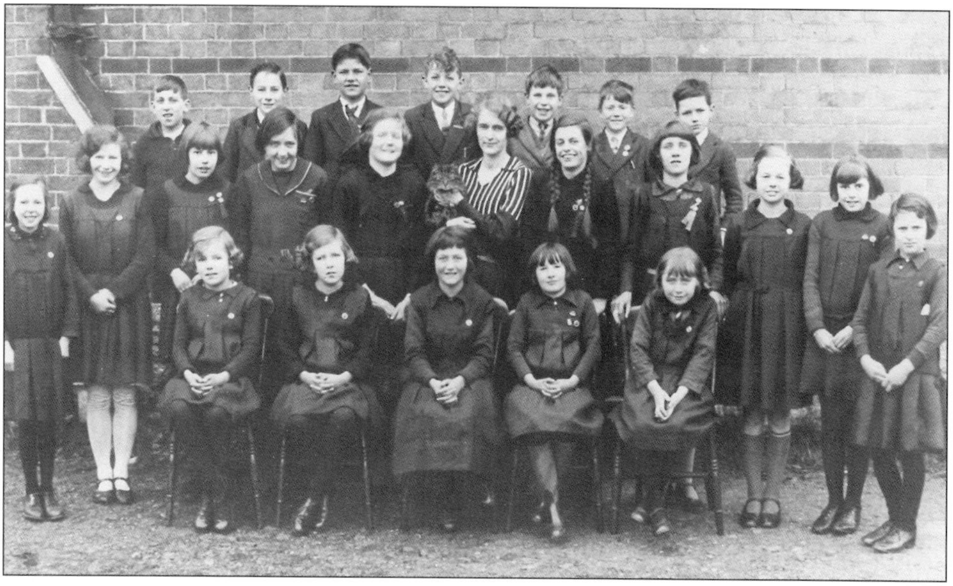

Miss Moody standing in the centre holding her cat and with her class gathered for a photograph taken in 1932.

North Wales for two weeks. Each child only had to pay ten shillings, all the rest of the trip was paid for them.

The old school log books provide a fascinating glimpse into the life of the school. The book was kept by the headteacher, who entered in it anything that deserved to be recorded. Only facts were to be entered, not opinions. Any reasons for closure were to be logged plus *'any deviations from the ordinary routine of the school!'*

The Second World War

Thanks to the log book we hear in 1940 about tar-macadam paths laid to the gates, Nurse King calling to inspect the children's heads, the rector visiting and, in December, *'Workmen are wiring the school for electric light!'*

In January 1940 there was a very cold snap. The temperature only rose to 36°F in the classroom on 17th January. *'The children were accordingly taken for an hour's sharp walk, and given a hot drink upon their return. No writing lessons were taken today. 18th January Morning walk as yesterday. Classroom temp. 40 degrees. The Rector called. 19th January Morning walk. Temp. 41 degrees. Report sent to the Director of Education.'*

Ella Butler remembers a tall, cylindrical container with a plunger that made hot Horlicks drinks for the children. At lunchtimes those who brought a packed lunch were able to give their pies or jacket potatoes to Miss Moody for her to heat up. The cold day walks included trips to the field below the church where the children could make snow slides on the steep hillside. Grace Davison remembers being a pupil in the 1930s when Miss Moody took the children down to Barton Manor pond which had frozen over and the children tried skating during lesson time!

Some of the comments in the log book during the Second World War make poignant reading. Air raids at night made the children very tired and sometimes they were allowed to sleep during the afternoon. Raids during school time were catered for by an air raid shelter located in the centre of the playing field. Miss Moody did not teach football, so this didn't matter. The children enjoyed playing rounders and there was still plenty of field for that.

The shelter was half underground and accessed by steps down. To the right were bench seats along the walls. The sound of the guns just across the main road at Whippingham Battery must have been deafening. Ella Butler, who started at Whippingham School in 1935, remembers being taught to knit by the light of an oil lamp while in the shelter. The first task was bedsocks on size 1 needles and then they progressed to red pixie-hoods, which involved pearl stitching. Ella decided she hated knitting!

The older children were taken out blackberrying for the war effort in September 1941, picking 20lbs of berries. Another task carried out by the children was the making of camouflage nets for the guns at the battery. They were given large pieces of open webbing material and then had to weave khaki and green strips of cloth in and out of the webbing. As soon as each net was completed, it was put in a wheelbarrow and two or three children would be sent across the road to the gate at the camp. A sentry would let them in and the net was gratefully received. Then the children would be taken to the sergeants' mess, where there would be an array of sweets and chocolate for the children to choose from. This was a great incentive for the next net to be completed and a different set of children to visit the camp.

On the night of 4th May 1942 there was a severe air raid on East Cowes and Cowes. Only five children managed to get to school the following morning, and three of the others were never to return. Mary and Vera Chiverton and Joan Abrook had lived at Point Cottages. Bombing to block the road to East Cowes had

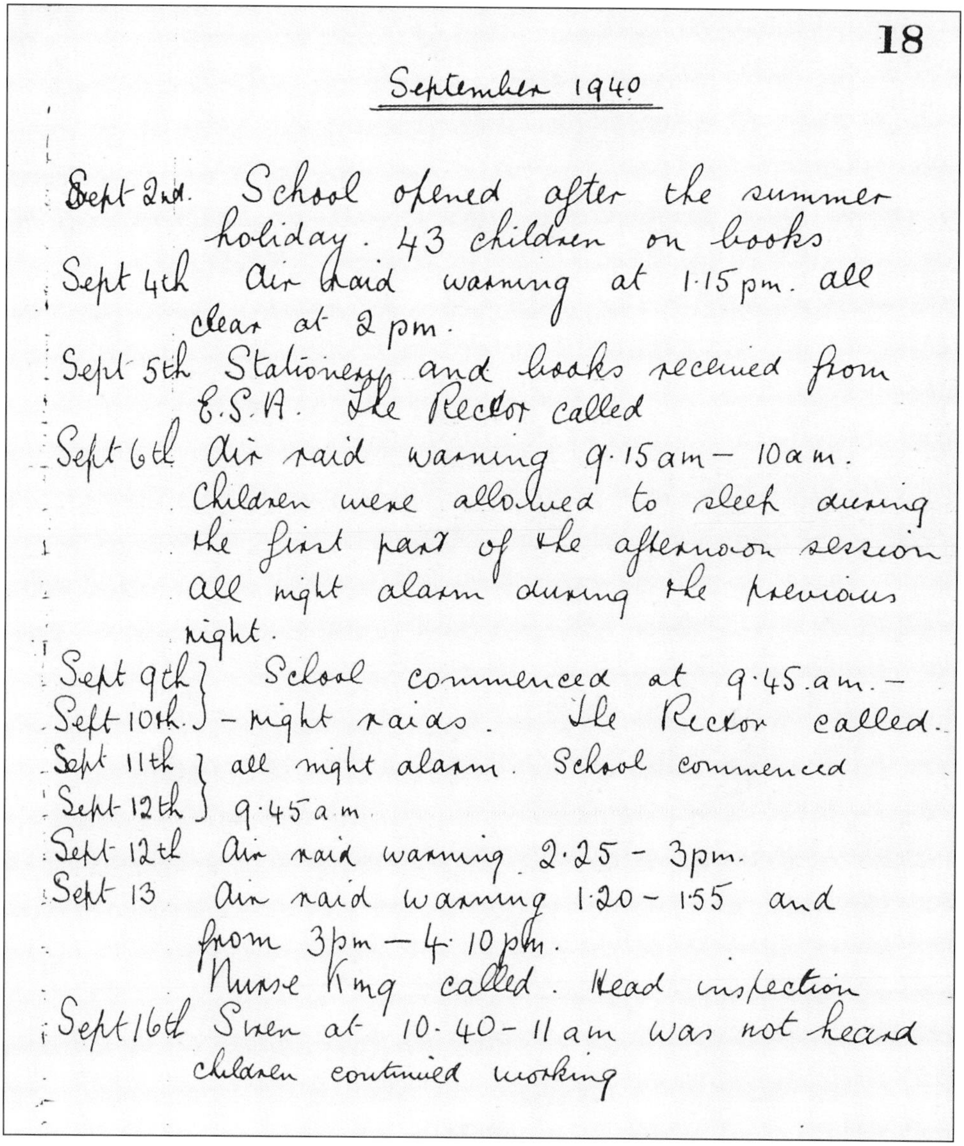

18

September 1940

Sept 2nd. School opened after the summer holiday. 43 children on books
Sept 4th Air raid warning at 1.15pm. all clear at 2pm.
Sept 5th Stationery and books received from E.S.A. The Rector called
Sept 6th Air raid warning 9.15am – 10am. Children were allowed to sleep during the first part of the afternoon session all night alarm during the previous night.
Sept 9th } School commenced at 9.45.am. –
Sept 10th } – night raids. The Rector called.
Sept 11th } all night alarm. School commenced
Sept 12th } 9.45 a.m
Sept 12th Air raid warning 2.25 – 3pm.
Sept 13 Air raid warning 1.20 – 1.55 and from 3pm – 4.10pm.
Nurse King called. Head inspection
Sept 16th Siren at 10.40 – 11 am was not heard children continued working

A wartime page from the school log book listing several air raids and alarms which disrupted the school and home life of the children.

destroyed their homes. Miss Moody informed the Education Department and received a kind letter back from the Director of Education, asking her to pass his condolences to the parents. There was no chance to do this as the whole family had been killed.

Post war activities

School plays were written by Miss Moody, who was very keen on theatricals. In May 1960 a pageant was performed to celebrate the centenary of the laying of the foundation stone of Whippingham Church. The stone had been laid by Queen Victoria. A message was received by the school on the occasion from her granddaughter, Queen Ena of Spain, who regretted that she was unable to attend.

All the children were superbly costumed. The Royal family of Queen Victoria were depicted and then the descendants of each of those children, including Queen Elizabeth and Prince Phillip. Famous Victorians in politics, medicine, science and literature were represented. The history of Whippingham Church was shown. Four pupils who were members of the church choir, were the final act. There were no speaking parts as the pageant took place outside in the grounds of the school, with Miss Moody broadcasting a commentary.

A tradition of annual Christmas plays continued. In 1956 Ella Butler had joined the staff of the school where she had been taught by Miss Moody over 20 years before. Mrs Butler wrote the plays from 1966 to 1985, when she retired. *The Bell that Cried* was performed in 1980. Another play involved a row of penguins. It was suggested that they should wear big rubber swimming flippers, but, as they were falling over their own feet anyway as they waddled along, the idea was dropped! The costume mistress at that time was the school secretary, Bernice Grist, who created costumes for Moley and Ratty for a production of *Wind in the Willows* in 1986. Mrs Butler remembers that one of the best productions was *Jack Frost*. Both she and the children enjoyed doing the Christmas plays. Headteacher Viv Maher continued the tradition.

In 1950 the present Community Hall was no longer needed by Saunders Roe for their offices. It was purchased from them by the Isle of Wight Council for £3,925 and used as an annexe by the reception and infants classes. The kitchens there were used to provide school lunches. Older children were still taught at the 'top' school, and marched in crocodile fashion down to the 'bottom' school at lunchtime. By 1956 Mr Darrington had joined Miss Moody on the staff. He worked hard on the football skills and achieved considerable success.

In 1966 Miss Moody retired, having been headmistress for over 35 years. Violet Coull took on the headship, helped in the 1970s and 80s by Maureen Smith and Ella Butler.

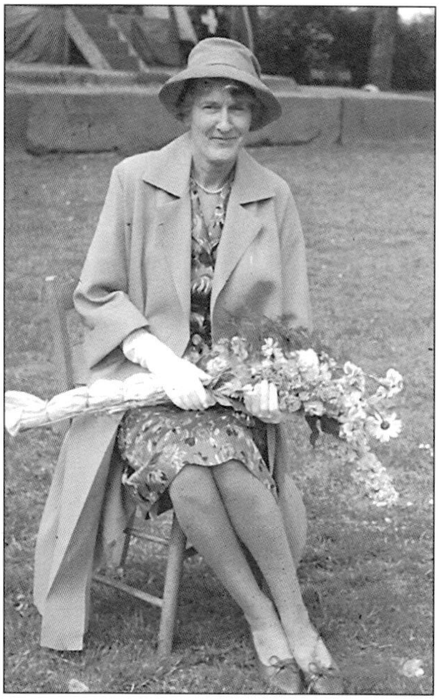

Headmistress, Miss Moody pictured on pageant day 1960. She retired from Whippingham School in 1966.

Ted Streets planted six flowering trees in the grounds to celebrate the Queen's silver jubilee in 1977, as the oldest of the local 'ex-Whippingham School' pupils. He had left school in 1903, aged 14.

The number of children in the village or in the catchment area south of Victoria Grove in East Cowes had diminished and in 1982 it was decided to move all the children onto one site. An extension was completed at the 'top' school in 1983 and the Community Hall was no longer necessary as classrooms. The hall had been a warm, sunny place for the children, with the infants having their own playground.

There were great advantages of having the school on one site again and in a well-designed building. The extension copied the original architecture of the old school, providing a new classroom for the top class. Cloakrooms and a new classroom were formed between the new part and the old.

In 1985 Miss Coull retired as headmistress. Her place was taken by Viv Maher. Over time, the numbers on the roll started increasing until three mobile classrooms were in use on the playground. Major remodelling took place in 1995/6, creating a new school hall and kitchens, so that the original hall could be divided permanently into two classrooms. Another classroom was added, with a new headteacher's office and secretary's reception area. The square hall had many advantages over the old long narrow rectangular one for any activity.

Many events have taken place at Whippingham School since Mrs Maher began in 1983, several with a Royal theme. One of these was the visit of Queen Elizabeth II to the Island in 1987. The whole school spent a week studying life at school in Victorian times, with all the children dressed in costume. The Queen was scheduled to drive past the school on her way to Osborne House and agreed to receive a posy. Many past pupils availed themselves of this opportunity to see their monarch stop outside 'Queen Victoria's school,' and joined the crowd of Whippingham folk there.

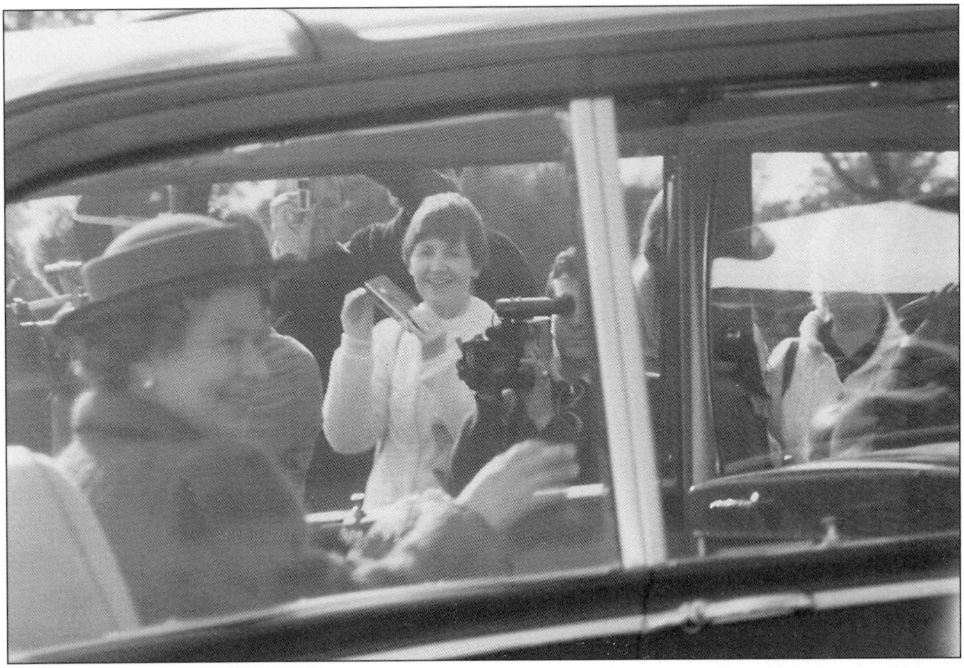

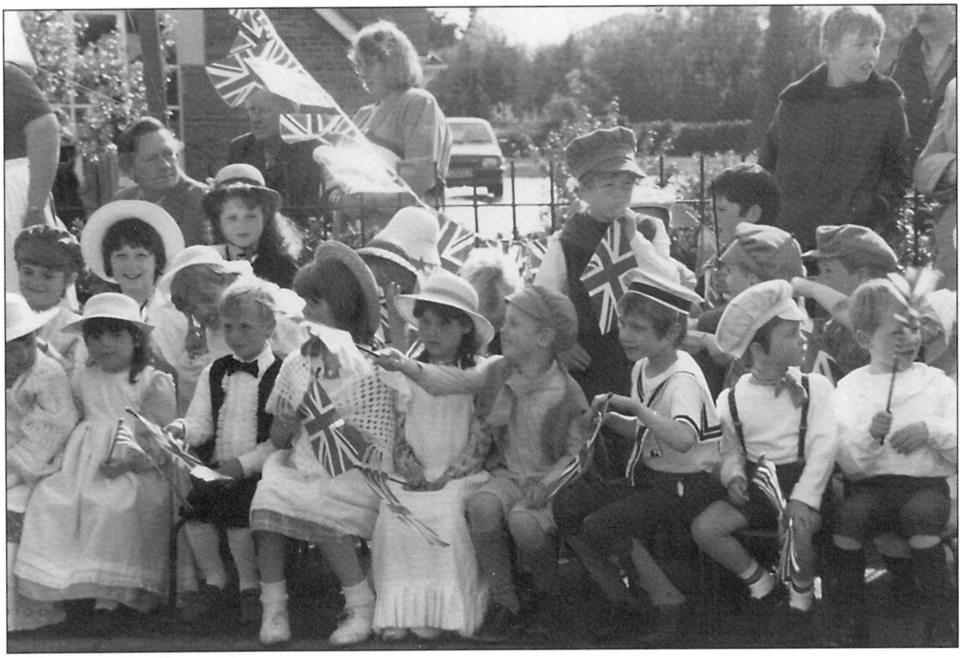

Queen Elizabeth II visited Whippingham School in 1987. Schoolchildren dressed in Victorian clothing and presented a posy to the Queen.

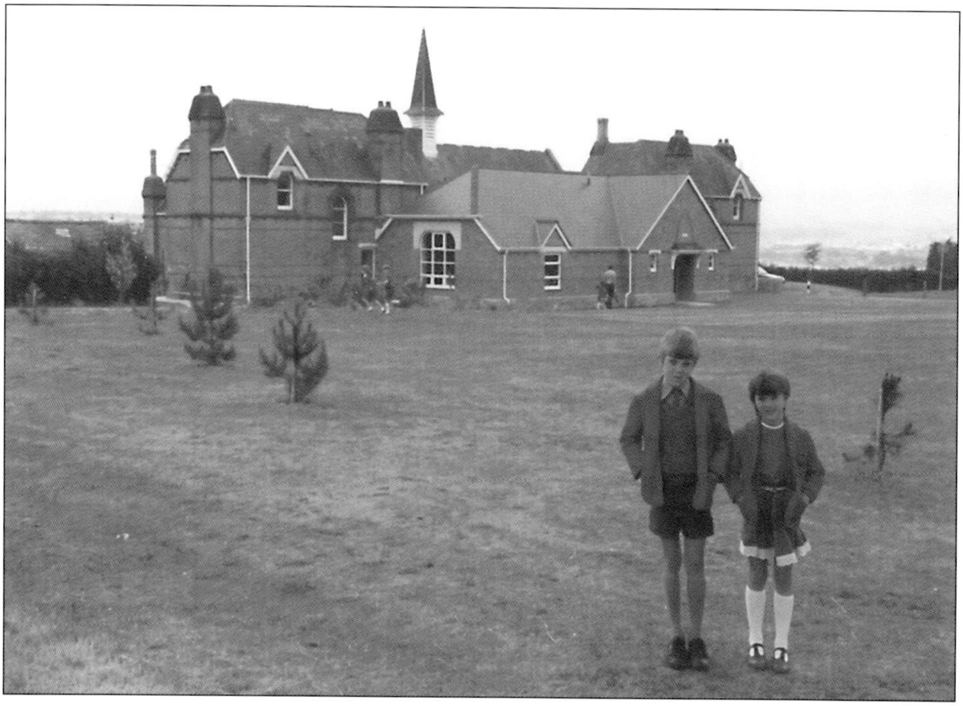

The first extension in 1984, with the author's children. A further extension was built in 1996.

In 2004 the school celebrated the 140th anniversary of the opening of the school by Queen Victoria. The pupils spent time dressing and working as the pupils would have done in 1864. The children found it an interesting experience to have to sit in rows and work silently, stand up when a visitor entered the room, and to see their headteacher walking around with a cane. At least one child was reduced to tears by a simple verbal reprimand! The author was invited to attend dressed as Queen Victoria and, helped by two of the children, planted a maple tree.

On the Beatrice Avenue side of the school two mobile classrooms provided the home for 'Chimneys', an educational play centre, from 1996 to 2010, accommodating up to 35 children. Chimneys took its name from the ornate chimney pots that once graced every chimney stack on the school.

In 2005 there were 140 children at Whippingham Primary School, coming from Whippingham, East Cowes and Wootton. A few walked to school, but most arrived by car. 140 years before, all the children would have walked, some from as far as Wootton as the Queen owned land on the far side of Palmer's Brook. Rain or shine, whatever the weather, Vicky Snow's mother walked down the hill to King's Quay, over a footbridge that used to be there, and up through both Woodhouse Farm and Barton Farm to get to school, perhaps a walk of an hour. In the 1980s the children living at East Cowes were put on the service bus by the school staff and then made their own way home. The way of life has changed.

In 1996, after 148 years, the old blackboards and chalk were replaced by whiteboards and dry-wipe markers. Subsequently they updated to interactive whiteboards linked to the teacher's computer.

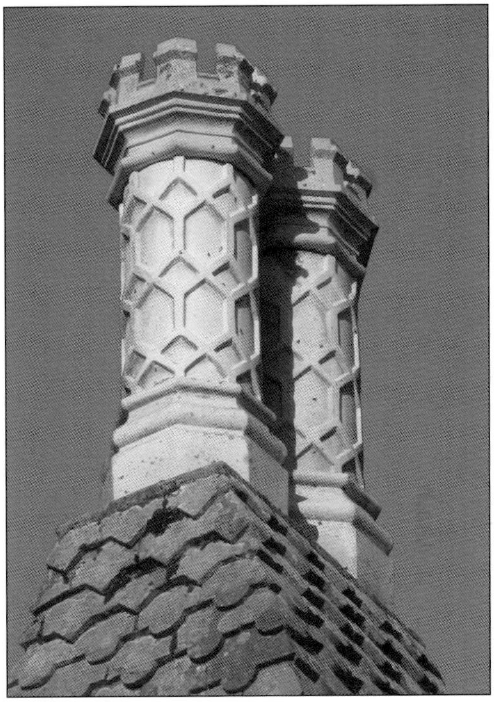

The decorative chimneys on the school.

The closure of Whippingham School

In 2010 the school system on the Island changed to a two tier model, middle schools being phased out. It was decided from September 2010 to amalgamate the two primary schools, Grange Road School East Cowes and Whippingham to relocate to the Osborne Middle School site when it became vacant. The name of the new school became Queensgate Foundation Primary School. For two years part of Queensgate was still at Whippingham School but in February 2012 state education moved out of Whippingham and Whippingham School was sold to the Priory School.

The Priory School of Our Lady of Walsingham

The Priory School is an Independent non-denominational Christian school. When Upper Chine School at Shanklin closed in 1993, Priory School took on the role of independent junior school in Shanklin and moved to Whippingham in 2012. A new reception unit and Sixth Form suite were added in 2014. Priory

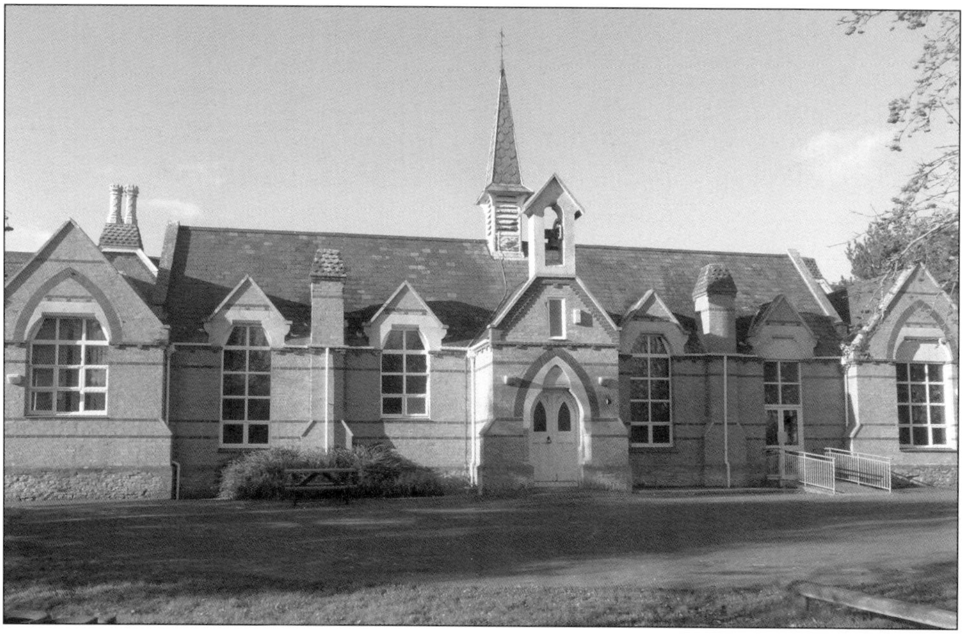

The present school building is now The Priory School of Our Lady of Walsingham, an independent, non-denominational Christian School.

School is committed to maintaining and developing this vital part of the village, the Osborne Estate and the Island's heritage.

In June 2014, HRH Princess Beatrice of York visited the school to unveil a plaque marking 150 years of continuous education in the same building, a building created by her four-times great grandmother. The school possesses the original of the deed of lease by King Edward VII granting the land back to the Rector of St Mildred's, complete with Royal seal.

The school has small classes, each with a maximum of sixteen students. It has pastoral flexibility with excellent academic results at GCSE and A Level. The Sixth Form sends undergraduates each year to universities such as London, Warwick, Exeter and Nottingham.

In 2012 there were just over 100 pupils when the school came to Whippingham. This rose to 150 in 2017, taught by over 35 members of staff. Many of the staff, as well as pupils, are local, continuing the tradition that reaches back to Victorian times.

It contributes to local and Island life, taking part in Isle of Wight Music, Dance and Drama festival and other academic and sports competitions. The

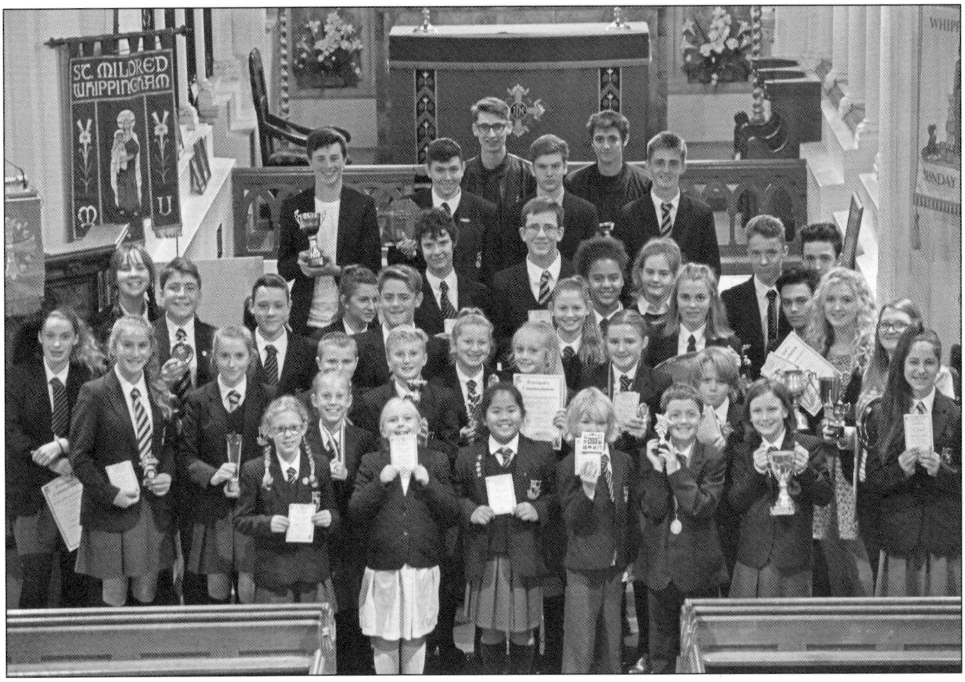

Some of the pupils of The Priory School at St. Mildred's Church on Prize Giving Day, 2017.

pupils have taken part in local activities, such as Isle of Wight Day and the 75th Anniversary of the East Cowes Blitz.

All the seasonal Christian services and special events such as Prize Day take place at St Mildred's Church, continuing a tradition that has lasted for many years. Priory School of Our Lady of Walsingham has both Anglican and Catholic Chaplains. Its dedication honours its Royal connection, as Walsingham in Norfolk was the Royal shrine throughout medieval times being visited by every king from Henry III to Henry VIII.

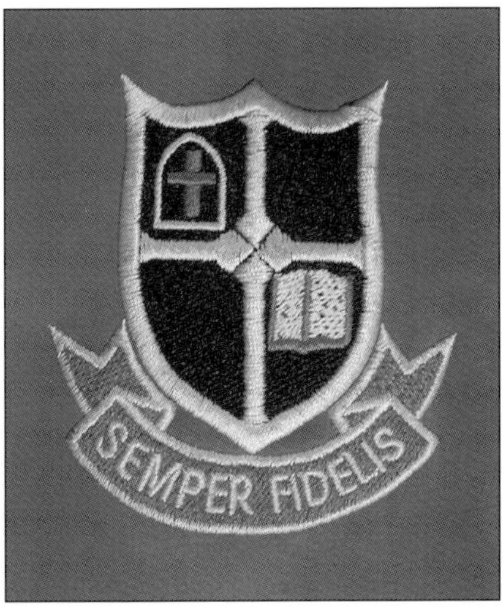

Priory School's role in the community can be summarized by the phrase: *"Built by the Queen of England: dedicated to the Queen of Heaven"*.

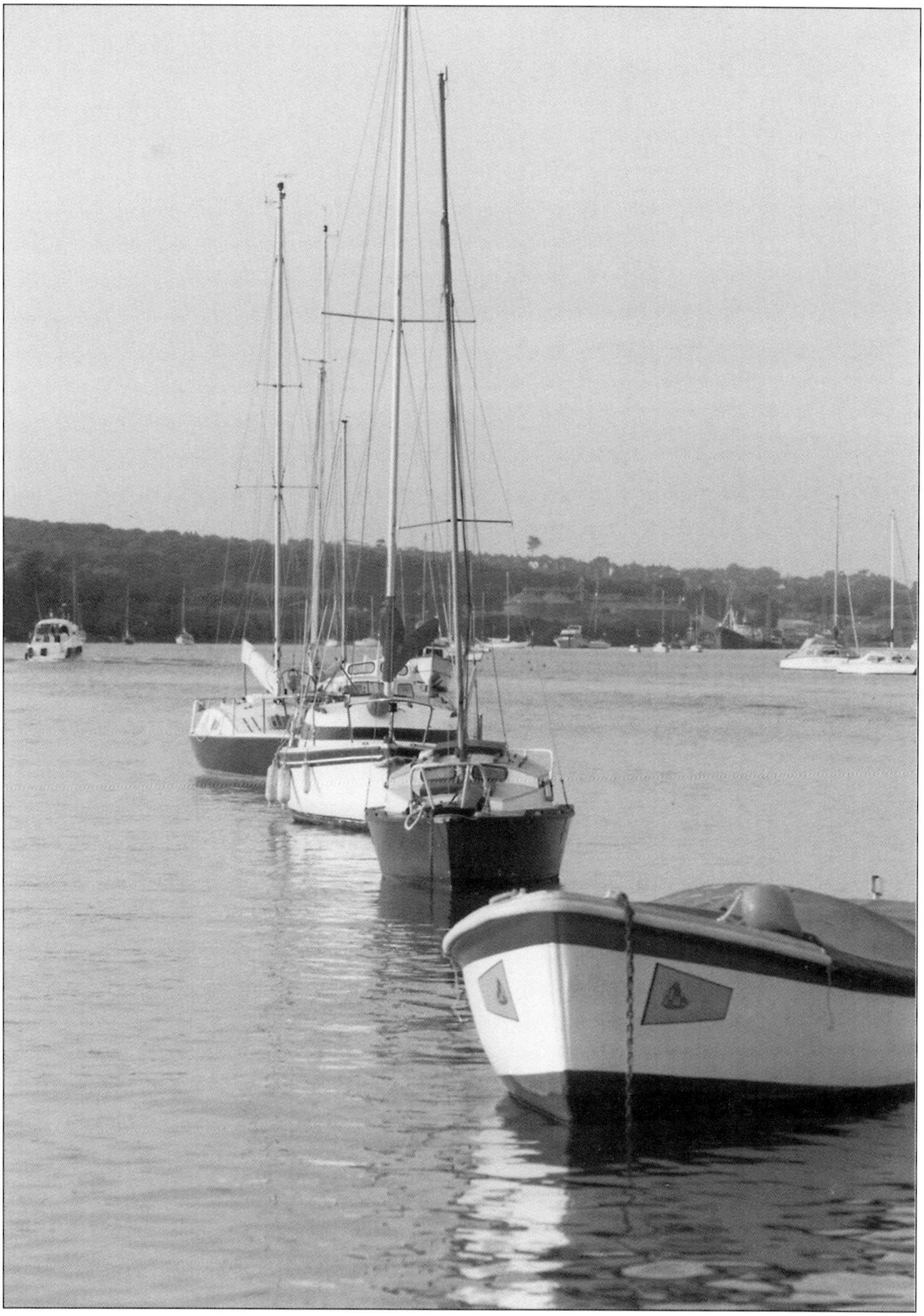

Folly Reach looking north down the River Medina.

Eleven

The River Medina & Railway

The tidal River Medina is four and a half miles long from Cowes to Newport. Extensive mudflats are revealed at low tide, when it is impossible to take anything other than a canoe up to Newport. At very low tides it is even possible to walk across the river at The Folly, although this is not recommended!

In 2017 the division between Cowes and Newport Harbour Authorities is The Folly pontoon. Boats can travel freely up and down the river and have always been allowed to do so. Whenever a boat moors up, however, the appropriate harbour authority takes its fee.

In the past, taxes were also liable on goods brought into the towns. In the late 1600s Newport complained to parliament that they were losing dues as East Cowes was being favoured by shipping. Parliament did nothing, so Newport built their own quay at East Cowes and charged ships to use it!

Newport also decided that they wanted the rights of usage of the river. They sold a lease in 1711 to William Cave, so only he could fish the river. This annoyed a lot of the local inhabitants, some of whom were oyster fishermen. John Redstone and Edward Faulkner were amongst these. They were using Claybrooks Luck [stream] for their oysters by permission of Mr Leigh at Heathfield Farm and Mr Barnard at Claybrooks Farm. This stream equates to the Island Harbour Marina today.

William Cave was under the impression that his new lease from the Borough of Newport gave him the rights to Claybrooks Luck so he took a pot-shot at the oyster fisherman and confiscated his oysters. The case went to court and Redstone and Faulkner's legal notes make amusing reading. What happened to the case we do not know. *'In the Parish of Whippingham there is a Rivelett of*

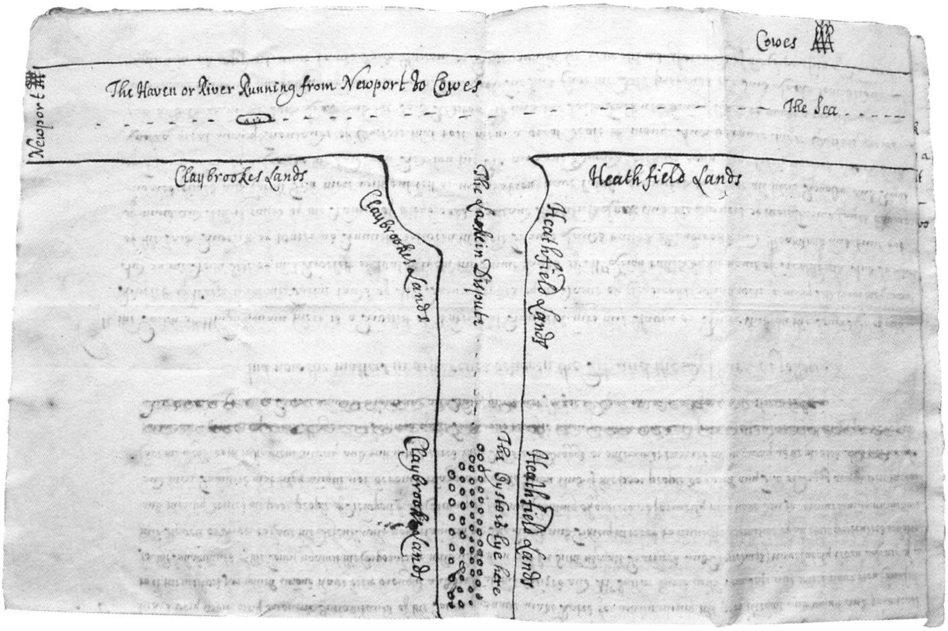

A map of 1711 showing the disputed oyster beds in the luck between Heathfield and Claybrooks land. (IWCRO)

water that Runneth into this ...River... it runneth between the said farmlands called Claybrooks and Heathfield and since time out of mind the owners of those farmlands having always fished there and catcht Fish there without lett or molestation they have lately granted by lease all their Royalty and Right of Fishery of the said Lucke to the said John Redston and Edward Faulkner who have lately throwed into the said Lucke a great many thousands of Oysters that cost them a great deal of money and because those oysters growe fatt and large in the said Lucke...Cave the defendant pretends the Lucke doth belong to him.

On the 1st of September 1711 Edward King did Dragg and Catch for the plaintiffs Two Thousand of Oysters in the said Lucke and while he was in the said Lucke the Defendant fired a gun which might have endangered his life some of the shot falling a very little distance from him and as the said King was Rowing in a boat with the said Oysters to Carry them to the plaintiffs at Newport the Defendant Cave....took away his said two thousand of Oysters...'

We read in the *Isle of Wight Herald* of 30th November 1867, *'For many years the oysters of the Medina have been noted and declared the best in England. Scarcely a day but that large quantities of oysters are forwarded to London and other parts of*

England.' It is known that there was an oyster company in the 1860s at The Folly, oysters were being farmed in 1711, and probably for many hundreds of years before that. In fact, it may have been during the time of the Romans that oysters were first farmed on the Medina.

Sadly the last oyster company on the Medina closed down in 2005, partly because there was little protection of the oyster areas. In 2014, oyster fishing was still carried out in season by a few people on the Medina. The river was classed as B grade water, so the oysters were sold to dealers who either put the oysters in grade A water for six weeks or treated them with ultraviolet light to kill off any impurities before selling them.

East Medina Mill

In 1790 William Porter had a causeway built across the mouth of Claybrooks (Great Luck) and a smaller luck to the south. William was a Newport baker and he constructed a tide mill. It was the time of the Napoleonic Wars and many troops were quartered locally at Parkhurst. These soldiers needed flour and bread, as did the men on ships moored in the Solent waiting to sail to war or the new convict colonies in Australia. Grain was imported to cash in on feeding this hungry market. At least five other tide mills were built on the Island at this time.

Mr Porter built a mill on the east side of the Medina, and another on the opposite bank a little further south. East Medina Mill was 300ft long, 30ft wide and four storeys tall. Unfortunately he was insufficiently financed and the banks who had previously supported him withdrew their funding. Within a year Mr Porter had died and the buildings were left empty.

Foreign mercenary troops, known as 'Hessians', from the German state of Hesse, were part of the British Army. They were quartered at East Medina Mill and over 70 men died there in a typhoid epidemic. The bodies were carried along the footpath beside the river and buried by Whippingham Churchyard. A couple of years later, French soldiers were held at East Medina Mill as prisoners of war. Many years later Queen Victoria's daughter, Alice, married into the Royal family of Hesse and on hearing the story had a plaque erected at the church to the Hessian soldiers.

By 1799 the mill was owned by William Roach, with James Roach running it. The building, kiln and machinery were valued for insurance for £2,000 which was a considerable sum in those days. The kiln would have made the bricks on site for the buildings.

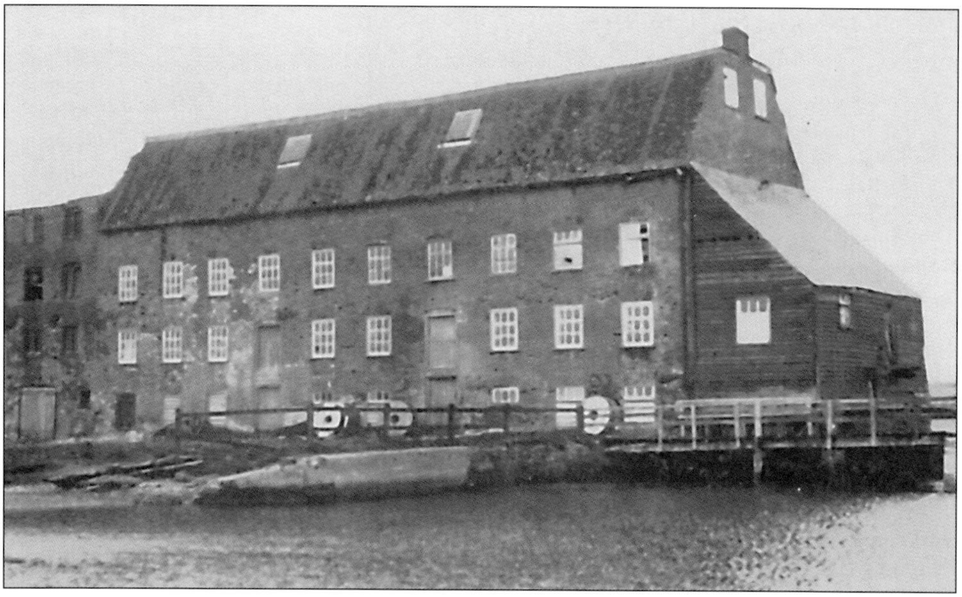

East Medina Mill pictured in 1936. It worked as a tidal mill using two mill ponds and the wheel was powered as the tide receded. (R Adams)

By 1850 many of the troops had left the Island and milling began to decline. Mr Roach put in new milling machinery at East Medina Mill made by Armfields, to improve his productivity over that of his competitors, and thus stayed in business. The Roach family continued to run the mill until it closed in 1939.

East Medina's tide mill worked on a simple principle. The tide was allowed to flow freely into the two mill ponds and when the ponds were full, the sluices were shut. The water wheel, a low breast-shot design, operated as the tide flowed out of the ponds. It could only turn on the ebb tide because of the shape of the buckets. This wheel, which was 15ft 6ins in diameter and over 6ft wide, had 30 buckets to catch the water and turn the wheel. This main wheel turned the pit wheel, and a shaft drove all the mill machinery, including the mill stones. The lock into the marina today stands on the site of the old water wheel.

In January 1930 there was a very severe storm. The storehouse roof, 90ft by 30ft, was lifted off by hurricane-force winds and hurled 40 yards through the air onto the two mill cottages causing severe damage. Thankfully nobody was hurt, the occupants had a lucky escape. The mill continued to operate.

After 1930 Viv Thomas remembered going to the mill to collect meal for his hens. The noise of the creaking machinery in the mill, cog against cog, wheel

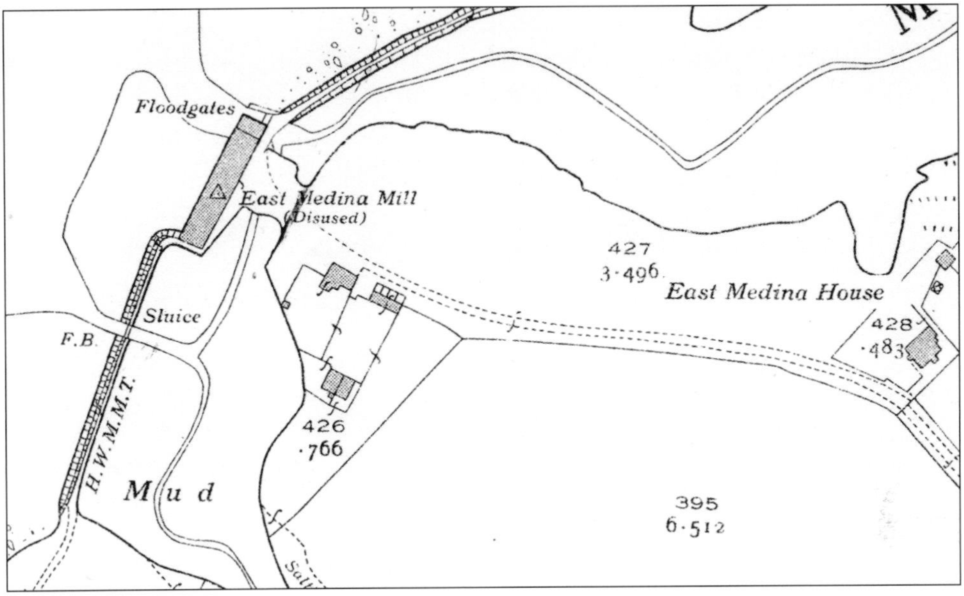

The disused mill shown on a map of 1939.

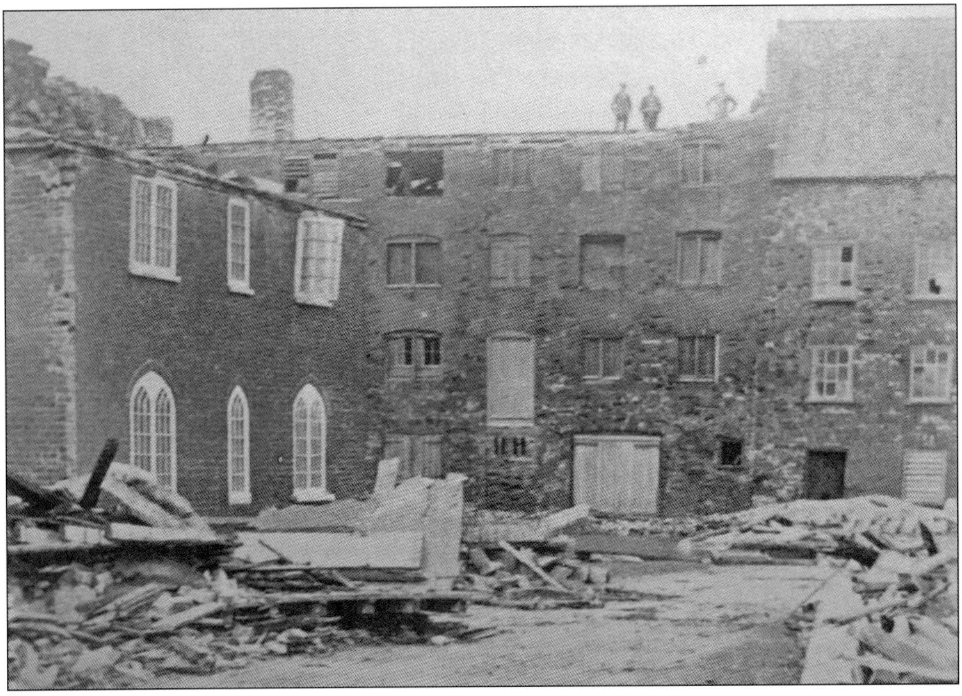

The damage caused to the mill in a storm of 1930 tore the roof off the storehouse onto the cottages below.

against wheel, remained in his memory. The mill struggled on until war came in 1939 and the machinery stopped for the last time. The Borough of Newport obtained the mill and used it as a store for waste material that had been collected for the war effort. At some time after this the mill caught fire and half was burnt. It remained derelict until 1950 when it was demolished.

The miller's house survived. Built of local red brick, it has a Georgian look to it and is listed Grade II. Passing the building today it is little noticed behind the trees and hedges on the right as one enters the present Marina, a small reminder of East Medina Mill.

The Marina

In the middle of the 1960s a consortium of local people leased the site to build a marina. It opened in 1965 as 'The Medway Queen Marina,' named for the paddle steamer berthed there. By 1971 the marina was known as 'Wight Marina' and later 'Island Harbour.'

Initially six fixed-concrete jetties were provided for boats. These were not all that successful as occasionally there could be a problem with the lock gates which lost water, leaving boats hung up on their moorings! Floating pontoons have since replaced the jetties. The lock enables boats to enter or leave for up to three and a half hours either side of high water. Shower and toilet facilities were provided and it was intended to provide a swimming pool, general store, chandlery, squash and tennis courts. Of these extras, only the chandlery appeared.

The *PS Medway Queen* was bought in 1965 and formed a club house for the marina. She had spent her working life from 1924 to 1963 as an excursion steamer in the Thames and Medway areas. In 1940 she was used in the Dunkirk evacuation, rescuing about 7,000 troops in seven trips. By 1972 the *Medway Queen* had rainwater dripping through the deck into the lounge. In 1979 she was removed from the smaller mill pond to the river in an effort to return her to the Medway for restoration by the Paddle Steamer Preservation Society. She finally left the Medina in 1984 and she has been totally rebuilt, returning to the Medway River in 2013.

In 1970 A H and C B Ridett bought the last paddle steamer to be used on the Ryde to Portsmouth route, the *PS Ryde*. She was built in 1937 for Southern Railway by William Denny and Sons of Dumbarton. 225ft long, with a gross tonnage of

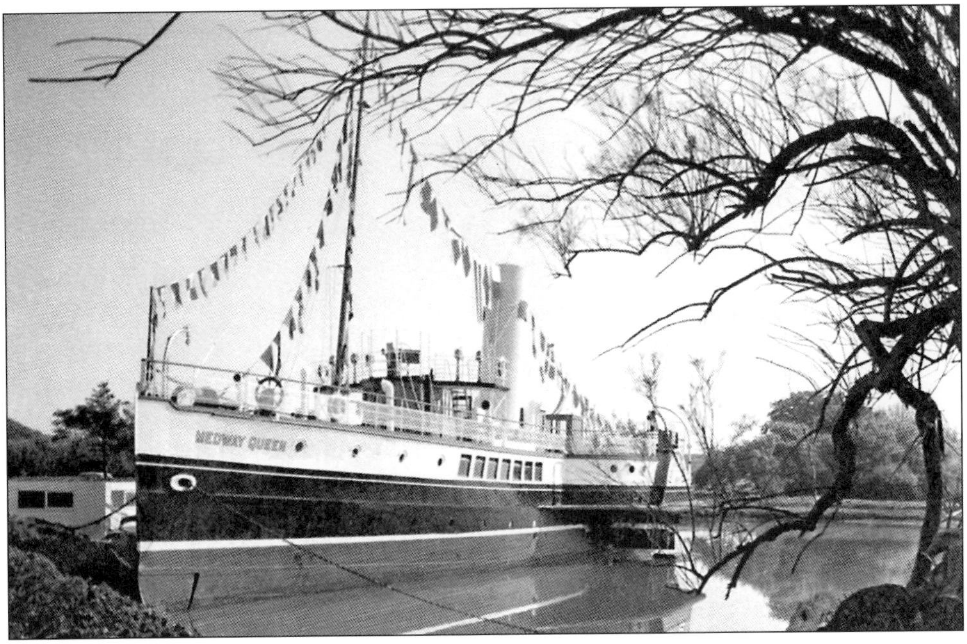

The Medway Queen was moored in the Marina and used as a nightclub. Now restored and working on the River Medway.

566 tons, she had a passenger capacity of 1011. *PS Ryde* saw service with the Royal Navy during the Second World War, being used for minesweeping duties in the Firth of Forth. After the war she came back to the Solent and operated for British Rail on the Ryde to Portsmouth route until 1969. She was renamed *Ryde Queen* and was put on a mud berth ahead of the already popular *Medway Queen* and was opened as a discotheque.

By 1972 the *Ryde Queen* was leased by Trusthouse Forte and turned into a floating hotel, or 'Boatel'. Luxuriously fitted cabins for 33 people, a classy restaurant seating 100, a bar on the saloon deck and below the restaurant a dance floor were all provided. The engines were exposed, to show their gleaming brass rods and shining mechanism.

Regrettably the 'Boatel' did not prove as popular as had been hoped, despite the good food, accommodation and position. Trusthouse Forte pulled out, and a discotheque moved into the *Ryde Queen*. In 1977 a fire caused damage to the vessel, which was repaired, but economics forced closure soon afterwards. A rescue effort was mounted by the PSPS, but negotiations with the owners broke down and *PS Ryde* is now a derelict hulk.

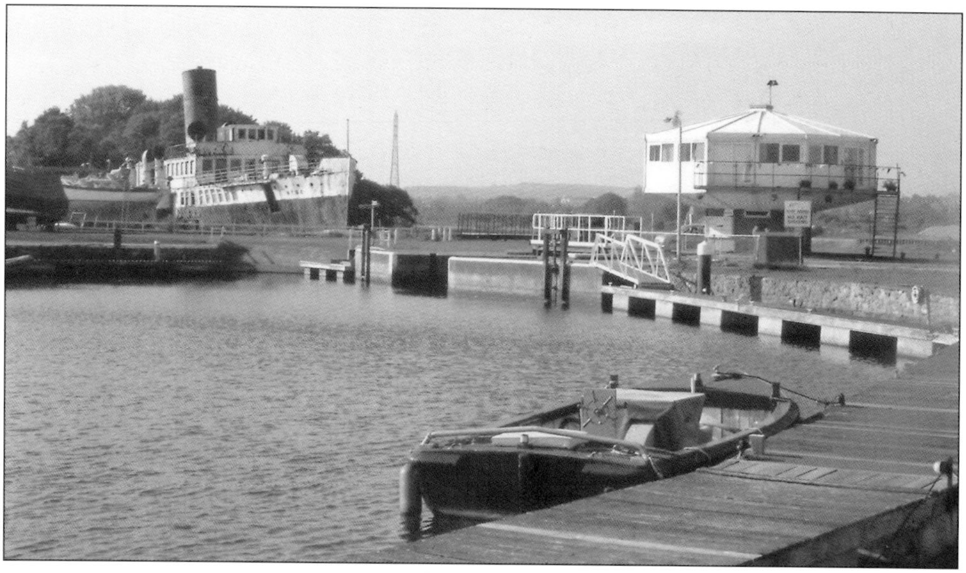

The Ryde Queen lies unused in 2005 near the lock-control tower of the marina.

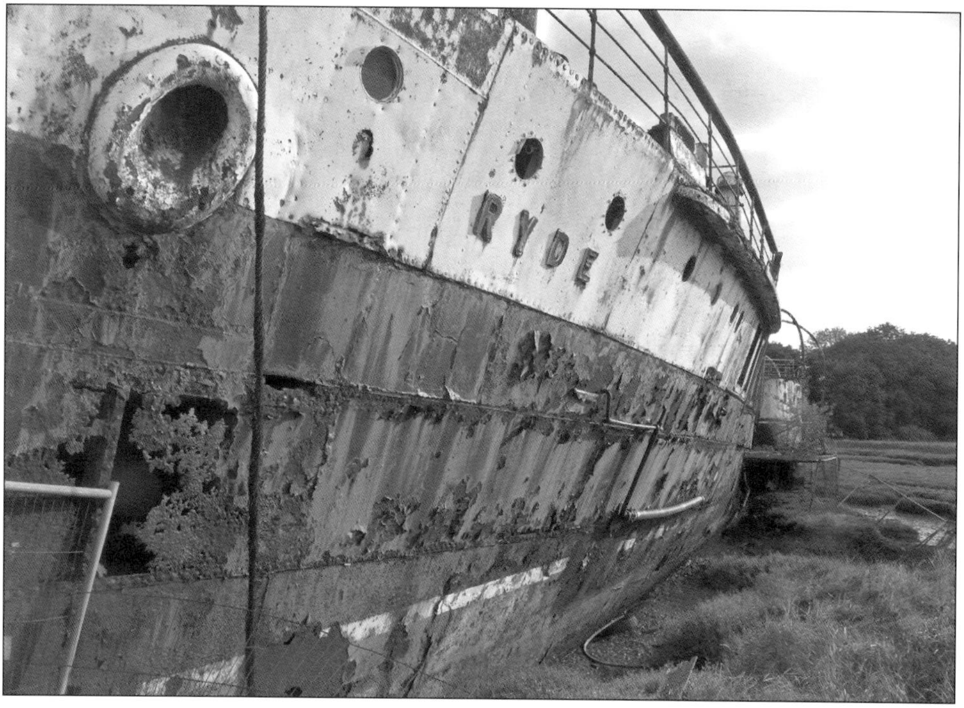

2017 and the Ryde has not moved and lies rusting at her berth. She is now probably beyond saving.

At the marina, a watchtower and lock-operating office was built in the shape of an enormous mushroom and a bistro was opened. Richardsons provided not only the chandlery for those working on their own boats, but a comprehensive yacht repair facility and cranes to lift up to 18tons. Many people stored their boats ashore to work on during the winter beside the rusting hulk of the *Ryde*, which provides them with a stark reminder of the ravages of weather on a vessel that is not maintained.

During the 1990s yachtsmen's cottages were built alongside Great Luck, and further housing stands on piles over the water. More new housing is under construction in 2017.

All those either living there or visiting the marina in their boats have the benefit of the beautiful country and riverside with a rich diversity of birds, of which more than 50 species may easily be seen.

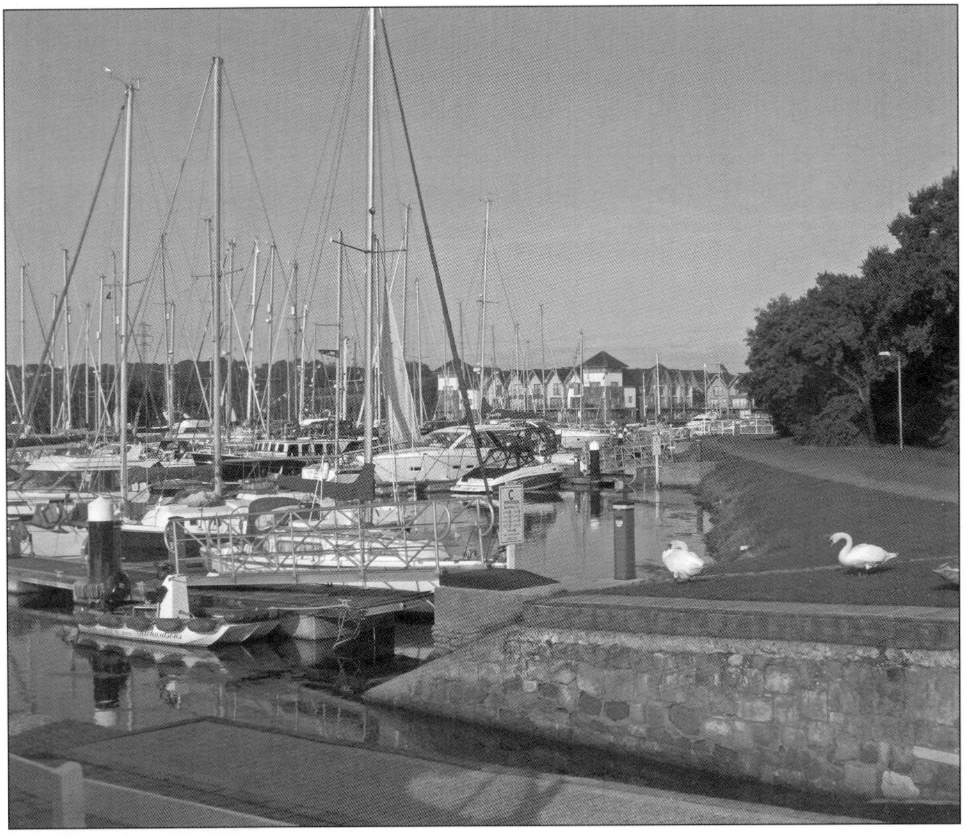

The marina in 2017 is a thriving area for boat owners and visitors alike.

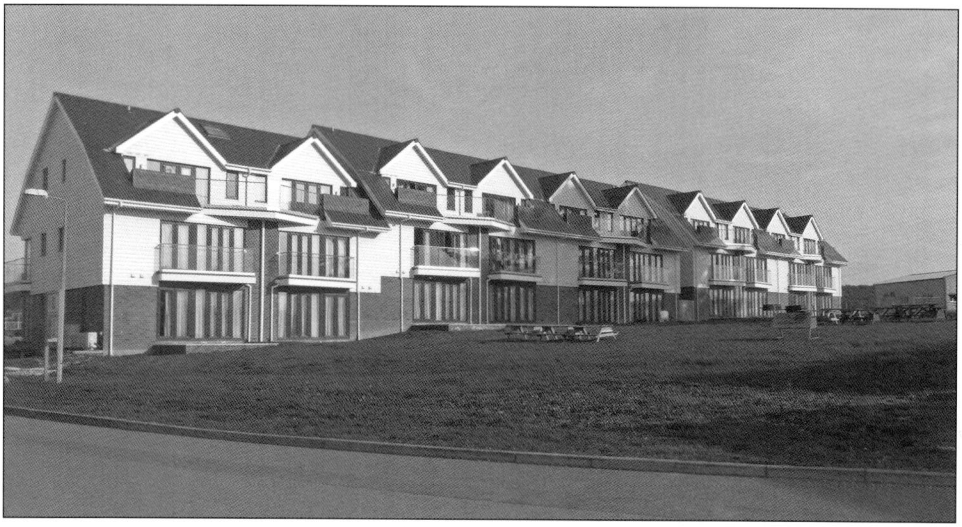

The start of new housing development by the Marina in 2017.

Whippingham Railway Station

The Ryde and Newport Railway Company constructed a station on their line at the nearest point to Osborne House, two and a half miles away. The village of Whippingham was over a mile from the station. The idea that the building was for the exclusive use of the Royal family can be eliminated, as it is believed that the Queen herself only used the station once. Many members of the Queen's court and government travelled by train to Portsmouth, caught the ferry to Ryde and then took the train to Whippingham. A carriage from Osborne would be sent to collect them. A private drive was made through the Queen's land and the distinctive entrance lodge with the Royal cyphers still stands today on the Ryde side of the crematorium roundabout.

The station was opened on 20th December 1875. The building was a mirror image of Ashey Station and both appear much too large for the communities they served. It was a roomy, two-storey building consisting of a stationmaster's house, booking office and signal box, waiting room, ladies waiting room, toilets and a luggage room. There was single platform 235ft long and a short siding towards Newport.

When initially opened there were seven trains each way on weekdays, and four on Sundays. Trains would only stop on request at Whippingham, and the station was announced as *"Whippingham for Osborne!"*

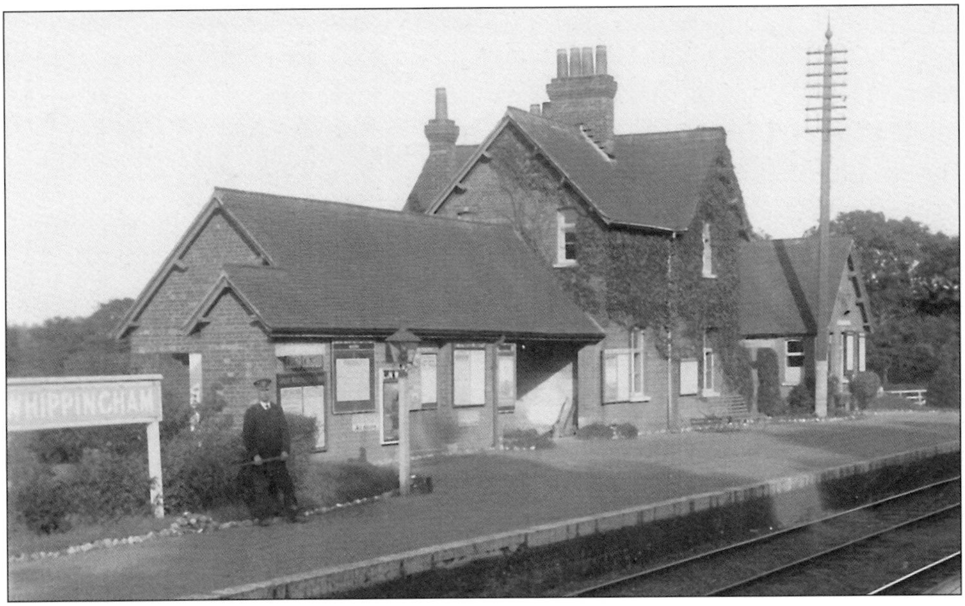

Whippingham Railway Station pictured in the 1920s. Trains stopped here on the route between Newport and Ryde.

In 1887 the Ryde and Newport railway amalgamated with other lines to form the Isle of Wight Central Railway. Henry Pinnock took over as chairman of the railway, having been a director of the Ryde and Newport Railway. He built Belmont Farm on top of the hill above Whippingham Station. The railway bridge over Belmont Lane at Binfield Corner was called Pinnock's Bridge. At the start of Mill Lane, down to the marina, stand a pair of houses proudly sporting H P in their brickwork.

Emily Merwood, the wife of James, a railway man, was given the position of station-mistress in the late 1890s. The couple had been living at the station house for about ten years and George Merwood, perhaps a relative, had been stationmaster. Emily Merwood adopted a white starched pinafore for her uniform, worn over a functional black dress, and a straw boater on her head. Various postcards were made of her, including one where she holds a staff. She was immensely proud of being in sole charge of the station. A ladies' journal of the time tells us that it would have been a brave man who would presume to offer Mrs Merwood assistance, so strong, capable and alert was she. Her civility was praised as being an example to all. Emily was a busy woman between trains, keeping the station clean, the flower beds and hedges neat, selling tickets, working the signals, answering the newly installed telephone and, in winter, keeping a good fire burning in the waiting room. She retired in 1912 aged 69, but continued to live at the station house with her husband and look after the new stationmaster, James Cooper. Emily died in 1929.

In 1912 a crossing loop was installed operated by an eleven lever signal frame. A new 242ft down-platform was built, complete with a second-hand shelter, possibly an old signal box from Wootton.

George Edwards became Whippingham's station-master in 1917. His daughter Marjorie Smith remembered, among other recollections of life at the station, that the young Louis Mountbatten used the railway just as an ordinary passenger. Other memories included the many, heated conversations between Whippingham Station and Newport 'A' signal box, where the signalman would often give preference to boats on the Medina River by opening the drawbridge rather than pass trains from Whippingham. She remembered helping her father to light the oil lamps along the platform at dusk and watching a fox trotting along the platform. These memories are recorded in *Once upon a line, Volume 4*, by Andrew Britton.

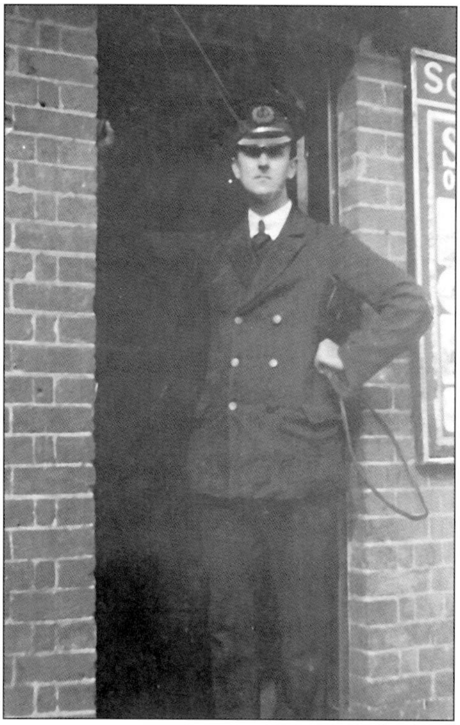

George Edwards waiting to hand over the single-line token to a train driver.

The Isle of Wight Central Railway was absorbed into the Southern Railway in 1923 and finally became part of British Railways upon nationalisation in 1948. The station was only to remain open for another five years, closing on 21st September 1953. Trains continued to run past the deserted platform on their way to Newport and Cowes. The loop was removed in 1956. Finally, the Ryde to Newport line fell under the Beeching axe and the last train passed Whippingham on 21st February 1966.

In 2017 the railway line from Whippingham to Wootton is a cycleway and popular footpath. Ideas are being considered to bring the railway back into operation.

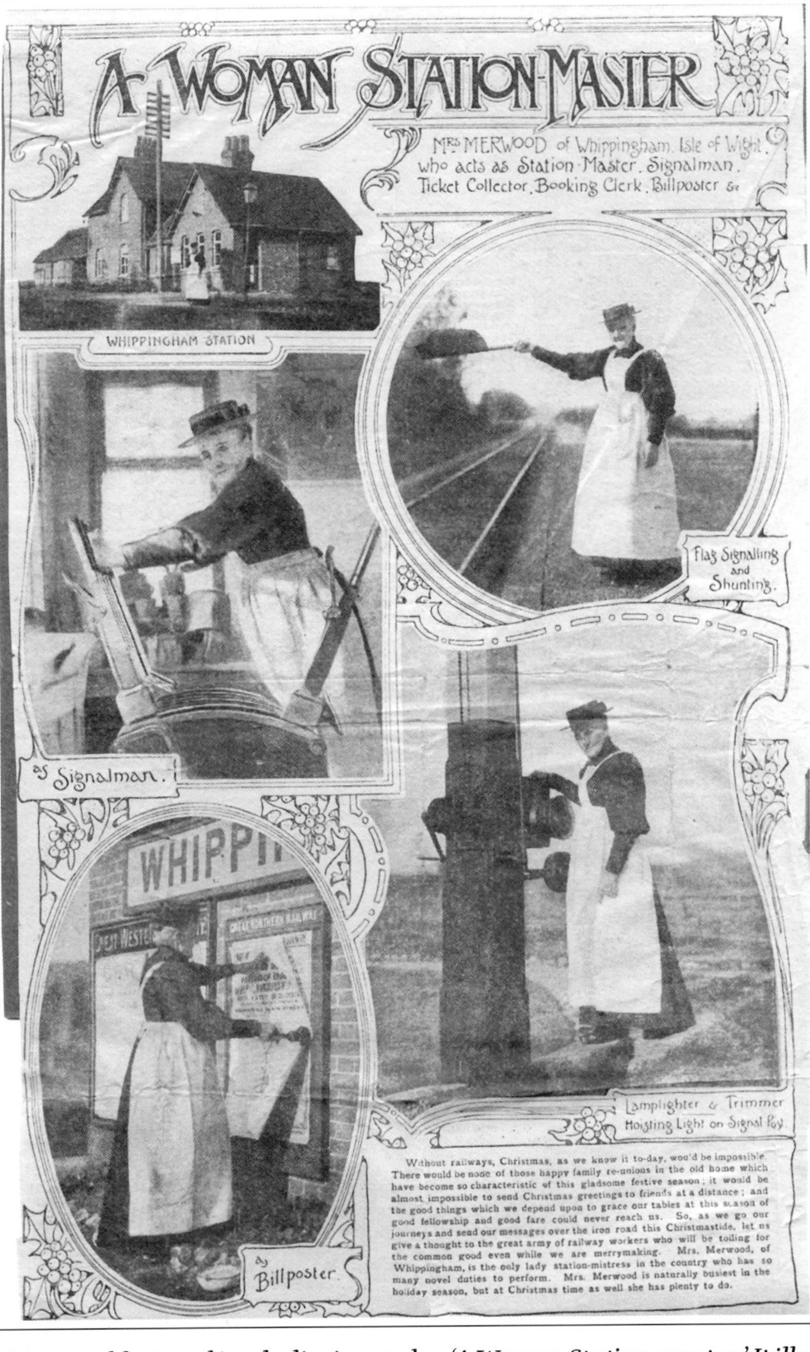

A Woman Station-Master

Mrs Merwood of Whippingham, Isle of Wight, who acts as Station-Master, Signalman, Ticket Collector, Booking Clerk, Billposter &c

Whippingham Station

as Signalman.

Flag Signalling and Shunting.

as Billposter.

Lamplighter & Trimmer Hoisting Light on Signal Post.

Without railways, Christmas, as we know it to-day, would be impossible. There would be none of those happy family re-unions in the old home which have become so characteristic of this gladsome festive season; it would be almost impossible to send Christmas greetings to friends at a distance; and the good things which we depend upon to grace our tables at this season of good fellowship and good fare could never reach us. So, as we go our journeys and send our messages over the iron road this Christmastide, let us give a thought to the great army of railway workers who will be toiling for the common good even while we are merrymaking. Mrs. Merwood, of Whippingham, is the only lady station-mistress in the country who has so many novel duties to perform. Mrs. Merwood is naturally busiest in the holiday season, but at Christmas time as well she has plenty to do.

Emily Merwood featured in a ladies journal as 'A Woman Station-master.' It illustrated all the tasks she had to perform to keep the station running.

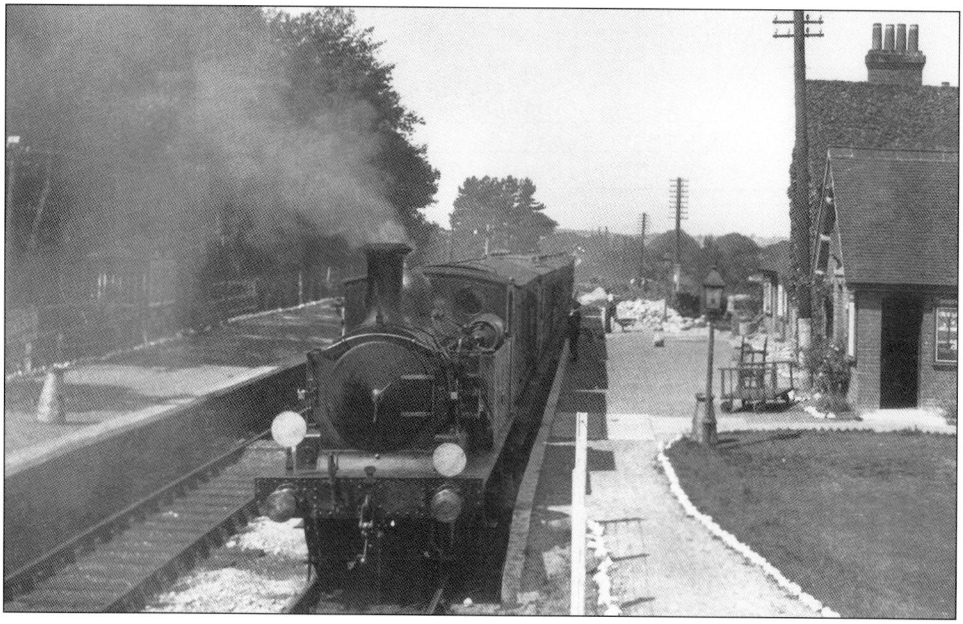

The train to Ryde at Whippingham Station in 1933. Note the milk churn standing on the opposite platform. (Andrew Britton Collection)

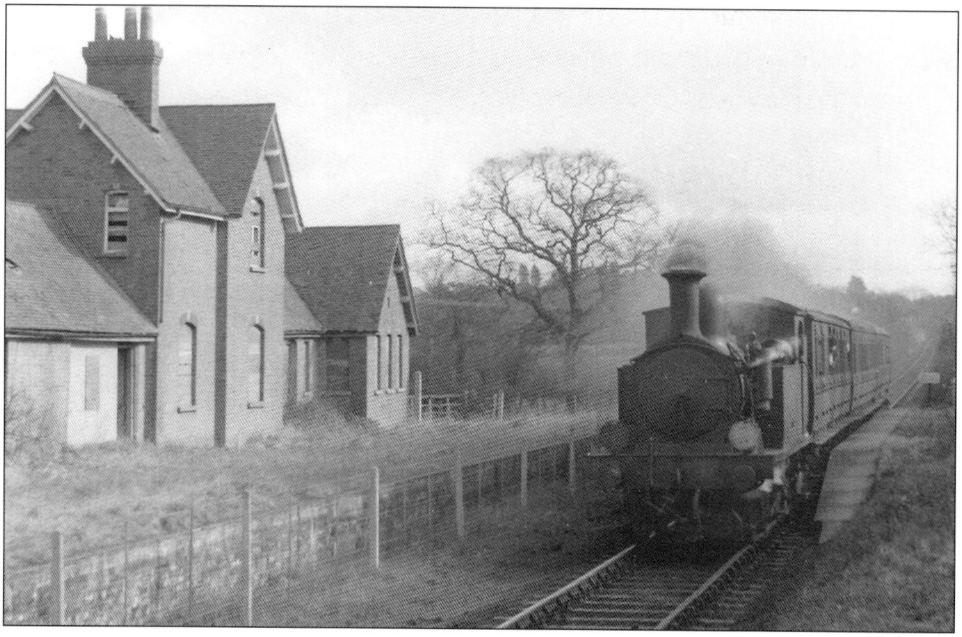

19th February, 1966. The 10.18 from Ryde passing the unused Whippingham Station two days before the closure of the line. (David Peters)

TWELVE

Sam Saunders & the Folly Works

In 1890 Sam Saunders was head of a firm constructing beautiful steam launches for wealthy people to use on the River Thames. He moved his centre of operations to west Cowes in 1901 and bought a redundant boat shed next to the esplanade in East Cowes in 1906 where he set about building fast petrol-driven launches for use in the Solent. The enterprise rapidly expanded and in 1935 the Columbine Factory was built on the site, which since 1977 has sported a huge Union Flag on its doors.

1906 was a time of rapid technological advances – man had just taken to the air and the internal combustion engine was improving all the time. Sam Saunders and his team of designers were developing new methods of travel.

The Heathfield Aircraft Sheds and airstrip

In 1909 Saunders formed a new department to design and build *'everything required for aero-navigation'*. He constructed two 6,000sq ft, lightweight aircraft hangars on the east bank of the Medina south of The Folly Inn. Today, you can walk south along the river bank from the caravan site, cross the stream by a wooden bridge, and enter the field which once housed the aircraft hangers next to the river. This field, part of Heathfield Farm, was large and flat enough for a rudimentary airfield to be made.

Sam was first involved in a surface-skimmimg hydrofoil designed by a Frenchman, Ravaud. Called the *Ravaud Aero-Hydroplane*, it was built at the Heathfield sheds in 1910, and must have caused a stir going up and down the Medina in tests early in 1911.

Sam had patented a very strong type of plywood sewn together with copper wire, called *Consuta*. It was used in the construction of not only his motor

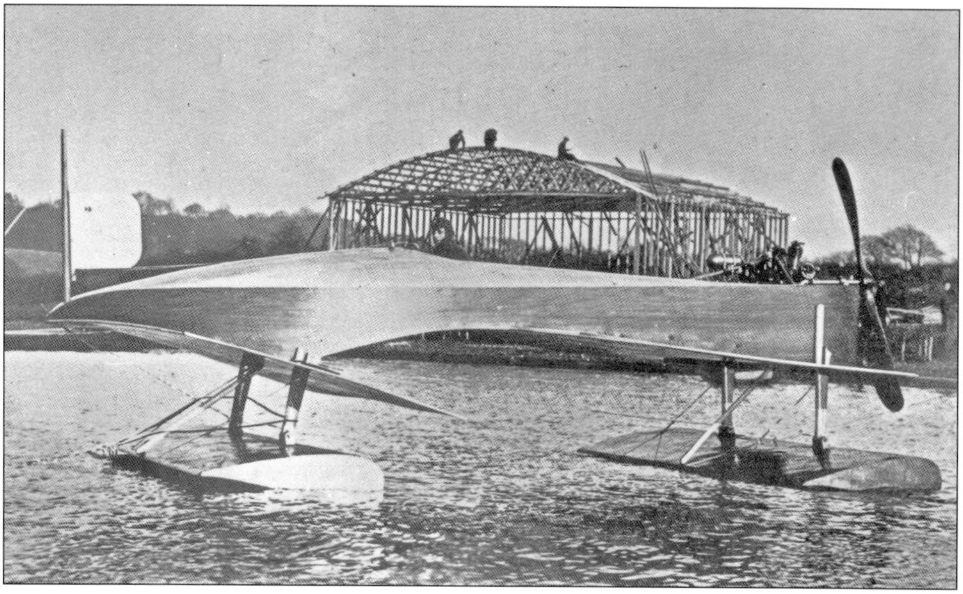

The Ravaud Aero-Hydroplane on the Medina in 1911. The aircraft hanger is being built in the background.

launches, but also of the floats and bodies of these early hydrofoils and seaplanes. *Consuta* was still being used in the 1930s.

In 1913, the *Sopwith Bat Boat* was assembled and tested from the Heathfield Sheds. Designed by Tommy Sopwith, it was the first successful European-built amphibious aircraft. Unfortunately it was left outside the shed one night and in unexpected strong winds the plane ended up upside down on the mud! It was soon mended and entered for the Mortimer Singer Flying Competition in 1913 with Harry Hawker as the pilot. This involved the *'planes making seven successive landings on land and on sea'.* Of all the planes entered, only the *Bat Boat* completed the course, and hence won the £500 first prize.

The *Bristol-Coanda No.120* was another plane assembled at the sheds. The original floats had proved to be too heavy, so *Consuta* ones were substituted. It flew on 15th April 1913, but the engine overheated and the plane crashed and disintegrated. The pilot, Harry Busteed was rescued.

Over 200 *AVRO 504s* were constructed by Saunders during the First World War. These were land-planes that used the Heathfield air-strip. In 1916 the sheds were dismantled. All that remains on the site today are the much-eroded vertical wooden planks that once held back the bank of the river beneath the sheds.

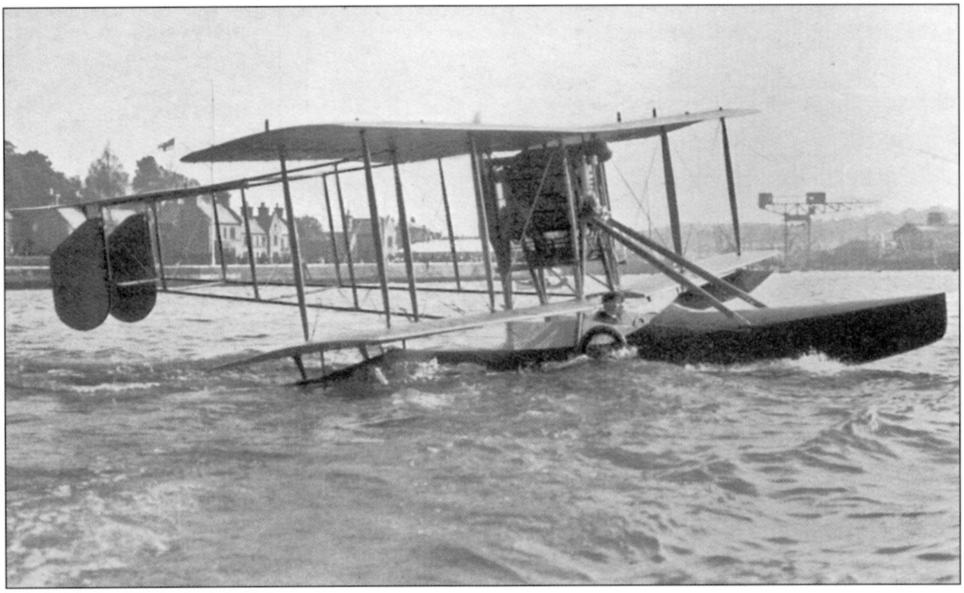

The Sopwith Bat Boat, the first amphibious aircraft in Europe.

Folly Works

In 1915, Sam Saunders bought the Padmore Estate for £6,000. The estate included the Queen Anne-fronted house, the lodge, cottage and stable block and land stretching down to the River Medina. Sam promptly sold 23 acres adjacent to the river to his company for £2,300.

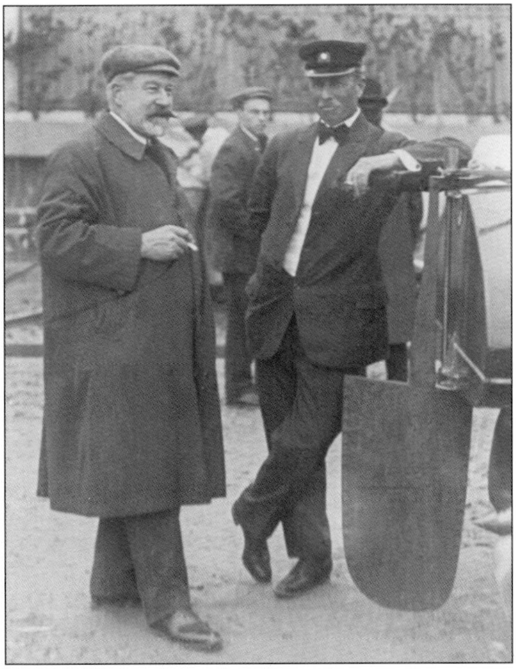

Sam Saunders and the Duke of Westminster in Monaco with the racing boat, Ursula.

Between 1916 and 1918 new wooden sheds were built at the Folly Works adjacent to the river. Saunders won a contract to assemble *Short 184* seaplanes. 30 of these were built for the Admiralty at a price of £81,000. The works had sliding doors fronting the river, with ramps for launching

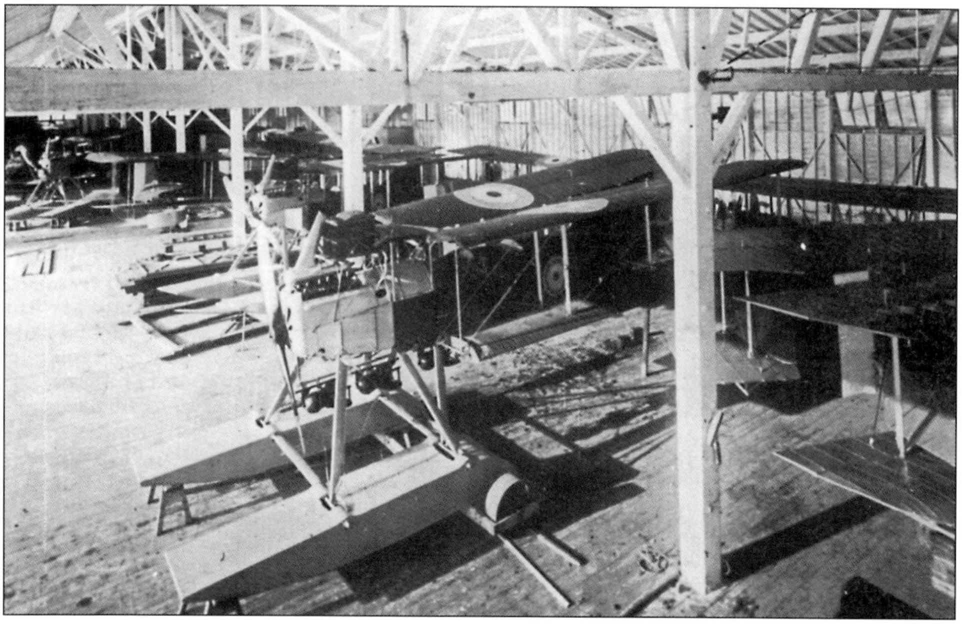

Short 184 seaplanes were constructed at the Folly Works site. They could be stored on ships with their wings folded.

the planes from any position along the factory. The remains of the concrete-reinforced river banks that were beneath this factory still exist in a somewhat crumbled state in 2017.

The Plywood Factory

The Folly Works became a major plywood factory as well as a manufacturing base when new sheds were constructed in 1919. The *Consuta* plywood made here was for general use, as well as for aircraft manufacture. The plywood factory was completed in 1921 at a cost of £43,905. The first superintendent of the new factory was Frederick Goatley.

Many of the workers were women, and this continued to be the case for subsequent years. Ada Carter, Fred's sister in law, was in charge of the girls, and she received the BEM in 1943 for her dedicated work.

Aircraft manufacture continued in the Folly Sheds during the 1920s and 1930s. In 1928, at the age of 78, Sam Saunders sold his shares in the company and Alliott Verdon Roe became the chairman. The company became known as Saunders Roe.

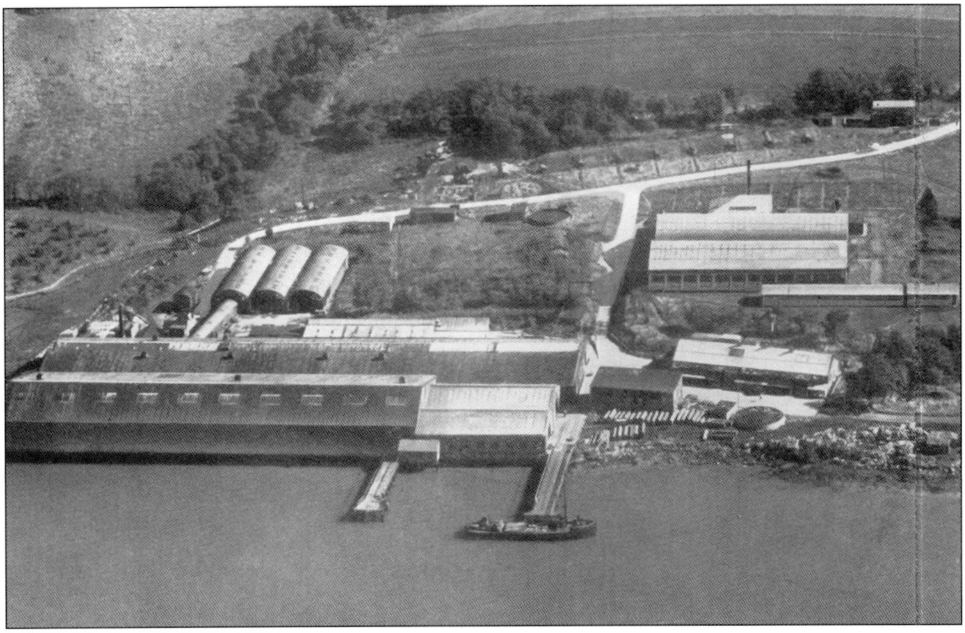

The Folly Works in the 1940s. Air raid shelters can be seen at the back of the site, each with a trench leading to the door.

Saunders Roe

Cutty Sark amphibious aircraft were built by the company, the wings being built at Folly Works in 1930. A total of 12 planes were built of this design, both for civil and military use.

A later design of sewn plywood manufactured at Folly was of three layers of wood, glued together with the direction of the grain at an angle to each other and reinforced by rows of stitching with a flax thread. Any thickness, from 1/16inch to 5/8inch, could be made and sheets up to 50ft long by 8ft wide. As glues improved, the need for stitching the wood diminished, and glue was applied either by large mechanical rollers or by sheets of 'film' glue being laid between each two sheets of veneer.

During the Second World War, Folly Works was producing 40% of the nation's plywood, much of it for aircraft construction. On the night of 4th May 1942 most of the reserve stock of plywood, which had been moved to 'safety', in the old college engineering sheds at Kingston, went up in flames when East Cowes was bombed. The government valued the work of the plywood factory so much that they installed a special power plant to ensure continuity of production should

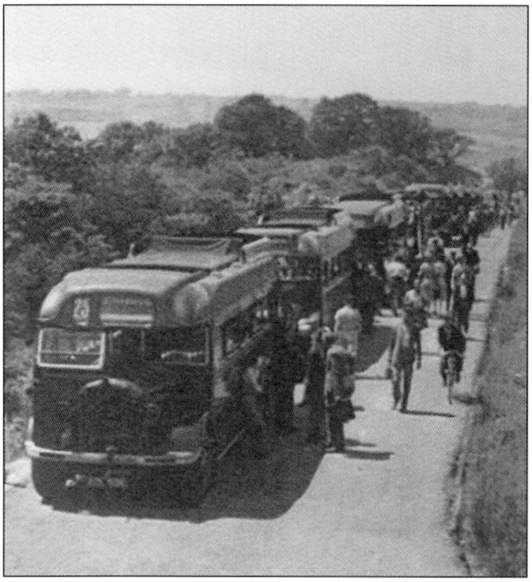

Buses in Folly Lane bringing workers to the site in the 1940s.

the main Island power station be damaged. There were two jetties which allowed barges to bring the veneers from the mainland ports and for the completed plywood to be shipped out to other factories. Railway tracks on site facilitated the loading.

Many of the workers required by the factory came by bus from further afield than Whippingham village. It was at this time that the road was widened around a big old oak tree, to allow the buses to pass one another. Until about 1900 there had been no road from Whippingham to The Folly. During the war, the shipyards and aircraft manufacturing works at East Cowes and Whippingham had first call on the Island buses. At one time 17 buses a day were bringing workers to the town from Ryde alone. Saro would provide their own bus drivers to cope with the early and late shifts, keeping the factories running 24 hours a day.

Dorothy Wilson remembered that working at the plywood factory was a very cold job during the winter months. She was employed to check the sheets of veneer for flaws. There were three shifts, the 6am-2pm, the 2-10pm and the night shift. They were on the night shift for three months at a time.

Many girls worked at the Folly Works, but there was little opportunity to mix with anyone other than personnel in your own workshop. The girls used to go to The Folly Inn for a welcome cup of tea. On a more sombre note, Dorothy watched the V1 doodlebugs flying over Fairlee, wondering where they would land.

The works had their share of high-explosive bombs, incendiaries and machine-gun attacks but very little time was lost as a result of these incidents. Despite a few casualties the spirit of the Saro team remained as high as ever. During one low-level attack by the Luftwaffe, the Saro Home Guard were credited as having damaged a Dornier with the factory's multiple anti-aircraft guns. The works fire brigade trained to a high standard and were provided with ample fire-

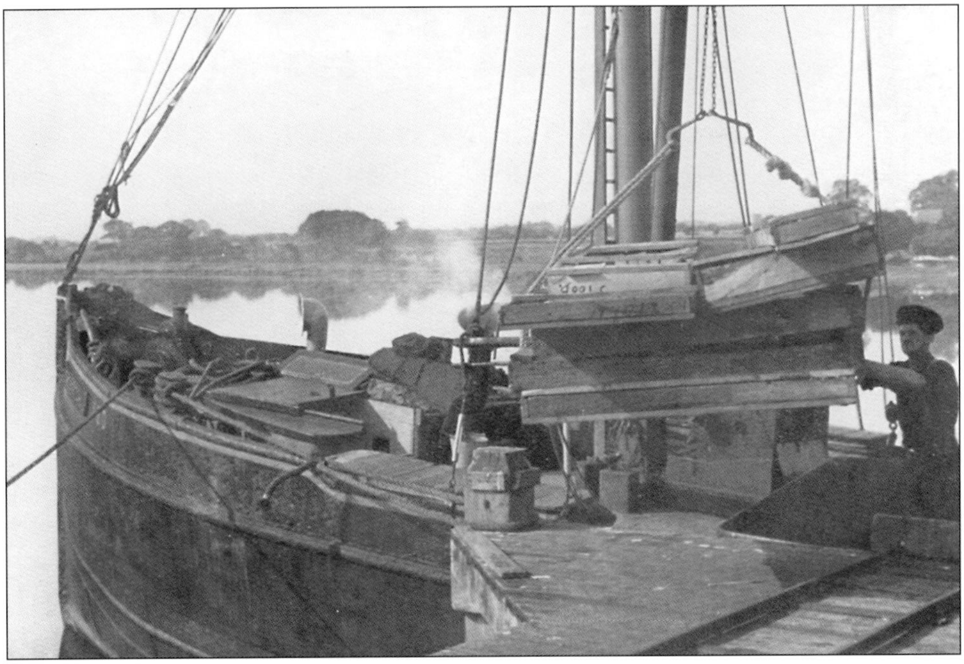

A cargo of veneers is unloaded from a barge in the 1940s.

fighting equipment and water storage in view of the highly inflammable stock of timber in the stores.

During the Second World War aircraft spars and pre-formed parts for aircraft were produced in great numbers. Prefabrication saved considerable time on the part of the aircraft constructors. Not only aircraft were made of plywood. Fred Goatley came out of retirement as Superintendent of Folly Works to design the collapsible two-man canoes needed for commando operations. The boats were used in Operation Frankton by the 'Cockleshell Heroes' and were built at Folly Works, as were a number of 16ft and larger folding assault-boats. Saro also produced plywood for air-sea rescue craft, motor launches and motor torpedo boats. The MTB decks were pressed in their full length of 75 feet.

After the Second World War more products were developed, from hockey sticks and golf clubs to plywood mouldings for train carriage finishes. The modern plant coated high-grade plywood with a hard gloss plastic which they designated *SaR-Ree Z*. The plywood was used for partitioning in offices, flats and factories. The part of the firm called Saro Structures went on to prefabricate aluminium roofs and domes, and radio masts, but this ceased trading in 1960.

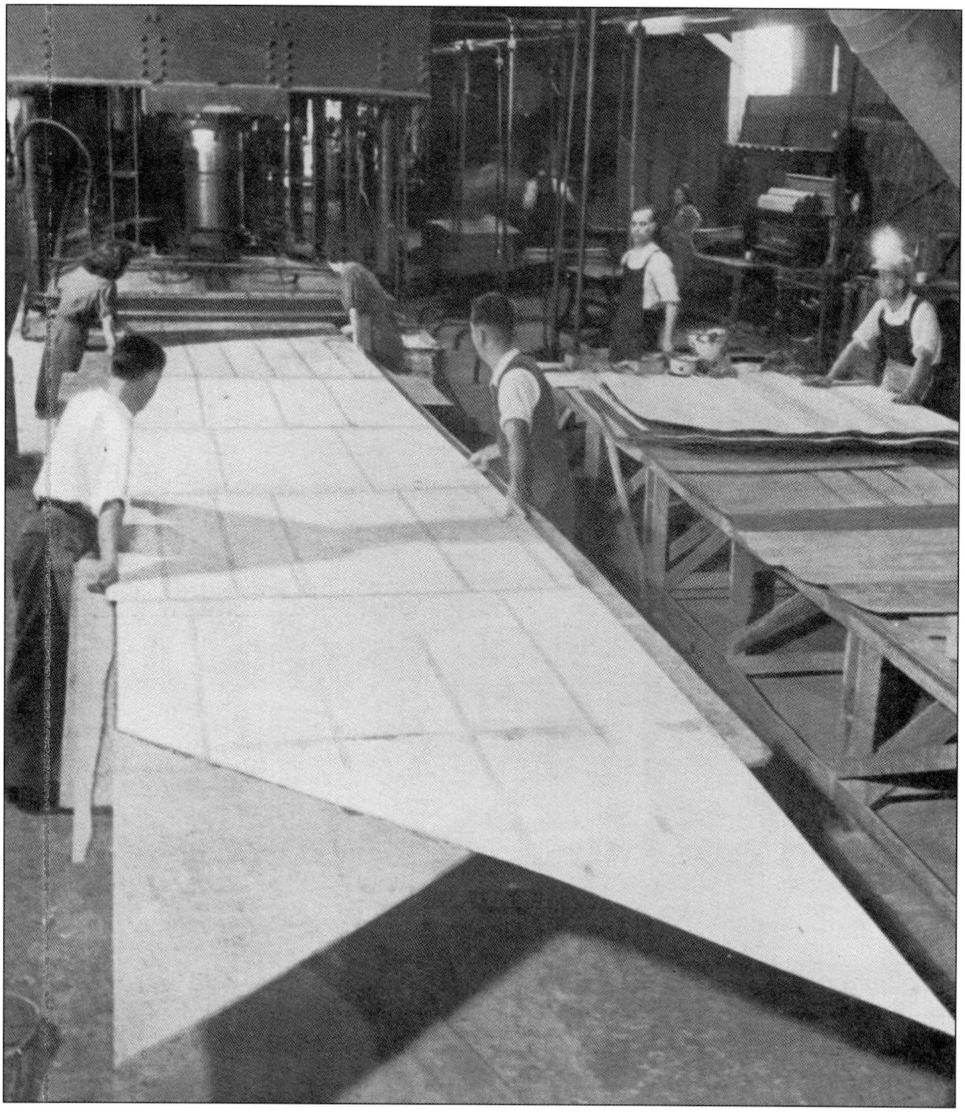

Plywood sections 75ft long, being constructed for motor torpedo boats during the war.

Plywood manufacture continued on this site until 1960, when a severe fire destroyed most of the works. Sue Rann at Old Post Office Cottage opposite the Forge feared the sparks would set light to her thatched roof, and Dorothy Wilson at King's Cottages by Barton Manor could see the red glow in the sky. The decision was taken not to rebuild the plywood factory, but instead to concentrate on the production of Thermo-plastics. Products such as linings for refrigerators

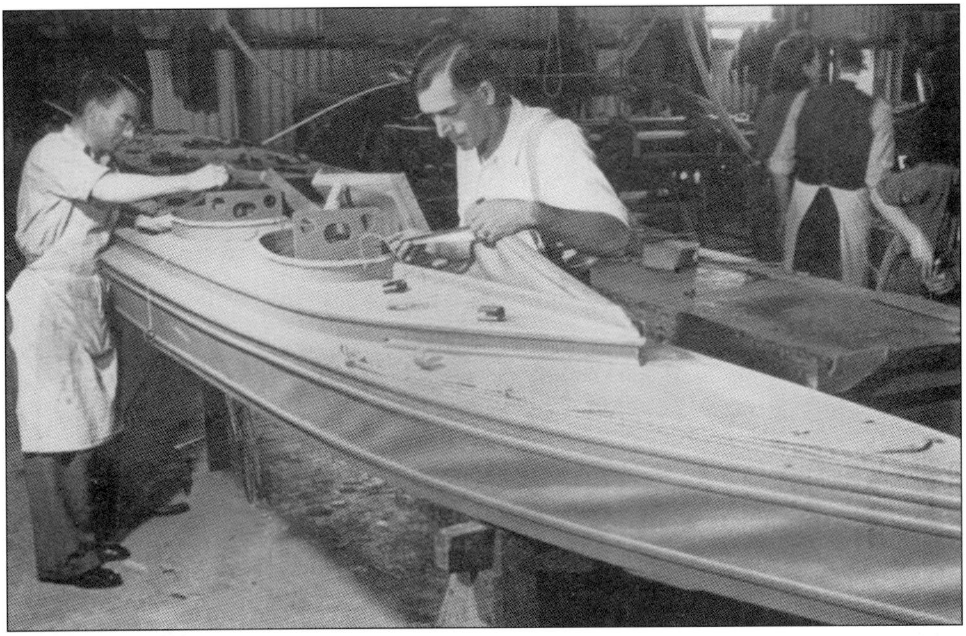

Two-man collapsible canoes which were used by Commando units such as in Operation Frankton were designed and built at the Folly Works.

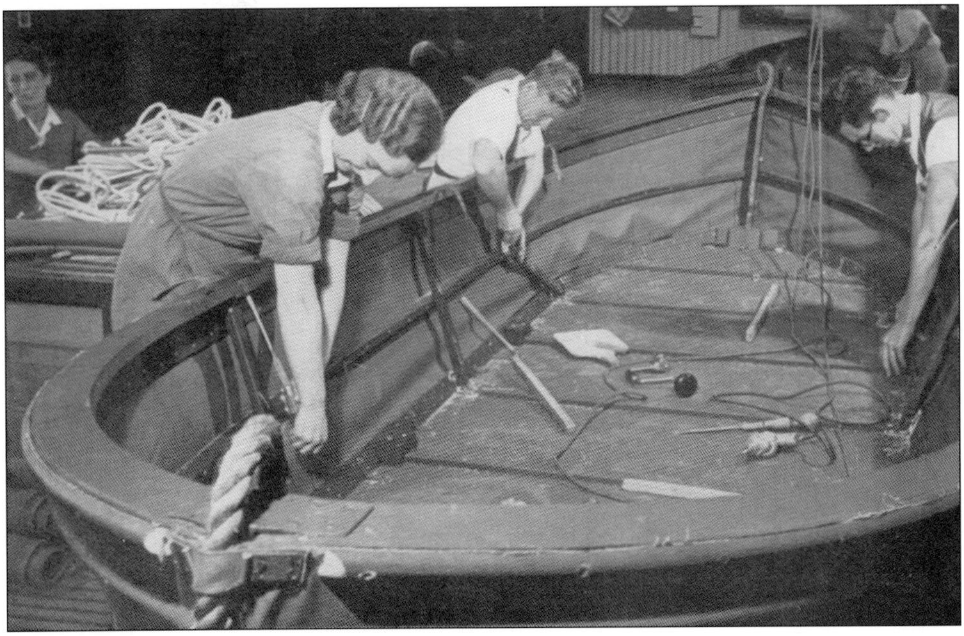

Canvas-sided assault boats were also produced here. Workers add the finishing touches before they leave the factory.

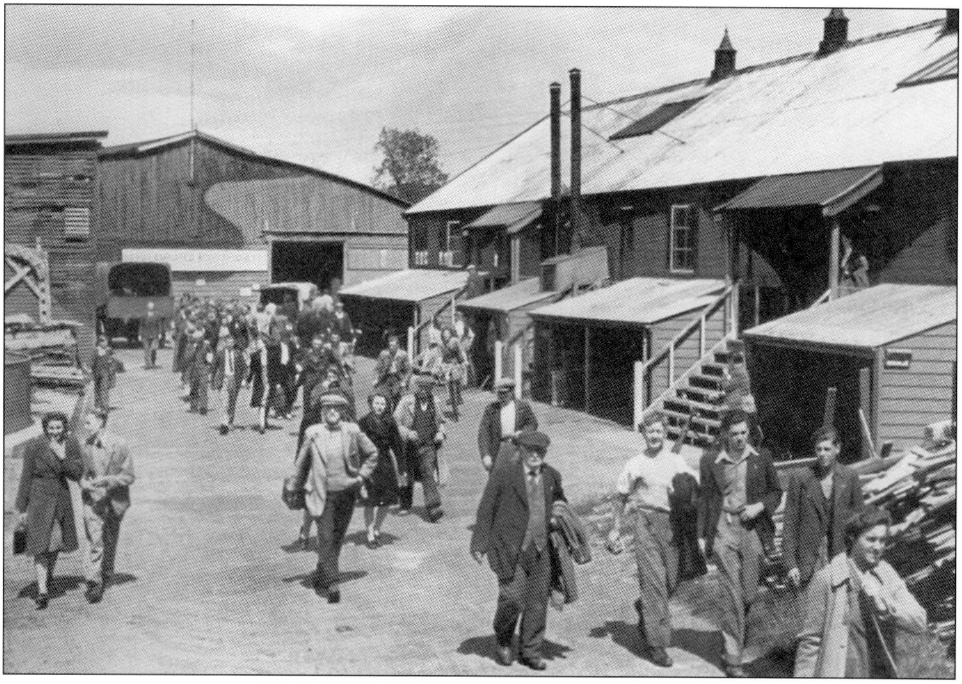

Workers leaving the wartime factory. Note the rudimentary camouflage to the wooden buildings.

and plastic punnets and boxes for retailing food were made. The factory finally closed its gates soon after 1993.

In 2017 the site is derelict. Plans have been approved for housing, a hotel and small business units but redevelopment has yet to start.

GKN Aerospace opposite Barton Manor

The company name on this Osborne Works site has changed from Saunders Roe via British Hovercraft, Westlands, GKN Westlands Aerospace to GKN Aerospace by 2017.

The workforce still deals with manufacturing components for the aircraft industry. These include engine nacelles, vanes, spars, winglets and a variety of other composite structures. The winglets have been proven to reduce fuel consumption. The chances are that the next time you fly, part of the aircraft may have been built here on the Island.

In combination with the GKN Falcon Works in East Cowes, there is a self-contained design, manufacturing, certification and maintenance facility. Products

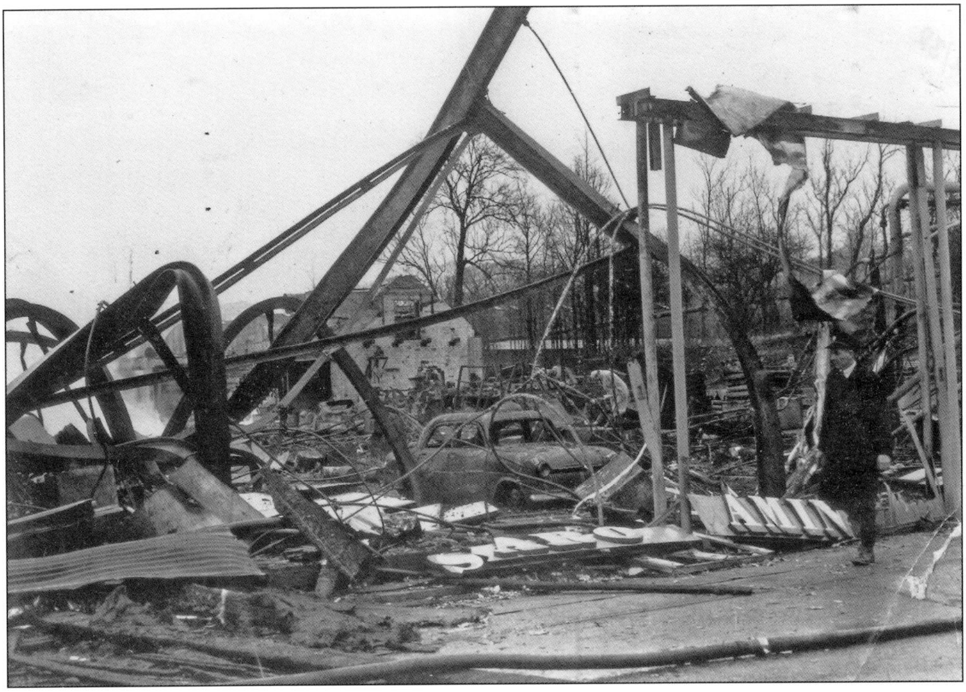

The aftermath of the fire in 1960. The Saro sign lies broken on the ground amongst the twisted metal spars.

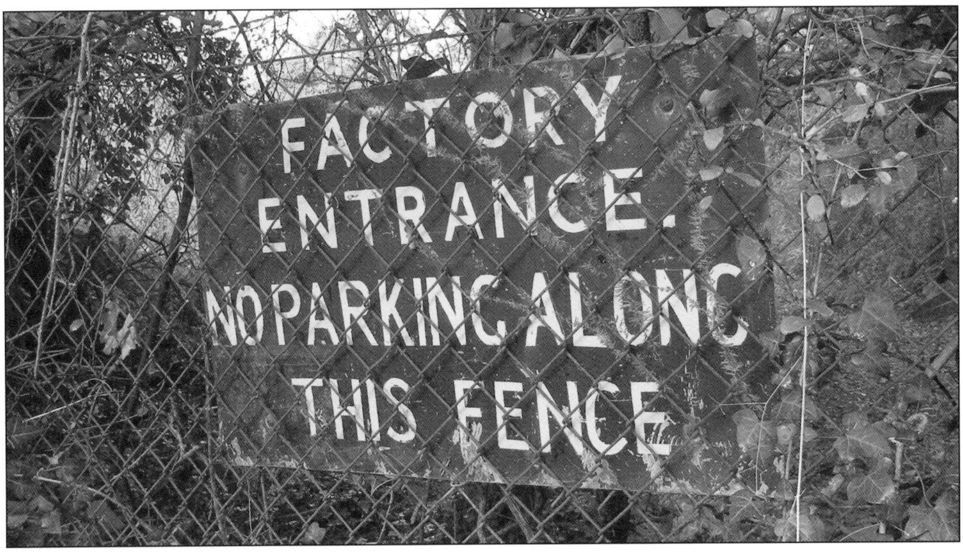

A sign remains on a fence in Folly Lane showing the location of one of the entrances to the Folly Works.

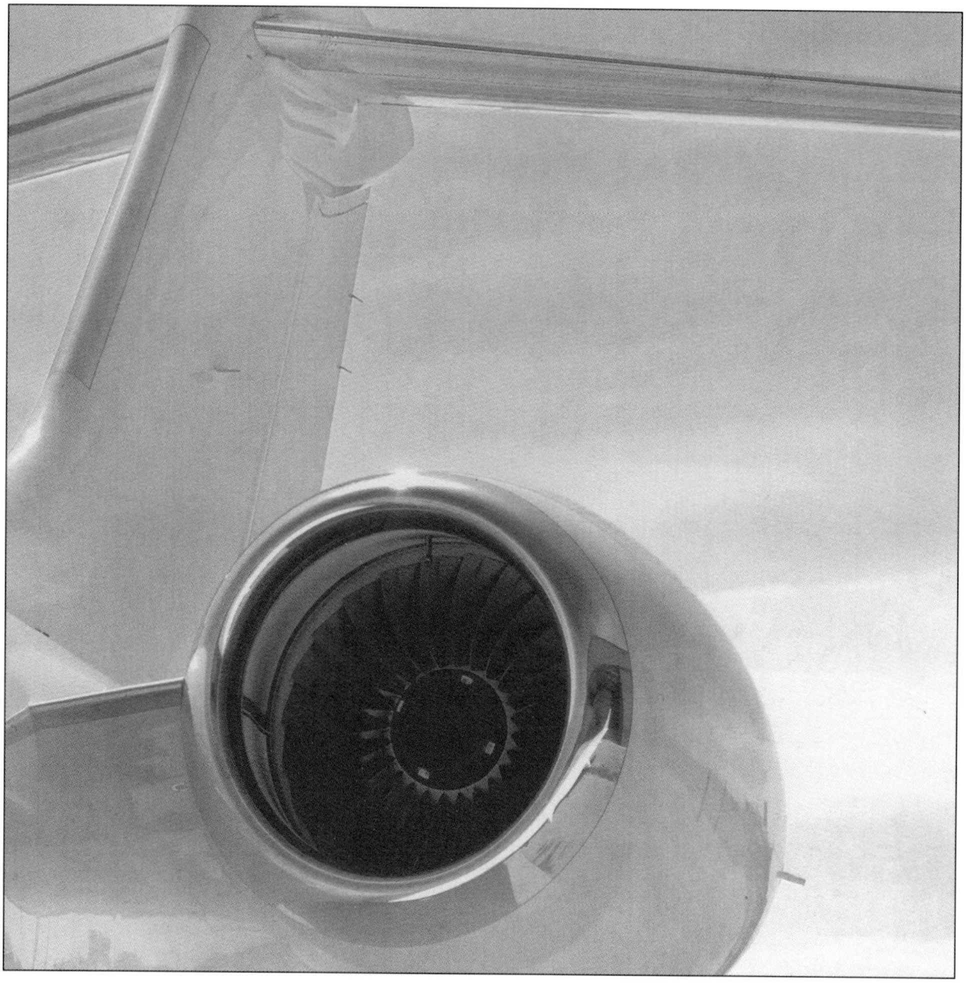

The GKN factory produces components for many of the world's commercial and military aircraft. The Bombardier Challenger 350 nacelle and pylon is shown here.

are made for companies such as Westland, Airbus, Boeing, Bombardier, Lockheed Martin and Rolls Royce. In 2010 around 900 people worked for the firm between the two sites, and there was a turnover of £148 million.

Advanced composite test facilities, autoclaves, and inspection equipment are installed at Osborne Works together with a Composites Research Centre, which is focussing on reducing the costs of composites through automation.

World class innovation and expertise in the aviation industry continues to exist here in Whippingham.

THIRTEEN

Royal Naval College Hospital

In 1903 the Royal Naval College Osborne opened. The college buildings were based around the stable block of Osborne House. Boys were admitted from the age of 13 years and spent two years here training to be officers before going on to Britannia College, Dartmouth. These officer cadets were given a good grounding in engineering at the Kingston workshops by the river with the intention of broadening their basic training in the hope of encouraging more boys to become engineering officers in the 'modern' navy and breaking down the existing social distinctions.

Among the cadets at the Naval College were several Royals. Future Kings Edward VIII and his brothers Albert, (George VI), and George, Duke of Kent, were at Osborne College, as was their cousin who later became Lord Louis Mountbatten, Admiral of the Fleet. They were among 4,000 naval cadets to be marched along the Cadet's Walk that crossed the Kingston Farm fields between the college and the riverside workshops.

While entry at 13 years old may have been a success, it meant that many boys started Osborne College straight from home tuition or small preparatory schools. Most had not had the opportunity to mingle with large numbers of their age group and consequently were vulnerable to many infectious diseases. A boy had only to return to the college carrying, for example, measles, for the whole of his class to catch it, with the likelihood of it spreading to other classes very rapidly.

As a direct result of a 'flu epidemic that spread through the college in 1910, resulting in 260 cases, it was decided that more hospital accommodation was required. So that year the 'Infectious Hospital' was constructed for the college

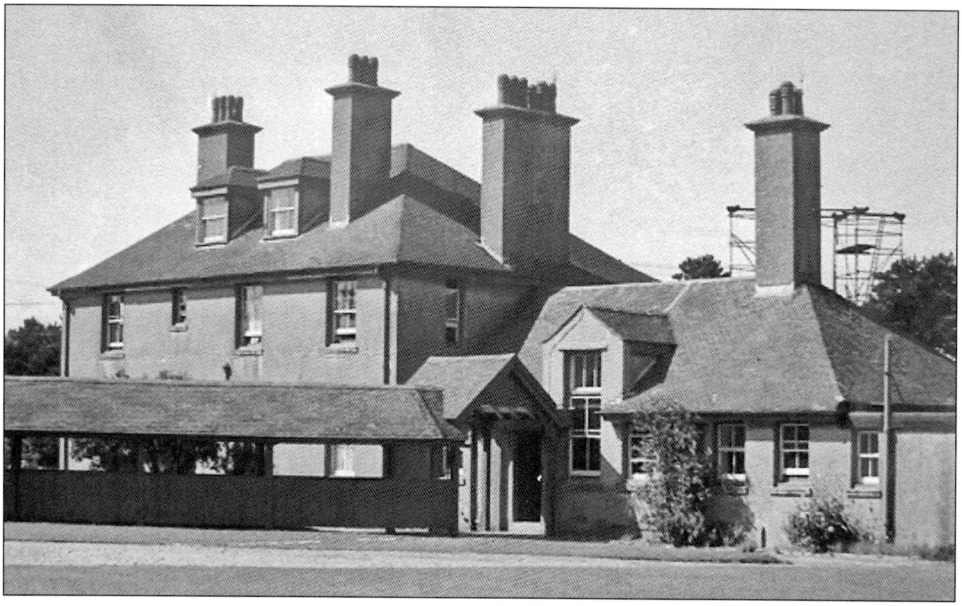

Staff accommodation for the Royal Naval College Hospital, pictured in 1956 when it housed Saunders Roe employees.

on fields opposite the gates to Barton Manor. Crown Estates transferred the land to the Admiralty and by 1915 there were four light and airy wards each capable of taking 20 boys. A substantial house was also added for the staff accommodation.

Cases of influenza, measles, German measles, mumps, and chicken pox were among those treated. The numbers of these could be alarmingly high. In 1911, for instance, there were 383 cases of infectious disease recorded, out of a total number of 440 cadets. In 1915, when a question was asked in the House of Commons, there were 136 cadets on the sick list that week. 106 presented with influenza, 12 with measles, 10 had conjunctivitis, five pneumonia, two with mumps and one had tonsillitis, among some 330 cadets present at college. The worst epidemic was in 1917 when a particularly virulent strain of measles struck. A considerable number of cadets succumbed to the disease, accompanied by broncho-pneumonia, which sadly caused six deaths. Three of these boys were buried at Whippingham Church.

According to the memoirs of Osborne cadets, many had experiences of the hospital and the boys were unanimous in their praise. The nursing staff were very efficient and looked after the boys well. Michael Partridge in his book *The Royal Naval College Osborne-A History 1903-21* includes some of these memories.

'The nursing was very good, they took great care to see that we were properly looked after whilst we had 'flu and in the post-'flu conditions, too, [they] made quite certain we were rehabilitated. They were very good nursing staff, I think. The surgeons were good too.'

'At the end of 1918 ...there was a terrible outbreak of 'flu. ...practically everyone went down with 'flu. Aspirin had just been invented and one of our really clever naval surgeons who was there insisted we were given aspirin and that did undoubtedly save a lot of lives...'

In 1921 it was decided to close the Naval College as Dartmouth now had sufficient capacity to house all the cadets required for the post-war navy. In 1934 many of the college buildings in the Osborne grounds were demolished.

The Infectious Hospital was valued at about £30,000 in 1921. The Admiralty was still working on 1914 prices so was not quite sure of the value. The hospital was just about to get a new lease of life.

East Cowes Holiday Camp

From 1927 to 1939 the Royal Naval College Infectious Hospital buildings were leased to be used as a holiday camp. The proprietor was Mr Allnatt, and his first intent had been to lease the Osborne Naval College buildings themselves for use as a camp. He offered to buy the whole college site in 1930 as long as he could have access to the sea at Osborne Bay, which was refused. The intention was to run a college for foreign university students, especially Austrian and German but the idea came to nothing.

Numerous young factory workers, school groups, church groups and youth organisations brought parties of youngsters here for an annual holiday at the old hospital site. Many of the youngsters were from London, so it must have been a wonderful experience for them to wake up in the countryside and walk through fields. The four hospital wards were used as dormitory accommodation, with the main house for the dining rooms and classrooms. Groups as large as 170 with nine teaching staff could be accommodated. Three of the Naval College dormitory blocks at Osborne were also rented in 1929 and this is probably how they put up a group of around 350 young people from Staffordshire.

Miss Allnatt, the daughter of the proprietor, was the camp nurse. She was described in one testimonial as *"so fascinating that any scratch was excuse enough to visit her!"* The manager was Dick Oldham, he took every care to make the holiday a delightful experience for everyone who stayed there. In the words of the captain in charge of the 1st Walthamstow Girls Brigade, *"He is a wonderful man, who is always sought after, always helping someone. His good nature is infectious and his helpers have caught it, the popularity of his staff is marvellous and every one of them is a friend."* Mr Oldham lived in the lodge, now demolished, opposite Barton Manor gates.

The cook was very highly praised in every letter. *"The food, both in the cooking and the quantity, have been of the very best." "The food - words fail to express our appreciation!" "Perfectly cooked and served up."*

Because the camp was in permanent buildings and the catering was supplied, life was perfect for these youth groups. They could make their own entertainment in the grounds. Football posts were erected in the field, which was large enough for several different games to take place at once and there was a small swimming pool. Groups could go for walks in the countryside and Osborne House was handy to visit.

Parties of children could walk down to the seafront to swim. Even groups of the Hitler Youth Movement stayed here, marching down to East Cowes beach from the camp, singing as they went. Mr Oldham would arrange coaches for outings to places more distant if required.

Mr Othen and his son, Frank, were running the eight-acre market garden to the south of the site. The swill from the holiday camp went to feed the 200 pigs they kept there, along with 300 fowls. These were fattened up for Christmas. Mrs Othen also worked in the market gardens. They had a round in East Cowes delivering fresh vegetables by horse and cart on Wednesdays and Saturdays. Some of the vegetables went to the holiday camp.

Young Frank Othen would go to Whippingham Station on a Friday with the horse and cart taking the bags and cases of the departing youngsters, who would walk to the station. He would then collect the luggage of the next visitors. Frank particularly remembered the girls from Cadbury's chocolate factory staying at the camp.

Several groups came back year after year. The young people so enjoyed the experience that the staff knew it was worthwhile. Many of these youngsters would have no other holiday, and would have spent a year saving up to be able to come. One of the groups, described as a welfare party, was from the firm Guest, Keen and Nettlefolds Ltd. of Birmingham. The firm who now operates from this Osborne Works site under their initials - GKN.

After the 1939 summer season, the holiday industry ceased to exist on the Isle of Wight as it became a prohibited area during the war. The Infectious Hospital was about to adapt to a third role.

Osborne Works – SARO to GKN

In 1941 the old Infectious Hospital site, of the Naval College, was taken over by Saunders-Roe, (SARO). They were given the use of the site for wartime production by the Ministry of Aircraft Production. Additional buildings were added at this stage for use by the firm. A raised aircraft-spotting post, to warn of air attacks, was built at the north-west corner of the site.

Some first toe holds on the hospital grounds had been achieved in 1939 when permission had been granted for the Saro Rugby Club to use the pitch west of the site. Saro Laminated Wood Products (SLWP) Sports Club were allowed a football pitch. The buildings opposite Barton Manor gates were called the Osborne

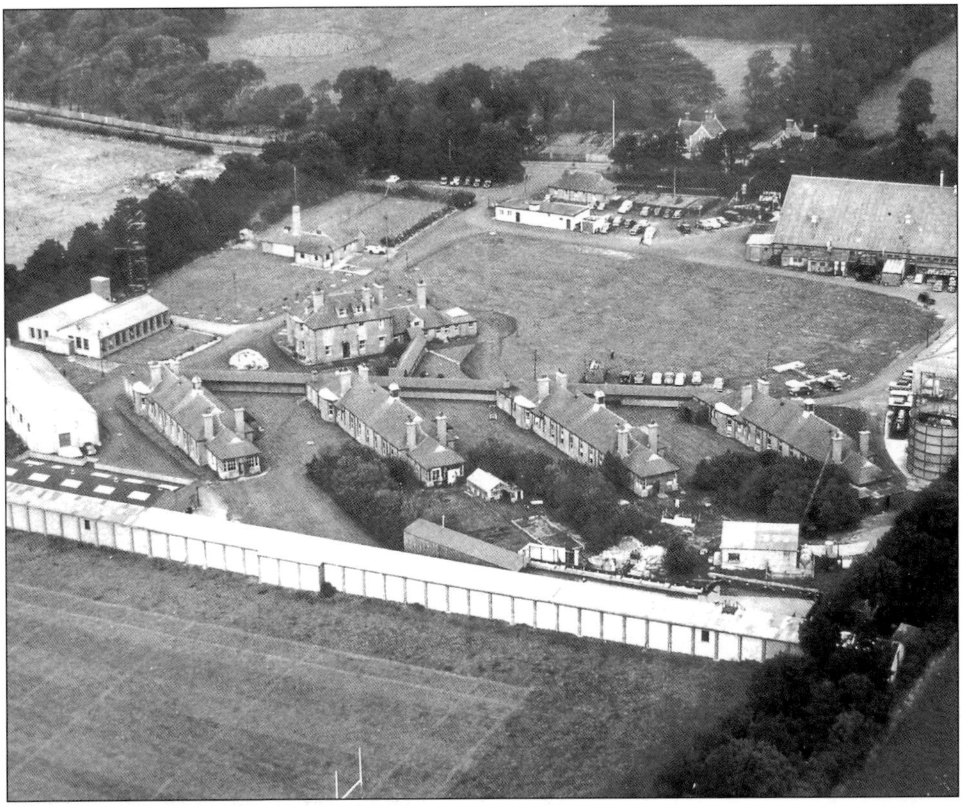

The Osborne Works site in the early 1960s.

Works. This caused some confusion as SARO also had its head office and design department at the Osborne House stables. After the war SARO leased these sites from Crown Estates.

Test Facilities

Hydrodynamic development of flying-boat hulls and high-speed craft led to a requirement for test facilities. Those created here at Whippingham were probably some of the most comprehensive in the country outside of government establishments.

The first indoor test tank for seaplanes and boats was constructed at the site in 1947. It was 618ft long, 8ft wide and had a mobile carriage running on rails over the water surface. The carriage not only supported the model plane or boat, but also up to four observers. The models, up to 6ft long, could be moved through the water at a speed from 0.05 feet per second up to 43 feet per second, (30mph).

The second tank, the 'Ditching Tank' which opened in 1950, was an open-air facility. It had a large gravity-operated catapult at one end, so that models could be launched at variable speeds, angles or rates of descent into a large tank of water and the results recorded.

The third, an indoor test tank, was built in 1956. 250ft long by 12ft wide, it had a monorail inside capable of moving an unmanned carriage at speeds of up to 50 feet per second, (34mph). All the sensor information was immediately relayed back to a central control console at the side of the tank. The operator not only controlled the model, but also had all the data presented to him immediately on dials and pen recorders. Another building housed a wind tunnel where

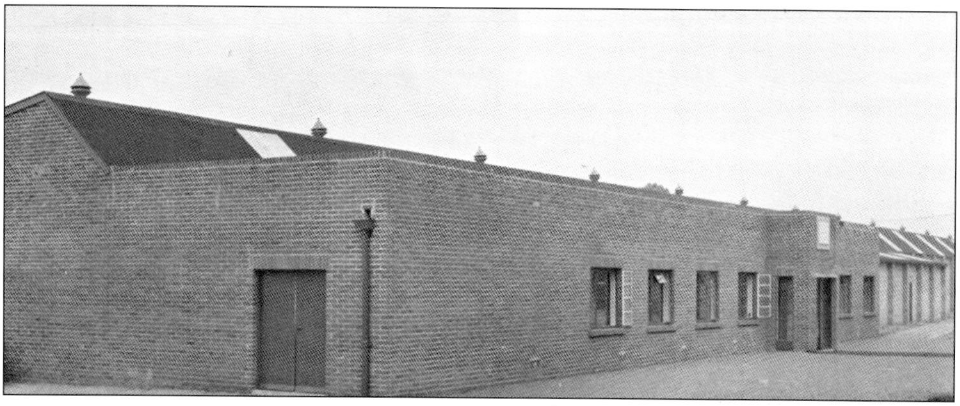

The third test facility, with a test tank, built at the Osborne Works site in 1956.

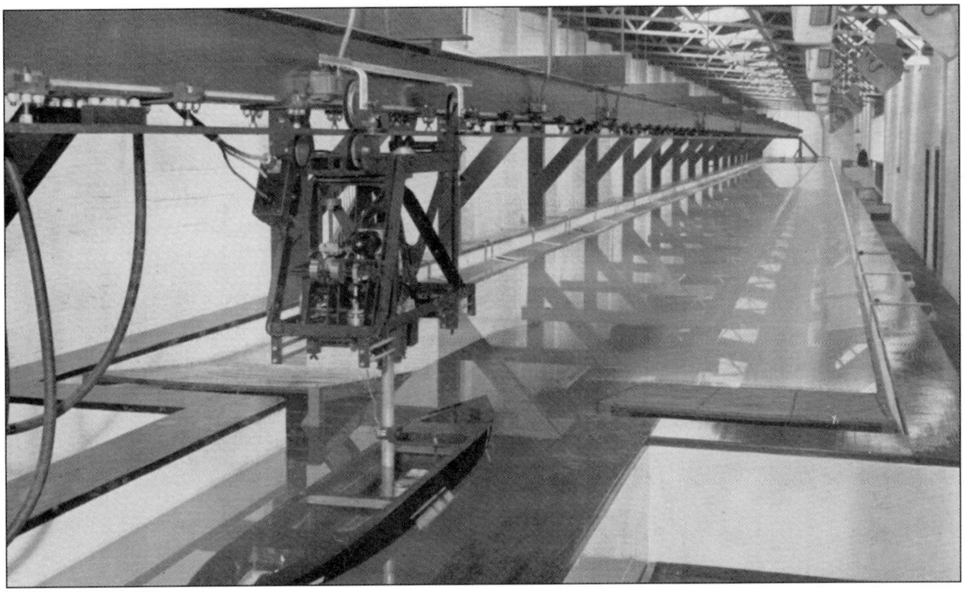

Inside the 250ft-long test tank. Models could be run at speed and tested thoroughly before full-scale production.

aerodynamic testing of models was carried out, the air flow eventually provided by a jet engine in the early 1950s.

In addition to these facilities the company also developed free-flight radio-controlled models so that other characteristics of the craft could be studied. Research and development facilities were set up in additional sheds. Equipment was installed for testing structures for vibration, fatigue and static loading on a rig known as the 'Elephant' together with the metallurgical testing of materials. For operations requiring a vacuum a large autoclave was installed in the main test house, which was also the home to the highly skilled model makers. Testing was also done on hydraulic and electrical systems. In fact all the 'behind the scenes' tests that need to be carried out before an aircraft part takes to the air took place at Whippingham.

In addition to the work for SARO, the research team at Osborne Works carried out work on a commercial basis for other companies. An example of this was the fatigue cycle testing of *Comet* fuel tanks for De Havilland after the early *Comet* disasters.

A full-size mock-up was built of the enormous *Princess* flying-boat fuselage in the late 1940s. This was housed in the largest shed at Osborne Works. When the managing director visited the mock-up his only comment was that the unusual spiral staircase between the two passenger lounges should be altered, because it had 13 steps. The designers had to work out how to fit a 14th step in.

A large cylindrical tank, quite a landmark, rather like a small gasometer, was built next to the eastern dormitory. This was used to pressure test, under water, the *Princess* fuselage and, later, the *Comet* fuel tanks. A smaller tank was built to test the *SR.53* and the *SR.177* fighter-jet cockpits. Also on the site in the late 1950s was a storage facility for the highly volatile rocket fuel HTP (High Test Peroxide) requiring very special precautions.

The Saunders Roe Apprentices School

Apprentices were an important part of the firm and facilities were soon made available at the Osborne Works for their training in the old hospital wards. The apprentices during war-time were generally local Isle of Wight lads, who would live at home. Any mainland apprentices during the war lived in digs in the town. An apprenticeship lasted five years.

Mr V T Stevenson was superintendent of training from 1940. In 1945 he improved the indentured apprenticeship scheme such that it became recognized in the industry as second to none. Apprentices attended technical colleges, and a full range of night schooling was provided and promising lads were encouraged to take university degrees. Stevenson played a great part in establishing the Isle of Wight Technical College, which opened in 1951. He retired in 1978.

In 1945 the Saunders-Roe Group Technical College and Apprentice Residential Centre was established. Initially this used two of the old hospital wards as dormitories with the Surgeon's house used as a dining room and accommodation for Stevenson's family. The remaining wards were turned into classrooms or workshops and the disinfection block was utilised as a hobby room.

'Pop' Stevenson, V T's father, was one of the instructors at the SARO Training School. He, and the other instructors, such as Frank Daltry, ran the workshop where the apprentices learned to achieve precision with the use of hand tools. There were also small machine tools for instruction in the basics of metal machining.

'Pop' was always ready to help the lads with their hobbies and past-times and, as he lived on site, he was always kept busy at weekends and evenings.

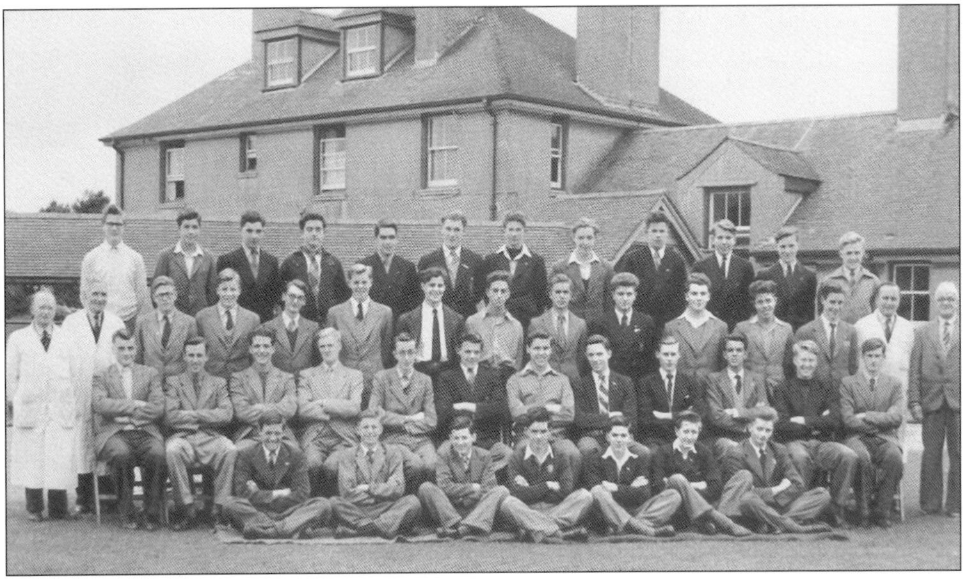

The 1954 intake of apprentices.

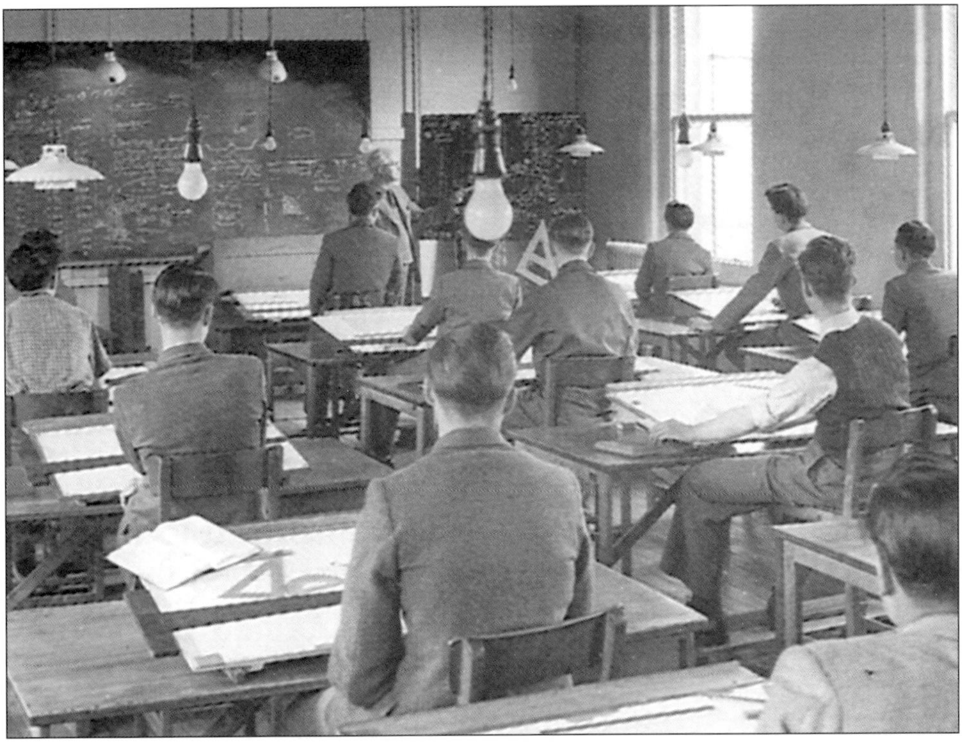

'Pooge' Saunders teaching technical drawing at the school around 1956.

Rosa Stevenson, VT's wife, supported her husband by running the apprentices' hostel. Her role would best be described as 'matron', but this title does little justice to her many tasks.

The number of apprentices increased sharply in the early fifties, when a third hospital ward was converted into another dormitory. The capacity of each dormitory was about 28 lads, utilising the side rooms for older apprentices and the single rooms for prefects. About 84 apprentices could be 'living in' and extra accommodation was developed for other seniors at Millfield House in East Cowes. A gymnasium and common-room were added in 1954.

Generally the hostel was a very happy place. In the mid-fifties the lads paid 30s for their keep out of their, initial, weekly wage of 45s, but they had to pay extra for their lunches and laundry, or do their own. Many of them received a small grant from the Ministry of Labour and National Service.

Ron Scruby, Chaplain to SARO Company in 1953, organized many activities for the apprentices, including football, rowing and trips to Loch Rannoch in Scotland. Two new gigs were constructed, *Ebb* and *Flo*. With these boats the lads were able to take part very successfully in local gig races. These included the 'The Head of the River' for all apprentices in Cowes. Other gig races were for the 'S E Saunders Cup', the 'Arthur Gouge Cup' and the 'Folly Challenge Cup'.

Roy Jones joined the training school staff in the early 1960s and became training manager in 1978 after V T Stevenson's retirement.

Due to the general malaise of the British aircraft industry after 1957, there was a gradual reduction in numbers of apprentices taken on by the company. The hostel closed its doors to residents in 1974 and the old hospital wards and Surgeon's house were demolished in the late 1990s. During its years as a training establishment, over 1,100 lads served their apprenticeship at Saunders Roe. These lads, trained in Whippingham, were to go on to become the renowned designers of planes, rockets and hovercraft, and experts in aircraft and other engineering disciplines.

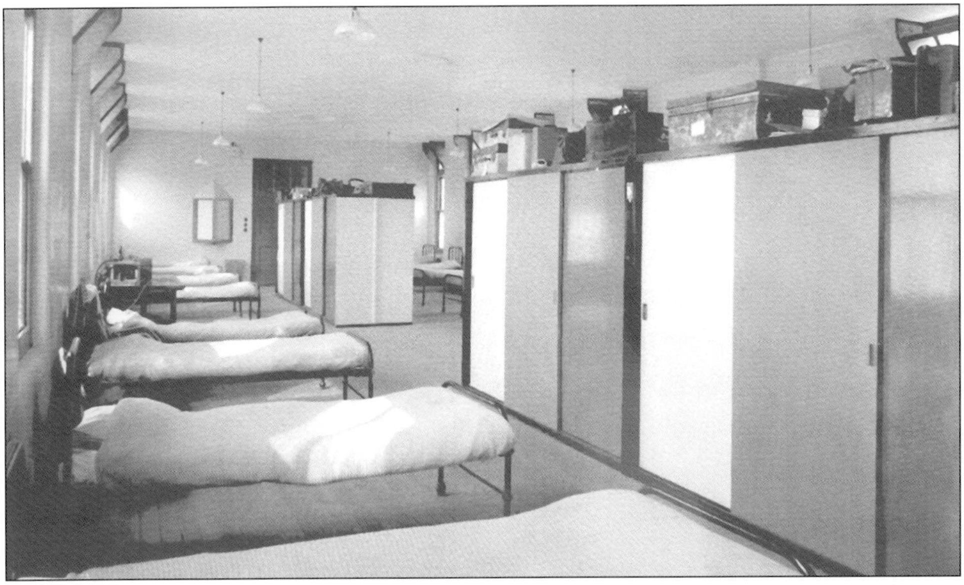

One of the dormitories for the apprentices around 1956.

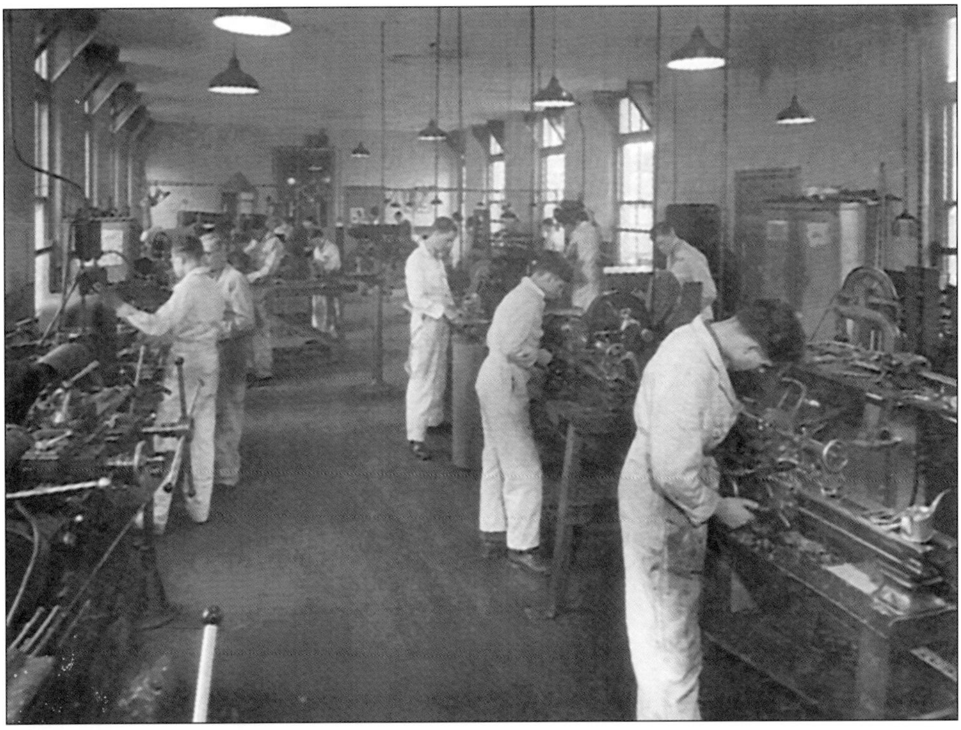

One of the old hospital wards was used as the training workshop.

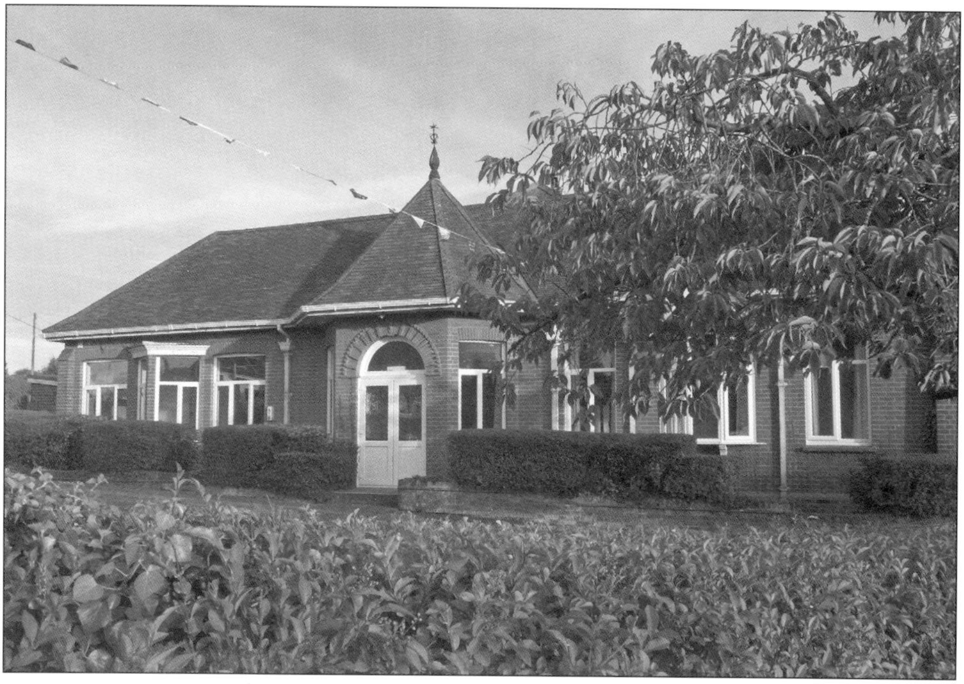

The Community Hall, built for Whippingham by Sam Saunders in 1931.

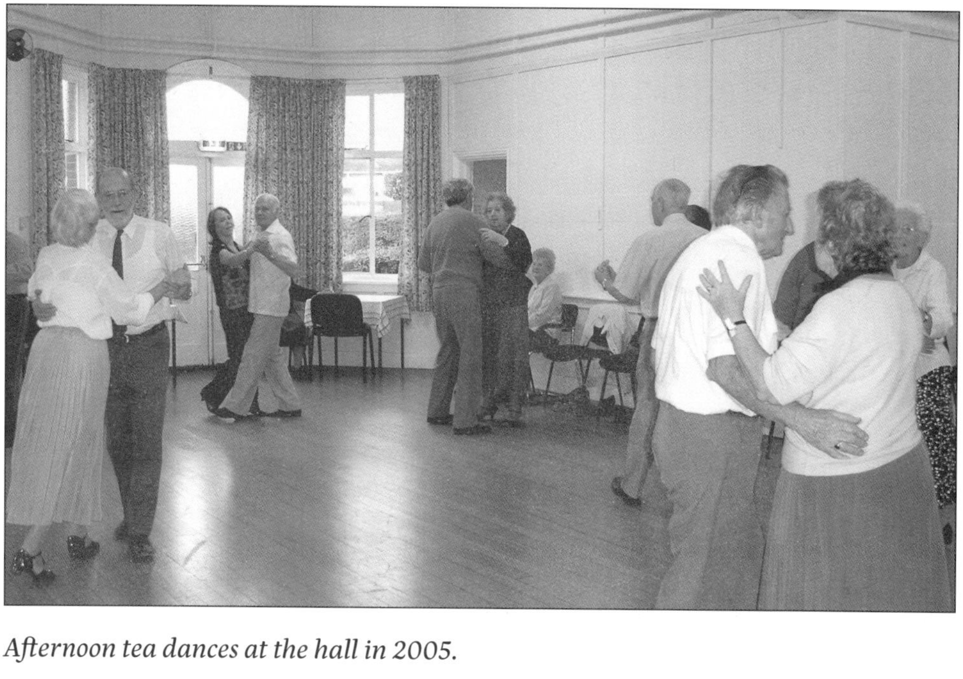

Afternoon tea dances at the hall in 2005.

Fourteen

The Community Hall

In 1930 Sam Saunders wished to present Whippingham Church with a church hall. The Vicar decided not to accept the building unless it was accompanied by a £5,000 endowment. Sam could not accept this condition and instead gave the spacious hall to the community, although the firm of Saunders Roe still held the lease.

It was completed in 1931, probably constructed of bricks from Sam Saunders' own brickyard at Gunville and was designed by the Newport architect Cheverton.

Queen Mary agreed to open the building during one of her fairly frequent visits to Cowes and they arranged to meet at Trinity Wharf at 11.00 am. Sam waited until mid-day and as there was still no sign of the Queen he returned to his house at Padmore. The local blacksmith, Frank Rann, promised to send his son, 12 year old Bob, to fetch Sam from Padmore if the Queen appeared. About an hour later the Queen arrived by car and Bob raced off. Unfortunately, Queen Mary immediately declared the building open and departed before Sam arrived. Bob Rann recalled that Sam Saunders was very annoyed, to put it politely!

The hall was used for various village events. There are tales of exciting dances held on Saturday nights for the villagers. One regular function of the hall from the earliest days was as a Working Men's Club. This provided relaxation and amusement for the men of the village for some years. Grace Davison understood from her mother that things became a little bit rowdy when drink was sold at meetings so the club came to an end before 1939.

The Barton and Whippingham Women's Institute started their meetings at the hall in 1934. Their meetings continued there until 1939, when the hall was no longer available for village entertainments. This was because the offices of

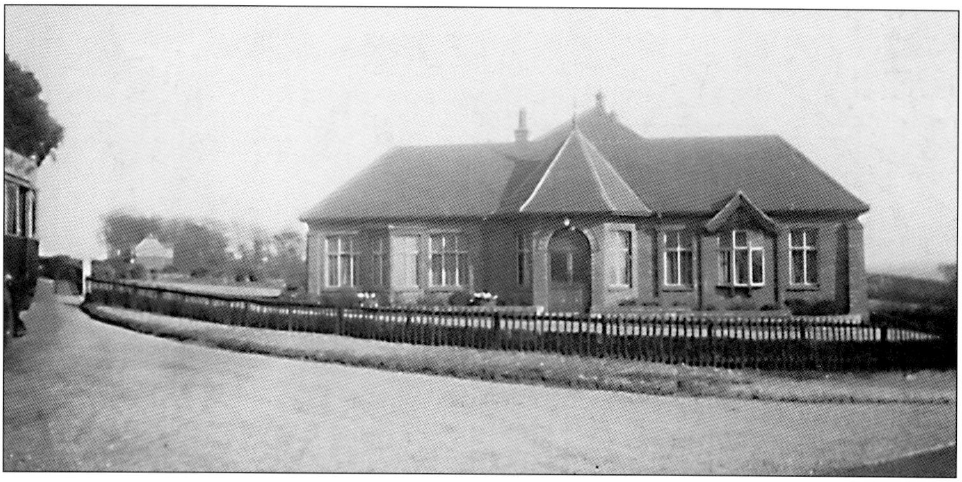

1930s photo captioned 'The Community Hall newly opened' including a glimpse of a bus passing on the left.

Saunders Roe were evacuated to the Island from London and took up residence in the hall. Staff both lived and worked at the Community Hall.

Five girls came down from the London office on 13th September 1939, ten days after war was declared. The side nearest the main road was altered for the girls, with partitions making three little single bedrooms and a twin room. Una Bennett, just 17 years old, shared the latter. Margery Hodgson, Joan Rice and Kathleen Kerr were three of the other Londoners. The kitchen and cloakroom facilities were available to them, with a dining and sitting room. Mrs Edwards, from Alverstone Road, came in every day to cook for the girls. The remainder of the building was one large room, used as the Saunders Roe office, where they were joined by several other Island girls.

Bob Rann put up the blackout boards daily, met Una, and two years later they were married. After serving in the navy for the duration of the war, Bob came back to work at the Forge with his father.

Una remembered her time living and working at the hall with some affection. The girls called themselves 'the evacuees'. They had guests to parties at the hall and made friends with numerous young men from the neighbourhood!

In April 1950 the building was purchased from Saunders Roe by the Isle of Wight Council and used as an annexe to Whippingham School. The eastern side of the hall was divided to make two classrooms, for reception and class one. School lunches were served there.

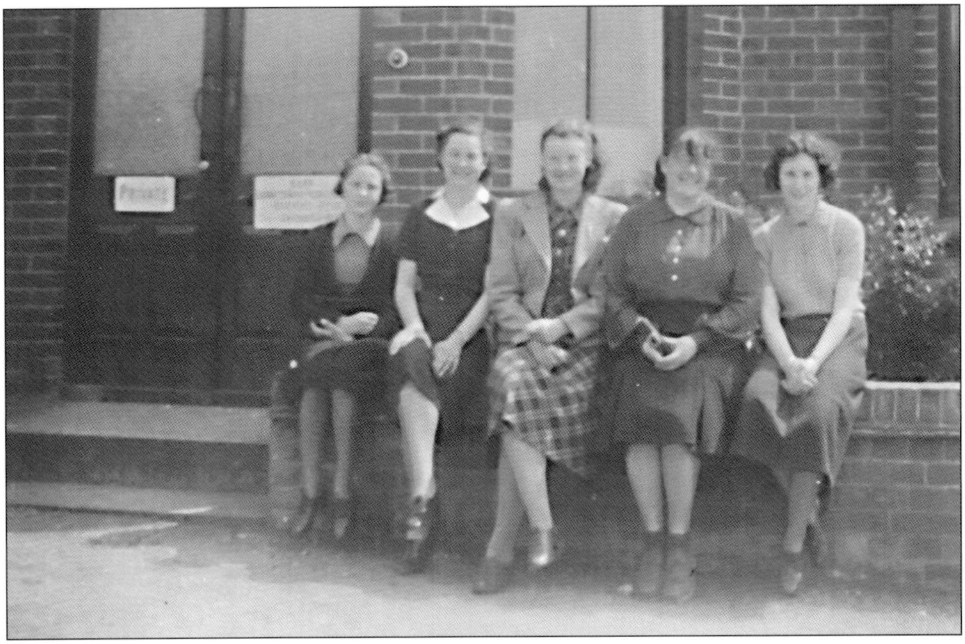

Some of 'the evacuees' who came down from the SARO London office in 1939 to live at the Community Centre. Kathleen, Kitt, Una, Margery and Dolly (from Whippingham).

In 1984 there was much discussion in the village as to what was to happen to the Community Hall when the school moved out. Some people felt that it should be returned to the community, while others thought it was unnecessary to keep the building. The county council had plans to sell it for conversion to two bungalows. A public meeting was held, and voted in favour of keeping the building as a community hall.

Whippingham Community Association was formed and, thanks to them, the village has a building for numerous functions which have enriched the lives of the community, such as a gardening club, tea dances, short mat bowls and talks.

The Association is entirely reliant upon lettings for its income. It has been the venue for public meetings on local issues. The Whippingham Partnership, which published a Heritage Trail around the village, met at the hall and now the Whippingham Parish Council meet there. The community hall continues to be used by the community as Sam Saunders intended.

The Women's Institutes

There has been a Whippingham Women's Institute group since 1934. They first met at the new community hall, although from the early days they saved for a hall of their own, selling dressed rabbit skins, jam and old newspapers. The wartime reports of the work of the WI are to be found on p. 205.
Meetings have moved from venue to venue, with church rooms at the rectory being used for 30 years. With the return of the Community Centre to general use in 1985 the WI moved back there.

The Women's Institute has long been active in encouraging improvements in the village, such as requesting a pavement along the main road, supporting a request that rural villages should have electricity installed in them, and organizing a bus shelter as a Coronation memorial in 1953.

Many local, National and International good causes have been helped over the years. For instance, silver paper and milk-bottle tops were collected for the Guide Dogs for the Blind fund, hot-water bottle covers knitted for the patients at Fairlee Hospital in 1958 and jerseys knitted for sending to Kosovo in 2000. 'Book Bags' were made for local schools, which contained numerous, wonderful props for telling a story to young children.

In 1965 Osborne WI was formed and work in the community has always been at the hub of their philosophy. From 1966 members arranged flowers at Frank James Hospital and this led to additional work serving evening suppers and clearing away. In 1970 members became involved with the campaign to gain pensioner concessions on Southern Vectis buses.

A choir and a drama group were established early in the 1970s. For several years in the 1990s their plays were one of the popular acts featured in the Old Time Music Halls held at East Cowes Town Hall as part of the annual Victorian Festival.

Other community action involved tree planting, especially at Osborne after the 1987 hurricane, trees at school, and planting bulbs in the village. In 1992, foetal stethoscopes were presented to St Mary's Maternity Unit and in 2005 Osborne WI successfully applied for a grant to enable 14 of the members to go to courses at Denman College, run by the WI.

Osborne WI has now closed and the remaining members joined Whippingham WI. The group continues to raise funds for good causes, hold craft events and talks. The ladies of the Women's Institute in the village are still as enthusiastic as ever and find true comradeship in their membership.

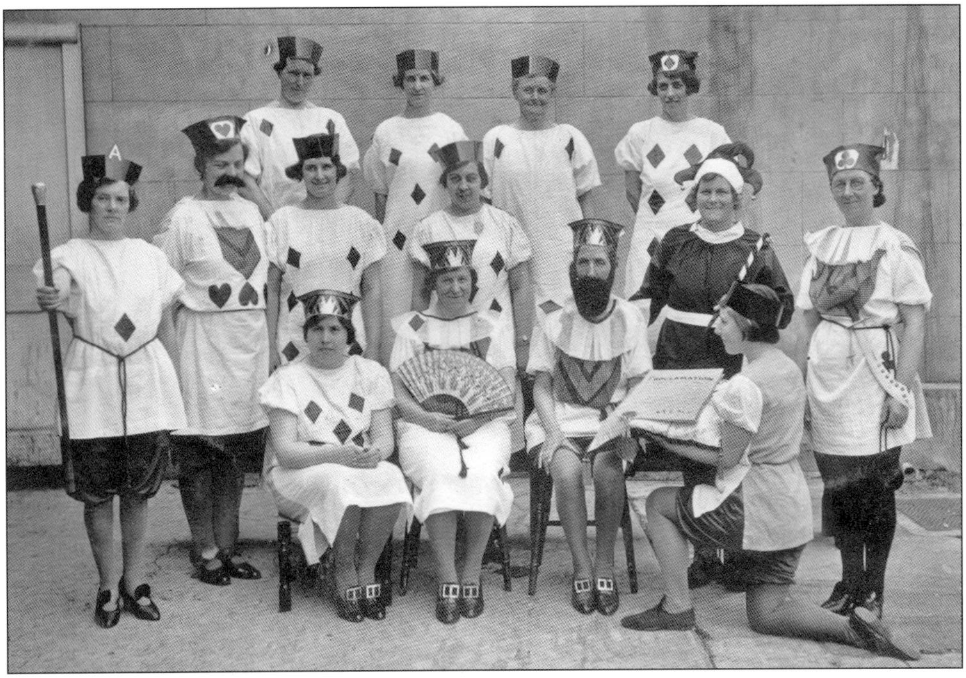

The cast of a pageant performed by Whippingham WI in the 1930s

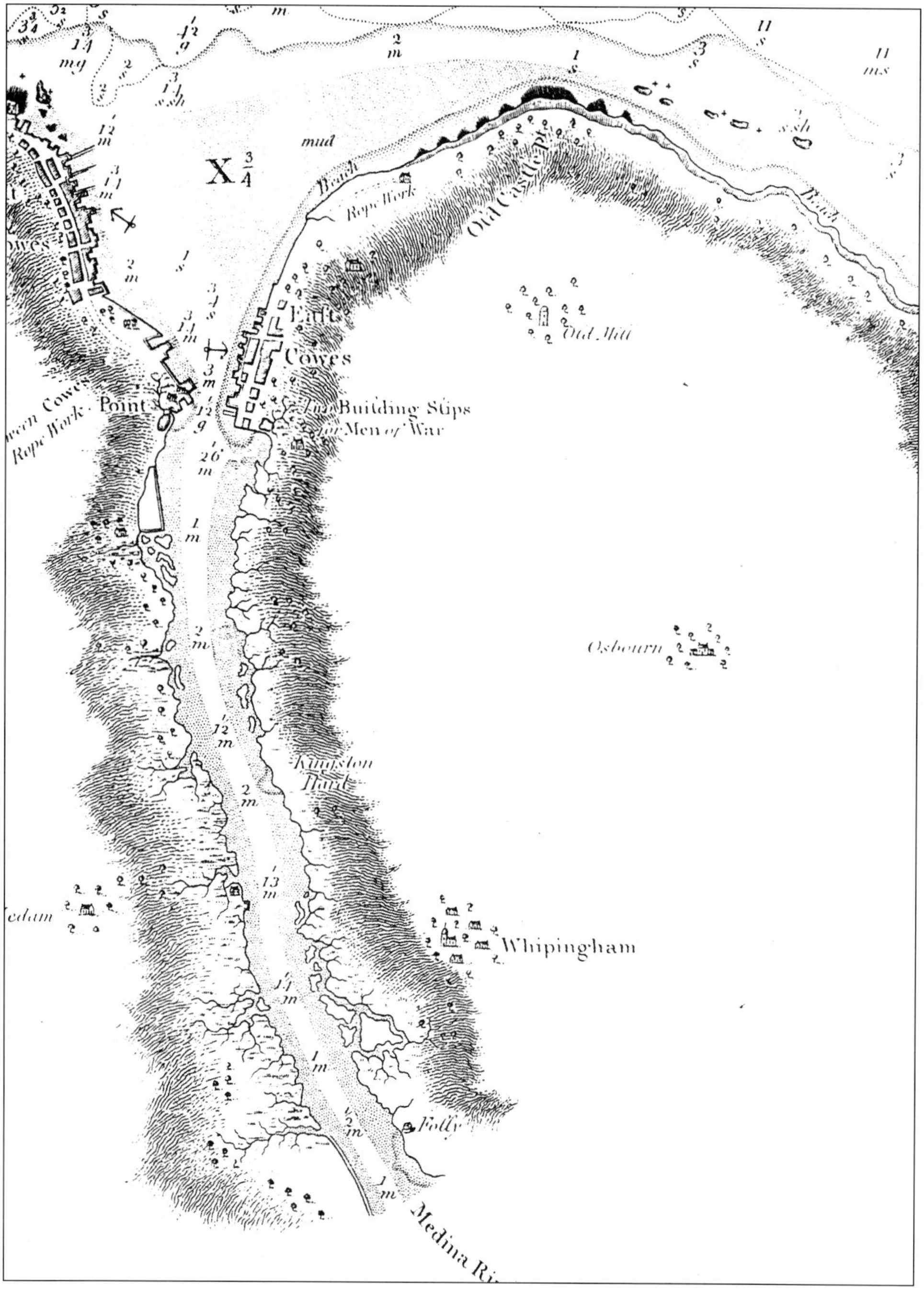

The Admiralty Chart of 1783 with The Folly marked south of Whippingham. (UK Hydrographic Office)

FIFTEEN

The Folly Inn & Regatta

The first known occasion that The Folly Inn is shown on a map is the 1783 Admiralty chart of the River Medina. Here it appears as a 'Noah's Ark' building with the name 'Folly'. It was on land belonging to the Padmore Estate.

According to the author of *'Sketches and Descriptions'* written in 1792, the name of 'The Folly' on the east shore of the river is derived from a barge, formerly moored near the side of the river, which used to be *'the scene of high entertainment amongst the bons-vivants of an earlier age.'* In 1792 the barge had been hauled up the gravel hard there and built upon.

The Folly was a vessel 60ft in length and had been in the Burnett family for many years. Captain Thomas Burnett had been the owner-master of several locally-built trading craft, including *The Three Brothers* and *The Bee*. He had the rights to several oyster beds in the river and owned seven oyster vessels. Captain Burnett employed a manager to run this remote inn in 1840. He died two years later and was buried at Whippingham Church. William Smythes took over the lease in 1842. From 1845 to 1856 James Smythes was paying rates for The Folly.

The story that the present inn is built over the remains of the vessel *The Folly* is true. When working on the reconstruction of part of the pub in the early 1960s, the ribs of the vessel were found and, until recently, a small section of this was exposed behind a glass panel in the floor for all to see. A deck hatch was found in situ during alterations to a ground-floor ceiling.

The 1853 Admiralty Chart gives us a clue as to why the inn prospered there. It is called 'The Folly Halfway House' on this chart, reminding us that it is half way up the river towards Newport. From East Medina Mill the river almost dries out at low water springs. Barges caught by the low water would wait in Folly

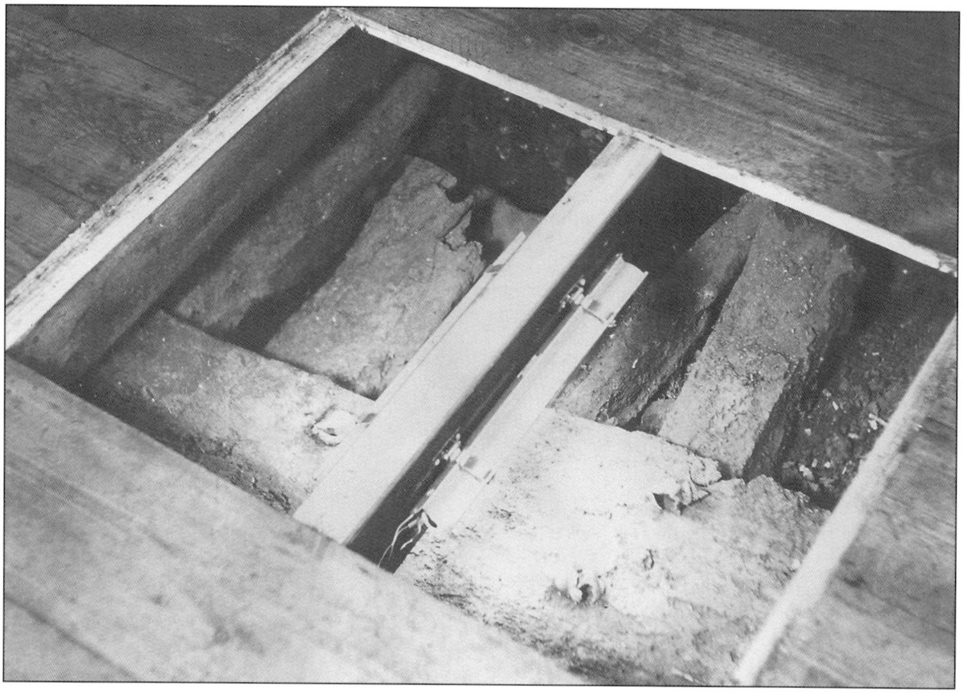

The ribs of the original boat, The Folly, were exposed during renovation work in 1964 and displayed behind glass in the floor of the pub. Now covered over.

Reach before proceeding up to Newport on the next tide and crews would be happy to partake of refreshment at The Folly.

By the 1860s the Jolliffe sisters owned the Padmore estate. They tried to negotiate a new lease so that the oyster company would take over The Folly, with the proviso that, *'no beer or spirits, or oysters or anything whatever to be sold at the premises.'* There was to be no access except by boat or from the public path to the south, which was to be fenced to enclose the footpath. Also it added that no-one could trespass across Padmore land. Obviously this agreement was never completed as The Folly continued to function as a public house through the century.

At this time there was no proper public access from the main road to The Folly, only footpaths along the river or over the fields. However, villagers certainly used the public hard at The Folly in 1860, as the ferryman Hollis called there twice a week to pick up passengers from Whippingham on his trips to Newport market. The hard spit of gravel made getting on board quite easy for much of the

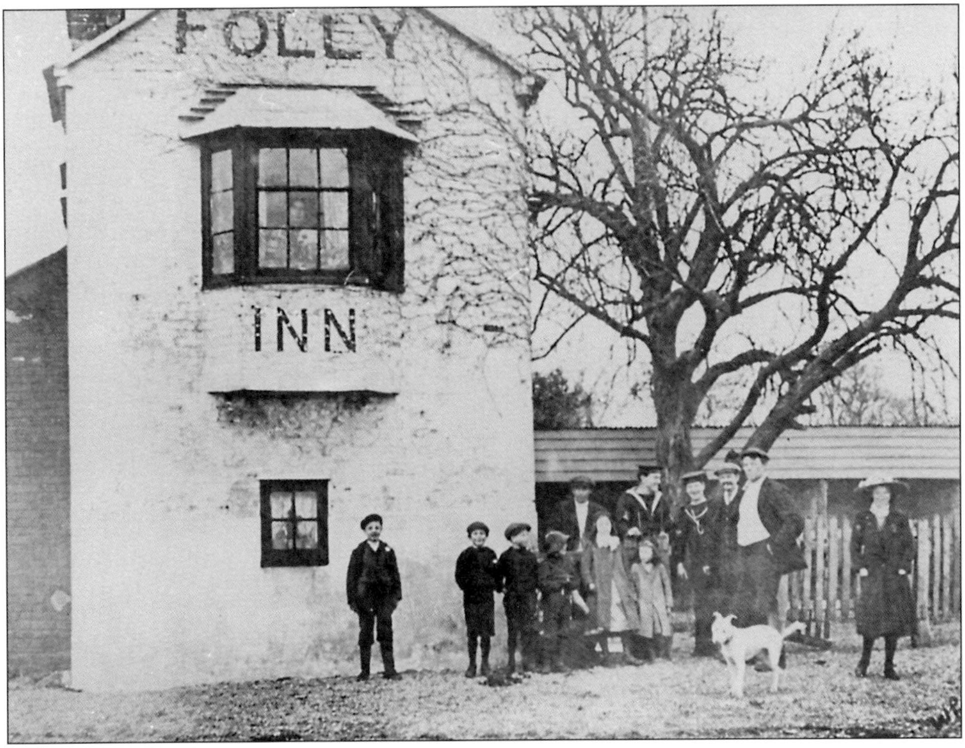

Visiting The Folly in 1910, possibly for a boiled egg tea.

tide. In the 1920s and 30s East Cowes people would row up the river to The Folly on a Sunday for a 'Boiled egg tea'.

A good landlord makes or breaks an inn. One of the many good ones at The Folly was Bob Savage. He was the tenant from around 1905 and had been a heavyweight boxing champion while in the Royal Navy. His relationship with the youngsters who frequented the river was good, although Uffa Fox talks of being caned by Bob for misdemeanours. Afterwards Bob would put the punishment aside and be friends with the boys again. He taught them how to box. Uffa tells of his first lesson when Bob spun Uffa round and round then invited the boy to hit him. Uffa swung a fist and promptly toppled over and Bob pointed out never to let your opponent make you dizzy!

Bob Savage was still the tenant in 1933 when the Padmore Estate was sold by Sam Saunders' trustees. He was offered the inn for £160, but thought it was a bit expensive. Instead the brewers Mew Langton bought The Folly for £185. Bob continued renting the inn from Mew Langton.

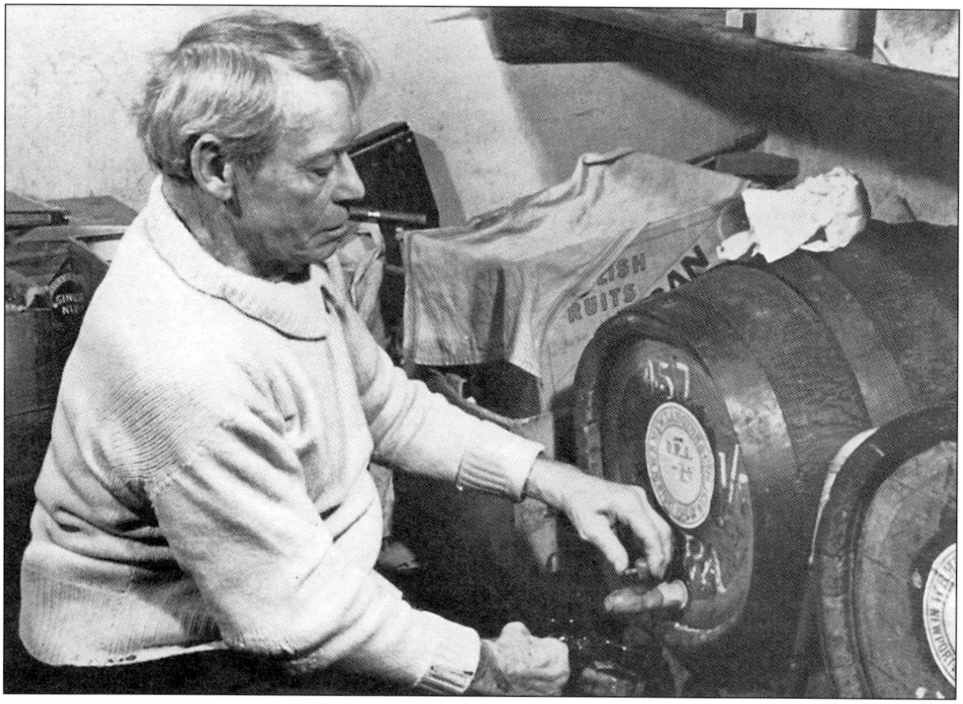

Bob Savage pulls a pint at The Folly in the 1930s.

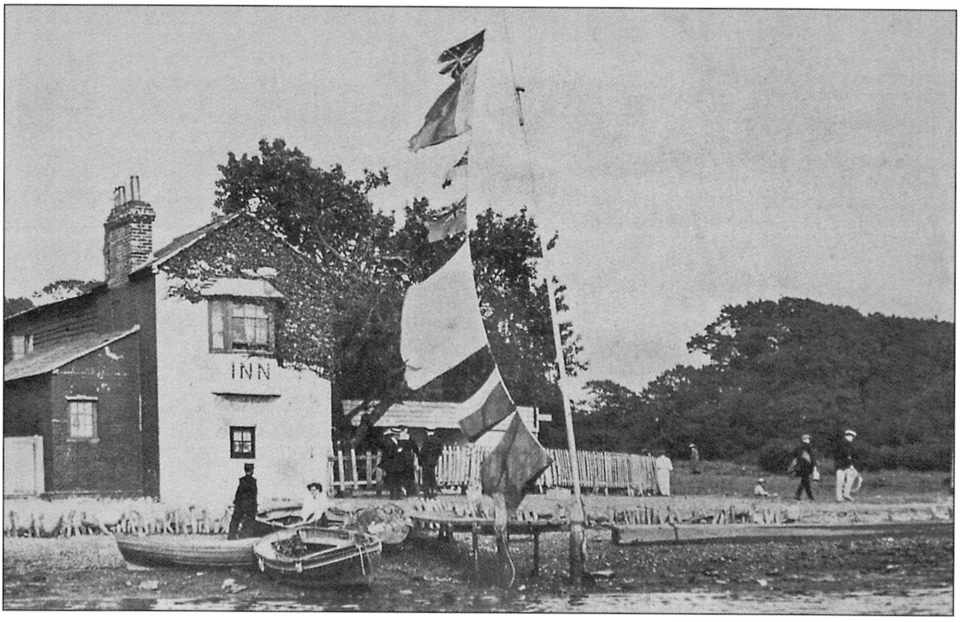

The Folly Inn pictured around 1910.

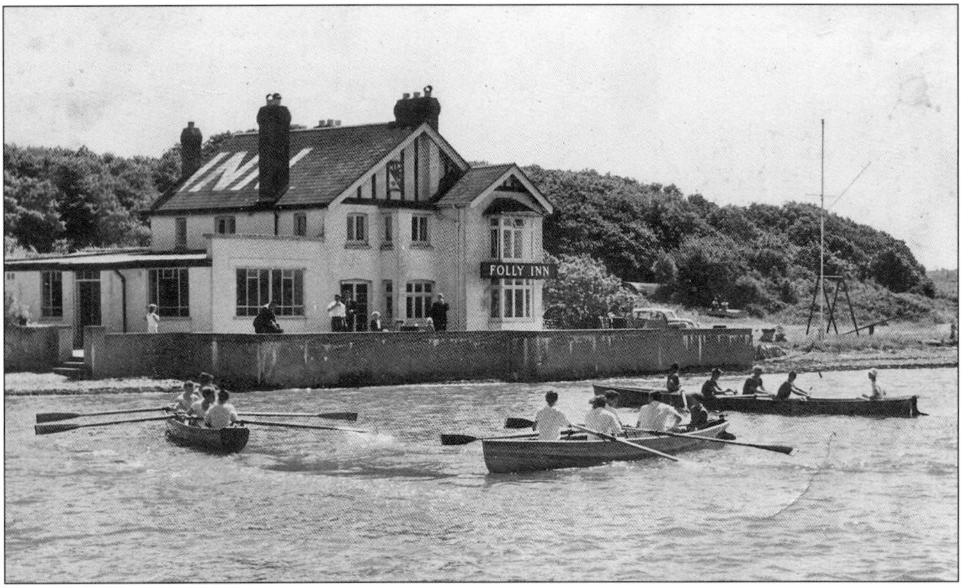

Gigs at The Folly in the 1950s. The ship and aircraft firms in East Cowes had gigs and their apprentices competed for trophies. The Scouts' Nissen Hut is among the trees.

A road had been made to the Folly Works in 1915 that also served the inn. An extension to the north side of the building was added in 1948/9 giving a much enlarged bar area. A protective wall and seating space was built on the riverside of the inn.

In 1960 there were just three permanent moorings laid down in the river. One was used by Mr Mew and the other by the boat *René Phillipe.* The *René Phillipe* came from the mainland, with Barry and Pat Stoneman, who set up a sailing school which operated from the boat, the pupils staying on board. Pam and Alan Cundall bought René Phillipe in 1963 and continued the sailing school successfully, with its fleet of dinghies. They could take up to eight pupils at a time.

In November 1960 Janette and Murray Dixon took on The Folly Inn. There had been a disastrous fire at the SARO Folly Works next door, cutting the work force from over 1000 to 120. The inn had depended heavily upon the workers for its income, especially the end of shift beers which had been good trade for them.

Mew Langton decided that the inn should now be developed to appeal to yachtsmen and Murray, nephew of Uffa Fox, was an ideal candidate as publican. On the first day they moved in, Janette had a party of eleven booked in from

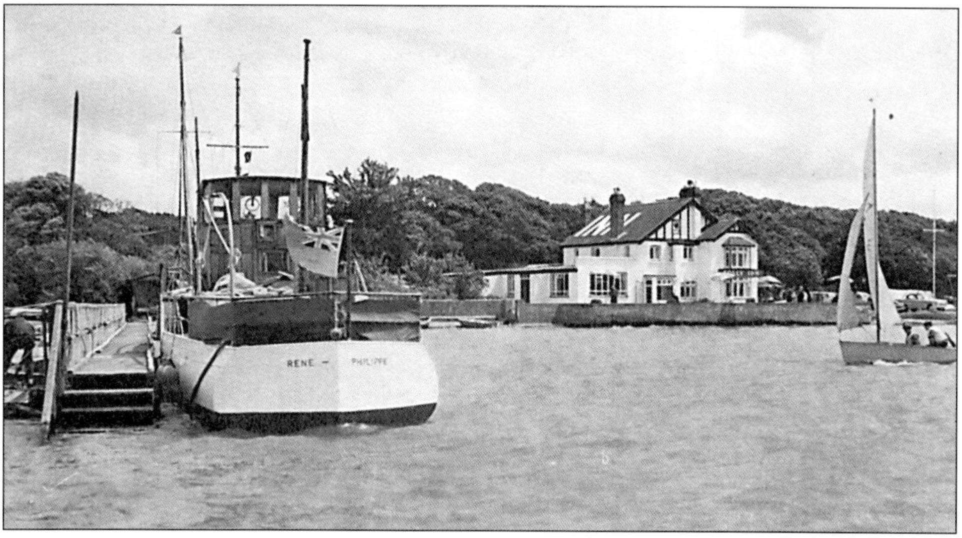

The René Phillipe tied up at The Folly landing stage in 1965.

SARO's for their lunch. She had only an Aga and a little Calor-Gas stove and went into East Cowes to buy a joint of beef. Somehow she coped.

A storm at the beginning of that November, which had flooded Mew Langtons Brewery at Newport, washed away numerous barrels of beer. The Dixons were still fishing these out of the river a month later!

Gradually the yachting facilities were improved and the pub started to increase its yachting clientele. The concrete scrubbing-off hard beside the jetty was made and concrete was laid down at the end of the gravel spit to the south. Outbuildings were converted to storage for outboard engines.

Increasing numbers of yachts anchoring in the fairways caused difficulties for the commercial traffic passing up and down the river. Murray Dixon suggested to the Cowes Harbour Commissioners that a string of visitor's buoys would ease the congestion, but they felt it would not be a viable proposition. Murray organised moorings himself and visiting yachtsmen put their contributions in a beer mug on the counter! This encouraged both Cowes and Newport Harbour Authorities to increase their mooring facilities.

The field at The Folly Inn, owned by the brewery, was a campsite at this time, licensed by the council. During Cowes Week families would sail over for the week and camp there. Sailing clubs from the mainland would organise dinghy weekends to The Folly and use the site.

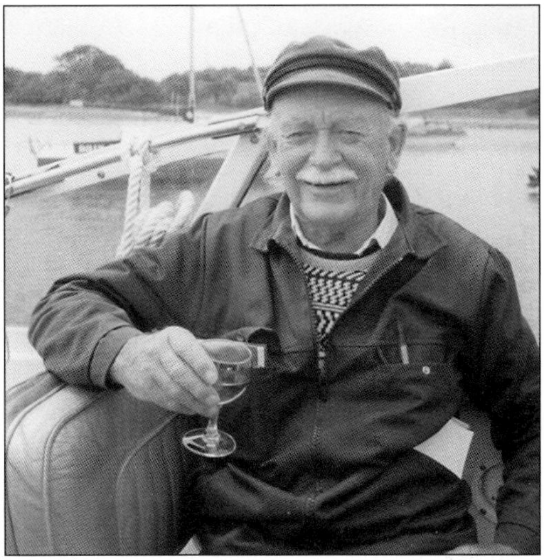

Alan Cundall - Folly Harbourmaster 1964-1998

In 1964 Alan Cundall became the first Folly Harbour Master, and for 34 years he could be seen cheerfully making the rounds of the visiting yachts, collecting mooring fees, checking boats after a storm and generally looking after the river craft and their users. He retired in 1998.

Pauline and David Faudrey managed The Folly Inn for a couple of years before moving to the Fishbourne Inn. After them in 1975, John McQueen Mason and his wife Lucy, (a niece of Uffa Fox), took over The Folly. It was then owned by Whitbreads, who had bought out all the Mew Langton public houses. The inn was extended to the south, with plush carpet on the floors and polished wood, so yachtsmen left their wellies lined up outside the door.

John and Lucy had been in partnership for a few years with Murray and Jeanette Dixon when they still ran Folly Inn. Whitbreads wanted to make it a managed house so John and Lucy went to the Clarendon at Chale. Later they returned to run the Folly when the Dixons left to set up Murray's Restaurant in Cowes.

John McQueen Mason remembered the occasion when he tried to call out the police launch. Trawling for fish was prohibited in the River Medina, but one night John spotted a trawler at work. He alerted the police, who instead of contacting the police launch *Ashburton*, sent a van with two men, which was not very useful in chasing a trawler!

After John and Lucy McQueen Mason left The Folly, the interior was given a 'make over'. Old timber was used to line the walls, ceiling and floor. The effect was very rustic and it took the locals rather a long time to get used to it. However it is very efficient as it has never needed repainting. In 1996 Andy and Cheryl Greenwood took on the pub/restaurant for Whitbreads and established themselves as firm favourites. Club outings of 50 or 60 boats visit The Folly at the weekends during the summer season, jostling for a berth six abreast on the visitor's moorings. Greene King now own the inn, which can seat 200 indoors and almost as many outside. Visitors arrive by boat, car, foot, amphibious vehicle, or even helicopter, and have included Royalty who appreciated fish and chips! A canoeist on a very high tide actually paddled in. Andy and Cheryl finally moved on in 2014 to Chale.

The ambience has grown on the locals, who continue to enjoy eating and drinking there. Whether sitting by the log fire on a winter evening, or by the window 'checking the boat' on a rainy day in spring, or basking in the summer sunshine by a sparkling river, the atmosphere is most enjoyable.

Medina Mariners' Association

As the yachting custom and fame of The Folly grew, more moorings were laid down by Cowes and Newport Harbour authorities. The Folly jetty is the dividing line between the two. There are many swinging and pontoon moorings attached to lines of piles. In the early 1980s a brick building was constructed as the harbour office near the slip, incorporating the office of the Medina Mariners Association.

The Medina Mariners Association (MMA) was formed in 1972 with Murray Dixon as a driving force and Norman Parr as the first President. Their aim was to preserve the River Medina in an unspoilt state. Islanders were becoming increasingly aware of the many developments that were spoiling the rivers on the mainland and they wanted to ensure the Medina remained with a green riverside.

Based at The Folly Inn, MMA run a variety of activities for members, as well as keeping to their brief to try, not always with success, to conserve the River Medina. MMA activities range from the provision of two dinghy parks, clearing rubbish from the banks of the Medina, cruiser races and outings, dinghy races, and winter talks on various nautical and conservation themes. Money has been raised by the club to send local people on *The Lord Nelson*, which is a tall ship specially equipped for the disabled sailor. MMA also ran The Folly Regatta for the last few decades.

The Regatta

The first Folly Regatta was held on the afternoon of the 20th September, 1913. Bob Savage took on the organisation of it and The *Isle of Wight County Press* reported the event.

The weather was perfect and there was a very large attendance both ashore and afloat. The nearby aviation grounds and sheds of Saunders and Co., from which Mr Hawker had started on his recent record-breaking round-Britain flight in the Sopwith Water Plane, had helped to popularise the locality. The firm helped with fundraising towards the cost of staging the regatta, together with various local dignitaries, such as Messrs Mew, T Sopwith, T Roach, and W Harvey, a popular local farmer at Kingston. Crouchers Ltd. of Newport kindly loaned their motor-barge Tally-Ho as a committee boat. Owing to the large attendance afloat it was often difficult to keep the course clear!

Races included a sailing handicap for members of East Cowes Sailing Club, four-oared galley and gig races, a punt race, a single-oared sculling race, a shovel race (two men in a boat with shovels instead of oars), a ladies paired oared race, a dinghy race for boys and one for bona fide bargemen, a boys swimming race and a ladies single-handed race. On shore there were even more amusements.

A large refreshment marquee was run by Bob Savage and the band of Princess Beatrice's IW Rifles played during the afternoon and through the evening for dancing. There was walking the greasy pole, a treacle bun eating competition for school boys, and a ladies tug of war, married ladies versus single and the latter won!

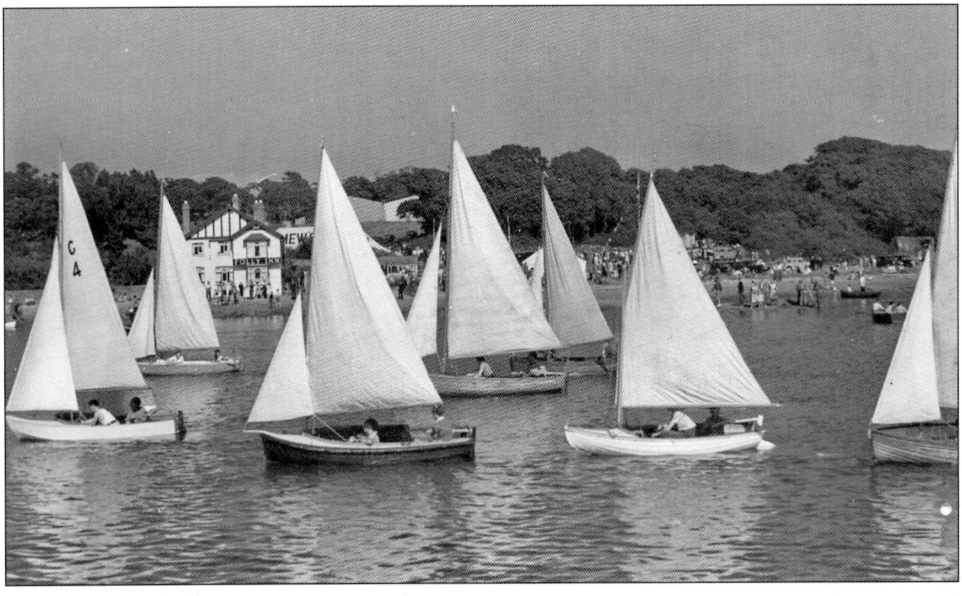

The 1948 Folly Regatta.

The success of The Folly Regatta in 1913 was short-lived as the Great War stopped events during the following years. It was revived at a meeting at The Folly in the mid-1930s. Uffa Fox was elected president of the committee and 22 of his friends were each given tasks to do on the premise commonly quoted as, '*You says it, you does it!*'

The posters were headed 'Fun and Frolic at The Folly' and advertised dancing on the spacious lawn. The lawn was the rough sloping grass field that had been scythed for the occasion and a brass band was seated on two farm wagons.

There were rowing races, sailing races, every kind of shore sport and fun for children and adults. A tub of beer was tied up on to a pile in the river, the rowing boats raced to the beer, and the first one to get the barrel won it. The innocent thought that all they had to do was to row to the pole, but the barrel was lashed so tightly that all the boats were jostling about under the pole before it was cut down. The river was soon full of sinking boats, swimming men, oars and paddles, and eventually all the men reached the shore swimming, pushing the barrel before them, and all shared in the contents.

The Championship of the Medina was a swimming race which started from the Cowes Floating Bridge, the competitors diving off from the top deck. Swimming up with the flood tide the racers were timed in when they arrived at The Folly by the Mayor of Newport, who also presented the trophies. In 1938 J Russell won in 59 minutes and V Thomas was second. Of the seven swimmers the only girl was Doris Toms, aged 15. She was last in 81 minutes. Both she and the winners received cups. Regattas ceased again during the next war, but were revived after the hostilities.

Medina Mariners Association took over organisation of the regattas in the 1970s. A popular race for the youngsters was a cork race, where one crewman rowed and the other collected floating corks that had been tipped on to the water. The winner was the boat which picked up the most corks, creating lots of barging, pushing and entertainment for those ashore as boats capsized! The Sea Scouts seemed to be quite good at this, probably practicing on their Wednesday nights sailing at The Folly during the summer!

As more moorings were laid down in the river by the harbour authorities the space for the regatta diminished. Races had often started with the Gurnard Sailing Club racing round and up the Medina to The Folly. Space for sailing races in the river was now much reduced and in 2005 problems concerning insurance meant MMA could no longer afford to run The Folly Regatta.

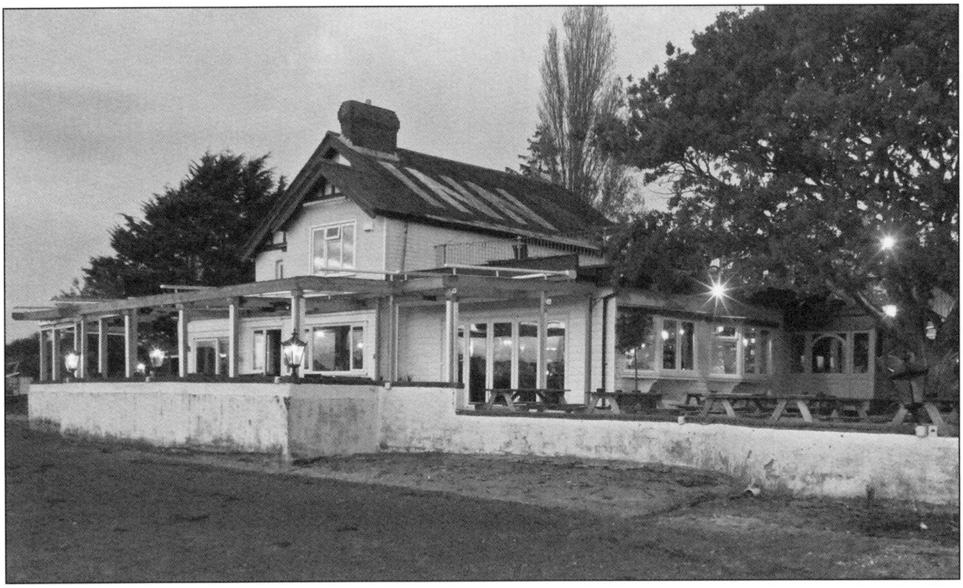

The Folly today is a popular riverside pub.

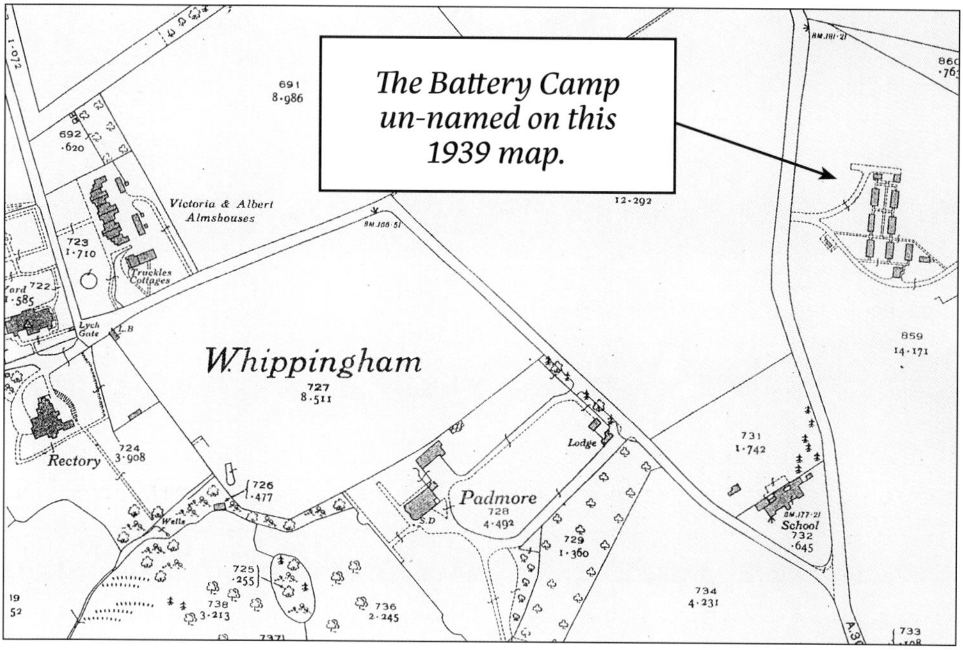

May 5th Only 5 children attended school
The Director of Education with the
County Architect visited the school
to ascertain damage. This was found
to consist only of fallen plaster,
loose or broken slates, and 7 broken
panes
3 children of this school have
lost their lives in the air raid
Mary Chiverton aged 7, Vera Chiverton
aged 4 and Joan Abrook aged 5, all
of Point Cottages Whippingham, which
received a direct hit.

The 1942 school log book, May 5th, describing the tragic results of the air raid over Whippingham the night before.

Sixteen

The Second World War

Whippingham, like many other villages, experienced great change during the war years. A large anti-aircraft gun emplacement appeared on the top of the plateau, now occupied by Whippingham Heights and Campfield Road housing estate. There were smaller guns elsewhere, large numbers of troops came and went at various times, and hundreds of workers travelled every day to the Folly plywood works. Air raid precautions were put in place throughout the village.

The air raid warden for much of Whippingham was Mr Brinton, from 'Astolat' on the East Cowes Road near Brickfield Corner. By day he was a turbine engineer at J S White's in West Cowes. His son, Roy, had the task at the start of hostilities of delivering a form to every house in the village. The home owner filled this in to detail all the people who lived there and whereabouts they slept in the house, in case there was damage to the property at night.

Sadly this information was needed in 1942. On the night of May 4th there was a concerted bombing raid on East and West Cowes. The routes into the towns were also hit in an effort to delay fire-engine access. Two families at Point Cottages received a direct hit from an armour-piercing bomb. The resulting crater was two storeys deep, so one can imagine the destruction. Mr Brinton, being the smallest of the local wardens, was given the unenviable job of crawling beneath the splintered roofs and floors to extricate the remains of the children and their parents. It took him a long time to recover from this grisly task.

In all, nine people were killed at Point Cottages. Three of the children there had attended Whippingham School. The worry and confusion created in the minds of those who lived through the raid is shown in the letter written from Four Cottages on the 5th May. *'It was a night and no mistake, hope you will understand as I don't know how to write.'*

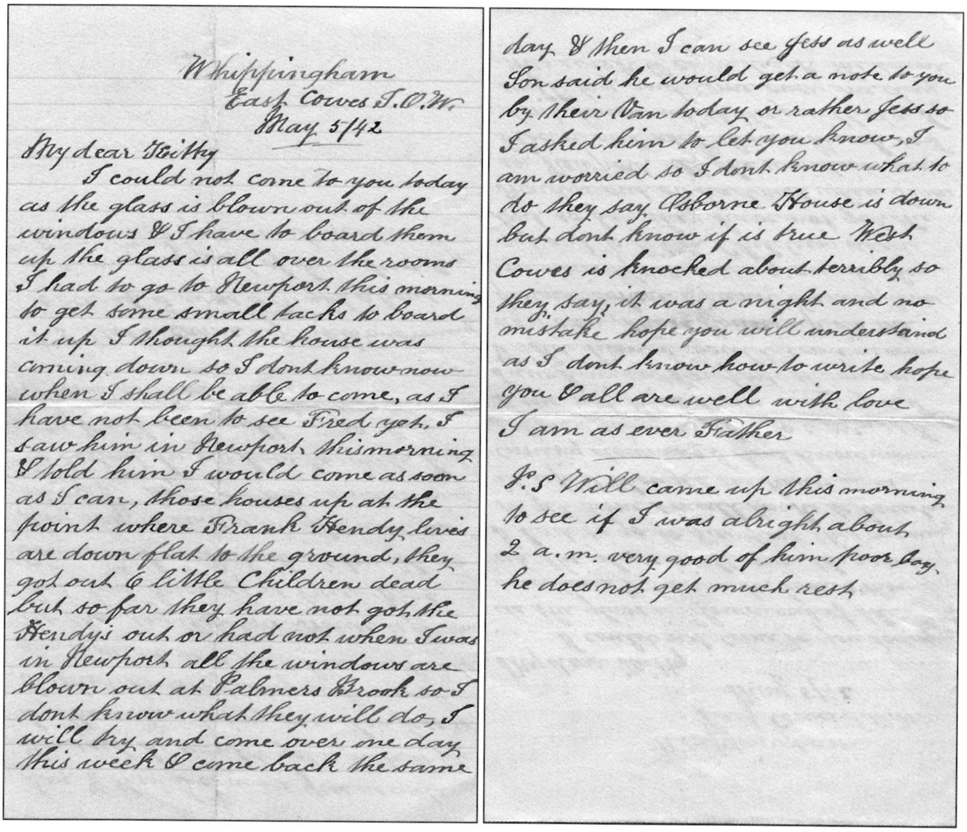

Whippingham
East Cowes I.O.W.
May 5/42

My dear Kitty

I could not come to you today as the glass is blown out of the windows & I have to board them up the glass is all over the rooms I had to go to Newport this morning to get some small tacks to board it up I thought the house was coming down so I dont know now when I shall be able to come, as I have not been to see Fred yet, I saw him in Newport this morning & told him I would come as soon as I can, those houses up at the point where Frank Hendy lives are down flat to the ground, they got out 6 little Children dead but so far they have not got the Hendy's out or had not when I was in Newport all the windows are blown out at Palmers Brook so I dont know what they will do, I will try and come over one day this week & come back the same day & then I can see Jess as well Son said he would get a note to you by their Van today or rather Jess so I asked him to let you know, I am worried so I dont know what to do they say Osborne House is down but dont know if is true West Cowes is knocked about terribly so they say, it was a night and no mistake hope you will understand as I dont know how to write hope you & all are well with love

I am as ever Father

P.S Will came up this morning to see if I was alright about 2 a.m. very good of him poor boy he does not get much rest

Mr Allam, of Four Cottages wrote this moving letter to his daughter at Chale after the 1942 air raid. "The glass is blown out of the windows and I have to board them up...I thought the house was coming down...it was a night and no mistake..."

The children suffered from lack of sleep during the frequent air raids and would arrive at school tired out. Protection during school hours consisted of an air raid shelter in the playground. It was a frightening time for the children when the big guns were firing only 300 yards away.

The chief air raid warden for the area lived at Summer Cottage, Binfield Corner. He was Mr Jolly, and had a car and a telephone. When the wardens were needed at a particular area, they would all pile into his car. One such occasion was the first hit by a V1 doodlebug in the area, just south of Mill Lane. The wardens happened to be having a meeting at the time at 'Astolat', so they got into the car and off they went. Roy Brinton followed on his bicycle. The only casualty, that time, was a cow.

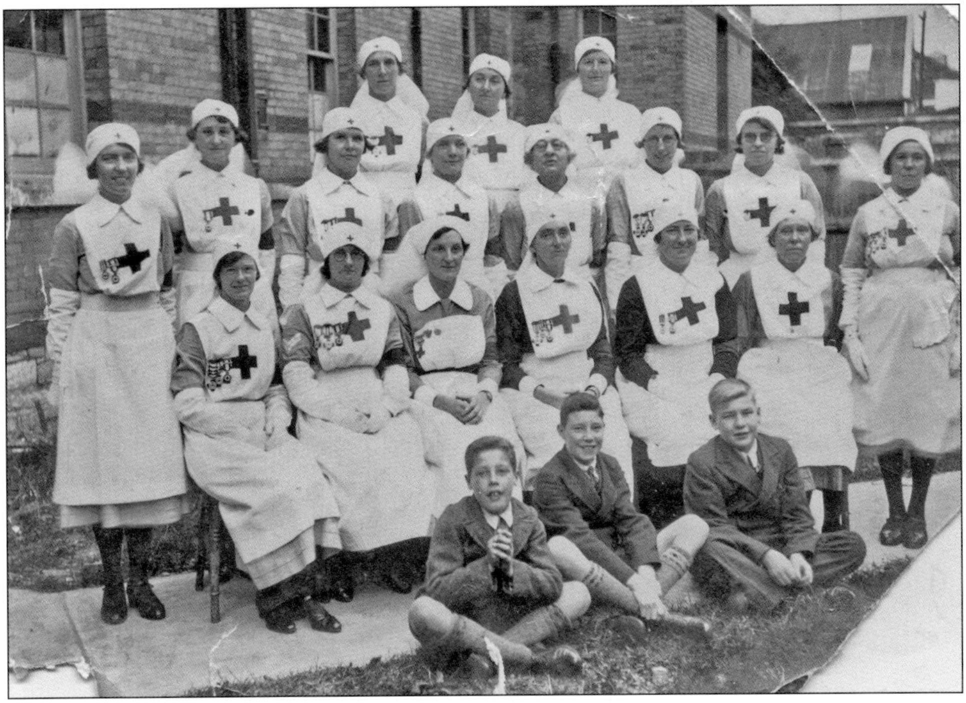

The VADs after inspection at Albany Barracks, East Cowes. They wear medals for examinations completed. Florence Jolliffe stands in the back row on the left.

Numerous bombs fell on Whippingham during the war. In August 1940 there was a raid on Folly Works when veneers, pontoons and boats were destroyed. Folly Works had their own fire-fighting crew, and fire-watchers at night. There was an unexploded bomb on the railway line near Whippingham Station, and a delayed-action bomb went off in the village in November 1940. An incendiary raid at Folly Works in March 1941 caused damage. In April 1941 over 50 incendiaries fell between the church and Kingston Farm.

Mrs Jolliffe and her daughter Phyllis both joined the Voluntary Aid Detachment, the 'VADs', part of the Red Cross. Nursing skills were taught at courses held at the Albany Road barracks in East Cowes. Mrs Pimm was their commandant. The 12th Field Ambulance HQ was at Barton Manor, run by Royal Army Medical corps personnel. Included here were Female Auxilliary Nursing Yeomanry, 'FANYs'.

By the present Forge bus stops there was a security checkpoint across the road. This consisted of a number of old oil drums filled with concrete, in which poles had been set. Wire was strung between the poles and the road was closed off to half its width. Vehicles had to negotiate a chicane and show their passes to the guard on duty. A pill-box machine-gun position was located next to it dug into the school grounds with a view down Whippingham Road.

Apart from the anti-aircraft battery at the Heights, troops were stationed in the Whippingham area on several occasions. Canadian troops trained in Whippingham for the ill-fated Dieppe raid in August 1942. They had to practice house-to-house fighting and used the empty cottages in the field immediately to the north of Whippingham Church for this purpose.

More Canadian troops were stationed in Whippingham ready for D-Day in June 1944. Many camped on the shore by Woodhouse Farm. Their tanks were drawn up under the trees – hazel paling fencing was laid down on the soft ground so that the tracked vehicles did not destroy the surface. Unfortunately the road between King's Quay and Barton Hard was seriously damaged by the tanks. On one occasion one of their lorries knocked a corner of a barn down at Woodside Farm and a calf was killed in the accident. The farmer was nowhere to be seen, so the carcass was rapidly removed in the lorry, barbecued and eaten. When the farmer arrived that evening searching for his calf, there was nothing to be seen.

All along Brock's Copse Road amongst the trees was a vast ammunition dump on both sides. This arsenal was guarded by one elderly gentleman who occasionally rode up and down the hill on his bicycle. His main task was to keep inquisitive young boys away from the shells. All this ammunition was destined for France with the troops, and disappeared on D-Day.

The build-up of craft in the Solent was remembered by all who saw it. *'There were so many ships out there it looked as if you could walk to Portsmouth.'* Then on the morning of 6th June 1942 suddenly they were all gone. *'It was so quiet, the Solent was deserted.'* Villagers had become so used to seeing the fleet when they looked out to sea that an eerie feeling descended on the area, and everyone listened to their radios for news.

Each member of the D-Day force embarking from the Isle of Wight wore a blue and white arm band, showing an angel protecting the Needles rocks. One is pinned into the school log book.

On the wall of the church is a plaque inscribed with the names of those Whippingham men who gave their lives in both World Wars. Jack Trusler was serving in the RAF when his plane was brought down in North Africa. His mother had been caretaker at the church for many years. Reverend Marshall

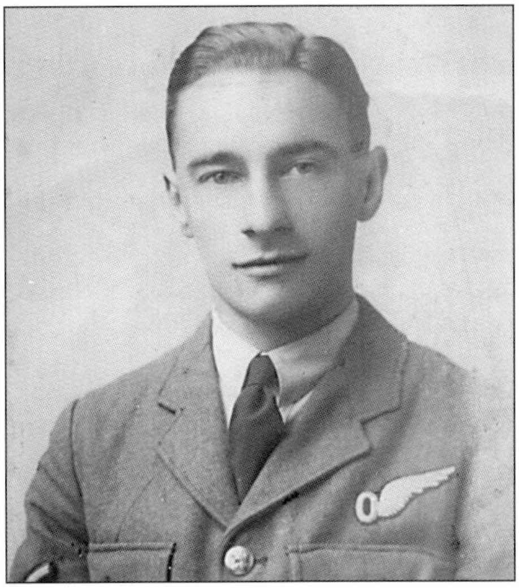
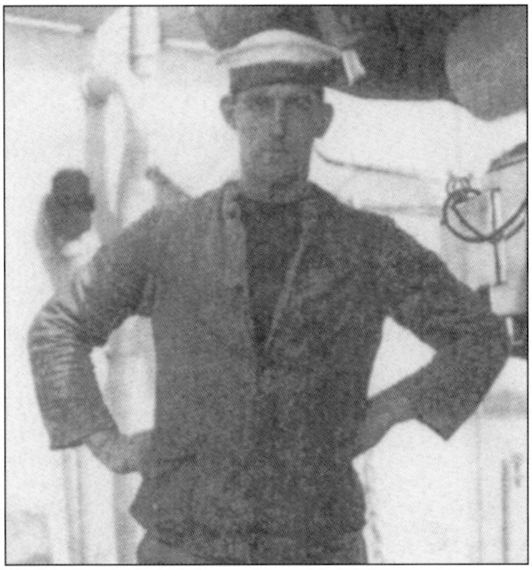

Left: Jack Trusler killed in North Africa. Right: Frank Rann who died in the sinking of the Royal Oak in 1939.

held a requiem service for Jack, with his RAF cap placed on the altar. Two of the Rann brothers are also remembered here. Frank Rann died when the Royal Oak went down in Scapa Flow in 1939, and his brother Alfred was killed in action in North Africa.

The Women's Institute, 1939 – 45

The Whippingham Womens' Institute lost their meeting room at the Whippingham Community Hall to Saunders Roe office staff in 1939. The WI moved to the Osborne Sea Cadets Hall, once Queen Victoria's stable block, later the Royal Naval College dining room. In 1940 Saunders Roe requisitioned the Osborne Hall so the WI moved again, first to Padmore House, then to the rectory and then to the billiard room at Barton Manor.

It was agreed at the outset of rationing that each member would bring a spoonful of tea and her own sugar to meetings. Special permission was given for the WI to serve refreshments, and they also had a licence from the Cowes Food Control Committee to hold their produce stall at each meeting.

For three years running the WI held a 'Dig for Victory' exhibition at Whippingham School showing trays of vegetables, fruits, jams, eggs, blackberries and so on. 'Thrift' handicrafts were displayed and also bundles of wood collected from the river bank. There were competitions for the children, such

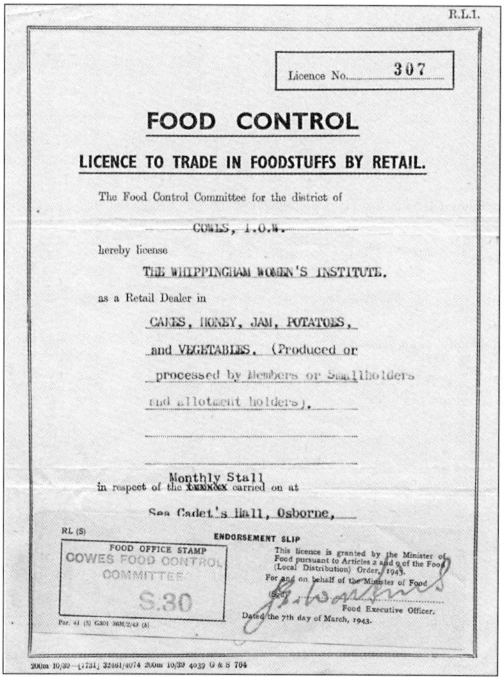

R.L.1.

Licence No. 307

FOOD CONTROL

LICENCE TO TRADE IN FOODSTUFFS BY RETAIL.

The Food Control Committee for the district of

COWES, I.O.W.

hereby license

THE WHIPPINGHAM WOMEN'S INSTITUTE.

as a Retail Dealer in

CAKES, HONEY, JAM, POTATOES, and VEGETABLES. (Produced or processed by Members or Smallholders and allotment holders).

in respect of the Monthly Stall carried on at

Sea Cadet's Hall, Osborne,

RL (S)

ENDORSEMENT SLIP

FOOD OFFICE STAMP
COWES FOOD CONTROL COMMITTEE
S.30

This licence is granted by the Minister of Food pursuant to Articles 2 and 9 of the Food (Local Distribution) Order, 1943.
For and on behalf of the Minister of Food
(Sgd.) ....
Food Executive Officer.
Dated the 7th day of March, 1943.

Par. 41 (5) G301 36M/2/43 (S)

200m 10/39—[1731] 32461/4074 200m 10/39 4039 G & S 704

Permission from the Food Control Committee for the Whippingham WI to sell produce at their meetings.

as the biggest marrow, rabbits and knitted dishcloths, with saving stamp prizes. In 1944 a produce market was held, which included a demonstration on the bottling of tomatoes.

Many of the monthly competitions for WI members had a thrift theme during the war. These included something made from unpicked wool, herbs from the garden, 1lb of blackberry jelly, a homemade calendar, and a patchwork cushion. Times were still difficult after the war, and it was not until 1954 that 'a fruit cake' appeared in the competitions.

In 1942 rosehips and horse chestnuts were collected in a national campaign, but only rose hips were needed in 1943. That year, in December, the WI members were asked by the WVS for help in collecting vegetables for Navy ships in the harbour each week. By January 1944 there is a comment that, *'green vegetables are very short, but even one cabbage would be gratefully accepted for the Navy!'*

Mr Thomas gave 100 seed potatoes each year for the WI members to grow in their own gardens. The resulting crop was brought to the meeting and the sacks were given to either a nursing home in Newport or to Frank James Hospital in East Cowes.

Presents to a retiring WI president or secretary at that time were extremely functional, such as half a dozen eggs, some seeds, or a bar of soap. Not until the mid-fifties do fancy gifts reappear – talcum powder or chocolates.

In 1942 Mr Bright of the Council for the Preservation of Rural England gave a talk on post-war planning. The minutes read, *'We hope in all we do to be given wisdom to make this country a better place for all and not to spoil England with ugly buildings in the countryside.'*

Links were established with WI groups in Canada and Australia and food parcels arrived to be shared among members. Tomato seeds arrived from Canada in February 1943, along with various tins and packets of food. In December 1945 two fruit cakes were received from Australia. Members cut one at that meeting and saved the other for the next! In March 1946 we read in the minutes, *'A parcel from Australia was opened during the social half hour; we each had a sweet.'* Parcels were still being received in 1951.

Soon after the war Whippingham WI were sending parcels to Holland to help the starving population there. Each member brought a tin of food and knitted clothes to send to them. A link was established, and four Dutch ladies stayed in Whippingham in 1947 for a holiday.

Throughout the war sacks of clothes were sent to Canning Town Settlement in London. Gifts were sent to wardened accommodation that had been set up. Bunches of primroses were picked by members and carefully packed and sent by post to Canning Town. The settlement was visited in 1947 by a member who brought back wool that had been donated to the home for Whippingham members to knit baby clothes to send back to London.

The WI members were only doing the same as other people in the community, although they received helpful hints through their organisation. Whippingham was a country village, and villagers had always grown their own vegetables and fruit. Queen Victoria had ensured that each cottage had sufficient land which meant that many residents were able to supplement their rations from their own gardens.

Whippingham Battery

Until 1939 this was just a field, part of Barton Manor Farm. During the preparations for war, the field was requisitioned and a battery built there for heavy anti-aircraft guns.

The surveyor for the work was an officer by the name of Norton Green. Accommodation huts were erected first, and appear on the 1939 Ordnance Survey map. Green then oversaw the construction for the installation of four 3.7 inch guns. These were in place by August 1939, manned by the Royal Artillery. They had a complement of 120 officers and other ranks of the 57th Regiment Heavy Anti-Aircraft 213 Battery.

Whippingham also had two low-calibre anti-aircraft guns. The first of these gave some protection to the main battery. It was sited at the lower end of the footpath leading west to the church across the field from the Battery. Another was positioned by the River Medina 100 yards north of the Folly Works. For a short time one was installed opposite the Brickfield Cottages. Mobile searchlight batteries were deployed at various places, including East Medina Mill.

By June 1942 a newly developed GL Mark II radar station had been added to the defences at the battery site. This was run by girls of the Auxiliary Territorial Service, ATS. Many London girls had volunteered as they felt that they would be protecting their families if they could help to stop the aircraft flying towards the capital. The ATS became the Women's Royal Army Corps, the WRAC.

One of the radar operators at Whippingham was Mary Skinner. She was in a team who had all worked together in Essex and Liverpool before being sent to the Island. They arrived in the summer of 1942.

The camp by this time was known as 526 Battery and was linked with another camp at Nettlestone. The radar installation consisted of a transmitter and power unit which was in a small cabin with two girls working it. The transmitter sent out a signal which bounced off the target plane and back to the receiver, 200 yards away. The receiver showed the target on a cathode-ray tube located in another cabin which housed three girls and their NCO. The first girl tracked the aircraft, the second fixed the bearing and the third girl (Mrs Skinner) fixed the elevation. A diesel generator provided power, but a handle had to be swung to start it, a tough job that the men would sometimes help with.

Signals were then sent to the predictors. A telephone had to be wound so many times in order to call the person at the other end. The predictor girls worked out in the open in all weathers, always wearing their steel helmets. They worked at ground level and underground cables ran down to the gun emplacements conveying the information for setting the guns before firing. If it all went correctly, the gun was fired and the shell exploded just as the plane entered that air space.

There were three teams of girls operating three shifts on the radar and carrying out their own maintenance. Cleaning and greasing the di-pole aerial was described as a horrible job.

By 1943 there were around 100 girls based on the site accommodated in wooden huts, 12 girls to a hut, with one stove and a bucket of coke for heating. By each bed was their 'soldier's box', which contained all their possessions. Each bed had a mattress made up of three separate sections, commonly known as 'biscuits'. These were separated out to form a mattress for the bed, but during the day they

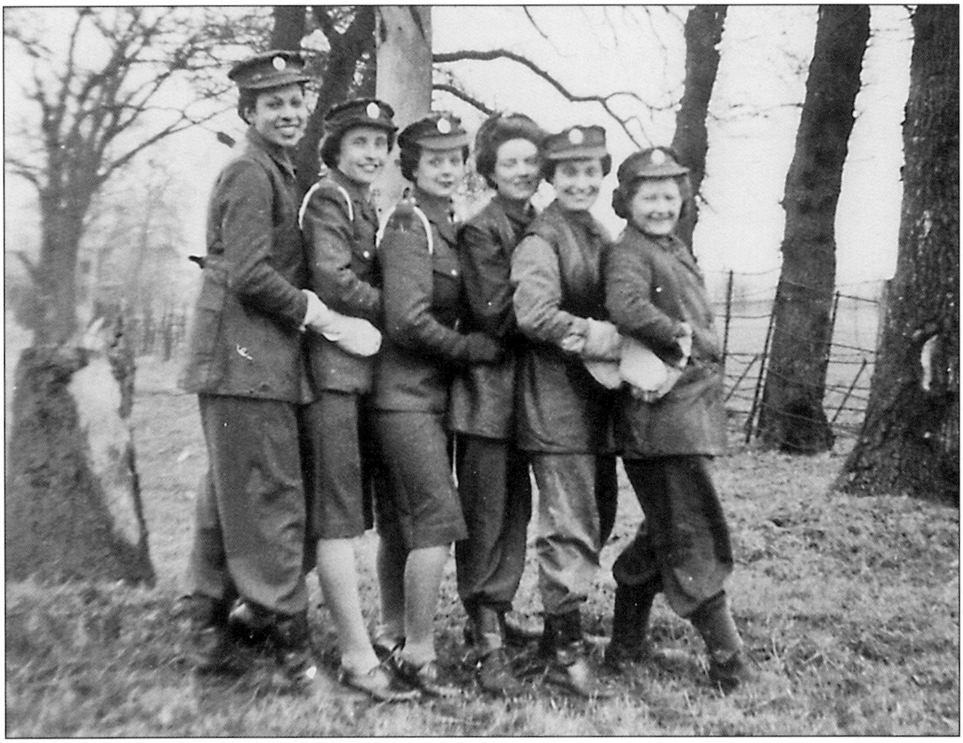

The team of radar operators who were sent to Whippingham in 1944. Mary Skinner stands second from the left.

had to be piled up one on the other, the pillow and sheets folded up on them and the two or three grey blankets wrapped around them in a neat roll. Those girls who had been on the 2am-6am shift could get a short sleep afterwards, but their beds too had to be rolled up by inspection time, between 10 and 11 o'clock every morning.

The girls' ablutions block had showers, but only the early birds caught the hot water and a bath was allowed only once a week. They did not have to do their own washing as it was all sent out to a local laundry. The daily work uniform was a khaki battledress top and trousers, boots, leather anklets, and sleeveless tan leather jackets. The khaki service dress, a skirt and jacket, had khaki lisle stockings which were *'horrible'* and the uniform colour was not attractive. A khaki hat or forage cap was worn.

In the cookhouse the eating was done in shifts. The food was very basic, but adequate and some ATS girls were assigned to cooking tasks. Everybody had their own cutlery, enamel mug and plate and did their own washing up at the end of the meal. There was usually porridge for breakfast, of varying quality, and the tea was kept in big churns and already sugared.

The ATS girls had to do guard duty on the gate to the camp sometimes, which Mrs Skinner didn't like. The men always did the night guard duty. Guard duty entailed standing by the long white pole across the entrance to the site, and opening it vertically to authorised personnel. Mrs Skinner was always afraid that she would not recognize someone whom she should salute, or that she would let in a lorry load of unwelcome visitors! It could also be a very boring job.

The wages of an ATS girl were 14s a week to start with. When the girls had passed their trade test this went up to 18s, paid weekly, in cash, the girls saluting to receive it. At the same time coupons were given to allow the girls to purchase soap or chocolate, unobtainable without coupons. The NAAFI canteen on site sold buns and cups of tea or coffee, together with things like soap, shampoo and toothpaste. Cigarettes, scarce in the shops, were also available at the NAAFI.

Iris Palmer worked at the Whippingham NAAFI canteen from 1942, as a member of the Women's Voluntary Service. At that time she lived in East Cowes and had a special permit to allow her to travel to and from the camp. Her work was described as being of 'National Importance' and to those who relied upon the NAAFI canteen it probably was.

The ATS women had a 24-hour pass once a week, 1pm to 1pm the next day. As Mrs Skinner's sister lived in Portsmouth and was expecting a baby, a visit to her was a break from the camp and the two expectant mums could exchange experiences. The girls didn't need to go off the site very often as everything came to them. Talks and entertainment were provided, and there were dances to which local girls were also invited.

Every three months the ATS staff were given leave of one week. As service personnel they did not have ration books but instead received a special form to give to whoever they were staying with so that additional food could be purchased. By December of 1944 Mrs Skinner left the ATS and Whippingham for the birth of her first child. Her husband was attached to a bomber squadron in Lincolnshire.

By June 1944 the guns at Whippingham had been upgraded to four, 5.25 inch turreted guns on extensive concrete bases. The noise they made when they fired was even greater than the 3.7s, and the sound could be heard, and felt, in Marks Corner, several miles away across the river in Parkhurst Forest. V1 flying bombs,

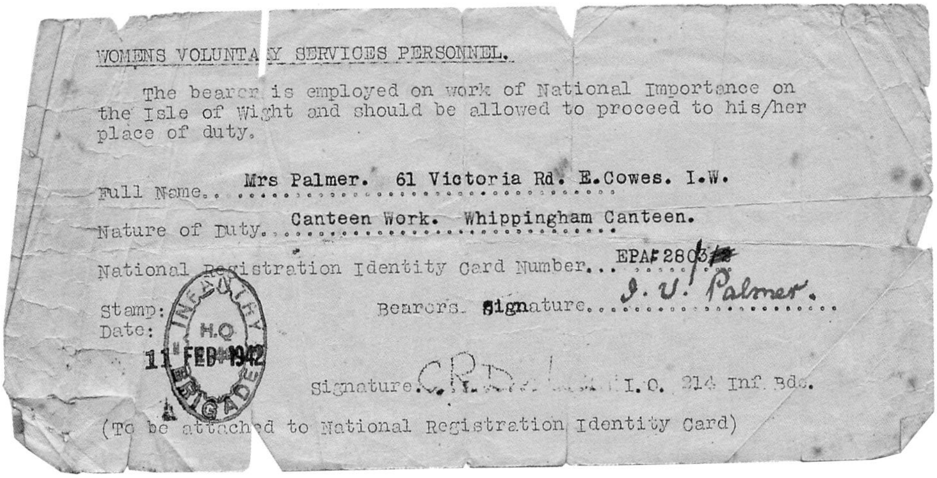

WOMENS VOLUNTARY SERVICES PERSONNEL.

The bearer is employed on work of National Importance on the Isle of Wight and should be allowed to proceed to his/her place of duty.

Full Name.. Mrs Palmer. 61 Victoria Rd. E.Cowes. I.W.

Nature of Duty.. Canteen Work. Whippingham Canteen.

National Registration Identity Card Number... EPAF 2803/[illegible]

Stamp: INFANTRY H.Q BRIGADE

Date: 11 FEB 1942

Bearer's Signature... I. U. Palmer.

Signature C.R.D[illegible] I.O. 214 Inf. Bde.

(To be attached to National Registration Identity Card)

Iris Palmer's WVS 'essential war work' pass to work at the canteen at the camp.

were passing over the Island from occupied France. These were rarely picked up by radar and were very difficult targets for the guns.

Much cleaning and polishing kept the guns of Whippingham immaculate, firing at any enemy plane that came within range, defending not only the Island but also Southampton and Portsmouth. The Whippingham Battery reportedly holds the record for the highest shot down aircraft over Britain during the Second World War, 37,000ft, (five miles) up in the sky.

January 1946 saw the guns of Whippingham removed and Viv Thomas pastured his cows around the empty emplacements and huts. In 1960 when Whippingham School held their pageant the army huts could still be seen in the background. Some of these buildings were occupied by local agricultural workers for several years after the war. The vast amount of concrete used for the gun mountings made it impossible to return the site to agriculture after the war and led to the development of housing in place of the Whippingham Battery in the late 1960s.

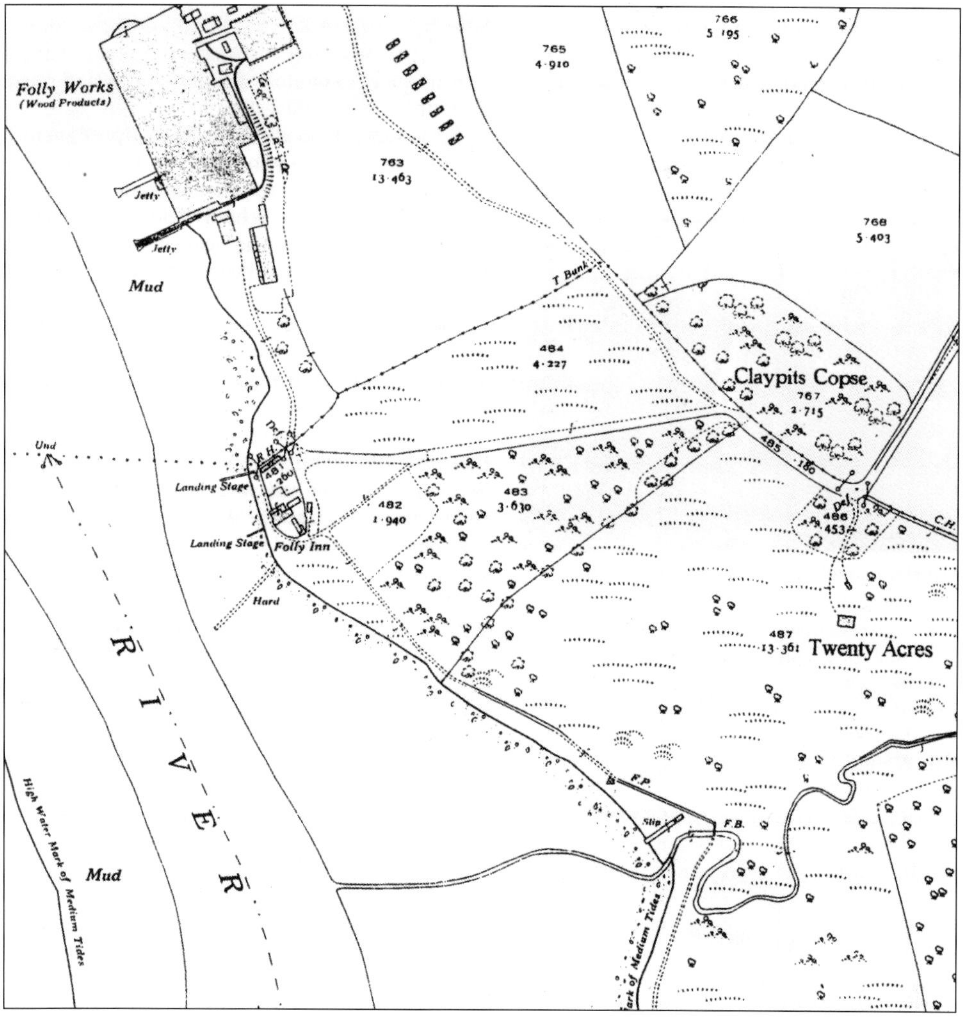

Special terms early and late visitors. S.A.E. Mrs. Cornwall Read, 26 The Dale, Widley, Portsmouth.—Tel. Cosham 75124

Medina Camps (I.W.) Ltd. Folly Lane, Whippingham, East Cowes

3/4/5-Berth Caravans. 6-Berth Chalets. Flush Toilet, Showers. Licensed Club with Communal Lounge. Modern, well-equipped Shop. Pretty wooded site sloping down to the Medina Estuary with 20 acres of playing space for children. Coach and Theatre trips arranged. Special low rates for early and late holidays.

Stamped addressed envelope for Brochure. *Telephone:* Cowes 759

Modern CARAVANS on the BEST ISLAND SITES

FOR HAPPY FAMILY HOLIDAYS Telephone Ryde 4295

Top: 1939 map shows Twenty Acres house and a slip on the foreshore, both constructed by Uffa Fox. Below: 1950s advert for the holiday camp.

SEVENTEEN

Twenty Acres & Medina Park

Until 1935 this land was part of the Padmore Estate, the one part of Whippingham that was not bought into the Queen's Estate. There had been some industrial use, as clay had been dug for the brickworks at Werrar on the opposite side of the River Medina. The use is remembered in 'Clay Pit Copse'. Werrar brickyard was still operating in 1935.

In 1935, after the death of Sam Saunders, Padmore was put up for sale. In the catalogue it was suggested that the area would be suitable for the development of a holiday camp. However, Twenty Acres by the river was bought by the yacht designer Uffa Fox, who set about building a house looking south up the river. He also brought his floating bridge workshop (and former home) and moored it by the river path through his land, just south of The Folly. On it he was designing and building world-class dinghies, with customers such as the Olympic yachtsman Sir Peter Scott, later well known as a naturalist and artist. Sir Peter wrote in his autobiography: [The dinghies] *'were built with the precision and artistry of a violin; Uffa had set new standards of workmanship in boat building, and to own one of his fourteen footers in the 1930s was to own the most perfect little boat in the world.'*

At Twenty Acres, Uffa created a self-sufficient house, with his own water catchment tanks to collect rain from the roof. It was a well insulated building with many novel ideas. The fireplace in the kitchen had a pit that the ash dropped into, ready to be raked out from outside once a month. All the fireplaces had an external coal bunker with a chute to oak-panelled lockers beside the fires, which avoided carrying coal in through the house. As befits a yacht designer, much of the furniture was built in and made of oak or teak, with the rooms panelled and floored with hardwood. No electricity was laid on to the house as Uffa wanted the house to remain isolated. Oil lamps and candles provided light.

In less than five years, Uffa sold Twenty Acres to Harry Dowsett. Uffa Fox went on to design, among other things, a lifeboat that could be dropped from a plane to enable a ditched aircrew to make their way back to English shores. Hundreds of airmen owed their lives to his design, and to Uffa's simple instructions printed on silk on how to sail the boat. A depiction of the lifeboat being parachuted to the sea is shown on his grey granite tombstone in Whippingham Churchyard.

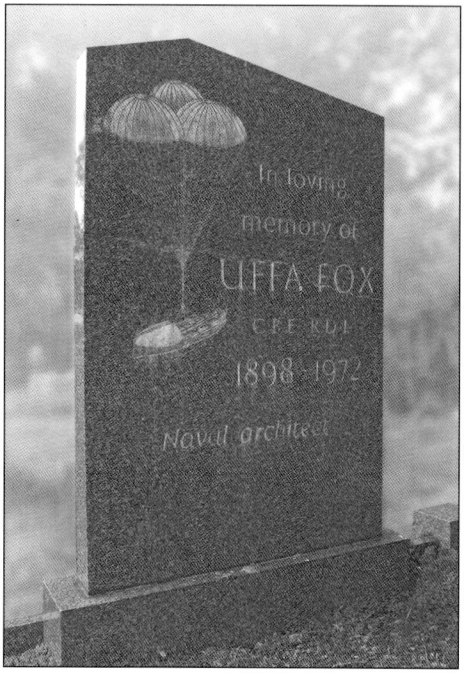

Uffa Fox's grave at St. Mildred's depicting his airborne lifeboat.

During hostilities, there was a large hut built on Twenty Acres to accommodate the soldiers manning the searchlight battery and small anti-aircraft gun north of SARO Works.

By 1951 the owner of the land was Arthur Guy who was raising pigs on the field. He took up the suggested holiday camp idea. The first field used was Clay Pits, then the 'Shop Site', where the leftover army hut provided some accommodation and more chalet huts were built, painted dark khaki green. Toilet and shower blocks were added and later the first caravans were introduced. These were placed between the oak trees and around two circular recreational lawns. A shop was provided and a telephone box.

In the 1960s the site gained residential status. By 1973 all but one of the caravans at the Clay Pits site on the north side of Folly Lane had its own toilet plumbed into a sewer. At that time each caravan was open to the wind beneath it and still had wheels and a tow bar. Gradually the undersides of the vans were boxed in, and new additions arrived on lorries. More areas of the field were developed and the number of caravans increased steadily. Each subsequent area of vans seemed more palatial than the previous one. For instance, in the early 1970s when the southernmost road was put in facing up the river, it was called 'millionaires row' by the other caravan dwellers!

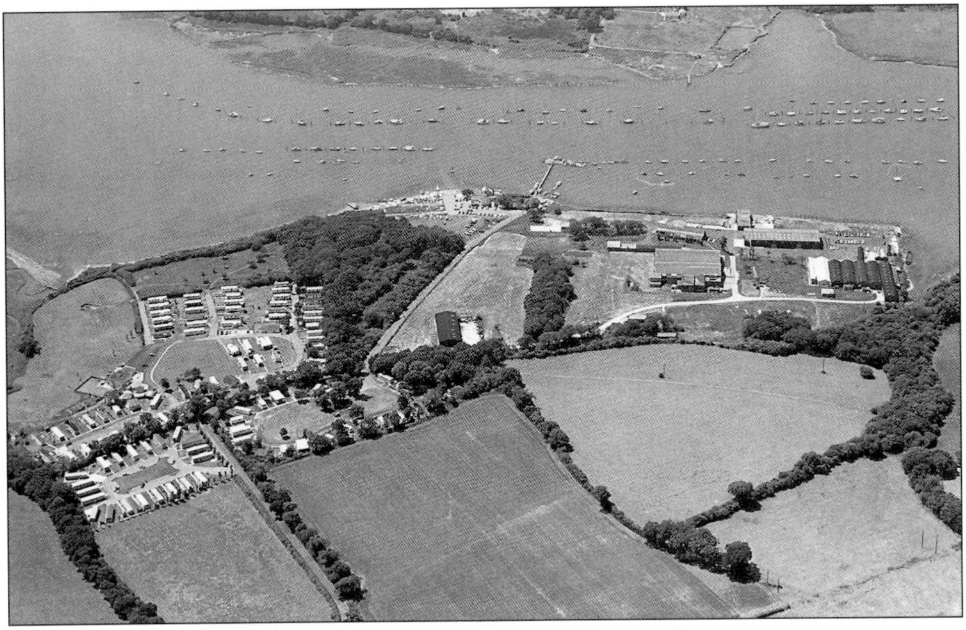

An aerial view of the Medina Park caravan site and The Folly in 1975. In 2018 the area of the caravan site has expanded.

At this time double caravans were introduced, which seemed enormous in comparison with the 30ft by 8ft singles, or even smaller original vans. The riverside field, where wild orchids used to grow in profusion, was the first to have mainly double vans, and by 1985 the 'pig field' uphill from the caravan site was acquired. The older, single vans were gradually sold off and were replaced by double vans. The latest developments have brick-built garages alongside each mobile home.

Now called Medina Park it is limited to those over 55 years of age. Families of all ages lived there in the early days. It is a beautiful place to live, close to the river, the boats, and the countryside with abundant wildlife. Squirrels are frequent visitors, and the calls of wading birds and geese drift up from the river. With 150 homes, Medina Park is a large community within the village of Whippingham, dependent on Folly Lane for road access. Planning permission has been granted for an hotel and housing on the site of the old SARO works. Construction has been delayed while the problems of Folly Lane are resolved.

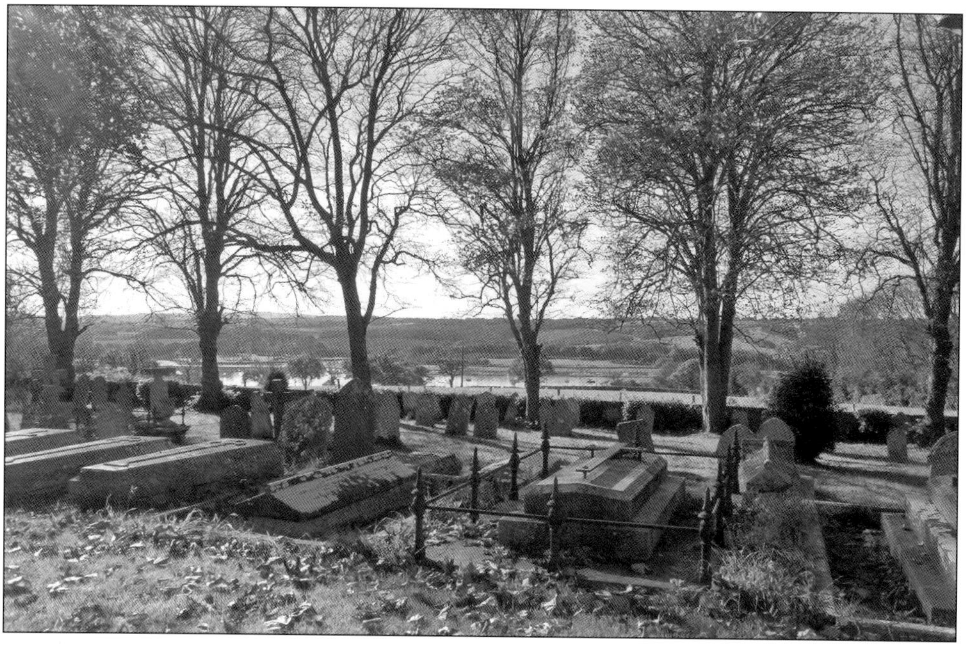

Autumn in the cemetery at Whippingham Church, with the peaceful Medina River in the valley below.

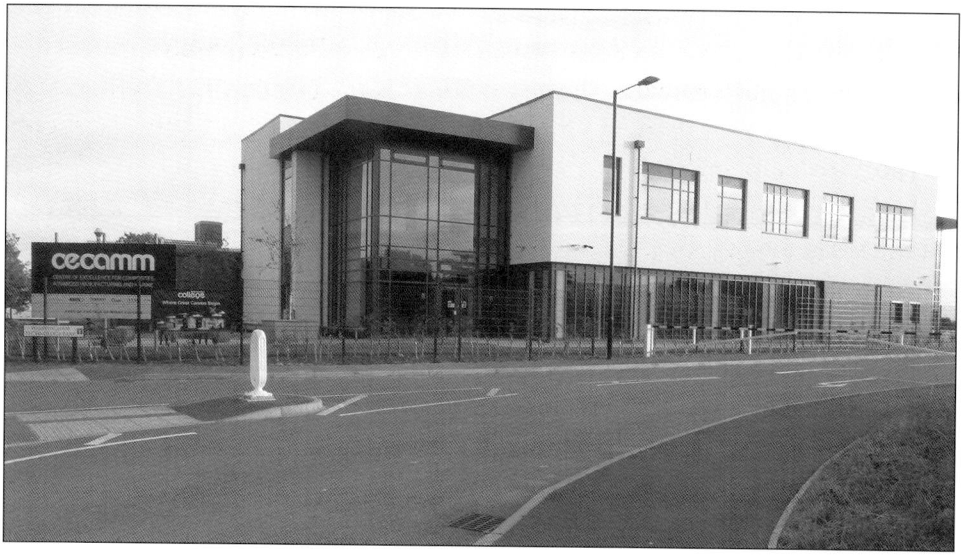

The CECAMM (Centre of Excellence Composites Advanced Manufacturing & Marine) is a campus of the Isle of Wight College which trains students for jobs in marine and aircraft technology. It opened on the Whippingham Technology Park in 2017.

Epilogue

Queen Victoria and Prince Albert had a huge impact on the village of Whippingham. They owned most of the village. Nearly every man, woman and boy worked for the Queen in some way or another. The Queen oversaw their schooling, their health care and their happiness. New housing was provided for the Royal Estate workforce and tenants were given every consideration.

This state of affairs was preserved for some time even after the death of the Queen. The Tillett family held the Barton estate together until 1953, and the other farms still remained as Crown Lands until 1956. Restoration of much of the Barton Manor farm buildings saved Albert's model farm. The estate roads, some of those 20 miles of private drives built for the Queen, still remain private. Consequently there has been a certain 'hibernation' of the whole estate, and much of the Victorian building is still intact. Unfortunately, some slight alterations are beginning to creep in, such as the removal of some of the redundant chimney stacks when in need of major repair. It may be desirable to arrange some kind of conservation area for much of the Queen's old estate of Whippingham, which would acknowledge how well the estate has been preserved. The Church and Almshouses are protected by a conservation area of their own already, as well as being listed buildings, but their environs may be affected by the encroachment of East Cowes further south in the future.

The Church remains a magnet for those interested in the Royal Family, and visitors come to see it from all over the world. Whippingham is proud to show the extent to which the rest of the village was linked to the Royal Estate. Exhibitions in the church and hall give a glimpse into the past.

The second impact on the area has been the industrial development. Aircraft hangars were built beside the Medina where flimsy craft took to the water and the sky. The Folly Works were built as this industry expanded. Despite the narrowness of the Folly Lane hundreds of people worked there during both World Wars. Saunders Roe had taken over the Naval College hospital site and created the Osborne Works and training establishment. Work continued there after the closure of SARO at the Folly. GKN have expanded the industrial activity at Osborne Works which continues with a new, adjacent Technology Park. Here the IW College, in conjunction with GKN, are improving training for apprentices by establishing the CECAMM building.

The Folly Lane remains private and narrow but the planned hotel and housing on the old Folly Works site may bring about dramatic changes to the road system, as well as the riverside character.

A third aspect has been the change in agricultural practices. From being a labour intensive industry, mechanisation has greatly reduced the number of workers involved in farming. The type of agriculture has also changed and there are no longer any dairy herds in the village. When you look at our countryside here in Whippingham, remember that you are looking at farms. To continue looking at farmland in the future, that land must produce an income, whether it is crops or pasture or some other activity.

Today, a fourth aspect has been the tourism and leisure facilities that are provided by and alongside the river. Many people come to the Medina, appreciating it as one of the more unspoilt rivers of the Solent, but with the Folly Inn and Island Harbour conveniently situated halfway up to Newport. An increased number of moorings, while providing additional income for the harbour authorities, may in fact ruin the character of the river. Trying to protect the river bank and the Sites of Special Scientific Interest for the future is also a cause of concern.

Expert studies of the wildlife along the river indicate it could be at risk from development. A decision in 1970 that a *'Country and Waterside Park'* should be established which would protect the whole of the Medina Estuary from development has been largely ignored in development plans produced for the Island since then, and in 2017 there is a suggestion that regeneration for the Island should be concentrated on the Medina envelope. Hopefully the authorities will realize the beauty of the valley before it is too late, and limit further development along the Medina.

This book cannot be a complete history of the village. The more one researches the more one finds that there is to learn. Here we have only touched the surface in an effort to record some of what is known, drawing together material from various sources and memories from those older residents of the village. There is a will to continue collecting information about our history, especially through East Cowes Heritage Centre. If you have more to add, please let us know.

We hope that this book will have broadened your knowledge of Whippingham and enabled you to understand how the village has developed. We hope you enjoy what the village has to offer, whether you live here, work here or are a visitor.

Acknowledgements

The author would like to thank the many people who helped in the creation of both this book and the previous *Book of Whippingham* by providing their photographs and memories.

The people of Whippingham searched through their old photograph albums and the Isle of Wight County Records Office (IWCRO) kindly provided many interesting old documents. Whippingham School still had their fascinating old Log Books when the research began. A two-day trip to the helpful Windsor Royal Archives was invaluable, examining Queen Victoria's original documents relating to Whippingham.

East Cowes Heritage Centre was the catalyst for the initial research about the village. We wanted to put on an exhibition about Whippingham, and it grew! The Workers' Educational Association (WEA) then asked me to run a course about Whippingham, which provided the impetus for further research in the 1990s. The need to write a book about Whippingham to spread the information to even more people became apparent.

A Heritage Trail and booklets, developed by the Whippingham Partnership, grew out of the first book. Oral History projects have been undertaken recording the people of Whippingham.

In particular my sincere thanks go to Brian Taylor who worked on many of the original photographs, and to Ken Wheeler who has taken on that role for this book. Ken also undertook all the page layout, guiding me towards a finished book.

If you think you have information that could be of use regarding Whippingham or East Cowes, please contact eastcowesheritagecentre@onwight.net

Sarah Burdett 2018

Index

Page numbers listed in **bold** indicate an illustration

Associated Reading

Brading, Rosetta, *East Cowes and Whippingham 1303-1914.* J Arthur Dixon, 1990

Brading, Rosetta, *East Cowes and Whippingham 1914–1939.* J Arthur Dixon, 1990

Brinton, Marion, *Farmhouses and Cottages on the Isle of Wight.* IWCC, 1987

Britton, Andrew, *Once upon a Line, Volume 4.* Oxford publishing Company, 1971

Burdett, Sarah, *The Book of Whippingham.* Halsgrove 2006

Burdett, S and Prior, M, *East Cowes.* Dovecote Press, 2011

Daniels, S.B., *Rescue from the Skies - the story of the Airborne Lifeboat.* HMSO 1994

Fox, Uffa, *Joys of Life.* George Newnes Ltd, 1966

Fox, Uffa, *More Joys of Living.* Nautical Publishing Company, 1971

Isle of Wight Women's Institutes, Within Living Memory. Countryside Books, 1994

Major, J Kenneth, *Mills of the Isle of Wight.* Charles Skilton Ltd 1970

Moore, Alice, *Arreton All My Days.* Homespun Publications, 1997

Partridge, Michael, *The Royal Naval College Osborne 1903-1921.* Sutton Publishing, 1999

Pevsner, N and Lloyd, DW, *Buildings of England- Isle of Wight.* Yale University Press 2007

Prothero, Rowland (Lord Ernle), *From Whippingham to Westminster.* John Murray 1938

Searle, Adrian, *Isle of Wight at War 1939-1945.* Dovecote Press, 1989

Tagg, AE and Wheeler RL, *From Sea to Air-The Heritage of Sam Saunders.* Crossprint 1989

Wheeler RL, *River to Sea – the Maritime Heritage of Sam Saunders.* Crossprint 1993

York, Sarah, Duchess of, *Victoria and Albert.* Weidenfeld and Nicholson. 1991